Stolen Wealth, Hidden Power

The publisher and the University of California Press Foundation gratefully acknowledge the generous support of the Anne G. Lipow Endowment Fund in Social Justice and Human Rights.

Stolen Wealth, Hidden Power

THE CASE FOR REPARATIONS FOR MASS INCARCERATION

Tasseli McKay

UNIVERSITY OF CALIFORNIA PRESS

University of California Press
Oakland, California

© 2022 by Tasseli McKay

Library of Congress Cataloging-in-Publication Data

Names: McKay, Tasseli, 1978- author.
Title: Stolen wealth, hidden power : the case for reparations for mass
    incarceration / Tasseli McKay.
Description: Oakland : University of California Press, [2022] | Includes
    bibliographical references and index.
Identifiers: LCCN 2021060594 (print) | LCCN 2021060595 (ebook) |
    ISBN 9780520389441 (cloth) | ISBN 9780520389465 (paperback) |
    ISBN 9780520389472 (ebook)
Subjects: LCSH: African Americans—Effect of imprisonment on. |
    Reparations for historical injustices—United States. | Imprisonment—
    United States.
Classification: LCC HV9950 .M394 2022 (print) | LCC HV9950
    (ebook) | DDC 365/.973—dc23/eng/20220228
LC record available at https://lccn.loc.gov/2021060594
LC ebook record available at https://lccn.loc.gov/2021060595

Manufactured in the United States of America

31 30 29 28 27 26 25 24 23 22
10 9 8 7 6 5 4 3 2 1

For Kyan, Delphi, and Seba
and in memory of Umar Muhammad

Contents

Preface

I was sitting in the kitchen when they gathered up what was left of my granny from the living room and carried her out of the old farmhouse where she had lived and died. Thankfully, I saw her again not long after, when she appeared in the passenger seat of the car I was driving. Her apparition was familiar and comforting, far less strange than the reversal of our roles as driver and passenger.

Death changes the shape of our intimacies and reallocates the work that is left to be done. The dead live alongside us, their actions and experiences shaping our choices in myriad conscious and unconscious ways. My immediate ancestors, my parents and grandparents, made my life and this writing possible in ways that words are too thin to carry. With the thickness of their love and labor came other inheritances, too: the get-out-of-jail-free card that is white skin in America and the perpetually unfinished human business of harm and repair.

And so, this book is a ghost story. An especially beloved ghost sat next to me as I wrote it, and she makes an invisible appearance in its pages. My granny, Elizabeth Foote McKay, filled my early days with sunlight, woodsmoke, pond water, and a supply of home-preserved garden produce that stood up to the long Vermont winter. With her love and care came the legacy of her people: well-intended Quakers, that outspokenly egalitarian Society of Friends, who advocated for incarceration as a humane alternative to more immediately brutal punishments. Helping to right the devastating harms of mass imprisonment that eventually followed in their wake is the work of more than a lifetime, and it comes to me in the blood of one of the people I have loved most.

Almost anything one could write about life in America is a ghost story. To be haunted here is not a nightmare but a way of waking up. May your own beloved ghosts sit beside you as you read this and accompany you in everything you do.

Acknowledgments

This work would not exist without the incredible data produced by the Multi-site Family Study on Incarceration, Parenting and Partnering. I am thankful for the insight and bravery of the families who participated and to the monumental effort and vision of my very dear colleagues and mentors at RTI (Chris, Anupa, Megan, Erin, Justin, and Stephen). Megan, in particular, was a fountain of inspiration, brilliance, and thoughtful feedback on this book, and Justin's research assistance was invaluable. I am grateful to the University of California Press team (especially Maura, for believing in the project from the start, and Madison and Emily for taking it to the finish), to the anonymous peer reviewers whose feedback strengthened the book, and to Michael for meticulous work on the references. I am also deeply grateful to William "Sandy" Darity Jr. for powerful and insightful feedback on an earlier draft and to Joseph T. Jones Jr. for the rich critical analysis he offered during an interview for the book.

I am indebted, in this and many other endeavors, to the guidance and generosity of my academic mentors (Chris, Leo, and Jon), who have improved and supported my work in countless ways. And I was fortunate to share parts of the book process with four of my oldest, dearest friends (George, Danielle, Ariyah, and Sam) and three fabulous, steadfast writing buddies (Cole, Geeta, and Kath). Support from the National Science Foundation and RTI helped to make the writing time possible, for which I am infinitely grateful.

In a dominant culture that tends to normalize exploitation, hoarding, loneliness, conventionality, and illusions of self-reliance, I am so thankful for a family life that keeps me knowing in my bones what else is possible. Three wonderful parents, six beloved grandparents, four fabulous siblings, a far-from-evil stepmother, and fantastic "out-laws" have each offered me much more than my fair share of love, encouragement, and inspiration. Dillyn, Grandma, and my parents have been priceless sources of support and encouragement on this book. I am equally blessed to share my life with a phenomenal queer chosen family, including my coparents and partners in life and land (Gretchen, Justin, Ava, Ryan, Jes, Hirsch, Alex, and Jlee), our little ones (Kyan, Delphi, Seba, and Wren), and my femme other half (Alba). I am inspired by each of you and how you are moving in this world. You make my life so incredibly sweet even when I am writing for hours on end: sharing cooking and childcare, bringing light and laughter, showing off the superpower of interdependence, and reminding me for what and whom we are fighting. The never-ending and awe-inspiring work of parenting our kids, and the indescribable honor and joy of being Kyan's mama, has held me in a state of wonder and general heart explosion for much of the last two and a half years. Finally, I am thankful beyond words to Gretchen, my partner in everything, who is an unflinchingly radiant human being, a joy to be with at every hour of the day or night, and has worked tirelessly to make this book and my life possible.

The mightiness of the people and cats who accompanied me in this work make it impossible for me to doubt Octavia Butler's famous insight: we change everything we touch. I am proud of what we are doing and undoing, and I offer this book as one tiny part of that massively daunting and infinitely possible collective work, which belongs to all of us.

1 Disremembered and Unaccounted For

> Disremembered and unaccounted for, she cannot be lost because no one is looking for her, and even if they were, how can they call her if they don't know her name?
>
> Toni Morrison, *Beloved*

In a nation built and maintained with racial terrorism, forgetting is no accident. At no point in history has America functioned without some of its people in shackles. Nor has there been a time when some measure of our public resources was not dedicated to the commission and enabling of racial violence. Ongoing racist atrocities carried out by predominantly white-controlled governments at the federal, state, and local levels have facilitated the theft of labor and land from Black and Indigenous communities, underwritten their physical containment in resource-alienated urban and rural spaces, and hobbled their political participation and resistance. Yet the cultural mainstream views itself as neither racist nor terrorist.

Carceral historians and critical legal scholars have meticulously detailed how America's brutal legacy of racist violence readied the ground for mass incarceration,[1] now the most pervasive form of racial terrorism in the United States. But a closer look suggests that it is not simply the persistent reality of racist violence in America that made mass incarceration possible, nor even the memory of such violence; rather, it is our persistence in forgetting.[2] Americans have hurried past genocide, enslavement, and each of the mechanisms of racist mass violence that followed them without reckoning or reparation.

This kind of forgetting is functional. In her canonical novel of the Reconstruction period, *Beloved*, Toni Morrison referred to it as "disremembering." The Pulitzer prize–winning author's unconventional verb slices through the possibility of a neutral memory failure; it evokes the process by which original acts of violence are reinscribed through efforts at their denial. Indeed, the larger-than-life ghost baby whom Morrison's novel resurrects represents not the horrific period of enslavement that some historians now call "the first mass incarceration"[3] but the failure to confront it in the time that followed. That pivotal failure of Reconstruction has been repeated each time a new set of racist horrors becomes history.

We are living in such a time, awaiting the seemingly imminent sunset of a four-decade program of state violence that has criminalized Black youth and ensnared incarcerated adults in a cycle of perpetual punishment, with rippling damage to families, communities, and the nation. As if it is a sort of national embarrassment, mass incarceration inspires widespread denunciation and dismissal but limited effort at collective remembering or official redress. Most of the policing and sentencing policies and practices that drove this blighted era remain in place.[4] If incarceration rates continue to decline on the present slope—which is far from assured given the haphazard origins of the decline and the law-and-order rhetorics that continue to pervade American politics—we will not return to pre-1980 rates of imprisonment until the year 2100.[5] Even the most numerically impactful reforms of the last decade and a half, such as California's 2011 Public Safety Realignment Act, have been designed primarily to limit the sprawling legal and financial liabilities of states operating mass-scale prison facilities.[6] Yet even those policy makers truly concerned with ending mass incarceration stop short of considering how we will correct the damage it has done.

This book takes up the charge of collective accounting for mass incarceration. Based on a large body of scientific evidence (drawn from my own research experiences in the Multi-site Family Study on Incarceration, Parenting and Partnering and the work of many other scholars), it argues that mass incarceration has consisted of a knowable and definable set of atrocities. It proposes that the harms sustained by Black individuals, families, and communities in this campaign of racist state violence can and must be repaired and outlines a program of reparation tied to concrete evidence of harm. Challenging the centuries-long logic of forgetting that much of our nation's history rests on, this work suggests that the shape of our collective future hangs on the willingness to take an intimate and honest account of the damage and to settle that account for good.

GHOSTS IN THE NATIONAL MACHINE

By the time mass incarceration arrived in American popular consciousness, it had already begun to disappear from view. Contemporary academic and journalistic works on the phenomenon are quick to remind audiences that mass incarceration is already fading into history. Criminologists Todd Clear and Natasha Frost, midway through writing their early critical assessment of mass incarceration, pivoted to reframe the country's inflated imprisonment rate as a "grand experiment" that was nearing completion.[7] Almost as soon as we recognized mass incarceration as a problem, it seems to have become a problem of the past. But is it?

Ironically, social scientific work on mass incarceration has contributed to the premature disappearance of its subject. For academics, the terms *mass incarceration*[8] and *hyperincarceration*[9] have become shorthand for America's globally and historically exceptional rates of imprisonment. The figures remain staggering: 2.3 million Americans are incarcerated, and American jails record almost 11 million admissions per year.[10] The United States continues to maintain the largest prison and jail population in the world and to incarcerate its residents at a rate higher than any other nation.[11] Still, looking only at the number of people behind bars suggests that mass incarceration has been in a slight decline since the carceral population peaked in 2009.[12]

For the "masses" of Americans who are directly affected by mass incarceration, however, prison and jail-cell counts fall far short of capturing the reverberation of criminalization and imprisonment across decades and generations. When we look beyond the time-limited experience of detention itself to the rippling consequences of justice system contact for individuals, families, and communities, the temporal landscape shifts. About as many Americans now have a criminal record as a college degree.[13] One in three Black men is living with a felony conviction.[14] In major American cities, approximately 44 percent of unmarried new mothers report that their baby's father has been recently incarcerated.[15]

The repercussions of imprisonment reach into every part of daily life: parenting and intimate relationships, health, education, employment, economic well-being, community safety, and wellness.[16] Its harms unfold across the individual lifespan, from cradle to grave. Damage accumulates at the local and national levels as well, manifesting itself in heightened infant mortality rates, diminished adult life expectancy, and greater racial disparities in each of these areas compared to other wealthy democracies.[17] By their very nature, the accumulated consequences of criminalization and confinement in targeted communities are unlikely to dissipate quickly.[18]

Many of us studying the repercussive effects of mass incarceration have been watching the wrong clock.[19] The breadth and magnitude of these repercussions at any moment in time is driven primarily by the number of former prisoners (and their family members) in our communities. This number will be rising for decades to come. As such, it is only in the years ahead that the consequences of America's punishment regime will fully come home to us. To understand (and address) them, it will be necessary to acknowledge that mass incarceration has been more than a terrible policy mistake or a grand experiment, as many critical scholars have previously suggested. The intentional, violent domination of poor, Black communities through intensive, racially targeted law enforcement and sentencing practices was and remains a campaign of collective, political violence: the use of force by a power-holding group to suppress or eliminate the power of another.[20]

In the United States, massive acts of state violence, and their specific deployment against Black Americans, have been normalized as an ordinary and necessary part of government operations. American police have served as agents of racially targeted collective violence for as long as they have existed. Southern police forces have their origins in slave-hunting patrols, and law enforcement agencies nationwide have participated not only in helping slaveholders to maintain violent control over their captives but in many subsequent forms of racial terrorism, from lynching to lethal police violence against Black children on streets and playgrounds.[21] Prominent legal scholars and historians from Michelle Alexander to Bryan Stevenson and Elizabeth Hinton have rightly argued that America's long history of racist atrocities helped to make the present era of mass incarceration possible.[22]

Still, it is not simply the fact of our brutal past but the persistent failure to grapple with and repair it that makes accounting for mass incarceration-era harms more difficult. The true damage wrought by the current regime of criminalization and punishment is both exacerbated and obscured by this more encompassing erasure.[23] Violence that occurs in "a context in which one group has the power to decide and enact what is to be validated as 'real' for all other groups" has been shown to inflict particularly deep and lasting damage. It erodes individual mental health and social functioning and inhibits collective cultural and social life and political participation.[24] In communities that have survived massive state violence and historical trauma, including Indigenous North Americans, these harms extend across generations.[25] Physiological markers of collective trauma are present even among children of state violence survivors who were born after the violence ended. Nevertheless, for Black communities that have survived and are surviving mass incarceration, the effects of sustained and systematic exposure to government violence have rarely been accounted for as such.

Writing of the Reconstruction era in Ohio, Toni Morrison suggests that the forgotten ghosts of slavery, far from receding, simply incorporated themselves into the climate of the place: "By and by all trace is gone, and what is forgotten is not only the footprints but the water too and what is down there. The rest is weather. Not the breath of the disremembered and unaccounted for, but wind in the eaves, or spring ice thawing too quickly. Just weather."[26] Efforts to reckon with the harms of mass incarceration, academically or otherwise, occur in the presence of ghosts like these—not the "spiteful"[27] kind of ghosts, emboldened to topple pots from the stove or dishes from their cupboards but the kind that have entrenched themselves so deeply in our collective consciousness and the machinery of our government that they are as normal and as encompassing as the weather.

CONFRONTING STATE VIOLENCE

Writing about the ways that slavery is remembered (and disremembered) in the contemporary American landscape, Clint Smith observes that the gaps and absences in our collective memory of injustice and atrocity are as significant as what we do know and see.[28] Lucid confrontation with the past is at the heart of a process that academics and policy makers call "transitional justice." Transitional justice generally refers to "a society's attempt to come to terms with a legacy of large-scale past abuses, in order to ensure accountability, serve justice and achieve reconciliation."[29] Applied around the world in scholarship on state violence and its aftermath, principles of transitional justice have yet to be embraced in the United States and are very rarely applied to consider the project of recovery from mass incarceration.[30] Transitional justice scholarship shifts our focus away from accountability for individual behavior toward reckoning with collective and institutional acts. It considers how to bring justice for harms committed by entire populations and the systems of government they control.

The persistent failure of the United States to confront and transform a succession of violent systems of racist domination is not the global norm. Worldwide, many democratic societies have made transitional justice a high priority in the periods of political and social transition that follow large-scale state violence. Research in contexts as diverse as Argentina, Germany, Rwanda, Indonesia, the former Soviet states, and South Africa points to several critical tasks that must be faced during such periods, including "truth-telling, restitution or reparation, and reform of abusive state institutions."[31] Such processes, though frequently framed in American media as bringing perpetrators of atrocity to justice, operate on a different paradigm from the retributive justice meted out by ordinary criminal legal systems. Unlike punishment-based retributive justice processes, transitional justice focuses on healing, closure, and transformation in the wake of mass-scale harm.

Transitional justice for the 1994 Tutsi and Twa genocide in Rwanda, for example, incorporated internationally recognized truth and reconciliation mechanisms, as well as traditional justice processes in local communities. Lay Rwandans viewed this work as having helped to rebuild trust among neighbors, bring a sense of closure for those harmed, and prevent future violence.[32] Research in other contexts—Colombia, Democratic Republic of the Congo, The Gambia, Lebanon, Palestine, and Uganda—suggests that the success of a transitional justice process depends on its internal integrity but also on its ability to shift the underlying attitudes and institutions that made mass violence possible. In periods of postatrocity reconstruction, opportunities are equally ripe for transformation or retrenchment in major social, cultural, and political institutions.[33]

The work of transformation after state violence is fraught, complex, and controversial. Even in the most favorable contexts, transitional justice efforts must reconcile "the grand ambitions of those seeking to build a new future and those struggling to restore their lives and repair the irreparable."[34] The experiences of Rwandan communities, while they represent a powerful example of a concerted commitment to national reckoning, also highlight the profound and inherent challenges and risks of transitional justice. Such an undertaking can retraumatize victim participants and observers, prompt retaliation against participants, and be co-opted to consolidate ruling party interests or enact purely retributive (punishment-oriented) forms of justice.[35]

Mass violence that occurs as part of a broader campaign of racial domination presents special challenges for the process of reckoning and repair. In the wake of large-scale acts of racist violence and abuse, survivors and perpetrators of group-based violence often retreat into deeper social segregation. For members of the victim group, social segregation may offer a partial refuge in which to rebuild a semblance of solace and safety. For members of the perpetrator group, however, social segregation may serve as further insulation from the experiences of the victimized. The social and informational insulation of the perpetrator group represents a serious impediment to transitional justice. The tendency in transitional justice work to emphasize reconciliation can further minimize the experiences of the victimized group and, ultimately, reinforce the status quo that made mass violence possible.[36] If not confronted in concrete, human terms with a basic understanding of the harms that victims have sustained, members of the perpetrator group will use their political, social, and economic power to discredit and undermine the project of repair.[37]

The success of transitional justice after mass racial violence hinges on whether members of the perpetrator group can develop greater awareness of what members of the victim group have experienced. Political scientist Joanna Quinn, founder of the Centre for Transitional Justice and Post-Conflict Reconstruction, calls this "thin sympathy," a minimal but essential cross-group awareness that must be actively cultivated among members of perpetrator communities.[38] Building a basic, shared understanding of the damages done to the target group supports a broader effort within transitional justice work "to make over the values and social codes that are prevalent within a society, taking away many of the beliefs that stand as impediments to any real process of transformation [and to] reform the policies or structures that hamper or block successful transitional justice."[39]

Among Americans who have not been personally affected by the deployment of our criminal legal system in service of white supremacy, "thin sympathy" for the victims of mass incarceration may be obstructed or overridden by a sense that criminals deserve punishment—and certainly not recompense. Two facts, each of which will be explored in greater depth in the chapters that follow, challenge this notion. First, our shared concepts of worth and deservingness and our collective belief in punishment are grounded in a false perception of badness or criminality as attributes of individuals and their behaviors. This perception is challenged by powerful evidence that supposed criminality is not a trait of individuals, nor even of their actions, but a weapon of social exclusion with a long-standing history of racist application. A social and political campaign of criminalization, levied against Black Americans and other communities of color, has been foundational to the project of mass incarceration in the United States. A key marker of its success is the fact that the experience of arrest has become widely decoupled from participation in illegal acts but strongly and consistently associated with race.[40]

Second, the idea that the harms inflicted on people of color in the context of mass incarceration represent punishments for crime is challenged by extensive evidence that such harms have also been leveled against unconvicted partners, parents and coparents, children, and even whole communities. The evidence assembled in this book indicates that, in fact, *most* of the damages associated with mass incarceration have been borne by people who have not been convicted of an illegal act. As such, the argument for reparations for mass incarceration must not be misconstrued as privileging those who have been convicted of crime over those who have not. The chapters that follow do not examine or quantify the damages of adjudication and punishment per se but rather those associated with the racialized deployment of systems of punishment and the imposition of extralegal damages that far exceed the bounds of statutory punishment.[41] It is this systematic campaign of political violence, directed primarily at Black Americans, that demands reparation.

Reckoning with the damage caused by racist brutality, transitional justice scholars agree, represents an especially steep climb in the settler nations of North America and Australia. In such countries, governments and economic institutions continue to be dominated by the same groups who were primarily responsible for major episodes of historical mass violence. State violence researchers Brinton Lykes and Hugo van der Merwe argue that in countries like these, "genocidal violence and its legacies have not only not been redressed but their underlying causes have been institutionalized in neoliberal economic and political systems. . . . These nation states have not 'transitioned' in any sense of the term."[42] The United States is such a nation.

Comparing government responses to illegal counterinsurgency efforts in the United States and South Africa highlights the challenge that settler nations face. In the middle and late twentieth century, each of the two governments used brutal and illegal tactics to destroy Black and Indigenous political resistance. In South Africa, the settler-controlled government that deployed such tactics was replaced in 1994 by the African National Congress (ANC). This new government initiated and stewarded a program of transitional justice. The ANC's efforts benefited from a powerful, central truth commission process that supported long-term efforts to expose the abusive tactics used by the prior administration, identify their root causes, and institute strong measures to ensure they would not be repeated. No such effort was ever made in the United States. Despite multiple changes in the federal administration, the United States remained in the hands of white-controlled political parties in the years following its racially repressive counterinsurgency efforts against Black and Native activists. While certain reparative gestures for these abuses have been mandated by the courts—for example, the American Indian Movement secured recognition in the United Nations and a large court-ordered payment to the Oglala Lakota—such actions were never initiated by the federal government. Indeed, they occurred in spite of it.[43]

SHIFTING THE BURDEN OF PROOF

The global transitional justice record emphasizes the special challenges that transitional justice presents in contexts like the United States, where there has been no "formal regime change"—that is, where the government that perpetrated or abetted a mass atrocity and the government that must work to repair that atrocity are effectively continuous.[44] Understanding the distinct challenges that face us in this regard need not be discouraging, however. To the contrary, it illuminates what has stood in the way of collective repair for the many racist atrocities that have marred American history—and what we can do differently now.

First and foremost, the international transitional justice record highlights the importance of addressing white Americans' relative isolation from information about racist harm. This is part of the symbolic and cultural work of reparations. The ferocious objections of many white Americans to the 1619 Project's frank framing of our nation's founding institutions illustrates the implications of the chasm that separates Black and white Americans' understanding of our racial history.[45] The chasm is also apparent in wide differences of opinion between Black and white Americans regarding present-day racism—differences that are largely due to deficits of factual historical knowledge among white Americans.[46] The yawning gap in popular information about racial harm, left uncorrected, helps to perpetuate the extreme social and political polarization that undermines American democracy as a whole. It also helps to perpetuate limited public support for any material forms of redress for racial injustice.

The information chasm represents a major impediment to sound official decision-making as well, given the ongoing dominance of white people (and predominantly white, class-privileged men) at all levels of American government.[47] White-dominated governments in the United States lack the factual information to make informed decisions on questions of repair and recovery from racist violence. From Nuremberg to Rwanda, formal truth-telling processes have been critical in furnishing such information in international transitional justice work. But in the case of mass incarceration, the very nature of the atrocity at issue makes the American government notably ill-prepared to gain the trust and guarantee the safety of victims for a public truth-telling process. Those targeted by the hypercarceral regime in the United States have learned from experience to regard government entities as agents of surveillance and violence rather than as sources of potential protection.[48] In such a context, building collective recognition and understanding of the harms of mass incarceration, without revictimizing or retraumatizing those who have been its targets, represents a formidable challenge.

Yet efforts to establish a collective memory of mass incarceration stand to benefit from one resource that many other transitional justice processes have lacked: extensive scholarly documentation of the harms sustained by the targeted group. Truth and reconciliation processes in other national and historical contexts have relied predominantly on truth commissions and trial or tribunal processes to build an account of harms, with scholarly work occurring contemporaneously. When it comes to mass incarceration in the United States, however, a rich and exacting account of these harms is already being assembled in research on the criminal legal system and its collateral consequences. The resulting body of evidence makes it possible to construct an authoritative account of mass incarceration's damages, in spite of the deeply divergent realities that this system (and the other forms of racial terrorism that have preceded and accompanied it) have fostered. Bringing scholarly evidence to bear on this process represents a viable and preferable alternative to transitional justice processes that burden survivors with creating an official record of their victimization for collective use.

Ample evidence indicates that the tough-on-crime policies begun under Presidents Johnson and Nixon and extended by each administration since have had devastating consequences for Black individuals, families, and communities. Scholars of the criminal legal system, as well as those who explicitly study the repercussions of mass incarceration for individuals and families, have built a rich body of evidence on its pernicious and lingering harms. Imprisonment erodes the physical and mental health, workforce and political participation, and long-term economic stability of those targeted for criminalization and imprisonment,[49] who are disproportionately Black men.[50] The experience of punishment radiates to the children and families of the imprisoned, as well, damaging the health of partners and other family members, increasing children's exposure to serious negative outcomes (including homelessness and abuse or neglect), and hampering their social and emotional development, school engagement, and achievement.[51]

Mass incarceration has also affected life in urban communities of color as a whole, even for residents whose own lives have not been touched directly. Law enforcement and punishment in the mass incarceration era are highly spatially targeted: the systematic surveillance, removal, and redeposition of criminalized individuals is concentrated in a relatively small number of American neighborhoods.[52] Those who live in targeted communities face elevated exposure to violence, infectious disease, and mental health conditions, as well as diminished educational engagement and achievement.[53] Consistent with the vision of white social and political domination that animated it,[54] mass incarceration has served at the national level to widen the gap between Black and white Americans' physical and economic well-being. High rates of imprisonment and the racial targeting of criminal justice contact has exacerbated racial disparities in infant mortality, child well-being, academic participation and achievement, and economic stability.[55] It also appears to have succeeded in curtailing Black political participation and political power.[56] This book will take up each of these bodies of evidence to suggest what they tell us about the racial harm of mass incarceration, how it might be repaired or redressed, and what a nation that has managed to settle these ugly accounts could look like for our children.

To embark on real reckoning and repair for mass incarceration demands more than just evidence on the nature of its damages, however. We must be able to identify precisely the individuals and communities who have borne these burdens so that our reparative efforts are directed appropriately. In other transitional justice initiatives, a lack of reliable documentation on who was harmed has presented a formidable obstacle, and it remains a potential challenge for reparations proposals aimed at descendants of enslaved people in the United States.[57] Fortunately (for this purpose, at least), the identities of those targeted for criminalization and imprisonment have been meticulously tracked by law enforcement and criminal justice agencies at multiple levels of government.[58] Public officials can enumerate each person who has been or is held in local, state, and federal correctional facilities; by extension, their family members and communities can also be definitively identified.

Transitional justice work presents undeniable challenges in any context, and efforts to address the harms of mass incarceration in the United States are no exception. It is equally undeniable, however, that the knowledge and data required to support this work are already at our fingertips.

FROM RECKONING TO REPARATION

The question of how to achieve "extraordinary justice" in the wake of what legal scholar David Gray calls "radical evil" has occupied legal scholars and political scientists for decades, even centuries.[59] Reparations, broadly speaking, are the means to this end: the material and cultural practices designed to achieve collective repair and closure following large-scale breaches of human decency and collective trust. It comes as no surprise that many policy scholars, historians, and economists have been calling for reparations to Black Americans since at least the late 1700s.[60] Among the most enduring political debates in American history, reparations proposals have been taken up in legislative sessions, adjudicated by courts, and debated in popular media since shortly after emancipation. Most such proposals focus on the idea of extending benefits to those targeted for enslavement (or their descendants) and the various forms of government-sponsored or government-abetted racial discrimination that have followed—particularly the legal discrimination of the Jim Crow era.

Opponents have been quick to dismiss the idea of reparations with references to its complexity: how could we possibly quantify the harms to be rectified, or determine responsibility for those harms, or agree on the mechanisms by which they will be redressed?[61] Each of these challenges is surmountable, however. Its existential unknowability notwithstanding, greater precision about racial harm in America is well within our reach, particularly in an age of rigorous social scientific research. Remaining in a state of perpetual doubt and ignorance about the history and nature of racial harm, whether we are laypeople or policy makers, is a potent choice in favor of the racial status quo. So, too, is the preoccupation with assigning (or rebutting) blame for racial harm. As Gray notes, "'I didn't do it' is a non sequitur in debates about reparations where the fundamental question is, 'How do we make it right?'" Every individual who reaps the benefits and privileges of membership in a collectivity, including a nation, must also accept a share of responsibility for its collective debts and transgressions—whether or not that individual was directly involved in incurring them.[62]

The contention that reparation is a nebulous concept, impossible to enact in practice, is equally distracting. The material and cultural work of reparations can be accomplished through a wide range of mechanisms, from "official acknowledgments of wrongdoing to reparations involving monetary compensation, government programs that invest in wronged communities, repatriation, or restitution of lost property or rights."[63] Any transitional justice initiative involves identifying the mechanisms best suited to repairing the particular harms at issue. Much scholarly work on reparations for racial injustice in the United States has focused on assessing the relative feasibility of legislative and judicial mechanisms. Work in this vein considers whether symbolic acknowledgment and material compensation for harm would be better achieved by pressuring elected officials to legislate it or by petitioning the courts to grant it. While neither strategy is uncomplicated or assured of success in the American context, adjudication carries the significant advantage of not requiring a shift in popular awareness of racial harm (particularly among white Americans). It also carries the significant disadvantage of failing to contribute to such a shift.[64] Reparation serves, ideally, as a project of both recompense and cultural transformation.[65] From this perspective, the transformative possibilities of grassroots mobilization and broad-scale, legislative action for reparations outweigh the potential pragmatic advantages of using the courts to secure compensation for victims.

Still, more than two centuries after the first documented proposal for reparations to Black Americans, a national reparations program remains unaccomplished. Continued inattention to righting racial injustice—and the ongoing apathy or opposition from white Americans that underlies it[66]—has far-reaching implications for American democracy and the well-being and life chances of all Americans. The more doggedly we ignore the ghosts of racist harm, the more fiercely they will haunt us. Engaging this irony in her preface to a reprint of *Beloved*, Morrison describes how, amid the Reconstruction-era refusal to reckon with the brutality of enslavement, "the order and quietude of everyday life would be violently disrupted by the chaos of the needy dead. . . . The herculean effort to forget would be threatened by memory desperate to stay alive."[67] Attempting to ignore a violent history so consequential, Morrison suggests, simply secures its prominence over the present. Left unaddressed, racism's enduring and subterranean harms quietly undermine a host of collective endeavors that should be well within reach for a country of America's wealth: achieving low infant mortality, ensuring all children are housed and fed, providing equitable access to education, and ensuring broad democratic participation. These basic milestones of human decency remain out of reach in the twenty-first-century United States, leaving the nation grossly out of step with its peers.[68]

For most of its history, reparations debate in the United States has focused overwhelmingly on the question of compensation for the labor and suffering of enslaved Black Americans prior to legal emancipation. Randall Robinson, a leader in the solidarity movement to end South African apartheid and an American reparations advocate, eloquently summarizes the argument of reparations-for-slavery scholars in his contention that no remedy save reparations could begin to right "the savage time-release social debilitations of American slavery."[69] As such, the unreconstructed harms of slavery have continued to compound under every American government since Lincoln's. At the close of Barack Obama's presidential tenure, economist Sandy Darity lamented that Obama had joined the ranks of every American president since the Civil War by failing to deliver meaningful economic reparations to Black Americans.[70]

Calls for reparations have drawn impassioned attention from a widening cast of supporters and opponents in recent years.[71] With this fresh debate has come new attention to the possibility of redressing postbellum racial harms. From segregationist housing and education policies to contemporary barriers to Black occupational attainment and economic security, reparations scholars and activists point to numerous other forms of racial violence and theft that demand official recognition and repair.[72] Still, despite expanded interest in reparations for postenslavement harm and growing recognition of mass incarceration as a weapon of racial destruction, the idea of reparations for mass incarceration has received very limited consideration.[73] The notion of bringing the "criminal justice system" itself to justice challenges the perverse focus on individual blame and punishment for transgression that has obsessed us as a culture and as scholars of crime and violence in particular.[74] We have poured stunning public resources into marginally effective strategies for correcting individual wrongdoing.[75] It is past time to confront and rectify our collective wrongdoing as well.

Accounting for and repairing the harm of four centuries of racial terrorism in the United States is no simple task. Ongoing racist violence by white settlers and the government they came to control has wrought catastrophic damage in Indigenous communities across the continental United States, Alaska, Hawaii, and Puerto Rico. State violence has also been heavily deployed to suppress ongoing contestation of the Mexican-American border by those who live south of it. Criminalization and imprisonment have been key tools in the US government's efforts to maintain repressive control of lands stolen from their original inhabitants.[76] This reality is reflected, in part, in the disproportionate confinement of Indigenous and Latinx Americans in jails and prisons.[77] Poor race and ethnicity data and small subsamples in major administrative and research data sets have helped to keep a rigorous quantitative accounting of harms to Indigenous and Latinx communities out of reach.[78] The broader work of redressing legacies of genocide, enslavement, and forced relocation of Indigenous peoples on this continent is urgent. Acknowledging and addressing the harms of mass incarceration for Black Americans is a timely and important place to begin.

The aim of this book, then, is to contribute to the broader project of reparations for racist mass violence in America by presenting the scientific case for reparations to Black Americans for mass incarceration. Robust evidence on the repercussive effects of mass incarceration for Black Americans, and the imperative of countering the pervasive marginalization and devaluation of Blackness, motivate the decision to center Black experiences in this book. The brilliant thought leadership and dogged persistence of Black activists and intellectuals in illuminating the harm of mass incarceration and arguing for its repair will be plainly apparent in these pages. The book aims to highlight their pivotal intellectual and strategic leadership while also encouraging white scholars and laypeople to shoulder responsibility for this work. Centuries of atrocities have sapped the material and psychic resources of communities targeted for racial violence on this continent. Accounts of the harms they have sustained are continually questioned and discredited by those who have benefited from, or been unaffected by, ongoing racial injustice. In this context, the task of making and justifying claims for reparations must not be left exclusively to those who have survived decades (or centuries) of racial violence; they must be shared by those of us whose complicity has enabled it.

The next six chapters offer a cradle-to-grave accounting of the harms of mass incarceration during the last half century. They draw on an extensive body of interdisciplinary research and interpret it with insight from non-academic formats and forums, including the cultural works and political protest of those with lived experience of criminalization and imprisonment. Recognizing that experiences of harm and of punishment unfold over the course of one's life,[79] the book is organized according to the life-course consequences of mass incarceration. It begins with the hypersurveillance, criminalization, and detention of children of color, the subject of chapter 2. Chapter 3 discusses the lasting harms of adult imprisonment and the protracted (and often perpetual) process of postprison reintegration for the convicted. Chapter 4 considers the inequitable burdens imposed on partners and adult family members of the convicted, while chapter 5 examines the intergenerational legacy of punishment among their children. Chapter 6 assesses the lasting consequences of mass punishment in targeted neighborhoods and communities and its detrimental impact on national measures of population health. Each of these empirical chapters uses evidence from the Multi-site Family Study on Incarceration, Parenting and Partnering, as well as other qualitative and quantitative research, to estimate the economic value of documented harms and to propose reparations strategies that could begin to address them. Chapter 7 surveys this cycle of harm, bringing the sum of the documented damages alongside the value of the Black-white household wealth gap. It suggests what the correspondence between these two figures implies for the possibilities that might await us in a postreparations America. Based on the assembled evidence, it argues for a national program of reparations to Black individuals, families, and communities that is commensurate with the scope and scale of the damages sustained.

Like our Reconstruction-era forebears, we live in a pivotal time for public policy and race consciousness. This time holds equal possibility of redoubling our violent commitment to white supremacy or undertaking its undoing in earnest, of maintaining our status-quo system of retributive justice (and the racial injustices it perpetuates) or of moving forward with reparative, transformative intent. As Morrison wrote of her heroine's frostbitten feet, "anything dead coming back to life hurts."[80] To peel back and examine every layer of racial atrocity that surrounds mass incarceration in America is an ugly undertaking. To attempt to measure and quantify the associated losses is excruciating but essential to the reparations project. In a country in which racist violence has continued with limited interruption or remedy for sixteen generations, this ugly work is our inheritance. The state-of-the-art scientific tools with which we now approach it do not make for a sterile operation. But it is only from this unsterile ground—soaked with the gross injustices and inequities that we have taken as irremediable, intractable, and even unremarkable—that the other country we have never known might spring.

2 "Institutionalized"

THE HYPERREGULATION OF CHILDHOOD CHALLENGES

On April 26, 2015, the night before Freddie Gray would be laid to rest in Baltimore's Woodlawn Cemetery, young people all over the city were mobilizing for another day of demonstrations. Gray's death in police custody a week earlier, deemed a homicide by the city coroner, had sparked righteous anger and rebellion in Baltimore's heavily policed Black communities. Michael Singleton, a soft-spoken, sixteen-year-old high school student, talked with his mother about taking part in the next day's protests around Mondawmin Mall. She told him to stay away.

The next day, three public high schools in the Mondawmin Mall area let out around the same time that Gray's funeral did. Singleton joined the protests. Asked later what he was thinking, he explained his intentions with a gentle and straightforward conviction: "I went because a lot of my friends been beaten, killed, abandoned, hurt by the police. So, I went down there just to fight for what I stand for: my Black people." On the streets and parking lots surrounding the mall, hundreds of youth and young adults faced off with lines of police officers in full riot gear. Some of the youth threw rocks at an impenetrable line of black-clad officers, whose riot shields formed a wall around them. Michael Singleton picked up a rock.

What happened next was caught on video by a bystander and seen all over the world. Singleton's mother, Toya Graham, plunged into the scene of the protest to grab her son, also clad in all black, by his neck. She swung him around, smacked his face and head repeatedly, and continued to follow him as he retreated, yelling and cursing at him for his participation in the demonstration and his contemplated challenge of the police officers. As the video went viral and was aired on several major news networks, Toya Graham became an instant national hero.

Commentators and news anchors lauded Graham for the sharp chastisement of her son, dubbing her the "Parent of the Year." National audiences saw her as taking a stand against the burning and looting that news coverage suggested was rampant in an apparently lawless Baltimore. Graham's confrontation with her son served as a conversation piece for many Americans looking for an opportunity to volunteer their thoughts on the futility of violence and destruction from the vantage point of comfortable homes far from Baltimore. Joining his mother for one of the many national television appearances that followed, Singleton was kidded for "getting whooped on television" and received advice on how to conduct himself from the women of *The View*. Talk-show hosts and audiences seemed to side unequivocally with his mother and urged him to express his views in "peaceful" ways. They probed and prodded Singleton about his decisions that day until he yielded up the admission of guilt that they and their viewing publics required: "I shouldn't have been there," he mumbled softly.

But it is unclear where, exactly, Michael Singleton should have been. This chapter examines the experiences of youth whose childhoods are lived out under a phenomenally high-stakes form of scrutiny. It considers the costs and consequences of wraparound surveillance and criminalization for the generations of young people of color who have been raised in an era of mass incarceration.

A CRIMINALIZED CHILDHOOD

When our team began interviewing several thousand people for the Multisite Family Study on Incarceration, Parenting and Partnering, we had no intention of learning about the criminalization of children. The study focused on partnership and parenting dynamics in families in which one parent was incarcerated. By the time we spoke with them, most of the men in these families had already served several years in prison. Like many other researchers concerned with the collateral consequences of mass incarceration, we were focused on understanding the effects of one particular experience with the system[1]—in this case, the state prison time that fathers were serving when they enrolled in the study. Following most families over a three-year period, we collected extensive data on how the father's incarceration had affected them. In the course of this work, we learned a great deal about how the harms of imprisonment extend long past the prison term and deep into the lives of those connected to the prisoner; I take up these topics in subsequent chapters.

As we continued to pore over the stories participants had shared with us,[2] we learned some other things we had not set out to find. To be sure, the men in the study had faced protracted suffering during their time as state prisoners. But their most damaging encounters with the criminal legal system seemed to have occurred long before we met them. Early life contacts with the system were generally briefer and ostensibly less brutal than the prison time men experienced as adults—but our qualitative analysis and structural equation modeling suggested that these youthful contacts may have wreaked lasting damage to men's behavioral health and ways of relating to their families. While any one such contact (for example, an arrest or a stay in juvenile detention) might have been relatively short-lived, the cumulative experience of childhood criminalization and punishment was linked to increased posttraumatic stress symptoms and social impairments in adulthood.

The surprising finding highlighted that our earlier understanding of children's exposure to the criminal legal system was incomplete. Certainly, we knew from earlier research that a school-to-prison "pipeline" tended to funnel children of color out of educational systems, into the juvenile justice system, and eventually into time in jail and prison as adults.[3] The alarm that this pivotal work sounded in popular consciousness focused on where the "pipeline" leads—that is, adult conviction and imprisonment. Yet it didn't always capture how surveillance and sanction might themselves undermine the experience of childhood, regardless of system outcomes. Whether it ultimately lands one in prison or not, spending one's childhood

years under high-stakes, racially targeted, institutional scrutiny is impactful in itself. Furthermore, the cumulative nature of these childhood contacts, like death by a thousand cuts, has been easy to miss in the prevailing
focus on measuring the effects of a single contact with the legal system (or
the fact of having any or no contact with that system). In attempting to
isolate the effects of a single event, we and some of our colleagues may have
inadvertently obscured the more pernicious, wraparound effects of the
carceral net—and missed the ways that it had quietly reshaped almost
every aspect of childhood for poor children of color.

Though seldom discussed as such, mass incarceration is, in large part,
a "childhood intervention."[4] Legal scholar Kristin Henning, director of
Georgetown University's juvenile justice clinic, argues that contemporary
youth of color are subjected to an unprecedented degree of surveillance
and scrutiny from criminal justice personnel: "Society has always tolerated some disruptive, and even delinquent, adolescent behavior without
formal state intervention and without significant cost or threat to public
safety. However, as is evident in data documenting the disproportionate
arrest and prosecution of youth of color, state actors appear particularly
unwilling to excuse and tolerate adolescent misconduct by Black and
Latinx youth."[5] Yet the same frontline government personnel who take
avid interest in monitoring boys of color for potential delinquency are
seen as relatively uninterested when they or their families are in danger.[6]
The combination of ever-present surveillance and absent protection suggests to young people of color that they are second-class citizens in the
eyes of the state.[7]

How did it come to this? President Ronald Reagan's widely publicized
declaration of the "War on Drugs" made official a set of federal, state, and
local government law-and-order agendas, begun in the Johnson and
Nixon administrations, that increasingly targeted poor communities of
color. The declaration furnished a name and a widely resonant ideology to
explain the militarized police presence that had already begun to descend
on urban Black neighborhoods nationwide.[8] Similarly bellicose declara-
tions have issued from the executive office during each successive presidential administration, with state and local political leaders also lending
enthusiastic support to a tough-on-crime agenda.[9] The increasingly harsh
sentencing policies of this period were accompanied and enabled by

a racialized shift in public infrastructure. A rapid expansion in local juvenile justice system infrastructure and state-level carceral capacity meant
that detention centers and prisons stood ready and waiting for youthful
guests to arrive.[10]

In the era of mass incarceration that tough-on-crime policies ushered
in, children of color do not experience "childhood" in any conventional
sense. In a letter to his young son, released the same year as Freddie Gray's
death, Ta-Nehisi Coates described it this way: "To be black in the Baltimore
of my youth was to be naked before the elements of the world, before all
the guns, fists, knives, crack, rape, and disease. And now, in your time, the
law has become an excuse . . . for furthering the assault on your body."[11]
Physical safety is a luxury that youth of color, particularly those in hyperincarcerated neighborhoods, do not enjoy. They face a stunning array of
physical dangers—from a robust (and increasingly militarized) police
presence in their neighborhoods and homes[12] to steeply disproportionate
risks of childhood homelessness,[13] violence and homicide victimization,[14]
and toxic lead exposure.[15] Rather than protecting children of color from
danger, however, mass incarceration–era institutions tend to treat them as
sources of danger to be controlled.

When evidence emerged of an epidemic of childhood lead poisoning in
urban Black communities, for example, the response from public health,
housing, and educational institutions was woefully inadequate.[16]
Protecting children of color from severe, lifelong cognitive and behavioral
impairments garnered much less interest from the public and policy makers than did the idea that they represented a so-called "demographic crime
bomb." John Dilulio's racist rhetoric was widely consumed by lay audiences
and was influential among policy makers in both political parties. Youth
raised in what Dilulio construed as the "moral poverty" of low-income
urban neighborhoods were supposedly most at risk: "Surrounded by deviant, delinquent, and criminal adults in abusive, violence-ridden, father-
less, Godless, and jobless settings . . . as long as their youthful energies
hold out, they will do what comes 'naturally': murder, rape, rob, assault,
burglarize, deal deadly drugs, and get high."[17] To eager audiences, Dilulio
figured urban children of color as a threat to public safety.

Racist notions of the supposed danger of urban youth assumed an especially prominent place in the Clinton-era political agenda. Dilulio was

invited to deliver an official briefing to the Clinton administration on the purported threat of young "super-predators." He alleged that this fast-growing group of youth had no regard for human life and committed egregious violent crimes with little cause.[18] The next year, First Lady Hillary Clinton described the imaginary young "super predator" in a New Hampshire speech on the White House crime-control agenda: "They are often connected to big drug cartels. They are not just gangs of kids anymore. They are often the kinds of kids that are called 'super-predators.' No conscience, no empathy. We can talk about why they ended up that way, but first we have to bring them to heel."[19]

The Clintons and their contemporaries in state and local policy making followed through on this rhetorical assault. Urban centers in the United States implemented and expanded a variety of intensive and hyperpunitive policing policies whose primary targets were children of color. These policies included widespread "zero tolerance" and "broken windows" policing in East Coast cities to gang injunctions on the West Coast that criminalized youth who gathered in public. Although diverse and jurisdiction-specific, they had the common effect of increasing warrantless and often causeless law enforcement contact with young people.[20] Under these various regimes, children were subjected to an array of day-to-day physical intrusions and assaults by public personnel.[21]

THE EXPERIENCE OF WRAPAROUND SURVEILLANCE AND SANCTION

Mass Incarceration and Youth Development

Mass incarceration–era policies have wound a restrictive net of social controls around the youth they target. Quantitative research on mass incarceration often tries to understand specific forms of justice system contact—police stops, arrests, convictions, imprisonment—and the consequences for those involved. In poor communities of color, however, the criminal legal system does not operate in such discrete ways. Living with the constant threat of police contact and (for many) the repeated exposure to arrest and detention is an experience not likely reducible to the effect of a singular police stop, an arrest, a conviction, or even a stay in detention.

We know relatively little about how the developmental timing and accumulation of events like these might shape well-being and development among youth of color.

When we surveyed Multi-site Family Study participants about their experiences with incarceration, we found that the prison terms men were serving when they entered our study were, for most, not a life event of singular significance. Rather, they were simply the most recent manifestation of a lifetime of surveillance, sanction, and social exclusion. Survey data told us that the typical participant had been arrested thirteen times and held in jail or prison an average of seven times over the course of his life—and that these experiences of arrest and detention began in childhood for most. Still, it was not until we conducted open-ended, qualitative interviews with a subset of couples around the time of men's release from prison that we began to grasp just how much the focus on a single, adult incarceration could miss.

The word *institutionalized* came up over and over as men and their intimate partners and coparents described the wraparound experiences of youthful punishment that had molded them. Particularly for those who had spent many of their childhood and young adult years in and out of confinement, extensive juvenile justice system exposure and the developmental effects of detention continued to define their adult lives. Partners explained how hard it was for men to function in the free world after spending many of their developing years in confinement. One interviewee put it like this: "He has been [in prison] since he was eighteen years old, and he has been in and out of juvi since he was little. So I feel like he's really institutionalized. When he's free, he doesn't know what to do." Violent, intrusive encounters with the criminal legal system during critical developmental periods, these interviews suggested, had shaped men's development. Such encounters often left them with severe posttraumatic stress and difficulty maintaining positive social ties, including nurturing relationships with partners and children. Affected men described being "institutionalized" as a form of inner suffering that made it difficult to navigate close relationships and ordinary social situations: "A woman has to have some type of understanding. . . . I was antisocial. . . . It's hard. I'm institutionalized. I'm f-cked up for real. Like I can't go in open places like that; if I do, I gotta sit in a corner. Loud noises affect me. Quick movements affect me. You know, it's like, it's f-cked up." Looking to our survey data to further understand this phenomenon, we constructed structural equation models using longitudinal survey data from both members of each study couple. Fitted models bore out the dynamic that participants had described in their qualitative interviews: men's childhood exposure to the criminal legal system predicted their adult posttraumatic stress symptoms, as well as how they approached close, personal relationships. Posttraumatic stress and a reactive, noncooperative approach to relationships, in turn, promoted dysfunctional couple conflict dynamics and ultimately abuse.

Coming of age at the height of mass incarceration, the men in our study had experienced forms of criminal legal system intervention during childhood that seemed to permanently alter their inner lives and personal relationships. But our own data stopped short of illuminating how this transformation occurred. The next four sections of this chapter turn to other valuable evidence to better understand how early-life surveillance and punishment shape the childhoods and life trajectories of American youth. The remaining sections attempt to quantify the racialized damage of a hypercarceral regime for youth and propose a reparations strategy for redressing it.

Aggressive Policing

Observing the day-to-day lives of boys of color in Oakland's flatlands, ethnographer Victor Rios documents how a "youth control complex" subjects them to constant, intensive monitoring. He describes this complex as "a system in which schools, police, probation officers, families, community centers, the media, businesses, and other institutions systematically treat young people's everyday behaviors as criminal activity"[22] Legal scholars and social scientists alike have documented the increasingly close regulation of adolescent conduct in the mass incarceration era and the disproportionate surveillance and sanction of youth of color within this regime.[23] Forms of verbal communication or even stylistic expression that violate stringent standards of conformity meet not simply with parental disapproval or informal correction but with various forms of official censure—including legal action.[24]

Youth, especially urban youth of color, routinely experience being stopped, questioned, and searched by police.[25] The rise of proactive policing in many American cities has meant that a variety of noncriminal behaviors can draw police attention and sanction. One can be legally cited for a variety of seemingly trivial transgressions, such as a "manner of walking" violation on the books in Ferguson, Missouri.[26] Measurably decoupled from individual behavior or neighborhood-level differences in crime,[27] police contact for trivial transgressions is indisputably racially targeted. This is particularly the case with formal sanctions for low-level misbehavior, as the Ferguson example illustrates: "Blacks totaled ninety-five percent of individuals charged with 'manner of walking,' ninety-four percent of individuals charged with failure to comply, ninety-two percent of individuals charged with resisting arrest, ninety-two percent of individuals charged with peace disturbance and eighty-nine percent of individuals charged with failure to obey."[28]

In East Coast cities, "zero tolerance" law enforcement, implemented approximately two decades ago, has encouraged mass arrests for minor crimes. Under zero tolerance policies, warrantless arrests encompass roughly 75 percent of all arrests in Baltimore. The practice of arresting and detaining individuals with no criminal charge at all (termed a "catch and release" arrest in Ferguson and a "walk-through" in Baltimore) subjects targeted individuals to many of the stressful and often violent aspects of law enforcement contact—arrest, booking, detention in holding cells, and eventual release—without a criminal charge.[29] A similar nickel-and-dime regime regulates the behavior of boys of color in Oakland's flatlands, where they are met with a steady stream of formal citations for trivial behavior: loitering, violating curfew, talking back to the school principal, wearing a poorly fitted bicycle helmet. As one study participant told Victor Rios after a highly invasive, warrantless encounter with law enforcement, "It happens every day."[30]

Proactive policing means that youth in targeted communities face not singular encounters with police but a barrage.[31] This form of policing draws boys of color into increasingly tight and increasingly consequential regulation of their day-to-day behavior:

> Minor citations for "little shit" played a crucial role in pipelining many of the
> young men in this study deeper into the criminal justice system. Some of the

boys missed their court dates; others appeared in court but could not pay their citations. This led to warrants for arrest or probation. Warrants and probationary status marked the young men for further criminalization. Police, school personnel, and probation officers would graduate the boys to a new level of policing and harassment. . . . When a young person is on probation, he is left with few rights; he can be stopped and searched for no reason, and he can be arrested for noncriminal transgressions such as hanging out with his friends or walking in the wrong part of the neighborhood.[32]

Ironically, contact with police in the context of minor misbehavior may be more damaging than contact associated with more serious transgressions, because of what being policed for apparent trivialities communicates to those targeted.[33] Taken together, such contacts curtail young people's access to physical safety and personal expression.

Indeed, frequent, low-level police intrusion, once hailed as a promising crime control strategy, appears to have a host of pernicious effects.[34] Racially targeted field interrogation practices telegraph an ugly message to youth of color about their presumed dangerousness and their subordinated place in society—a message that youth pick up loud and clear.[35] Exposure to violence at the hands of police places young people at heightened risk of depression and suicidality.[36] A single arrest diminishes educational outcomes and reduces asset accumulation in adulthood by approximately one half.[37] Even stop-and-frisk encounters and other comparatively low-consequence forms of police contact have been shown to damage young people's physical health and psychological well-being.[38] Citywide, implementation of such tactics is associated with a global decrease in standardized test scores among Black boys.[39] Not surprisingly, the experience of being policed for trivial behavior also tends to make targeted young people more likely to engage in serious transgressions in the future.[40]

School Pushout

More a hub than a pipeline, schools are physically and temporally central in the day-to-day lives of youth. They are also a defining feature in the landscape of social exclusion. The forms of surveillance and punishment to which youth of color are subjected in ostensibly educational settings do powerfully condition children's future life chances (as in the pipeline anal-ogy). But they are also harmful in themselves, regardless of where they lead or originate. While sanctioning on the streets and in community set-tings reaches into schools, damaging educational engagement and per-formance, school-based sanctions radiate into the community through administrators' contacts with parents and law enforcement.[41]

In public education, as in policing, the mass incarceration era has been a heyday for zero tolerance policies. Zero tolerance rule enforcement and other high-consequence behavior-control strategies in schools are informed not by pedagogy but by the criminal law enforcement logics of deterrence and incapacitation.[42] Students who fail to conform to school expectations meet with a range of quasi-criminal sanctions, including confinement in detention rooms and exclusion from the school commu-nity through suspension and expulsion.[43] In addition, almost three-quarters of public middle and high schools report a regular police pres-ence on school grounds, typically a sworn school resource officer (SRO). SROs are more likely to be deployed to schools with sizable proportions of low-income students and students of color.[44] Where SROs are present, students are more likely to be disciplined for low-level conduct violations and to be arrested for subjective charges.[45] This increased regulation of minor transgressions is disproportionately directed at Black students.[46]

The school climate fostered by SROs and other deterrence-and-incapacitation-based strategies is difficult to reconcile with cultures of learning and care in which many educators and school administrators are deeply invested.[47] Acknowledging this disjuncture matter-of-factly in arguing for the need for SROs, the National Association of School Resource Officers warns that "anyone who hasn't received the extensive training provided to law enforcement officers will likely be mentally unprepared to take a life, especially the life of a student."[48] This assertion underscores how incompatible schools' stated goals of educational oppor-tunity and inclusion are with a school-policing approach that requires the presence of staff who are trained and prepared to kill students. Students exposed to SRO programs in middle school are significantly less likely to graduate from high school or enroll in college.[49]

An exclusion-oriented disciplinary environment can exacerbate other barriers to school attendance that young people face, such as trauma, mental health conditions, learning difficulties, and residential instability. Youth with mental health– and trauma-related needs are at heightened risk for school truancy, yet schools' responses to truancy regularly sidestep these root-cause issues. Youth who are truant are often suspended from school, formally filed as status offenders, and placed on juvenile probation. These consequences, in turn, make it likely they will be found delinquent by the court and less likely they will be able to return to school.[50] Among youth with trauma histories, such treatment is especially counterproductive; for them, school can become just another hostile or unpredictable environment that is best avoided. Schools focused on punishment also systematically miss chances to connect trauma survivors and youth experiencing other mental health difficulties with the early intervention resources they need.[51] The underlying challenges that punitive approaches leave unaddressed often prevent young people from being able to persist in school.[52]

Classroom environments and the disciplinary practices that bind them can create a developmentally counterproductive feedback loop of negative experiences among children whose unaddressed mental health disorders are incompatible with rule compliance in a highly proscriptive, group educational setting. For children whose underlying challenges manifest as symptoms of high impulsivity and low self-control, the school environment tends to promote escalating deviance and disengagement.[53] The increasingly close integration of school discipline processes with law enforcement means that unaddressed emotional and behavioral needs like these can bring rapid and devastating consequences in students' lives.[54] Children who are subjected to exclusionary discipline practices are two to five times more likely to become involved with the justice system compared to similarly equipped students whose needs and behaviors are addressed in other ways.[55] Even a single disciplinary incident in a punitive context can be impactful: exposure to an out-of-school suspension, for example, puts students at sharply increased risk for subsequent arrest, school disenrollment, and eventual incarceration—even among students who had not engaged in *any* form of serious delinquency prior to suspension.[56]

The tandem problems of neglected trauma and harsh, exclusionary discipline are heavily racialized. Students who are poor, male, or Black or

Latinx are disproportionately targeted for disciplinary sanction in school, including exclusionary and zero-tolerance discipline practices.[57] Black students receive a markedly disproportionate share of general disciplinary attention and harsher forms of disciplinary sanction from their schools: "Even while controlling for effects of misbehavior, attitudes, academic performance, parental attention, school organization, and economic disadvantage and poverty, black students receive harsher school punishments."[58] Staff are especially likely to underdiagnose problems like attention-deficit hyperactivity disorder among Black children, underrefer them to treatment, and overpunish them at school relative to their peers.[59] Teachers and administrators are more motivated to work out nonpunitive disciplinary strategies for white, middle-class children with behavioral issues than with children of color or low-income children.

Among staff, educators, and administrators (who, of course, vary widely in their perspectives on punitive discipline), support for punitive discipline may be driven by racialized perceptions of students' dangerousness.[60] Schools with larger populations of Black and low-income students are disproportionately likely to implement punitive and exclusionary discipline policies.[61] Quantitative research confirms that the perceived threat of students in predominantly Black schools drives the overuse of harsh disciplinary practices, even after controlling for school-level delinquency, crime salience, socioeconomic status, gender, degree of urbanization, and staff training practices. The imagined racial threat posed by a majority-Black student body not only predicts greater use of punitive discipline but also reduced use of restorative approaches to misbehavior, regardless of the prevalence of such behavior and independent of students' economic disadvantage.[62] Of course, the only individuals actually endangered by racial threat in educational settings are the students of color whose education and life chances it foreshortens.

Social Exclusion and Disconnection

Trouble at school radiates into other life domains, putting opportunities for social connection and contribution further from reach for troubled students.[63] Family relationships and domestic life, rather than furnishing a refuge from punitive schools and streets, can be profoundly undermined by processes of institutional criminalization. School and justice system personnel may actively recruit parents, neighbors, and community support systems to confront and monitor youth, infusing key relationships with shame, fear, and suspicion.[64] Parents' fearful and often harsh reactions to their children are founded in a frightening reality: the delinquent label signals their children's heightened risk of exposure to potential street violence and violent encounters with police.[65]

When legal epidemiologist Erin Kerrison and her team talked with two generations of Black Baltimore residents about their experiences of policing in 2015, they did not set out to investigate parent-child relationships per se. But many older interviewees, in describing the kind of danger children in their communities faced, focused on the high-profile story of Toya Graham and the parental concern and responsibility for which she seemed to stand. Their reactions to the triangular confrontation among police squad, mother, and son at Mondawmin Mall highlight the omnipresent and formidable threat of arrest, police violence, and incarceration from which parents of color are impossibly tasked with protecting their children. Lifted up as exemplary by other adults who shared her desperate concern for her children's survival, Toya Graham's actions typify "the urgency that Black parents feel to rescue their children from impending lethal state-sanctioned violence. . . . Parents prefer not only that the beating come from them instead of a police officer, but that it serve as enough of a 'taste' of rage that their child will be stunned into self-preservation lest they meet a greater violence at the hands of someone else."[66] Graham herself saw the celebrated beating she gave her son as neither heroic nor praiseworthy but simply necessary—her duty as a parent. It highlights the impossibility of the task, set before her and other parents, of somehow nurturing children's healthy development and self-expression while also teaching them to dodge bullets.

Outside of families and schools, structure and support for youth tend to be lacking. Many urban communities offer some free activities and spaces for youth, such as youth development or empowerment programs, sports, and drop-in centers. But in the mass incarceration era, many such spaces prioritize more carceral objectives in their dealings with youth.[67] Youth on probation, for example, may be required to meet with their probation officers onsite at the local youth community center or be tracked into exclusively juvenile justice-oriented programming (such as anger management classes) within such spaces.[68] Co-locating youth services with juvenile probation may be done with the best of intentions, such as making sure that delinquent youth have access to the supportive services they need. But the goals of monitoring youth for potential parole violations and of creating a welcoming, affirming, and nonstigmatizing environment for those who are struggling appear fundamentally at odds. The culture of criminalization that characterizes the mass incarceration era thus contaminates almost every space—home, school, community—in which youth spend time. The wraparound reality of "multispatial criminalization"[69] ushers many youth into another space that we claim we don't want them to go: court.

Legal Adultification

The presumption of diminished child culpability and the directive of rehabilitation on which juvenile courts were founded have been functionally eviscerated by the racialized crime-control imperative of a hypercarceral era.[70] Separate juvenile courts, equipped with specialized juvenile court judges, staff, and procedures, were established on the premise that young people's welfare, confidentiality, and need for rehabilitative services require special attention. Early juvenile courts recognized that the developmental differences between youth and adults limited youth culpability. Beginning in the early mass incarceration era, however, juvenile courts came under pressure to deprioritize youth welfare and rehabilitation in favor of a primary focus on safety and crime prevention.[71]

A racialized rhetoric of youth dangerousness drove the increasing adultification of youth in contemporary judicial process. Such rhetoric figures delinquent children not as deserving of special protection and disposition, as in earlier concepts of juvenile justice, but as "dangerous and irredeemable."[72] John Dilulio, the academic darling of tough-on-crime policy makers, relied on explicitly racist reasoning. He famously described "the black kids who inspire the fear" as "not merely unrecognizable but alien." He also publicly suggested that "all that's left of the black community in some pockets of urban America is deviant, delinquent, and criminal adults surrounded by severely abused and neglected children."[73] The racist rhetoric of DiIulio and his contemporaries helped to convince politicians and the general public that youth of color deserved fear and punishment, rather than care, from adults.

As Hillary Clinton's New Hampshire speech clearly communicated, what the administration had in mind for delinquent young people of color was not a rehabilitative path toward a promising adult future. By the mid-1990s, juvenile courts had come to focus less on rehabilitation and more on deterring and incapacitating youth through harsher punishment. Despite the pseudo-academic arguments used to justify the punitive turn in juvenile justice, it appears to have been more a matter of political strategy than evidence-based policy. Indeed, it directly contradicted the official position of the National Research Council at the time, which was that harsh, punitive youth sentencing was unsupported by evidence.[74]

Predicated though it was on the specter of youth aggression and violence, newly harsh juvenile sentencing has overwhelmingly targeted minor property or drug offenses. Nationally, fewer than one-quarter of crimes for which minors are arrested are crimes against persons. The majority do not involve direct harm or threat of harm to other human beings; they are criminalized acts involving property, psychoactive substances, or status offenses, such as truancy.[75] In many states, youth charged with more serious acts are tried as adults—receiving even harsher (and less developmentally appropriate) treatment from the courts. Almost a tenth of detained youth are held in adult prisons, which seriously endangers their well-being.[76] Minimum ages for adult prosecution range from ten years old in Kansas to sixteen years old in the Dakotas, District of Columbia, and South Carolina, with a mean transfer age of fourteen.[77] Even when youth remain in juvenile courts and are tried as minors, children as young as ten years old can be sentenced to serve time in a juvenile detention facility. Furthermore, despite Supreme Court interventions and a consensus among legal scholars that life-without-parole sentences are fundamentally inappropriate for young people—whose cognition and decision-making are still developing—judges retain the ability to impose such sentences where the court determines the child to be "irreparably corrupted."

The developmental inappropriateness of contemporary juvenile justice is exacerbated by gang-related sentencing enhancements in many states.

Such enhancements allow prosecutors to pursue far heavier sentences, as many as five to ten additional years, for individuals who commit a crime that is determined to be for the benefit of a gang. Such policies don't simply fail to accommodate developmental differences in youth cognition; they invite prosecutorial abuses that actively exploit these differences. In a common practice known as overfiling, juvenile prosecutors file charges on which they are unlikely to obtain a conviction. Youth are informed of these charges and threatened with serious prison time. They may also be counseled by their attorneys on the implications of a gang-related charge for the trial process; that is, evidence that would otherwise be considered prejudicial becomes admissible. Gang-related enhancements help to create an environment that pushes youth, even those who believe or know they are innocent, to plead guilty.[78]

Even under ordinary circumstances, with no gang charges involved, developmental differences place youth at a measurable disadvantage during plea bargaining—the stage at which more than 90 percent of cases are settled. Youth are highly susceptible to false confessions and false guilty pleas.[79] Youth commonly plead guilty to crimes of which they believe they are innocent.[80] Moreover, defense attorneys report accepting guilty pleas from adolescent clients even when they believe that a client is not competent to comprehend the plea decision and its often-permanent consequences.[81] Defense attorneys are often ill prepared to communicate effectively with their clients about these issues.[82] Differences in frontal lobe development make adolescents less able to understand and weigh the long-range consequences of a conviction against the immediate desire to resolve a frightening charge.[83]

By systematically constructing youth of color as threatening predators who are beyond the purview of adult protection, mass incarceration era sentencing confers a racialized adulthood that deprives youth of color of developmentally appropriate responses to misbehavior and harm. Black youth have been increasingly prosecuted for drug-related crimes during a period in which their overall rates of drug use remained relatively unchanged.[84] Black children who come before juvenile courts, particularly Black boys, are less likely than other youth to receive rehabilitative treatment options and more likely to receive exclusively punitive sanctions.[85] State records show that Black and Latinx youth are disproportionately likely to be transferred to adult courts, and Black youth are twice as likely as their peers to be sentenced to life without parole.[86]

As in the school system, the punitive focus of contemporary juvenile justice leaves young people's trauma and mental health needs grossly underaddressed. Trauma histories are normative among youth in contact with the juvenile justice system. Common histories among system-involved youth include traumatic loss or bereavement (reported by 61 percent of youth in the juvenile justice system), the impairment of a parent or parent figure (reported by 52 percent), violence in the home (reported by 52 percent), emotional abuse by a caregiver (49 percent), physical abuse by a caregiver (39 percent), and exposure to community violence (34 percent). About one-third of justice-involved children report severe and chronic trauma—that is, having experienced multiple serious, traumatic events every year from their early childhood through adolescence.[87]

Multiple trauma exposures make youth substantially more likely to develop mental health conditions, tripling their risk of posttraumatic stress disorder (PTSD) and doubling their risk of major depression.[88] Indeed, most youth in contact with juvenile court or placed in detention have at least one mental health condition; the most comprehensive study found that 70 percent of such youth reported a mental health condition.[89] Rigorous mediation analysis demonstrates that trauma exposure promotes the development of mental health conditions and that such conditions (in turn) increase a young person's likelihood of reacting aggressively in the face of challenges.[90] If uninterrupted by treatment and supportive services, this cycle carries children from early mistreatment to later experiences of labeling, punishment, and ongoing harm. Youth who have mental health conditions are more likely to be arrested, have poorer outcomes in juvenile courts, and are more likely to be found in violation of court requirements.[91] They are also significantly more likely to experience continued arrest and legal-system involvement into young adulthood.[92]

In contrast, youth who receive treatment for mental health needs early in their juvenile justice system involvement are less likely to be rearrested.[93] But far too few youth receive these services. Eighty percent of youth with mental health conditions who are involved with juvenile courts and 85 percent of youth with mental health conditions who are detained reported that they did not receive mental health treatment.[94] Justice-involved adolescents report widespread barriers to mental health treatment.[95] Boys, particularly Black or Latinx youth, are particularly unlikely to receive these services.[96] These youth face the widespread barriers to behavioral health care, like stigma and shame, that curtail access in the general population. But research suggests that, for Black boys in particular, additional deterrents discourage seeking behavioral health care—among them, past exposures to ineffective treatment and a learned mistrust of the service delivery system.[97] Racial and gender disparities in mental health treatment, evident at multiple stages of juvenile justice processing,[98] may exacerbate racial and gender disparities in legal-system involvement.

ADDING UP THE HARM OF YOUTH CRIMINALIZATION

Policy makers bent on bringing fearsome children "to heel" did succeed in incapacitating many young people. Whether they ever got around to "talk[ing] about why they ended up that way" (in Hillary Clinton's choice words) is another matter. While policing and pipelining have wrought undeniable damage, a somewhat less-discussed hallmark of mass incarceration has been the malign neglect leveled at low-income youth of color. Needs for preventive or supportive intervention to address traumatic experiences, treat mental health conditions, or address environmental toxin exposures have been left unmet in the overwhelming institutional focus on punitive responses to young people's behavior. The cost of public neglect for the more than forty birth cohorts of Black children born in the era of mass incarceration has not previously been tallied.

With regard to environmental lead exposure, the price of neglect has been astronomical. In the decades since Hillary Clinton's infamous speech, robust evidence on the proliferation of lead poisoning in low-income urban communities furnished a partial answer to the question her husband's administration didn't care to answer. The much-touted (though modest) rise in youth violence during his administration has since been linked to peak lead exposure in low-income urban areas. Lead poisoning remains the second-most-common preventable disease among American children.[99] Affected children struggle with cognition and impulse control and are more likely to experience poor academic performance, school suspension, truancy, and dropout, as well as addiction, aggression, and other behavioral issues.[100] The Centers for Disease Control and Prevention (CDC) deems there is no safe level of lead in children's blood.[101] High levels (>70 mcg/dL) induce profound neurological debilitation, seizure, coma, and death—a common occurrence in the pediatric units of urban hospitals in the latter half of the twentieth century.[102] But even levels considered "low" until recently (<5 mcg/dL according to CDC's 2012 guideline) are now understood to produce permanent neurological damage and behavioral disorders, including aggression, in children.[103]

Children affected by lead poisoning attract the attention of the juvenile and adult justice systems. Spatial and temporal variation in air-lead levels is strongly correlated with rates of violent crime and juvenile delinquency, even after controlling for a variety of other environmental and structural influences.[104] Decades of data in Atlanta, Chicago, Indianapolis, Minneapolis, New Orleans, and San Diego show that metric tons of air lead for a given year predict later increases in rates of aggravated assault when those exposed as infants and toddlers became young adults. Differences in air-lead levels explain a stunning 90 percent of the variation in rates of assault across American cities.[105] Lead exposure also strongly predicts rates of violent crime arrest among boys, children in low-income households, and children in low-income neighborhoods.[106] What might have been different if policy makers had mobilized a fraction of the massive public resources that they dedicated to punishing youth toward responding to the public health catastrophe that underlay many children's impulsivity and aggression? The cost of preventable lead-related developmental disability, cardiovascular disease, and behavioral difficulties in just one birth cohort of American children was conservatively estimated at $43.4 billion in 2002[107] (or $62.8 billion in 2020 dollars).

Yet the price of malign neglect for Black children born in the mass incarceration era becomes even steeper when we consider the chronic disconnection from schooling and employment that tends to follow young people's neglected educational and behavioral health needs. When youth between the ages of sixteen and twenty-four are detached from both education and employment, the immediate and lifetime consequences are profound, both in social costs to youth and others in their communities and in direct public expenses.[108] An in-depth, national economic assessment conducted by a team of researchers at Columbia University and the City University of New York found that a cohort of 3.46 million youth who spent their late teens and early adult years chronically disconnected (reporting no participation in formal employment or schooling after age sixteen) paid an average of $1,680 less in taxes per year than they otherwise would have and incurred an additional $12,220 in yearly direct taxpayer costs for expenses such as Medicaid-billed health care and juvenile and adult detention. Net the amount that public educational systems "saved" by neither providing these youth with a complete public secondary education nor subsidizing any college expenses for them, these yearly direct fiscal costs totaled $13,900 per chronically disconnected youth (or $16,091 in 2020 dollars). Such youth incurred an additional $37,450 in indirect social costs, such as lost wages and the costs to victims of their involvement in harmful activity (or $43,352 in 2020 dollars).

Across a lifetime, chronic disconnection among just one cohort of young people (3.46 million of them in the cohort on which Belfield and colleagues focused, who reached age twenty-four in 2009) will rack up $3,359,568,832,439 in lost personal and public resources. Underattachment to schooling and the workforce, estimated to affect another 3.3 million youth per cohort, is associated with $2,104,274,076,083 in lost personal and public resources over a lifetime.[109] Combined, the lifetime costs of educational and employment disconnection in late youth and young adulthood for this single cohort of youth will total approximately $5.46 trillion ($5,463,842,908,522) in 2020 dollars.

Racial disparities in unaddressed childhood trauma and mental health issues and racially targeted school pushout mean that youth and young adults of color experience disproportionate disconnection from prosocial institutions. Although Black and Latinx young people make up 15 and 18 percent, respectively, of the US population ages sixteen to twenty-four, Belfield and colleagues note that they make up 32 and 22 percent of those disconnected from work and school—disparities that are not attributable to differences in youth misbehavior.[110] Racial disparities in youth and young adult disconnection are even sharper in certain urban areas. In Atlanta, Boston, Chicago, Dallas, Houston, New York, Los Angeles, Miami, Philadelphia, and Washington, DC, for example, Black and Latinx youth are 300 to 600 percent more likely to be disconnected from work and school than their white peers.[111]

What do these figures tell us about the damage associated with racialized criminalization of young people in the mass incarceration era? To approximate the harm caused by treating youth of color as dangerous, pushing them out of public institutions, and neglecting their need for care, I first calculate how many fewer youth of color would have experienced disconnection from work and employment if such risk were unaffected by race. If the youth of color in Belfield and colleagues' 2009 cohort of 38.9 million sixteen-to-twenty-four-year-olds were only as likely as their white peers to become disconnected, just 11.8 percent of them would have experienced disconnection from both school and work—that is, 688,530 of the 5,835,000 Black youth in the cohort and 826,236 of the 7,002,000 Latinx youth in the cohort. Comparing these figures to the actual numbers of disconnected youth (2.144 million Black youth and 1.474 million Latinx youth) suggests that 1,455,470 Black youth and 647,764 Latinx youth in the 2009 cohort were "excess" disconnections that arose in the context of racially targeted criminalization and neglect. Over a lifetime, the costs of these "excess" disconnections (which average $810,049 in 2020 dollars for each youth who does not participate in education or work) would total $1,179,002,656,986 for Black youth and $524,720,864,807 for Latinx youth in the 2009 cohort (a total of $1,703,723,521,793).

Examining the timing of changes in national and local criminal justice policies and policing strategies reveals that four other cohorts of American youth are likely to have been affected by racial criminalization in similar ways as those in Belfield and colleagues' study: those who were sixteen to twenty-four years old in 1982, 1991, 2000, and 2018. Although we lack cohort-specific estimates of racially disproportionate disconnection for these additional youth, for purposes of estimation, one might imagine that the magnitude of racially disproportionate disconnection for each was proportional to the prison population in that year (as proxy for the population reach of hypercarceral policies and practices at a given point in time) and to the proportion of the youth population that was Black and Latinx. Estimating the cost of youth disconnection in each of the other four cohorts as a function of these demographic variables suggests that the inflation-adjusted cost of excess disconnection would be approximately $6.09 trillion ($6,085,783,435,849) in 2020 dollars across the five cohorts. Of this figure, roughly $4.31 trillion ($4,307,612,644,035) is associated with the excess disconnection of Black young people.

The $4.31 trillion estimate represents a lower bound of the personal and public losses associated with racial criminalization of Black youth in the mass incarceration period. No such estimate can be exact, and this one is likely conservative for several reasons. First, Belfield and colleagues exclude costs associated with disconnection prior to age twenty-four. Second, I use the average lifetime cost of youth disconnection, although Belfield and colleagues estimate that the yearly and lifetime costs for Black youth are considerably higher than lifetime costs for their peers. As such, the estimate offers a valuable starting point for grasping the magnitude of harm to disconnected youth across four decades of racial criminalization and the extent of reparative effort that will be required to correct it.

REPAIRING HARMS TO CRIMINALIZED YOUTH

The institutional policies and practices of the mass incarceration era have deprived youth of color of many of the essentials of a healthy childhood: room to make mistakes, care for physical and mental well-being, equitable access to tools and skills for forming and pursuing long-term goals, and a supportive community of adults to undergird and affirm that pursuit.[112] Restoring these losses is impossible—but a sincere effort to make it right would include reparative investments on par with the magnitude of the harms sustained, as well as a multilevel and multisectoral policy commitment to promote and honor the leadership of youth of color. Consistent with economist Sandy Darity's vision of a reparations "portfolio,"[113] reparations for the racial harm of mass incarceration would ideally include both individual and collective compensation. For directly affected individuals, cash-value payouts could be distributed on a monthly or lump-sum basis at the individual's option. Alternatively, individual trusts could be created on behalf of affected persons for use in a variety of stabilizing or asset-building endeavors: physical or mental health care, education or training expenses, small business start-up costs, a down payment on a mortgage loan, or subsistence expenses in retirement.

Individual restitution for those who came of age in the mass incarceration era should be accompanied by "institution building" investments at the local and national levels.[114] Guided by the evidence on chronic disconnection, this work could focus primarily on programs that support reconnection to education, meaningful life's work, and a positive long-term future. Efforts to help youth rebuild or remake their connections to education and employment recognize that such connections are central to long-term social and material well-being in the current political economy. Sadly, federal funding for programs that serve disconnected youth have fallen precipitously. An annual reinvestment of just $6.5 billion (a $4 billion annual increase over current funding levels) in such programs could serve to reconnect one million youth per year.[115] Community-based youth organizations that operate outside of the school and juvenile justice systems represent a top priority for reinvestment. Though often financially strained and underequipped, these organizations have a critical role to play in reconnecting youth of color who have been marginalized in, or pushed out of, mainstream institutions. Collaborations between local grassroots organizations that have built trusted relationships with young people and the mainstream educational and workforce institutions (which control and distribute key resources that many youth need) have great potential to benefit marginalized youth.[116] Critically, many such programs also center youth and community leadership and accountability.[117]

The history of the youth-initiated and community-guided YouthBuild program offers an instructive example of what it looks like to bring such a program to national scale. In 1979, a newly formed collective of youth of color in East Harlem called the Youth Action Project founded the program in collaboration with longtime educator Dorothy Stoneman. The founding youth collective shared a vision of transforming their immediate neighborhood by rebuilding deteriorating homes and taking back empty buildings. As a start, they successfully renovated an abandoned, ten-unit apartment building in the neighborhood. Today, YouthBuild programs operate in most of the fifty states, with each program engaging anywhere from twenty to two hundred local youth and young adults who have not completed high school, many of whom have histories of arrest and adjudication.[118]

Similar to JobCorps and AmeriCorps, YouthBuild provides full-time, wraparound programming that includes education and employment opportunities alongside structured support for community engagement. The wraparound model shows considerable promise for countering the equally wraparound experience of "multi-spatial criminalization"[119]— effectively reengaging youth whose access to traditional education and employment pathways has been blocked or interrupted.[120] For YouthBuild participants, youth-driven educational activities (in and out of the classroom) are combined with on-the-job construction training (through renovating a home for a low-income family); community service projects; case management and leadership development, including the development of a personal growth plan; and connections to other supportive services, such as counseling, housing assistance, and childcare.[121] A randomized controlled trial found that youth who participated experienced higher civic engagement, education and vocational training attainment, and higher wages and earnings.[122] But at the program's current funding level ($89.5 million in annual support from the US Department of Housing and Urban Development), YouthBuild programs are unable to keep up with demand among youth. Indeed, youth demand so steeply exceeds program capacity that local programs must turn away an average of three interested youth for every one they serve.[123]

Radical transformation of educational institutions represents another key target for institution-building reparations. The classrooms of the mass incarceration era have played a central role in the replication of social inequality and exclusion, but they also hold extraordinary potential to alter young people's habituated understandings of themselves and their life prospects. Indeed, an adaptation of the YouthBuild model to twenty-nine diploma-granting educational institutions illustrates what is possible when youth and young adults of color are supported in remaking mainstream educational institutions.[124] The initiative—which combined wraparound supportive services with meaningful opportunities for youth contribution and leadership—demonstrated that schools "can be sites where existing hierarchies are reproduced and they can be places where these very same hierarchies are disrupted and possibilities for class mobility are created . . . sites where [transformations] in students' fundamental beliefs about themselves and the world around them can occur."[125] Actively affirming, community-contribution-oriented, and youth-driven educational experiences represent a promising model for future schools that prioritize all students' educational needs.

Countering negative expectations of students of color held by white teachers, which measurably depress student achievement,[126] is also imperative. Youth of color deserve culturally based education and support to counter harmful racial messaging from the cultural mainstream. Cultural identity development is closely linked to resilience among American youth of color.[127] Youth who are able to develop strong cultural pride fare better in many domains than those who do not.[128] Efforts by youth development programs to support positive cultural-identity development show great promise for helping young people to realize their life goals in the face of culturally and racially targeted adversities.[129] Schools, because of their unmatched reach and their historical role in affirming white cultural supremacy, offer an important and promising venue for such work.[130] To interrupt the lifetime domino effects that often begin with school discipline issues and juvenile arrest, interventions could leverage broad-reach settings like schools and engage teachers and other potentially supportive adults in supporting positive cultural identity and cultural pride for youth of color[131]—beginning in the very settings in which their cultural experiences have traditionally been pushed to the margins.

Schools also hold great untapped potential to support young people in navigating their trauma and mental health needs.[132] Therapeutic interventions represent a positive and effective alternative to punitive practices, but accessing therapeutic services outside of the school building and school day presents formidable challenges to many of the youth who most need these services.[133] School-based mental health programs that target externalizing problems (such as aggression) and are delivered several times per week, are integrated with academic instruction, and focus on youth who demonstrate the most need (rather than universal prevention approaches delivered to all students) are effective at addressing students' mental health symptoms.[134] School-based trauma interventions developed by and for low-income communities of color, such as the Cognitive Behavioral Intervention for Trauma in Schools, can support youth in developing healthy coping options while engaging parents and teachers in creating environments where healthy coping is truly a viable option.[135]

Recognized as promising by multiple federal agencies, the framework includes culturally responsive and affirming practices for adaptation to diverse school contexts.[136]

Of course, specific reparative initiatives in the school setting and beyond will be of limited use without a broader effort to transform school cultures of punishment and marginalization into cultures of mutual respect, affirmation, belonging, and collaborative problem solving that promote equitable outcomes for students of color.[137] Even modest, incremental efforts by schools to transform school cultures in this way demonstrate success in shifting the pattern of school pushout.[138] As long-term transformative efforts unfold, they can be enhanced by other simple measures: greeting all students at the beginning of the school day, creating opportunities for them to share their stories, and offering positive feedback early and often. Such acts send a message of welcome and repair in communities recovering from institutional maltreatment.[139]

ENGAGING THE POWER OF YOUTHFUL CHALLENGE

The malign neglect leveled at youth of color in the mass incarceration era has sidelined their contributions in many arenas. Replacing the web of surveillance and sanction with a youth-supportive culture will involve improving direct services to youth but also a systematic effort to "respect and embrace the work that young people do for dignity and freedom . . . decriminalizing young people's style and noncriminal actions, listening to young people's analysis of the system, and asking them how to develop programs and policies that can best help them."[140] Remaking community institutions to center the leadership of youth of color will require concerted, community-wide effort on a massive scale.[141]

A healthy oppositional identity and connections to nonmainstream activities and organizations can play a powerful role in cultivating youth well-being and resilience.[142] For youth of color whose experiences have been marginalized in mainstream institutions, reconnection may involve explicitly affirming their own worth in the face of, *and in opposition to,* injustice.[143] In articulating and publicly enacting an oppositional consciousness, young people rematerialize themselves and relegitimize their lived experiences in the civic body. Protest actions that allow youth to deliver an oppositional perspective to those with political or economic power thus represent an essential form of civic engagement and participation. Such work draws on young people's prior experiences of being excluded, devalued, and othered as a critical resource rather than ignoring or perpetuating those experiences.[144]

Despite heavy impediments to youth political participation and the "declining representative capacity" of American democracy,[145] many young people go to great lengths to contribute to civic life through protest and critique. The fact that individuals who have lived entire childhoods in the face of pervasive social exclusion would opt to invest their time in collective political action should command our respect—but it is often met with further harassment and punishment: "Symptomatic of Ferguson's reflexive use of its criminal justice system was the wholesale arrest approach on display during the protests that followed [Mike Brown]'s killing. Many individuals who were speaking, videotaping or standing in silence, including news reporters and photographers, were arrested and then released without being charged and without any paperwork."[146] The cathartic, communicative, and participatory impulses that motivate protest engagement for many youth are often ignored, negatively interpreted, or even criminalized by adults in their families and communities.[147] Yet many youth involved in street protests, having been actively and systematically pushed out of a wide array of domestic, public, and institutional spaces, have little recourse to other forms of expression or participation. Their engagement in protest often represents a brave, positive, and creative response to their situations. It may also be an expression of last resort. Whether such acts are met with respect and responsiveness or with further criminalization and exclusion may be pivotally important—not only for the futures of the youth concerned but also for the future of a nation that has silenced them for too long.

CONCLUSION

On February 24, 2016, Hillary Clinton's campaign tour made its way to Charleston, South Carolina, the historical Wall Street of the American trade in human beings and site of innumerable atrocities against Black Americans. In a city whose white residents clung to the domestic slave trade until halted by military force, neither contemporary white residents nor visitors appear willing to relinquish the touristic exploitation of that legacy. Tourists who have exhausted their interest in the human auction grounds and Old Slave Mart of the central city are encouraged to "experience the opulence of early Charleston" on display in the many lovingly preserved plantations that dot the surrounding countryside—which describe themselves as "lush," "grand," festive places to explore, vacation, and wed.[148]

Ashley Williams, a Black queer activist from Charlotte, North Carolina, visited Charleston in 2016, not to "experience the opulence" but to meet Hillary Clinton on the campaign trail. Williams approached Clinton in the middle of her address to the donors who had assembled with her in a duly opulent Charleston home. Williams opened a small banner that read, "We have to bring them to heel" and asked for an apology for Clinton's role in the criminalization of Black youth.

WILLIAMS: We want you to apologize for mass incarceration. I'm not a "super-predator," Hillary Clinton.

CLINTON: We'll talk about it. OK, fine, we'll talk about it.

WILLIAMS: Can you apologize to Black people for mass incarceration?

CLINTON: Well, can I talk? And maybe then you can listen to what I say. There are a lot of issues in this campaign. The very first speech that I gave back in April was about criminal justice reform.

WILLIAMS: You called Black people "super-predators."

AUDIENCE MEMBER: You're being rude!

AUDIENCE MEMBER: That's not appropriate!

WILLIAMS: She called Black people "super-predators." *That's* rude.

AUDIENCE MEMBER: You're trespassing![149]

Williams's exchange with Clinton ended with a familiar and predictable sight: a Black young person being hauled away. In this case, Williams's forcible exit ensured that the rest of the assembled guests might proceed uninterrupted with the more predictable form of political conversation they had intended. Despite being a paying guest at a small function in which candidate conversation was encouraged, being better informed regarding Clinton's political history than were other political analysts at the time, and making a calmly assertive request—this during a campaign in which overtly "rude" exchanges among and between candidates and reporters were commonplace—Williams was immediately and harshly shut down and physically removed.

Rhetoric about encouraging youth civic engagement and democratic participation notwithstanding, Williams's short-lived "trespass" into political debate and the blatantly criminalizing response it received reveals much about our ingrained notions of where young people of color belong—and don't. If we truly wish to make reparations for the harms done to youth by a racist and politically opportunist vision of law and order, we must cease to fetishize the narrow version of civic engagement favored by many adults: watching the nightly news, making polite conversation about current events, and casting a vote for a party-nominated candidate on the appropriate day. We must also cease escorting from the proverbial building those young people who aim to participate in our political process in more challenging, confrontational, or inconvenient ways. Democracy is better served by recognizing and responding to the bravery, intellectual engagement, and dedication to collective betterment that Ashley Williams and other young activists have offered than by shutting it down. If the election season that inspired Williams's protest (and the presidential reign of terror that followed it) is any indication, the preservation of our most basic rights and freedoms may depend on it.

3 "More than a Shell"

PERPETUAL IMPRISONMENT

Since his release from more than two decades in California prisons and jails, American artist Gil Batle has been etching the experience into eggshells. His bas-relief carvings, rendered with a dentist's drill, depict scenes from life inside prison in sharp and visceral detail. Studying the *Sanctuary* egg from his *Hatched in Prison* series, the eye goes to a crown of flying birds and open sky. Their finely cut wings stand out sharply where the surrounding shell has been drilled away to let in light. Directly beneath the birds, correctional officers restrain and assault prisoners in a set of harsh, muscular, tightly interlocking scenes. Batle says that the egg is "about how most convicts are never free. Doesn't matter if they are on the streets or in prison, they are never free. . . . It's only a matter of time when they will be back in the joint or on the streets. Both are terrifying."[1] Above the flying birds, an unbroken sequence of tally marks wraps the top of the egg, suggesting no end to the counted days (fig. 1).

The commentary, drilled into eggshell by an artist whose postprison life looks a lot less bleak from the outside than those of most returning prisoners whom I have interviewed, is stark. Batle's work suggests that the moment of release that all prisoners await is a mythic one, that every person imprisoned is, in effect, sent away for life. This chapter examines the

Figure 1. Gil Batle. *Sanctuary,* 2014. Carved ostrich eggshell. 6.5 × 5 × 5 in (16.5 × 12.7 × 12.7 cm). Private collection. Image courtesy of Ricco/Maresca Gallery, © Gil Batle.

experience of former prisoners in the era of mass incarceration to understand whether the convicted ever get a fair chance at freedom and to weigh the burden of their ongoing losses.

A REGIME OF NEVER-ENDING PUNISHMENT

The sense of permanent damage, the tenuousness of life outside prison, and the ongoing specter of captivity evoked in Gil Batle's egg reverberate in the lives of many other formerly incarcerated people. Batle's assertion that "convicts are never free" resonates with an extensive body of research on prisoner reentry. By the three-year anniversary of their release, for example, almost two-thirds of former prisoners have been arrested again. The majority (56 percent) have already been convicted, sentenced, and readmitted to prison by that time.[2] For those who do manage not to return to incarceration, lingering behavioral health challenges and long-term social and economic marginalization await. Returning prisoners who have finished serving their time are not freed; they are transferred from one punitive and controlling environment to another,[3] taking their places in what sociologist Reuben Jonathan Miller describes as a "lineage of control" extending back to enslavement.[4]

Still, among almost two thousand former prisoners who participated in the Multi-site Family Study, everyone was hoping to find freedom. They had ample reason to try: all the men in the study were in committed relationships, and most were fathers. The typical participant had a long-term partner or spouse who had stuck with him through years of prison time, as well as two or more minor children awaiting him on the outside. Most expected they would live with their partners (83 percent) and children (78 percent) when they got out of prison, and almost all (92 percent) planned that they would financially support their children. Men expressed optimism about their prospects for finding and keeping employment and strong confidence in their chances of avoiding a return to prison. Their partners' expectations—informed, perhaps, by prior experiences of release and return to prison—were more measured.[5]

Though we often speak of imprisonment as a singular experience, attempts to cordon it off are challenged by its ever-trailing effects and by the circularity of the experience itself—the so-called revolving door of American prisons and jails. Attempting to capture the experience and consequences of confinement is challenging in this context. Many rigorous studies, the Multi-site Family Study included, focus on understanding a single incarceration experience. But such an experience is very unlikely to be a study participant's first (or last) encounter with incarceration. For many prisoners, then, the starting point against which we measure change during and after an incarceration may already reflect the damage of prior confinements. The lack of novelty of the experience, for the prisoner and also for the prisoner's family and community, may also attenuate its effects. From a research perspective, this suggests that the powerful evidence we already have on the harmfulness of mass incarceration may grossly under-estimate its cumulative harms. From a policy perspective, too, it presents the worrying possibility that the ostensibly varied and finite prison sentences that judges hand out every day are all, in fact, for life.

THE EXPERIENCE (AND AFTERMATH) OF IMPRISONMENT

A Perpetual Confinement

The expanded imposition of imprisonment has coincided with shrinking academic interest in the inner lives of prisoners and ex-prisoners. Prison ethnographies, once an important fixture in sociological scholarship on the relationship between individuals and the state, receded from prominence just as national incarceration rates approached their peak.[6] The disappearance of intimate accounts of prison life has occurred in parallel with a basic tactical shift in public policy: from the use of imprisonment as a last-resort tool of individual incapacitation[7] to its application as an instrument of mass political warfare. In contemporary America, the criminalized and imprisoned have become (of political necessity) so thoroughly other—and the prospect of them ever truly rejoining the mainstream so distant—that their inner lives figure as a relatively remote concern. But if we are to quantify the harms of imprisonment and consider how they might be repaired, we must bring this hidden damage into clearer view.

American prisoners face notably more "extreme" prison conditions than those found in other wealthy democracies.[8] The repercussions of such conditions for well-being during and after incarceration are not yet fully understood.[9] But severe overcrowding and the use of segregation or solitary confinement—each commonplace in US prisons[10]—appear especially damaging.[11] So, too, do the social and material conditions in the communities to which most prisoners return upon their release—a process one American criminologist has aptly termed "reentry to nothing."[12] To begin to convey the inner and outer aftermath of incarceration for prisoners, the next four sections of this chapter examine how time in prison affects physical and mental health, interpersonal relationships, economic well-being, and connections to institutional forms of support. The following section systematically estimates the cost of the lingering harms and perpetual catastrophes to which prisoners are routinely subjected after having served their legally imposed sentences.[13] The chapter closes with strategies for bringing this regime of racially targeted, extralegal punishment to an end and repairing the damage it has caused.

Physical and Social Precarity

Returning home from prison, an experience infused with hope and fear alike, presents a potent touchstone for "human frailty": it is a period of inner and outer tumult, of long-awaited reunion, of bitter personal, social, and material struggle.[14] Given the extreme stress of incarceration and of release, it is hardly surprising that returning prisoners face a host of stress-related physical and mental health conditions.[15] Their mortality rates are stunningly high: three to thirteen times that of the general population.[16] Former prisoners are more likely to develop high blood pressure and left ventricular hypertrophy (a heart disease precursor) than peers of similar physical and socioeconomic status. And because they have poorer access to health care than their peers, former prisoners may also experience disproportionate mortality from these conditions.[17]

Reentry from prison is often a time of intense inner turmoil as well. Psychological and interpersonal adaptations to prison life, combined with underlying behavioral health vulnerabilities, can foment tremendous suffering. Many prisoners experience a loss of joy in living and a general deterioration of their mental health during and after prison.[18] The lingering pains of imprisonment and the formidable structural barriers to freedom after release cast a long shadow on efforts to rebuild connections to family, community, and meaningful work.[19]

Without a government safety net, released prisoners depend on close personal relationships for survival.[20] The state of these relationships is pivotal in their efforts to repair their inner and outer lives.[21] But prolonged separation from the home and community and the secondhand strains of stigmatization and punishment can severely strain these essential ties.[22] The experiences of Multi-site Family Study participants suggest that many former prisoners, navigating the lingering psychological and interpersonal effects of confinement, may be ill-equipped to repair or maintain the human relationships they need for successful recovery and reintegration. Derrick, who enrolled in our study about a year into his four-year prison term, fared better than most. Incarcerated individuals are three times as likely as their peers to divorce,[23] but Derrick and his partner of thirty years maintained their relationship throughout his prison stay. When he spoke with a study interviewer soon after his release, it was clear that this one relationship connected Derrick to every material and social asset he had.

Derrick's wife, who completed a graduate degree and became a teacher during his incarceration, had also managed to set up a stable home for their children. This is the home to which Derrick returned when he came back from prison. Although he reported having struggled to find decent employment, and his access to resources outside of the relationship was severely limited, Derrick had not spent time on the street nor worked in the illicit economy since his release. Rather, he had been supported by his partner's income and absorbed into the domestic routines she created. As a result, Derrick's description of his day-to-day life sounds remarkably stable: "Basically, you know, Friday, everybody gets off work. It's dinner and a movie or pizza or—you know, pretty much the kids do their own things, normally. . . . When there's nothing to do she'll watch *Criminal Minds* and I watch sports. Company here and there. Pretty much might get the shopping done and Sunday we try to go to church together. Or if my daughter got a basketball game somewhere, we go watch basketball."

Underneath his account of domestic stability and community integration, however, there is a quiet threat. Derrick's emotional distance and tendency to withdraw are starkly evident as he describes the conditions he coped with in prison. His struggle with hypervigilance surfaces throughout the study interview. He asks to skip over several questions, stating that they make him suspicious; repeatedly halts the conversation to question the interviewer's motives; and shares candidly how the conversation reminds him of being interrogated:

> What kind of police sh-t is that you asking?
> You sound like you're repeating and you want me to fumble my words or something.
> I don't like these f-cking tape recorders in front of me because it feels like we're in a [police] interview room.

Derrick's stories of family life make it clear that the inner reverberations of his criminal legal system experiences not only make for an uncomfortable research interview; they cause extreme difficulty in his family relationships. He doesn't enjoy talking, and he expresses especially strong distaste for conversations about the kinds of sensitive or painful issues that families must navigate during and after an incarceration: understanding what the prison time was like for everyone involved, strategizing about challenges in intimate and professional relationships, making mutual adjustments in household authority and routine. Observing matter-of-factly that he became self-centered, defensive, and noncommunicative during his time in prison, Derrick mentions that his family tells him he acts like he is still in prison. His detached and dismissive description of his children and life partner is difficult to reconcile with the fact that his survival and daily routines appear to depend entirely on his relationships with them:

> A relationship, a woman, ain't going to make and break me. [Partner] can leave me today. Best wishes . . . that is your choice. I don't—I'm not about to sit here and beg you to be with me. I'm not about to sit here and not be myself. . . . Going to jail—it made me more aware of myself than others. I had to look out for myself. . . . It made me more to myself. More than a shell, like—I really wasn't a talker, so now I really, really ain't a talker. And I don't really let no one see my feelings. I'm not an emotional feeling type person.

Derrick's frank description of the worldview, mental health symptoms, and ways of relating that he developed while in prison make his approach to human relationships quite understandable. But his astute awareness of the brittle veneer of inner and outer coping that he calls "more than a shell" has not made it possible to break through it—despite the obvious threat it poses to the only thing keeping him from homelessness, hunger, and total disconnection.

Long-Term Economic Exclusion

Managing inner struggles and the pressures of family life in whatever ways they are able, most released prisoners turn with urgency to the search for employment.[24] Many see work as central to their dignity and survival and essential to staying out of prison.[25] Others respond to the urgent expectations of resource-strapped family members who are unable to continue supporting them indefinitely. Much in the lives of returning prisoners depends on the outcome of their search for employment.[26]

Job prospects for people returning from prison are very poor. Employment skills and professional networks have often deteriorated or become outdated during the prison term,[27] and reentering individuals have much lower-than-average levels of formal education. In the contemporary American labor market, which puts less-educated workers in competition for a shrinking number of secure, full-time, living-wage jobs, these disadvantages present a formidable challenge.[28] When they are compounded by the widespread (and mostly legal) practice of discriminating against job applicants on the basis of criminal conviction history, the results can be devastating.[29]

Eliminating job applicants on the basis of a felony record is a widespread practice. Even when employers say they are willing to hire individuals with conviction histories, applicants who report such a history are less likely to be called back.[30] They do not compete successfully against other applicants with identical skills and educational qualifications but no conviction history.[31] Although almost a third of Americans have some form of criminal record, individuals who are Black and who have felony records are most heavily affected by conviction-related discrimination.[32] In many parts of the country, municipal ordinances further exclude those with conviction histories from a variety of small-scale entrepreneurial endeavors, such as food carts, street vending, and taxicab or rideshare driving. Such individuals may also be excluded from the kinds of Small Business Administration loans that would otherwise help make an entrepreneurial livelihood possible.[33]

Challenges with finding work far outlast the immediate reentry period. Research with prisoners returning to several large American cities found that most had no formal employment a year after their release.[34] Impacts on the ability to earn a legal income persist far longer.[35] An incarceration history exacerbates the disadvantage of individuals who already fare less well in the labor market because of racial discrimination, educational disadvantage, and struggles with mental health and addiction.[36] A National Academy of Sciences review of evidence on incarceration and workforce participation emphasizes that incarceration "both reflects and exacerbates persistent labor market inequalities." But even after accounting for all the disadvantages that predate their time in prison, former prisoners earn lower wages for their work, have lower annual incomes, and are less likely to be employed than their never-incarcerated peers.[37] They also have fewer economic assets.[38]

Talking with Multi-site Family Study participants gave a human dimension to the grim statistical view of former prisoners' chances in the workforce. Many expressed great anguish and distress about their uphill battles to find employment or other legal income and avoid a return to prison. Anthony, a father of five, struggled to find work after his release from a four-year stay in prison. He felt frustrated and hopeless in the face of his bleak prospects and was angry about repeated experiences of hiring and housing discrimination that appeared to block his dream of a normal life outside prison: "I would love to work a nine-to-five. I would love to grow old and watch my children grow up and graduate and maybe have grandkids one day and stuff like that. But how can I ever do that if I don't get a chance to stay away from [prison], you know what I mean? It is crooked, man. There is no job opportunities out there for us, there is no living arrangements out there for us." For many released fathers, high-stakes obligations to the criminal justice and child support systems combined with pressing family responsibilities (particularly young dependents) make these obstacles even more overwhelming. If Anthony wanted to remain out of prison, he had to deliver the monthly fees levied for his parole monitoring ($50) and his monthly child support obligation ($300). He also had to comply with all of his parole conditions and the monitoring requirements that accompanied them. Unemployed and with no transportation or housing of his own, Anthony was unable to create a stable day-to-day life. He worried about missing a payment or a monitoring visit with his parole officer:

> I feel like I rehabilitate and I feel like I learn something and now I got this guy on my back saying, "Well, make sure you come see me or you are going to jail. If you don't come see me twice a month you are going to jail." I don't have a vehicle. I got to get people to bring me here ... and then it is like, okay well, I am showing you these applications that I done put in and people telling me that they not going to hire me because of my felony. Now I can't

get a job here and I still got to pay you. You know what I mean? I still got to pay $50 a month [for parole fees]. And it is like, I don't get it man. It is so [much] stress and pressure on somebody coming home from prison nowadays.

Anthony's growing sense that the deck was stacked against him was confirmed when a neighbor with whom he had "exchanged words" telephoned his parole officer. Though he had not violated the law, Anthony was found in technical violation of his parole conditions and sent back to prison. Beneath his critical account of the event lies a palpable sense of futility and utter devastation:

I get took away from my family, my children, everybody who care about me, who will believe in me, who keep telling me to keep doing right and keep my head up afloat, now I have to come back [to prison]. You know what I mean? And that don't do nothing but tear me down even more, like "Well, f-ck it, man, this time when I get out, I am going to just go ahead and do this, or I am going to go ahead and do that." I don't even care anymore. It makes you not want to care. You get what I am saying? It makes you overlook the five little young faces that I do have looking up to me. . . . I mean, it takes away your self-respect. It takes away your self-esteem, your self-encouragement. It takes all of that from you.

Anthony's experience was far from unique. Many of the stories Multisite Family Study participants told us of their attempts to find work and stability after release from prison were exceedingly bleak. Searches for employment, housing, and some normalcy took on a desperate, despairing quality when long-guarded hopes and plans—nurtured while surviving an extended separation from home and family—were soundly and repeatedly crushed.

An Unsafety Net: Surveillance Instead of Support

The relative absence of a social safety net in the United States is keenly felt among returning prisoners, who face urgent needs for food, shelter, and transportation on their release. Researchers who inventoried the available supports for returning prisoners in the United States found that, even in major urban areas, public infrastructures were "quite primitive" and sometimes so inadequate as to cause harm.[39] Another study, among the biggest ever conducted of supports for returning prisoners, found that most available services were of limited use and that some made things worse.[40] Programs designed to prepare people for the practical challenges of returning home (such as employment assistance, life-skills education, and reentry preparation classes) didn't make them any more likely to succeed when they got out of prison. In fact, those who participated fared worse than their counterparts, experiencing a higher chance of being rearrested after their release.[41] It seems that such initiatives might raise people's hopes and expectations for postrelease stability and success without actually bringing it within reach.

When we spoke with Multi-site Family Study participants after the release from prison, former prisoners and their partners could rarely think of any program or resource that had been at all helpful. During the postrelease interview, we prompted them in half a dozen different ways to identify any public agencies or programs that had made the reentry from prison easier. Interviewees gave stilted answers that contrasted with the detailed and reflective accounts they offered elsewhere in the interview. When pressed, some observed that formal support in their communities was scarce or nonexistent ("You're on your own") and that the only thing that had helped them was their own inner strength or the support shared by family members. Others detailed the extensive efforts they had made to connect with recommended services or follow up on the lists of employment opportunities to which prison or parole staff directed them. When they tried to make contact, however, many learned that the information was out of date or inaccurate: "They give you this list of all these people—places hiring ex-offenders. And then when you go to these places they're like, 'We ain't—we're not hiring offenders.' And [they] never call you. . . . They ain't hiring no felons, no offenders." Supposed employers were not actually hiring or were not willing to consider people with criminal histories. Programs were either no longer in operation, or study participants didn't meet their eligibility criteria. Because ex-prisoners in the study lacked their own transportation, their fruitless efforts often came at a steep cost to their own and their family members' time.

Unhelpful encounters with formal institutions took an emotional toll as well. Sometimes, individuals recounted these unhelpful experiences with public agencies and programs matter-of-factly. But many became frustrated, immobilized, or cynical as repeated experiences with help-seeking proved pointless or disappointing:

INTERVIEWER: Have there been any human services programs that affected your reentry?

INTERVIEWEE: You want it in all honesty? (Pause.) How do you put it bluntly without cussing? These reentry programs out here, you go to them, they don't follow up. . . . They point you [to] all of these programs and seven out of ten won't help you.

Such experiences, it seemed, eroded people's ability to even imagine that services *could* be helpful. When we asked one recently released person (who was ultimately quite articulate about how badly reentering individuals needed assistance with employment, housing, and maintaining family relationships) what kinds of programs might be helpful, his first response was, "Oh, my God. I don't even know how to answer that." These experiences reinforced Multi-site Family Study participants' understandings that public servants who might offer to help them rarely delivered.

But returning prisoners faced more than an absence of helpful services. Rather, their narratives evoke a sense of "distorted responsiveness," a pattern that researchers at Yale and Johns Hopkins discovered when studying how residents of urban communities of color describe their encounters with the police. Analyzing data from hundreds of conversations between individuals in different urban neighborhoods, the team found an ugly paradox: "Suffocating police attention to paltry offenses stood in stark contrast to participants' accounts of deafening silence in situations of serious need."[42] For returning prisoners and their family members in the Multi-site Family Study, this paradox was not limited to police encounters but characterized their contacts with a wide range of public institutions, including parole offices and a variety of health and human services agencies. Government agencies seemed ever-present and even intrusive in monitoring released men and their families for compliance with parole conditions, child support payments, and welfare regulations—but nowhere when those same individuals struggled to find food, housing, employment, health care, or other necessities.

Struggling to meet basic needs and with the state as apparent adversary, the returning prisoners we interviewed often concluded that their freedom was never meant to last. "The system," however they conceived of it, appeared to have set them up to fail. William, a father who had struggled to stay out of prison amid ongoing employment and housing difficulties, spoke for many others in the study when he suggested that "society should quit looking at us as animals, cruel, or just straight-up criminals.... You know, society got to—not make it easy, but give us the same rights." He went on to explain how the fundamental idea that a person could pay a debt to society in prison and then be free was undermined by government-sanctioned social and economic exclusion after release. William summed up this last point tersely: "They ain't playing fair, man."

ADDING UP THE PRICE OF PERPETUAL PUNISHMENT

Millions of people leave prisons and jails each year. Few of them ever arrive at freedom. For Multi-site Family Study participants, the return from prison followed such a consistent script that it often seemed rigged for failure. Families on the outside awaited the release date with high hopes that their imprisoned family member would recover from the experience, find work, avoid legal trouble, and be able to fulfill his commitments to the family. Most men and their families devoted tremendous joint effort toward these goals. When barriers became insurmountable in one or more domains, however, many returned either to the illicit economy (and the legal problems that came with it) or to long-term economic dependence on impoverished family members. Weathering this failure sequence, as most families in the Multi-site Family Study had done repeatedly, was draining and devastating. It corroded their trust in the system and often their trust in each other, too.

Understanding exactly how much the regime of perpetual punishment drains the resources and well-being of the imprisoned is a challenging task. Those targeted for imprisonment often already face a host of disadvantages, including low incomes and limited formal education.[43] The best estimates of the toll of a prison record rely on two large, national data sets produced by the National Longitudinal Survey of Youth (NLSY) and the Fragile Families Study. Using ordinary least-squares regression with Fragile Families data collected from 1999 to 2002, Charles Lewis and colleagues estimated a roughly 28 percent difference in annual earnings (amounting to a mean $10,000 per year gap, or $14,474 in 2020 dollars) between formerly incarcerated fathers and similar fathers who had never been incarcerated.[44] Applying propensity score matching to the Fragile Families data to isolate the influence of incarceration itself from the other forms of disadvantage that are associated with it, Amanda Geller and colleagues determined that formerly incarcerated individuals were significantly less likely to be employed than similar, never-incarcerated peers. Among those who did have jobs, formerly incarcerated individuals made significantly less per hour (a $10 mean difference in hourly wages; range = $16.41 to $26.39) compared to their never-incarcerated counterparts.[45] Using NLSY data, and controlling for other differences between ever- and never-incarcerated sample members, Bruce Western estimated that incarceration reduced wage growth by 30 percent over a fifteen-year period. The effect of incarceration on employment status diminished over time, but its effect on wages persisted. When formerly incarcerated people manage to avoid reincarceration and succeed in finding legal work, they do so in low-wage jobs with very limited growth potential. Thus, as Western's work shows, the earnings gap between them and their never-incarcerated counterparts widens with time rather than narrowing, as one might otherwise expect.[46]

Most prisoners experience their first prison stay in early adulthood and accumulate substantial earnings losses over the remainder of their lives. I estimate these losses with a focus on men, for whom better incarceration-related data are available. From 2020 Census data, we know that there are 126,329,864 living adult men in the United States. Applying the Bureau of Justice Statistics (BJS)'s estimate that 4.9 percent of adult men have ever been incarcerated (a rate that has actually increased since 2001, when BJS made the calculation),[47] I estimate that there are 6,190,163 living adult men in the United States who have spent time in prison. The average age at which Americans leave prison is 35, and the average age at which they leave the workforce is 57.8.[48] I therefore estimate that each of these formerly imprisoned men will earn approximately $330,007 less than a similarly educated counterpart over the course of his postprison lifetime. This means that the total earnings penalty for the cohort of ever-incarcerated men still living today is approximately $2.04 trillion ($2,042,797,121,141) in 2020 dollars. Owing to the extreme racial targeting of mass incarceration, more than half (52.54 percent) of these earnings losses, or $1.07 trillion ($1,073,285,607,447), will be sustained among Black men.[49]

My estimate of the collateral consequences of incarceration for postrelease earnings is conservative. It excludes women, who make up about a tenth of the incarcerated population and represent an even higher proportion of the formerly incarcerated owing to their shorter average sentence lengths. It uses a 4.9 percent estimate for the lifetime prevalence of incarceration among adult men, despite BJS projections that this rate has risen. And it assumes that formerly incarcerated individuals are as likely as never-incarcerated individuals to be in the workforce in the years following their release, despite evidence for an elevated risk of unemployment and of a return to prison in the immediate postrelease years. Though no approach to estimating these losses will be perfect, $2.04 trillion offers a useful starting point for understanding the magnitude of reparative effort that is called for to redress the ongoing, racialized harms of mass imprisonment among the formerly incarcerated. Such an effort could help to ensure that Americans who have completed the terms of punishment to which they were sentenced have some chance at freedom in the life that remains.

REPAIRING HARM TO FORMER PRISONERS

The racially targeted overuse of imprisonment has inflicted devastating harm—much of it sustained long after the prison term ends. Even for those who would embrace the idea of imprisonment as punishment for crime, there is no justifying the extreme racial disproportionality nor the unending social exclusion and economic subjugation of former prisoners. Darity and Mullen propose that an effective reparations program should be designed to be final and complete in itself; that is, it should be constructed such that no further claims of damage would be anticipated or relevant.[50] To meet this standard will require individual and institution-building reparations to the former prisoners already affected by the racial harm of mass incarceration, but it also demands timely intervention to keep the millions yet to be released from prison from sustaining these same harms. To accomplish the latter, we must reimagine an approach to public safety that is not made in the image of slavery and Jim Crow, shackling or shutting out a part of the population whose freedom is figured as a threat. And we must meet the coming era of decarceration with robust new forms of support for individuals who have survived a term in prison.

Even in the United States, where transitional justice work lags behind international models, strong precedent exists for making financial reparations to survivors of racially and politically motivated detention. The Civil Liberties Act of 1988, signed into law by President Reagan (and carried out largely under the George H. W. Bush administration), authorized the contemporary equivalent of $3.5 billion in direct payments to Japanese Americans who had been detained during World War II. Acknowledging that the survivors of wartime incarceration had been racially targeted, the federal government established the Office of Redress Administration to distribute $20,000 payments to each internment survivor.[51]

A similar program of cash-value compensation for Black Americans imprisoned during the mass incarceration era could help to mitigate the massive, extralegal harms that Black former prisoners sustain even after serving their legally imposed sentences. It would also offer a concrete opportunity for individual apologies and amends to those most directly harmed by the anti-Black racism that has driven the policy and practice of mass imprisonment. As with strategies for compensating criminalized youth of color (described in the preceding chapter), individual reparations to Black former prisoners could be distributed in a variety of forms at the recipient's option, including monthly or lump-sum payouts, the creation of interest-bearing accounts, or access to trust funds for asset-building activities.

An effective reparations program must include institution-building investments, as well. Providing for a humane reentry for all returning prisoners represents an urgent policy task in a time of mass decarceration. The number of former prisoners in American communities already far outstrips the resources available to them, and that number will continue to rise for at least the next several decades.[52] The nation's largest reentry initiative, the Department of Justice's Second Chance Act program, has funded almost a thousand programs in forty-nine states since its inception in 2009. Yet neither this nor any other federal initiative has ever been able to mobilize reentry support resources on an order of magnitude matching that of the social and economic catastrophes they attempt to mitigate, which the estimates presented in the preceding sections of this chapter suggest exceed $2 trillion. Thus, providing for a fair and humane return from prison will require a massive correction of scale.

Reducing or preventing ongoing harm to former prisoners further demands an earnest reengineering of current prisoner reentry program models. Rigorous experimental and quasi-experimental research indicates that many existing reentry program models have weak positive effects at best, harmful effects at worst.[53] Such programs must be remade to target more precisely the mechanisms that shape postprison economic and social outcomes and to build the delivery capacity of trusted community-based organizations.

Sociologist Devah Pager's work on former prisoners' economic participation could help to guide a more effective approach. Pager's experimental research shows how a history of incarceration interacts with racial discrimination to disproportionately exclude Black former prisoners from the workforce. Pager identifies three potential mechanisms that could shape poor workforce outcomes for former prisoners and postprison challenges more broadly: selection (who is targeted for incarceration), transformation (how prisoners are changed by the experience of imprisonment), and labeling (the ways that those with prison records are identified and stigmatized).[54] Evidence across many separate studies supports not one but all three of these mechanisms, which may help to explain the striking lack of success of previous reentry initiatives. Initiatives that attempt to interrupt *only* selection, transformation, or labeling effects, carried out without careful attention to the others, could inadvertently exacerbate harm (or at least fail to avert it). Indeed, undertaken in isolation, prior efforts to divert convicted individuals from being sentenced to incarceration, to reform prison environments in ways that lessen their harmfulness, to offer programs to support employment and reintegration after imprisonment, and to reduce the consequences of criminal-record-related labeling have each fallen short of ameliorating incarceration's massive, destructive effects on economic participation.

First, so-called selection effects—namely, the systematic selection of economically marginalized individuals into arrest and incarceration—can and must be addressed. People who are unable to find adequate work in the legal economy are more likely to engage in criminalized activity and become incarcerated.[55] Preventing this selection into incarceration before it occurs would involve moving substantially upstream to improve the employment prospects of those who would otherwise be targeted for arrest and imprisonment. Large-scale interventions that make it easier to enroll and stay in formal education, to acquire job-relevant skills, and to build soft skills that affect labor-market competitiveness are needed before individuals are drawn into heavy criminal legal system contact. Such efforts should be designed by and for those who are systematically edged out of workforce opportunity, particularly young adults of color.[56]

Broader federal initiatives to transform racially and economically hostile labor-market conditions are also needed. Systematic efforts to eliminate racial employment discrimination, expand living-wage jobs for workers with less formal education or work experience, and promote labor practices that boost income security for low-wage workers could all reshape the landscape of workforce inopportunity that has channeled economically marginalized individuals into repeated cycles of arrest and incarceration.[57]

Second, transformation effects must be addressed. Evidence suggests that serving a term in prison depreciates job skills, erodes social and professional networks, and promotes forms of psychological and interpersonal coping that interfere with participation in work.[58] The debilitating changes that many individuals undergo during confinement might be partly ameliorated upstream by addressing prison conditions that damage mental and social health—particularly practices like solitary confinement and chronic prison overcrowding. In addition, prisoners and former prisoners need robust psychosocial supports to help them cope effectively with the trauma of imprisonment and to maintain strong, healthy ties to loved ones and community.[59] Persistent, unmet need for mental health treatment in prisons and in the low-income communities to which prisoners return must not be tolerated.

Just as the Veterans Administration offers specialized, lifelong physical and behavioral health care to those returning from combat, a postincarceration treatment system could engage formerly incarcerated individuals with services specific to their unique (and intensive) needs. To succeed, such a system must be clear about its mission to support and not to surveil: a thirteen-study review of initiatives designed to engage former prisoners in mental health treatment found that some programs made them *more* likely to become reincarcerated, likely because they exposed them to heightened scrutiny from the criminal legal system.[60]

Efforts to prevent transformation effects by diverting those convicted of criminalized behavior away from imprisonment are also crucial. But many such efforts replace carceral forms of punishment with noncarceral ones (such as community supervision, probation, parole, or so-called preventive policing practices like stop and frisk)—representing a troubling example of a unidimensional approach. As many scholars have begun to document, the intensification of noncarceral control over the convicted could actually expand, not lessen, the collateral harms associated with criminal legal system involvement.[61] As legal scholar Allegra McLeod argues, these strategies still impose criminal labeling and surveillance, even on those who have not been fully and meaningfully adjudicated.[62] In so doing, they actually widen the carceral net and expand the adversities associated with surveillance.

But diversion can succeed, too. Model programs do not simply offer alternatives to criminal punishment; they replace hypersurveillance with active care and support. Miami-Dade County's Criminal Mental Health Project, a model for such work, diverts individuals with serious mental illness and addiction issues from criminal prosecution by addressing the root-cause issues that contribute to criminalized behavior. The program delivers intensive support and proactive street outreach—including peer-to-peer care from other individuals who have experienced behavioral health challenges and criminal legal system involvement—and helps those who are unable to work to enroll in appropriate disability benefits and health coverage using the Social Security Outreach, Access, and Recovery model.[63]

Third, labeling effects must be addressed. Individuals with incarceration histories are discriminated against by prospective employers and others in ways that affect their mental and social health and their ability to secure and retain meaningful work.[64] The overdisclosure and misuse of information about conviction histories presents a serious problem for those working to rebuild their lives. Robust experimental evidence indicates that prospective employers are less likely to hire those with even low-level conviction histories.[65] We also know that such workers perform at least as well on the job as those without conviction histories.[66] Yet efforts to prevent conviction-related hiring discrimination must be implemented with acute awareness of the reality of ongoing racial hiring discrimination. Ban the Box initiatives, designed to reduce labeling effects by restricting what employers can ask applicants about their conviction histories, appear to have exacerbated discrimination against Black applicants, as employers opt to use race as a proxy for criminal record.[67] (Such initiatives are discussed in more detail in chapter 6.) Promising alternatives include expunging conviction histories, eliminating the use of stigmatizing language in reference to such histories (e.g., away from the term *offender* toward "person with a conviction"), reducing public access to conviction records, and offering incentives to employers for hiring individuals with conviction histories, all of which could help to make hiring procedures and work environments less hostile for returning prisoners. Federal and local legislative initiatives are needed to remove entrepreneurial and educational exclusions, such as Pell grant and small business loan exclusion, that keep former prisoners from pursuing important educational and vocational goals.

Income support will be essential for individuals pursuing such long-term goals and also for those who will remain outside the formal workforce because of disability (including those who have become physically or mentally disabled during incarceration[68]), older age, or the choice to prioritize nonremunerative forms of care work. A stronger social safety net, including universal basic income and high-quality universal physical and mental health care, is essential to our collective well-being and integral to recovery from mass incarceration. Decades of research have shown us that no singular program or initiative, regardless of its scale or sophistication, will single-handedly reverse the complex of racial and economic harms that the incarcerated have sustained. But the policies and programs described here, if implemented in concert and with the leadership of those who have been directly affected by incarceration, hold substantial promise for bringing these cycles of harm to an end.

Work to ameliorate the social and economic aftermath of imprisonment must be accompanied by a fundamental systems transformation aimed at ending the use of prisons altogether. It is time to discard the carceral paradigm, which inflicts violence and harm in the name of safety, in favor of one that actually protects the vulnerable. We can work systematically to make carceral justice obsolete by constructing what McLeod calls a "grounded preventive justice" framework. Her vision builds on the foundational insights of W. E. B. Du Bois, who made the critical observation that outlawing forced labor would never, in itself, end slavery. Rather, Du Bois argued, slavery would only truly end when the economic and governance structures on which it had rested had been remade and the resources stolen through enslavement had been redistributed to the formerly enslaved.

Drawing from Du Bois's insight on the failures of the Reconstruction Era, McLeod proposes that the process of ending mass incarceration must involve systematically displacing or obviating each of the functions of the current system—that is, deterrence, incapacitation, rehabilitation, and retributive justice—through preventive and reparative social welfare practices and the strengthening of noncarceral responses to harm. She describes a process that consists of "meaningful justice reinvestment to strengthen the social arm of the state and improve human welfare, decriminalizing less serious infractions, improved design of spaces and products to reduce opportunities for offending . . . proliferating restorative forms of redress, and creating both safe harbors for individuals at risk of or fleeing violence and alternative livelihoods for persons subject to criminal law enforcement."[69] Individual reparations for the racialized harm of imprisonment are critical, as are efforts to support a real homecoming for those who have been locked away from their families and communities. Yet the most important repair strategy by far is our collective commitment to cease harming one another in the name of justice and safety.

CONCLUSION

What prisoners and former prisoners have already suffered in the name of mass incarceration will not be undone. But we cannot afford as a society to continue carrying these damages forward. Expressing the difference between freedom and its opposite, Maya Angelou looked famously to birds. "A free bird leaps," she wrote,

> on the back of the wind
> and floats downstream
> till the current ends
> and dips his wing
> in the orange sun rays
> and dares to claim the sky.[70]

Her verse rushes with open light and a sense of bold, sweeping movement.

Birds were also there when a formerly incarcerated interviewee tried to describe the feeling of life beyond prison to the Multi-site Family Study research team. But the texture and feeling of his expression could not differ more from Angelou's. It is "more than a shell," Derrick explained to us—this sense of separateness, of hardness, of imminent fracture. For Gil Batle, too, the bird and its egg offer not just an artistic medium but a metaphor. The artist seems to have finally made it to freedom, living with family in the Philippines and earning a livable income from his craft. But when he talks about life after prison and the precarious nature of the work on which he depends, it's clear that freedom is tenuous. "The shell of an egg," he explains, "is about a sixteenth of an inch, and if you go past that sixteenth of an inch, you practically destroy the egg. And I think that kind of fragility is where I stand."[71] Even for a person who has spent ten years outside prison racking up accomplishments exceptional enough to merit national news coverage, the prospect of catastrophic failure and punishment still looms close. After so long, and in the context of so much apparent success, one must wonder when that looming prospect will dissolve, if there will ever be real light and space for movement, or if the cage bars have simply been carved away into a sharper and more brittle form of confinement. The question will be decided, perhaps, by what the rest of us make of the opportunity for repair.

4 "I Always Put the Burden on Her Shoulders"

THE INVISIBLE WEIGHT OF MASS INCARCERATION

On any given day, thousands of women leave homes across America and enter prison voluntarily. They furnish their own transport, often traveling for hours on public trains and buses. They clothe themselves and their children according to the correctional dress code and submit to searches of their bodies and belongings and myriad forms of intimate regulation and humiliation. To refer to these mothers, grandmothers, partners, and coparents of the imprisoned as "visitors" is to miss most of what is happening as they circulate in and out of prison facilities en masse. Their movements constitute what the scholars and activists of Essie Justice Group aptly describe as "another Great Migration."[1] They have wrapped their lives around the prisons that hold their loved ones, navigating a uniquely mobile, but still punishing, form of confinement.

For the women who visit it regularly, the prison becomes a "domestic satellite" within which much of the business of family life must be conducted.[2] But prisoners' family members have even less claim on carceral space than do the convicted. They have access only to the periphery of the prison and only for short and intensively regulated periods. Nor are they permitted, even in this visual age, to photograph the brief scenes of family and domesticity that they are able to stage with their loved ones in prison visiting rooms. Governed as minutely by correctional facilities as every other activity and document within their walls, photographs are made only for a fee: portraits of prisoners and those who visit them may be taken on prison-owned cameras in front of false, pictorial backdrops constructed for the purpose. Collected in Alyse Emdur's *Prison Landscapes,* the highly regulated embraces of prisoners and their visitors are flatly surreal.[3] Clothed in prison scrubs and street clothes, couples stand before bucolic scenery and urban skylines. Often hand-painted by other prisoners, these background scenes serve a dual purpose: they offer a partial escape, the chance for couples and families to depict themselves together somewhere other than the prison. They also prevent visitors from gathering photographic documentation that could be used to facilitate an actual escape from the prison or to otherwise weaken the hold of penal authority within its walls.

Like the painted backdrops, the partners and family members who appear in visiting-room photographs are interpolated in a pair of irreconcilable tasks: helping to sustain prisoners through their confinement and connecting them to the possibility of freedom. This chapter examines that impossible burden, its surprising implications for the gendered impacts of mass incarceration, and how a comprehensive reparative effort might begin to lift it.

MASS INCARCERATION AND WOMEN'S INVISIBLE LABOR

The logic and practices of racialized punishment reach well beyond the prison. As an institution, prison shapes life far past the concrete walls and barbed-wire fences that define correctional borders; it reaches into streets, schools, and communities. It also reaches deep into the lives and homes of the families that prisoners leave behind and sets the rules for life in the households to which they return. Ethnographer Megan Comfort has explored these dynamics in depth during several years of participant observation with women who were visiting their imprisoned loved ones at California's oldest prison. Spending time with the partners, coparents, and mothers of many San Quentin prisoners, Comfort observed that the conditions of their lives were thoroughly remade by the prison system.

Calling the phenomenon "secondary prisonization," she compared it to the process of prisonization described in Donald Clemmer's early prison ethnography, by which incarcerated individuals came to adapt their values, worldview, and social behavior to fit prison life.[4] The lives of the overwhelmingly female-identified visitors who spoke with Comfort in the narrow visitor holding area of San Quentin were governed and circumscribed by the same penal restrictions to which their imprisoned kin were subject. The minutiae of prison living conditions, the vagaries of the daily prison routine, visitation procedures and restrictions, and intensive communications monitoring shaped every aspect of couples' relationships. The prison defined the terms of their ostensibly private domestic lives and controlled myriad aspects of women's movements, garb, schedules, finances, and personal lives.[5]

Mass incarceration has produced a new body of invisible labor at the place where prison and home meet. Multi-site Family Study participants' stories suggest that the daunting task of tending to home and family, now stretched across the boundaries of prison and community, has been absorbed into women's uncompensated domestic work. Carried out primarily on behalf of partners and children, this distinctive form of women's work serves the immediate purpose of supporting loved ones' survival and well-being during and after incarceration. On a broad scale, however, it represents a quiet privatization of the expense and labor required to maintain an oversized carceral state. Offloading much of the true cost of imprisonment onto women and families helps to obscure just how costly (and damaging) mass incarceration has been. The full scope and extent of this transference, as with domestic work generally, has remained conveniently out of sight in policy discourse and even in critical research.

Scholarship on the role of the prison in the gendered "discipline" of women has tended to focus on women prisoners.[6] Yet American women are vastly more likely to be connected to incarcerated or formerly incarcerated male partners, coparents, and adult children than they are to go to prison themselves. Men are incarcerated at twelve times the rate of women,[7] and most depend heavily on female-identified partners, coparents, mothers, and grandmothers for support during and after the prison stay. Two in five American women have experienced the incarceration of an immediate family member, including one in five who has seen an intimate partner or coparent sent to prison or jail.[8] The vast scale of women's connectedness to incarcerated men intersects in damaging ways with another defining feature of the American political economy: the feminization and "invisibilization" of reproductive labor, the myriad non-income-generating acts of care that keep us alive.[9]

The stories that women in the Multi-site Family Study told us illuminate how systems of penal regulation that target poor men of color are extended and sustained through the emotional and material labor of the women closest to them. The experiences of prisoners, former prisoners, and their partners and coparents suggest how much of the physical, emotional, and material fallout of hyperincarceration among men is absorbed by their partners. Deeply entrenched heteropatriarchal norms of women's caretaking, even in less-traditional families, help to silently relocate a large share of the damage associated with men's criminalization and imprisonment. Women's coerced work on behalf of their partners and families may be effective at keeping the unsightly damage of mass imprisonment largely out of public sight. It may even, sometimes, succeed at providing a modicum of physical, emotional, and material stability for those they love. However, this work is undertaken at great physical, psychological, and material cost to women themselves.

BEHIND THE GENDER PARADOX OF MASS INCARCERATION

The Other Face of Imprisonment

Most research on the consequences of mass incarceration has concentrated on effects on prisoners and former prisoners, overwhelmingly men. The Bureau of Justice Statistics estimates that one in fifteen Americans will be subjected to imprisonment in their lifetimes. The racial targeting of imprisonment quintuples that rate among Black men, with approximately one in three predicted to serve prison time at some point in their lives.[10] Though the experience of imprisonment is much rarer among women, it is indisputably significant. Women's incarceration rates grew at roughly twice the rate of men's from 1978 to 2015. Recent, tentative moves toward decarceration have largely passed over women.[11]

The potent and unrelenting significance of prison in the lives of the convicted and confined has focalized their experiences for scholars of mass incarceration. The burdens shouldered by partners, coparents, and other family members, surfacing as early as the late 1980s in works by Creasie Finney Hairston and other scholars,[12] have generally been presumed secondary to the experiences of prisoners themselves. But emerging quantitative research on the repercussions of imprisonment presents a challenge to this long-standing presumption. The unexpected evidence comes from criminologist Christopher Wildeman's rigorous investigation of the population-level health consequences of mass incarceration. Wildeman examined the relationship between changes in the national imprisonment rate and changes in American life expectancy, a central indicator of overall population health. He uncovered an apparent paradox: increases in the male incarceration rate have depressed women's life expectancy more than they have men's.[13] The next three sections of this chapter examine the realities that underlie this paradox: the social and economic losses that women sustain while supporting a loved one through incarceration and reentry, the coercive conditions under which their labors are extracted, and the ways they are physically harmed. It considers how these harms challenge the very logic of individual punishment and how we might begin to make them right through individual and institutional reparations.

Multidimensional Losses

Women's relationships with incarcerated men are a site of profound social, emotional, and financial loss. Incarceration and release from prison are heavy financial stressors. When a partner or coparent becomes incarcerated, many women not only lose another adult's financial contributions to the household but find themselves with an array of new expenses associated with supporting him in prison. Representative data on the costs of supporting prisoners do not exist; however, research with national convenience samples has produced staggering estimates. Among 1,080 families of prisoners surveyed for the Who Pays Project in 2014, two-thirds had trouble meeting their own basic subsistence needs, like food and housing, owing to their family member's incarceration. Court fees and fines, ostensibly assessed against convicted individuals, are most often paid by family members, as the convicted person's assets and income are almost always severely curtailed during and after incarceration. Such family members are overwhelmingly women with very limited resources themselves. In the Who Pays sample, family members who kept in touch with an imprisoned loved one (83 percent of whom were women) paid $13,607 on average for that loved one's court fines and fees. For the largest group of families in the study, who had annual earnings under $15,000, the cost of court-related expenses alone came close to one year of household income for the family.[14]

Women assume the further financial burden of maintaining their own and their children's relationships with their imprisoned loved one and meeting his basic material needs during incarceration. Qualitative research and preliminary survey data suggest that the high costs of receiving prisoners' telephone calls and traveling to the prison for in-person contact are shouldered primarily by partners, coparents, mothers, and other female family members.[15] Telephone rate-gouging for calls from prisons has been enabled by long-standing monopoly agreements between correctional systems and telephone carriers that allow the imposition of additional fees. In part as a result, families spend approximately $1 billion per year to receive telephone calls from incarcerated individuals.[16] An early survey of women visiting Black men at San Quentin found that the poor women in their sample spent a quarter to a third of their incomes on such communications.[17] Many family members, including over a third of those in the Who Pays study, take out loans specifically to cover telephone and visitation expenses.[18]

Even after a family member's time in jail or prison ends, women continue to be affected by severe economic strains from the incarceration. Formerly incarcerated fathers contribute 25 percent less financial support to the mothers of their children than similar never-incarcerated fathers.[19] Their households also experience greater material strain and housing instability than those of similar never-incarcerated fathers.[20] Multi-site Family Study participants saw men's incarceration and return to the family and community—a cycle that many couples had experienced multiple times—as exacerbating chronic material deprivation and household instability. Families suffered serious financial setbacks as women attempted to support the household alone while also covering the costs of visiting prison, receiving collect phone calls from prison, and putting money on men's prison accounts for supplemental food, clothing, and toiletries. One imprisoned father explained, "They've gotta do this, they've gotta provide this. They've gotta do extra stuff, you know. And it's a burden. It hurts."

Partner imprisonment affects women's social health as well. The removal of a partner to prison disrupts committed intimate relationships, damages relationship quality, and promotes greater sexual risk-taking.[21] Many women report deep social isolation and disconnection during and after their family member's imprisonment, as the physical absence of the loved one is compounded by broader social alienation. When Essie Justice Group surveyed 2,281 women with incarcerated loved ones in forty-six states and Puerto Rico, most reported they felt compelled to hide their experiences and struggles from others, had a general sense of emptiness, and experienced extreme loneliness and social isolation. On the multi-item loneliness measure that women completed, which measured "subjective feelings of loneliness as well as whether women have enough people whom they can rely on, trust, and feel close to," the largest subgroup of respondents received the highest possible loneliness score.[22] (This finding is even more striking given the specific group of women from whom the researchers were hearing: surveys were administered to a convenience sample recruited by Essie and twelve partner organizations in the US states with the highest incarceration rates or largest incarcerated populations. Such methods would be expected to underrepresent the most isolated and disconnected women.) Amid heightened isolation and with limited social support, many women face the added labor and pressure of single-parenting the incarcerated person's children—a responsibility that can make social isolation even worse. (Parenting stress and its implications for children are discussed in detail in the next chapter.)

Sociologist Hedwig Lee and colleagues highlight the fact that Black women bear a disproportionate share of the multidimensional losses associated with mass imprisonment. Nationally representative estimates from the Family History of Incarceration (FamHIS) Survey indicate that one in five women in the general population has experienced a partner or coparent's incarceration (in jail or prison) at some point in their lives—and this prevalence jumps to one in three among Black women.[23] Furthermore, even Black women with high levels of formal education remain unprotected from the experience: approximately 60 percent of college-educated Black women experience the incarceration of an immediate family member, comparable to the proportion of white women who have not completed high school.[24] Estimates using 2006 General Social Survey data suggest that racial disparities in connectedness to imprisoned family members are even steeper.[25] Lee and Wildeman point out that "so long as the fate and well-being of black women remains closely linked to that of black men, then they are also disadvantaged by the problems and issues that black men face"—and mass incarceration is no exception.[26]

But the racialized impact of mass incarceration among women is more than simply a function of its prevalence among Black men. For Black women, the incarceration of partners, coparents, and other family members compounds the vulnerabilities introduced by their own, multiplicitous experiences of racialized and gendered social disadvantage.[27] Growing recognition of Black women's vulnerability to the harms of mass incarceration has prompted some scholars to begin examining unique mechanisms of harm among women of color. To date, however, such work has tended to leave aside questions of women's agency (and constraints on that agency) in relationship with their partners, families, the state, and the broader political economy.

Coerced Labor

Academic and advocacy work on labor exploitation in the era of mass imprisonment has focused heavily on prison labor.[28] The coercive and exploitative nature of prison work and its contributions to the broader political and economic apparatus of mass incarceration are well established. Prisoners' wage labor occurs largely out of the public eye, is grossly underpaid, and helps to subsidize the untenable public expense of operating mass-scale correctional facilities.[29] The focus on prison labor, however, has perpetuated the invisibility of a second, and perhaps even more significant, form of labor exploitation in the penal state: women's support for incarcerated and formerly incarcerated family members. Women's extensive unpaid work on behalf of imprisoned family members, like the wage labor of prisoners themselves, is formally voluntary but undertaken under duress. Offered up in a context in which choices are profoundly constrained, such work must be understood as coerced.

The stories of returning prisoners and their partners suggest that—far from being a natural or automatic product of men's and women's "linked fates"—the harms of imprisonment are transferred from imprisoned men to their female family members systematically, through a set of extractive interpersonal and structural conditions. Women in the Multi-site Family Study supported their partners and coparents out of concern for them and their children. But men's interpersonally controlling behavior, the abject dependency and vulnerability imposed on them in confinement (and following release), and the tenuous social and material conditions of their households combined to extort a level of support well beyond what the women in their lives could afford to provide. Thus, the tremendous labor and material support that women funneled through their partnerships to men had a decidedly compulsory element.

During the incarceration, men often attempted to extend the authoritarian control under which they lived in prison over their partners on the outside, drawing financial and emotional support from them through tactics of interpersonal control. Although male participants spoke of this dynamic less often than did their partners and coparents, one characterized it as very widespread among his incarcerated peers: "People are more controlling in jail than anything. People be on the phone cussing their girls out, threatening them. . . . 'Put money in this phone.' Want to talk to them all day on the phone. All day. 'Why I didn't get no letter? Why didn't you answer the phone?'" Desperate for more contact and more material support than loved ones on the outside could afford to provide, men applied a variety of strategies to obtain it. According to women, these control tactics often included verbal harassment and emotional abuse.

Alicia, a Multi-site Family Study participant who lived in poverty during her ex-partner's incarceration, described the emotional pain of being continually berated by him for being unable to offer material support during his prison stay: "He would write me really bad letters because I wasn't helping him with whatever he needed over there, you know. If I didn't have money, how am I going [to] send you money or clothes or booze or food or whatever? And, you know, it would hurt because I'm over here—I tried to send him as much as I could, and he still wouldn't appreciate it.

So, what could I do, you know?" Some men backed their demands with threats, accusations, or other forms of psychological abuse. They also applied "jail talk," a term used by interviewees to describe the practice of telling women what they might want to hear, including poetic expressions of love and commitment, to manipulate them into providing ongoing support during the prison stay.

Regardless of the interpersonal context that surrounded it, women's support for their imprisoned partners was proffered under a more structural form of duress, too. The onus of prisoners' basic needs, when left unmet by the prison, was effectively shifted to their female family members through relationships of familial care. As Comfort's ethnographic work documents, women assume the cost of an array of basic food, clothing, and toiletry items. Rather than obtaining these basic necessities at prison expense, men receive them from their female partners in highly regulated care packages or by purchasing them from the prison using funds that women deposit in their prison commissary accounts. Shoes, soap, toothbrushes and toothpaste, over-the-counter medicines, writing paper and envelopes, and many other apparent necessities of life are effectively furnished not out of the correctional budget but from the personal funds of very low-income women. The deprivation that many women endure in order to cover these transferred costs can be extreme; for example, participants in the Multi-site Family Study and the Who Pays project described going without their own medications or even without electricity in order to meet the needs of their incarcerated loved ones.

The financial drain of men's imprisonment for women often continues long after their release. In some Multi-site Family Study couples, men continued to use tactics of interpersonal control to maintain a grip over the women in their lives, who also represented their primary connection to the resources needed for survival on the outside. For Alicia, whose partner had been highly controlling during his prison stay, the controlling behavior became even harder to tolerate after his release: "He calls all the time . . . like where am I at. . . . If I go somewhere, he just, oh my god, he just makes a big thing about it. . . . He just gets upset if I go anywhere. He's just real possessive. That's how he is, you know . . . probably because I been with him for so long and I've always done what he said."

For many women, however, postrelease material support was extorted not through interpersonal control tactics but structural pressure. Multisite Family Study couples viewed the ongoing material burden that women shouldered after men's release as a product of men's institutionalized dependency. As discussed in chapter 3, men face significant barriers to formal economic participation after their release that often bar them from assuming the provider role that many couples hope they might take up. Multi-site Family Study participants also argued that men's long-term "institutionalization" helped to position them as permanent dependents in their families after release. One former prisoner described the post-prison adjustment especially sharply: "In [prison] . . . you're just living free like a little baby. Out here, it's 100 percent real." Partners concurred, though most offered a somewhat gentler view: "He was just on pause. There was no nothing happening, no maturity, no growth, no—no development. It was just like, like he was just paused, he just lived. He survived. Like physically—physiologically he survived his [incarceration], you know what I mean? He did the seven and a half years but other than that, there was nothing." Men who had served a long time in prison, whether in a single bid or "in and out" over many years, often occupied a childlike role in the household after release. Unable to contribute financially and requiring extensive scaffolding to fulfill their parenting and household responsibilities, they struggled to interface independently with the outside world.

Men's extreme dependency and hobbled interpersonal and occupational capacities after the prison stay made "women's work" into a full-time job for many Multi-site Family Study partners. Women often served as sole financial providers for their households after men's release while also assuming overwhelming responsibility for parenting and domestic life. But they also took on other uncompensated roles, functioning as unpaid case managers, mental health workers, and first responders for their returning partners. Women assisted men with telecommunications, transportation, job-seeking, obtaining public benefits, and managing their physical and behavioral health and health care. Many also actively supported or even managed men's interactions with children, employers, peers, and the rest of the outside world.

Women's caretaking functions extended beyond the jobs left undone by an inadequate social services infrastructure to include the complicated task of keeping their partners and coparents "out of trouble" with the state. In the heavily surveilled environments where they lived, it was a formidable task. Hoping to protect their partners and families from what they understood as the far-reaching ramifications of further criminal legal system contact, Multi-site Family Study women put great effort into helping men avoid police and stay in compliance with parole conditions—for example, remitting required fees, providing transportation to and from monitoring, and providing a home that met parole conditions. Alicia, who had privately endured physical violence and controlling behavior from her partner for more than two decades, nevertheless maintained a strong sense of personal responsibility for keeping him from drawing the attentions of the system:

INTERVIEWER: How do you think your relationship with him affected him staying out of trouble with the police?

ALICIA: I always kept him out of trouble. I'm the one that has. Even his dad said [after he was arrested] "Oh, my God. Why did he get in trouble? Where's Alicia at? She always kept him out of trouble.'" . . . I mean, I've never let him get into trouble. . . . He wanted to start a fight with somebody, stuff like that, [but] I'm like, "Come on, let's leave," you know.

Sociologist Beth Richie describes this dual labor of caretaking and legal system intermediation as the "new burden" managed by poor women of color in the era of mass incarceration. In hyperincarcerated communities, she argues, women balance "the constant work that they are required to do to keep their family members from the long reaches of the criminal justice system" with "pick[ing] up the slack" for atrophied social welfare and human services systems.[30]

Gendered ideals of social care intersect with racialized inequality and community norms to refigure women's superlative and sacrificial forms of devotion as ordinary and unremarkable. Women's commitment to their partners and relationships is shaped by their understanding of racism in the criminal legal system, as well as bleak social conditions and the pervasiveness of legal troubles in their communities.[31] Such conditions normalize the painful and draining dynamics of women's relationships with their partners, other criminalized and convicted family members, and the legal system itself. Women in the Multi-site Family Study, like the female visitors to San Quentin whom Comfort observed, often considered themselves fortunate by comparison with others they knew or relative to the circumstances of their own prior relationships. One Multi-site Family Study participant, whose partner had been in and out of prison for many years and was unable to contribute financially to the household, summed this up when she commented, "We are the ideal couple around the area, the neighborhood. . . . I couldn't see myself with anybody else because he is a nice guy. He doesn't abuse me."

But couples in the Multi-site Family Study did recognize the sharp asymmetry of their respective contributions to their partnerships or coparenting relationships. Both couple members often regarded their domestic and financial arrangements as placing an unfair burden on women. In describing his hopes for a more equitable division of labor in the future, one father summed it up simply: "She had endured enough. . . . I always put the burden on her shoulders to carry the load." Yet men faced serious legal and structural obstacles to the kinds of legal breadwinning that they and their partners envisioned would help to better distribute that burden. In the context of men's perpetual economic and social exclusion after incarceration, the fact that each partner recognized the unfairness and untenability of the load women carried did not mean that they succeeded in relieving it.

The heteronormative ideals and expectations that couples bring to partnerships and parenting not only help to compel women's care but often allow them to make peace with arrangements that appear stressful (at best) or exploitative (at worst). The women visitors to San Quentin, who widely acknowledged feeling "depleted" by their relationships with imprisoned men, "often refer to popular culture enjoinments to follow the gender role of loving and devoted female." Such ideals helped to motivate their persistence in what one woman referred to tersely as "doin' your wife job"—but few were so matter-of-fact.[32] Among the diverse domestic scenes that women recreated in the prison visiting room during Comfort's observation was Thanksgiving dinner, a feat that one study participant achieved by cooking all the traditional dishes at home, wrapping them in tiny folded packets, smuggling them into the prison in her pantyhose, purchasing decoy food from the prison vending machines, replacing that food with the homemade dishes, reheating it in the prison microwave, and keeping it concealed from guards while serving it to her imprisoned partner at the visiting-room table.[33] Though the scene ended in gendered success—the man got to eat his turkey—the partner in question was near emotional collapse from the stress of her task.

Indeed, women's gendered obligations expand to untenable proportions in the context of men's incarceration. For the Thanksgiving dinner smuggler and many others, efforts to keep the men in their families well-fed and clothed, to maintain emotional closeness, and to shield men's debilities from the rest of the world take on a fraught and frantic quality that highlights their high stakes. Men's well-being and women's gendered identities are each riding on women's ability to achieve near-impossible feats of care for their loved ones—whether during, after, or between incarcerations. As the partner of a man who was frequently in and out of jail explained to Comfort (in another study of family relationships affected by incarceration), "The feminine one in a relationship is always the caregiver—you know, you do more of the taking care of. This is my first [relationship] where it's actually been, you know, a twenty hour a day job."[34] Still, women focus on the idea that if these efforts succeed, they might someday have the picture-perfect family life that beckons on the horizon—what one Multi-site Family Study participant referred to as "one little family and the white picket fence and everything."

Writing of the necessity of women's domestic labor in capitalist economic systems, Silvia Federici suggests that "we are not speaking of a job like other jobs. . . . We are speaking of the most pervasive manipulation, and the subtlest violence that capitalism has ever perpetrated."[35] Read alongside the narratives of the Multi-site Family Study couples and other women affected by family-member incarceration, Federici's perspective emphasizes that the harms of mass incarceration for women do not simply arise as a natural by-product of their interdependence with men but are produced (and required) in the context of heteropatriarchal social organization and the structural conditions of racialized capitalism. Women's expanded labor in their private lives—essential to the survival of their families and to the ongoing functioning of the prison itself—is simultaneously required, devalued and obscured by the interpersonal and structural conditions under which they offer it.

Damage to Physical and Mental Health

The body registers its losses and labors, even when no one else does. The harms sustained by women with incarcerated and reentering loved ones, though they are kept well out of public view, do not disappear. In households affected by incarceration, women's work expands even beyond the untenable "second shift" of reproductive labor imposed on women in other households.[36] It fills every crevice of time and draws up all available energy and resources, leaving little to spare. It reaches beyond the boundaries of traditional domestic spaces and roles into extensive caretaking responsibilities in public and carceral spheres. Invisible to the formal economy and devalued within the correctional and social services systems that make it necessary, this labor takes a quiet mental and physical toll.

Supporting an incarcerated or returning family member can sap women's health and well-being in multiple and complex ways.[37] The economic and social losses and increased labor burdens that women shoulder, particularly the work of parenting and grandparenting, appear to make them more vulnerable to behavioral health problems.[38] A longitudinal cohort study of Black mothers found that sons' incarceration predicted mothers' subsequent psychological distress. The effects of a son's incarceration on the mother occurred via mothers' financial distress and increased grandparenting burden.[39] Another analysis found that mothers in the Fragile Families study who experienced the incarceration of the father of their children were more likely to report major depression and diminished life satisfaction at a subsequent survey wave (even after controlling for mothers' overall mental health). Just as among the mothers of incarcerated sons, negative effects of coparent incarceration on women's well-being appeared to be mediated by women's diminished economic stability and increased parenting burden.[40] The strain of partner incarceration also appears to make women more vulnerable to addiction and substance misuse, although this connection is less well studied. Women whose partners have been recently released from prison report very high rates of smoking, heavy drinking, and illicit substance use.[41] Constructing lagged dependent variable models with propensity score matching using Fragile Families data, Bruns and Lee found that coparent incarceration predicted mothers' illicit substance use, with effects concentrated among Black women.[42]

Family member incarceration also brings physical strain. The imprisonment of a son, for example, is associated with long-term declines in mothers' physical health.[43] Family-member incarceration appears to put women at particular risk for stress-related health conditions, including diabetes, hypertension, and other cardiovascular problems.[44] Risk for stress-related conditions may be further heightened by the increased burden of uncompensated labor that women assume on behalf of their family members. To better understand these connections, Hedwig Lee and her colleagues constructed logistic regression models with nationally representative, cross-sectional data from the National Survey of American Life. The research team adjusted for an extensive battery of socioeconomic and physiological variables, as well as women's other adverse life experiences. They found that women who had a family member imprisoned experienced significantly poorer physical health than other, similar women. They were almost twice as likely as their peers to report being in fair or poor health. Women who had faced family member imprisonment were also two and a half times as likely as their peers to have experienced a serious cardiovascular event, such as a heart attack or stroke.[45]

Beyond the mental and physical stresses and strains that many women face during and after a family member's incarceration, the partners of incarcerated men also bear more intimate forms of physical risk and harm. Such risks appear to arise through the complex dynamics of intimate relationships interrupted by incarceration. Multi-site Family Study qualitative interviews and Megan Comfort's ethnographic works suggest that men in prison may rely on multiple relationships to meet needs that one partner, usually a single mother living in poverty, cannot possibly sustain single-handedly: sending packages into the prison, writing letters, paying for collect telephone calls, visiting the prison in person, putting money on men's prison accounts, and bringing other children to visit. On the outside, women left behind sometimes seek relationships with other men to provide what a prisoner physically cannot: physical protection, housing, help with bills, physical intimacy and companionship, and support in raising their children. After the male partner's release, couples are faced with the complex task of rebuilding their relationships with one another, redefining or ending any new relationships, and often navigating existing, ambiguous (and potentially competing) relationships with the other parents of their children. Among Multi-site Family Study participants, all of whom had weathered prolonged physical separation during the male partner's imprisonment, it is unsurprising that even partners in highly committed, long-term romantic and coparenting relationships expressed deep uncertainty and insecurity regarding their relationship status and agreements.

The mutually uncertain relationship situations that prisoners and ex-prisoners navigate with their partners leave women physically vulnerable when men return from prison. Although research in this area is not sufficient to support strong causal claims, women with formerly incarcerated partners do appear to be at heightened risk for human immunodeficiency virus and other forms of sexually transmitted infection.[46] They may also be at heightened risk of physical violence. The prevalence and etiology of partner violence victimization among women with recently imprisoned partners is unknown, but fully 50 percent of Multi-site Family Study couples reported physical violence in their relationship after the male partner's release.[47] Their qualitative interviews suggest that the experience of imprisonment and release tended to foster, suppress, and then abruptly unleash forms of relationship conflict that outstripped couples' coping skills.[48] These dynamics parallel those documented in earlier qualitative research with couples reuniting after prison.[49] Among Multi-site Family Study participants, women's vulnerability to violence at the hands of their partners appeared to be further exacerbated by men's material and emotional dependency. Women's high-stakes responsibilities as social workers and caretakers in their partnerships made them less able and less inclined to act in their own self-interest. Their sense of the institutional forces that constrained men's household contributions and hobbled their interpersonal capacities, and the perpetual anticipation that these institutionally and structurally determined adversities might someday relent, compelled women's continued participation in a perpetually extractive (and sometimes physically harmful or dangerous) arrangement.

ADDING UP THE INVISIBLE BURDEN

Women's labor on behalf of their incarcerated loved ones is free to the state, but it comes at high personal cost to women themselves. The narratives of Multi-site Family Study participants, read alongside prior research on women's experiences with family member imprisonment, help us make sense of the gender paradox observed in population-scale studies of incarceration's collateral consequences. In the context of heteropatriarchal norms that shift men's social and material burdens to their female partners and family members, mass incarceration extracts labor and material resources from poor women—particularly women of color—that they can scarcely afford to spare. As Beth Richie argues, "Against the backdrop of divestment of basic services in low-income neighborhoods and mass incarceration, women of color are now burdened in ways that have untold costs and consequences."[50] Like the labor of prisoners themselves, the uncompensated work that women perform in service of their incarcerated loved ones' survival and well-being is both invisible and necessary to the hypercarceral project.

Valuing and compensating women's work on behalf of loved ones affected by incarceration will be an especially pivotal task in the coming period of decarceration. Qualitative research suggests that female family members provide extensive case management, mental health care, housing, job searches, and transportation assistance on behalf of their incarcerated and reentering loved ones, as well as laboring to keep them out of trouble with police and parole officers. Unfortunately, existing data do not allow us to quantify the magnitude of women's labor on behalf of incarcerated and formerly incarcerated partners, coparents, and other loved ones; the sum of their financial investments in visitation and subsistence during incarceration; or the fines, fees, food, housing, and transportation they cover on behalf of those loved ones after release. The several studies that have investigated the economic cost of women's support, discussed earlier in this chapter, used convenience samples. While they create a valuable picture of the intensity of effort and spending involved in supporting current and former prisoners, their results cannot be formally extrapolated to the general population.

Nevertheless, available evidence does support initial, conservative estimates of some of the caretaking labor carried out by family members on behalf of incarcerated and reentering individuals. Examining year-end national prison population totals from the Bureau of Justice Statistics, I estimate that American prisoners collectively served 45,362,759 years of prison time from 1978 (the accepted beginning of the mass incarceration period) to 2018 (the latest year for which Bureau of Justice Statistics data are available).[51] Representative data from a midwestern state suggest that approximately 41 percent of these prisoners would be visited in a given year.[52] Data collected from a convenience sample of prison visitors suggest that, focusing solely on the prisoners who do receive visits, female family members expend roughly $5,594.16 per year (in inflation-adjusted dollars) to maintain communications with the prisoner, including visits, telephone calls, and mail. Therefore, over the four focal decades of the mass incarceration period, the adult family members of prisoners (predominantly women) have expended at least $104 billion ($104,044,278,074) to maintain contact with incarcerated loved ones. The racial composition of American prison populations during the focal four-decade period suggests that at least $39.5 billion ($39,536,825,668) of these expenditures were made on behalf of Black prisoners.[53]

To create a lower-bound estimate for the intensive reintegrative support that many women provide for family members returning from prison, we can draw on cost estimates associated with providing professional case management for returning prisoners. In most jurisdictions, such services are reserved for those with health conditions that require close continuity of care, particularly people living with HIV or serious and persistent mental illness. Reentry consortia and pilot initiatives, however, have begun to offer them to the general population of reentering state prisoners in some jurisdictions. The Maryland Reentry Partnership Initiative offers a useful model for understanding the cost of delivering case management services to a general population of returning prisoners—those who might be most comparable to individuals receiving informal, uncompensated reentry support from their partners, coparents, mothers, and other relatives. The Maryland program delivered a modest set of practical supports for all individuals returning from state prison, including a case management session immediately before and immediately after release and assistance accessing other services and benefits during the reentry process. The average annualized cost of these services per participant was $6,900 in 2004 dollars[54] or $9,505 in 2020 dollars. Summing the annual number of individuals released from United States prisons for the years 1978 to 2018 indicates that 20,459,069 releases from prison occurred during this period.[55] Assuming conservatively that each prison release event necessitated the equivalent of the light-touch forms of reentry support delivered by the Maryland initiative from family members, the inflation-adjusted value of this labor would be about $194 billion ($194,463,450,845). Of this figure, roughly $73.9 billion ($73,896,111,321) of this labor value has been expended on behalf of Black reentrants.

Recognizing the costs of mass incarceration for women's health is critical as well. Quantitative research on health and well-being among adult family members of the incarcerated is in its nascency; many of the health impacts that women appear to sustain during and after a family member's incarceration, such as diabetes and HIV, have not yet been studied in ways that enable us to isolate the excess incidence among women that is associated with the racially targeted incarceration of their family members. But Lee and colleagues' nationally representative estimates of cardiovascular event risk, which controlled for a robust set of potential confounders, do make it possible to examine this question in a reasonably rigorous way. Their analyses suggest that family member incarceration (in jail or prison) more than doubles women's risk of a heart attack or stroke (odds ratio = 2.53).[56] This burden lands disproportionately on Black women. Results from another nationally representative study, the FamHIS survey, indicate that 64 percent of Black women have had a family member incarcerated in jail or prison, compared to 46 percent of white women.[57] Extrapolating the FamHIS estimates to population data collected by the United States Census Bureau suggests that 9,964,906 adult Black women and 51,533,810 adult non-Black women alive today have experienced family member incarceration. I estimate that this experience is associated with a total of 9,040,311 excess incidents of heart attack or stroke, including 1,464,841 excess incidents sustained by Black women. The health care costs and lost productivity precipitated by a typical cardiovascular event are estimated at $213,333.[58] We can, therefore, expect that adult women alive today have sustained approximately $1.93 trillion ($1,928,596,666,563) in monetizable damages from the cardiovascular burden of family-member incarceration, $312 billion ($312,498,925,053) of which have been borne by Black women.

The incarceration of a partner or coparent also increases women's risk of behavioral health problems, including major depression. Nationally, the twelve-month prevalence of major depressive episodes among women is 11.1 percent, and the prevalence of partner incarceration among adult women in the United States is 14 percent.[59] Using Wildeman and colleagues' figures for the increased odds of a major depressive episode among women who have experienced the incarceration of their children's father,[60] I estimate that American women alive today have likely experienced approximately 488,559 major depressive episodes associated with the incarceration of a partner or coparent. The average economic burden associated with a major depression event, including both health care costs and productivity losses, is $82,157 (converted by the author to inflation-adjusted US dollars).[61] The combined cost of such events is roughly $40.1 billion ($40,138,541,763). Of these costs, at least $7.7 billion ($7,695,892,661) are associated with partner incarceration-related depression episodes among Black women.

Estimating the costs to women of family member incarceration necessarily involves imprecision. But these particular estimates are relatively conservative. First, they focus exclusively on women's unpaid labors and health consequences, omitting entirely the direct financial expenses that women incur to maintain communication with incarcerated family members, ensure that prisoners have adequate food and toiletries, and pay their court-imposed fines and fees during and immediately after incarceration (when the incarcerated individual has no meaningful income). Qualitative data and surveys using convenience samples suggest that women's direct financial expenses on behalf of their loved ones are enormous, but the lack of generalizable quantitative data necessitates their exclusion from the present calculations. Estimates of women's unpaid labor and health consequences are also partial. Estimates of uncompensated labor account only for women's unpaid case management services and not for the many other well-documented, unpaid labors that women perform on behalf of imprisoned or recently released family members. In addition, my estimates exclude the excess wage labor that many partners and coparents perform during and after the loved one's incarceration to support their households and children without that person's financial contribution to the household. Although we know that not every incarcerated person receives such help (and that some receive it from someone other than a female family member), available research suggests that most do. Furthermore, with regard to health, the estimates presented here focus exclusively on the costs of two health conditions (cardiovascular disease and major depression). Strong evidence suggests that family-member incarceration exposes women to other costly and consequential health risks as well, whose costs cannot yet be estimated. The likely net result of these assumptions and omissions is that the sums presented here are much lower than the actual price that women pay.

REPAIRING HARM TO PARTNERS AND PARENTS

The private subsidies and uncompensated labor extracted from prisoners' family members have not only supported present and former prisoners themselves. They have subsidized an otherwise untenably overblown carceral project. And they have compensated for the shortcomings of the public services and systems that fail to support people returning from prison. The unwieldiness of the burden carried by prisoners' family members, overwhelmingly poor women of color, highlights two urgent policy tasks: making individual restitution to them as victims of the political violence of mass incarceration and developing an adequate public safety net that does not depend on women's costly invisible labor.

Repaying the resources that have been extracted from Black women under the current punishment regime and compensating women for damages to their health and well-being are a critical part of bringing the age of mass incarceration to a close. Black women have been especially harmed by the racially targeted use of mass incarceration as a tactic of political violence against their communities. They are owed individual restitution. Individual restitution must be undertaken thoughtfully, however, as women's losses themselves highlight the gendered social and economic relations that quickly redistribute assets and burdens within familial and social networks. As such, the segment of the American population whom qualitative research suggests has gone without basic medicines or utilities to ensure family members' well-being is especially likely to shift some or all of the cash-value assets they receive to loved ones in need. The calculable

portion of women's economic losses associated with the mass imprisonment of Black men (estimated in the preceding section of this chapter at
$434 billion) would ideally be returned to them in ways that are not sim-
ply appropriated to the care of other vulnerable individuals—individuals
whose care must be made a public and collective priority instead. To ensure
that women of color themselves reap the benefit of restitution, trust funds
could be established for affected women, with the annual interest accessible for any purpose the recipient desires and the nontransferable principal
value of the fund available for covering women's major costs of living on
retirement or other exit from income-generating work (such as the birth of
a child or the advent of a disability). Some portion of women's reparative
entitlements might also be invested in individual health care spending
accounts to be used for the care of the recipient's own physical and mental
health and well-being.

Institution-building reparations that end public cost-shifting to all poor
and working-class women should accompany individual reparations to
affected Black women. Fundamental transformation of public safety, correctional, and human services systems is needed—eliminating the coercive
use of women's uncompensated, private labor to fulfill essential public
functions. Law enforcement practices that oversurveil and underprotect
poor communities of color deputize women to keep men "out of trouble"
while failing to support women's safety. They must be radically remade.

The powerful roles that individual women—and the strong neighborhood social networks primarily maintained by women—have long played
in preventing violence and injury should be reimagined as appropriately
remunerated work. Women who have played these informal, unpaid roles
during the mass incarceration era, particularly poor women of color,
transgender women, and those living in hyperincarcerated communities,
must be kept at the forefront of efforts to design new public safety and
first-response systems operated by and for their communities.[62] Through
the long-standing national leadership of Critical Resistance, founded in
1997, a host of potential alternatives to incarceration have been developed and tested across the United States, including the Harm Free Zone
communities and other grassroots work. Large-scale public investment
from all levels of government is needed to further implement and evaluate
these strategies.

The mass-scale correctional systems of the current era are wholly unsustainable without gendered labor exploitation. Women have been unjustly burdened with a set of near-impossible tasks: sustaining men's physical and mental health under brutal conditions of deprivation and violent control; maintaining family relationships in the context of intensive contact restrictions, communication surveillance, long travel distances, unreasonable costs, and formidable logistical barriers; fulfilling the crushing array of private and state-imposed financial obligations left behind when men are forcibly removed; and providing intensive reintegration support when they are redeposited, empty-handed, in their communities. Given that current levels of correctional expenditure are already widely regarded as untenable and unsustainable by the state governments that fund them,[63] it is extremely difficult to envision how our current correctional systems could be made to operate humanely without massive underwriting from poor women. They should be eliminated.

Robust public investments in community behavioral health services are critical to enable the safe dismantling of correctional systems and to unburden poor women from the work that such systems impose on them. Significant public investment in residential treatment services represents an essential component of successful systems transformation. Smaller-scale, trauma-informed, restorative forms of residential care (including involuntary commitment for those whose behavioral health issues put others or themselves in danger) will be key in the new behavioral health infrastructure. Broadening the availability of no-cost, intensive outpatient and residential mental health and substance abuse treatment services is also crucial for supporting women's recovery from the behavioral health damage that mass incarceration has wrought.

To help meet the burgeoning need for behavioral health services that respond to clients' cultural contexts and life experiences, specialized student loan repayment programs should be developed to support those who have frontline experience with mass incarceration (including women who have been criminalized themselves and those who have supported incarcerated loved ones) in designing and delivering next-generation mental health care and addiction treatment. The Federally Qualified Health Center primary care model could be adapted to make such services widely, freely, and locally available in urban communities that have been targeted for mass incarceration. These same communities will serve as the front lines for the massive project of decarceration, and they urgently need public infrastructures to support healthy integration for former prisoners.

The long-awaited transition from an era of mass incarceration to one of mass decarceration will be socially and economically disastrous for women if an inadequate social safety net and community-based supports for returning prisoners are not addressed. We must begin to replace the vast architecture of private supports that women construct around their loved ones with a robust health and human services infrastructure capable of supporting the needs of all families. Modeling such systems on the needs and visions of those who have been affected by mass incarceration will help to ensure that they effectively serve the vulnerable and marginalized more broadly. The institution-building investments discussed in the preceding chapter would also help to shift the burden of supporting community reintegration for ex-prisoners away from struggling family members and back onto the public systems responsible for removing people from families and communities in the first place. Basic social welfare programs must be expanded or restored to meet the long-term needs of poor and working-class women (disproportionately women of color) in the context of the tremendous caring responsibilities that they shoulder. The overriding, intensive focus of contemporary Temporary Assistance for Needy Families (TANF) "workfare" policies on pushing poor mothers into low-wage shiftwork is incompatible with the heavy demands of their uncompensated care work. Federal intervention to broaden the availability of free childcare for low-income families could help bring economic stability within reach for more women and families. So could federal and local initiatives to address the urgent need for safe, affordable housing in urban communities (discussed in more detail in chapter 6).

The unwieldy and surveillance-oriented process of qualifying for and accessing benefits from public programs adds to the invisible labor that poor women undertake on behalf of returning prisoners and their children. To help alleviate the burdens of unpaid casework that fall on female family members of current and former prisoners, benefits eligibility and receipt must be streamlined. Cost-effective and viable strategies for modernizing the enrollment and delivery of benefits (like food stamps) exist but were largely halted under the Trump administration, based on unsubstantiated claims that they made it easier for people to receive a benefit "when they clearly don't need it."[64] Such strategies could be revived and reinvigorated to ease the gratuitous labor burden they place on poor women.

But even the most streamlined set of public entitlement programs is a less-efficient mode of support than cash-value, recurring income payments with no strings attached. A basic guaranteed income program could radically strengthen and streamline the social safety net while eliminating the need for poor women's administrative labor to access support for themselves and their loved ones. The Magnolia Mother's Trust, a pilot basic guaranteed income program, provides $1,000 in monthly cash support to low-income Black mothers in Jackson, Mississippi, for twelve months. Launched by Springboard to Opportunities, the trust imposes no restrictions on how funds can be spent or on how mothers use their time while receiving the support. It aims, instead, to "provide the necessary freedom for participants to define meaningful work for themselves."[65]

The Economic Security Project, which supports and studies guaranteed income programs like these, suggests that community-based programs like Magnolia Mother's Trust could be effectively brought to scale through state and federal income tax reform. Their proposed Cost-of-Living Refund policies would modify the federal Earned Income Tax Credit (EITC) to provide an $8,000-per-worker credit to low- and middle-income households. It would also expand EITC to include families without children and those performing important work outside the formal economy, such as full-time caregivers. It would also modernize the benefit to enable automatic filing and allow families to elect monthly payments rather than an annual refund for continuity of income.[66] Together, these efforts could help end the extortion of women's labor and resources that has defined the hypercarceral era, restore to women some of what they have sacrificed, and perhaps even build a new public infrastructure based on the intimate ethics of care.

CONCLUSION

The hand-painted river and mountains behind a visiting-room portrait of Genesis and Catrina draw the eye off into an imaginary horizon (fig. 2).

GENESIS & CATRINA

Figure 2. Alyse Emdur. *Genesis Asiatic* (left), Powhatan Correctional Center, State Farm, VA, 2013. Image courtesy of the artist.

Still, beneath the artist's careful efforts, the concave lines of mortar that hold the cement blocks of the prison in place are clearly visible. Visible, too, are the regulations on physical contact, which define the awkward angles of the couple's embrace and the strain on Genesis's face. But Catrina's shining face transmits none of this. Without her, the picture is impossible. With her—with the possibility of human wholeness and closeness that she has somehow smuggled through metal detectors and past prison guards—the whole scene is different. Still, just as thousands of pounds of concrete underlie the painted veneer of the photo backdrop, beneath the sweetness of Catrina's face is an architecture of bone, muscle, and blood; the raw materials of a massive support infrastructure that she and millions of other women have been holding up with their ostensibly free bodies.

The pioneering member-led collective of women with incarcerated loved ones, Essie Justice Group, has released a statement of demands on behalf of themselves and their loved ones. The demands reflect the particular boundary-crossing insight that women have built as they travel into and out of correctional institutions and labor on both sides of the prison gates for the possibilities of life and freedom:

> We demand the immediate return of our loved ones . . .
>
> We demand an end to all predatory and discriminatory laws, policies, and practices (including in the criminal, welfare, and immigration systems) that target, harass, and instill fear in us, and remind us every day that we are not truly free.
>
> We demand that every woman with an incarcerated loved one has access to healing and care [that acknowledges] ongoing negligence and harm experienced by Black and Brown women . . .
>
> We demand restitution from the state and all corporate beneficiaries of prison labor for their attacks on our professional development, educational opportunities, and other opportunities for access to social and economic well-being . . .
>
> We demand that criminal justice, racial justice, gender justice organizations, and organizations serving victims and survivors of violence recognize women with incarcerated loved ones as a highly impacted and impactful constituency [and prioritize] women with incarcerated loved ones for hiring and leadership . . .
>
> We ask to be held as we endure the deep pain of having our loved ones incarcerated and as we challenge the system that continues to harm us and our families.[67]

All the demands, as of this writing, remain unmet. But even in the demanding, something changes. The Essie women name forms of pain and labor that are supposed to go unnoticed, that women are expected not simply to endure but to conceal. They ask to be compensated for losses that have been left off of the collective ledger entirely, to reclaim resources that have been extracted by force and then dismissed as being of no value.

Resurfacing the vast, submerged edifice of women's work in families and communities affected by incarceration makes the gender paradox of mass incarceration's consequences suddenly intelligible. The untenable burden that family member incarceration places on women explains how it is that increases in the male incarceration rate have harmed women's health and well-being more than men's. Such an understanding also points to the imperative of reparation and the urgency of fundamental change in public safety, correctional, and social services systems. But perhaps most important, it reveals the extent of ingenuity and generative force that poor women of color have mobilized for collective survival during a deadly campaign of political violence. Born of systematic captivity, the feats of transportation, of construction, of transfiguration that women have enacted between and across carceral and domestic spaces also point unmistakably to the technologies of freedom.

5 "They Needed Me There"

THE MASS REMOVAL OF PARENTS

Thirty-five years into the American campaign of mass incarceration, a character on *Sesame Street* sang to comfort a Muppet child whose parent was in prison. The refrain was sweet and equally chilling:

> You're not alone.
> I've been there, too.
> Many children have.
> Many are like you.[1]

Far too many children have been there. In fact, at the time that *Sesame Street* composers produced the song, the number of American children with incarcerated parents had risen by 80 percent in just two decades—a fact they cited as the catalyst for the program.

One in fourteen American children is separated from a residential parent by incarceration at some point in childhood, and many more see a nonresidential parent sent to prison or jail.[2] In 2016 alone, 8 percent of minor children in the United States experienced the incarceration of a parent or guardian.[3] The targeting of Black and poor communities for arrest and imprisonment has placed poor children of color at astonishingly high risk. In such communities, having a parent in prison has become as much a fixture of childhood as *Sesame Street* itself. The majority (62 percent) of Black children whose parents did not complete high school are expected to experience parental incarceration at least once during their childhoods. Black children growing up at the height of mass incarceration had a one-in-four chance of having their fathers imprisoned before their fourteenth birthday, slightly greater than their chances of having a father who completed college.[4]

Children's emotional, physical, and economic well-being is inextricable from that of their parents. Parents know it intuitively, but years of psychological and sociological research bears this out.[5] Indeed, the design of our health and human services infrastructure is largely premised on the fundamental inseparability of child well-being from parent well-being. But the linked fates of children and parents raises an unsettling question for the penal arm of government: Are the pains of imprisonment[6] suffered by adults inevitably passed on to their children? And if so, what does this mean for the idea of individual punishment for crime and the broader legitimacy of the criminal legal system? This chapter examines this question and its far-reaching implications for the Black and low-income children whose parents have been targeted for incarceration. It attempts to quantify the harms they have experienced and to consider how those harms might be repaired and redressed.

THE REFERRED PAINS OF IMPRISONMENT

Almost two decades ago, theorist Nicola Lacey criticized what she saw as "penal philosophy's strongly individualistic presuppositions about the nature of human beings and social relations."[7] Lacey points to the fundamental fallacy of a scholarship and practice of punishment that "focus[es] on the individual offender and his or her relationship with the state" while excluding from its purview the other social connections interpolated by the relationship between the convicted person and the government. As her argument suggests, there is a damning contradiction embedded in a criminal legal system that individualizes culpability and accountability for harm, while imposing forms of punishment that radiate beyond the individual to others (including children) who have never been convicted of a crime. Caroline Lanskey and colleagues describe this phenomenon as the referred pains of imprisonment.[8]

Our ability to overlook the pain of prisoners' children is a product of two related oversights and elisions in scholarship and policy. First, critical penal theorists have focused on interrogating the exercise of state authority in relation to individuals, on the one hand, and to the entire collective social and political body, on the other. With a few notable exceptions,[9] critical scholars of penality have traditionally paid much less attention to how relations between the state and the criminalized subject might also involve intermediate social relationships, such as family ties. Such ties have received burgeoning attention from researchers concerned with childhood and parenting in families affected by incarceration. But most scholars of incarceration and the family have, for their part, focused primarily on understanding these experiences in order to guide parenting interventions, clinical treatment, and other services for affected children. Only recently have scholars in this space truly begun to foreground the challenge that their evidence presents to the very logic of the criminal legal system.[10]

Second, the mass removal of incarcerated parents from their children's lives has been made easier by a wider tendency not to acknowledge that such parents were ever there. Incarcerated and formerly incarcerated parents are overwhelmingly fathers (rather than mothers or parents of other genders), disproportionately fathers of color. Dominant images of home life and domestic work systematically erase these parents' domestic and nurturing contributions. Even prior to imprisonment, many such parents did not participate in family life in the ways that are most legible in the mainstream—for example, as formally employed, wage-earning providers or as legal husbands to the mothers of their children. Ironically, the same feminization and invisibilization of reproductive labor that compromises women's well-being (discussed in the preceding chapter) also helps to obscure many of the meaningful ways that fathers operating outside the formal economy contribute to their children's lives.

Dominant racial discourse figures Black men, in particular, as threatening and unwelcome anywhere that their labor is not being exploited for profit. In this framework, the unmonetized time that many fathers (particularly the low-income fathers of color disproportionately affected by incarceration) give their children holds no value whatsoever. Such fathers, at least from a dominant-culture perspective, exist at the margins even of their own families and homes. And having figured fathers of color as "deadbeat," irresponsible, or irrelevant to domestic life, we can hardly grapple with the meaning of their absence.

Thus, we have effectively masked the profound social and material losses that children sustain when their parents (overwhelmingly, their fathers) are imprisoned. For the parents whose children sit in the cross-hairs of the state, however, the fallout from imprisonment is much harder to overlook or underestimate. Incarcerated fathers and their coparents are acutely aware of the ways that fathers' imprisonment puts children in harm's way. The thousands of parents whom we surveyed for the Multi-site Family Study acknowledged many serious concerns about children's well-being during their fathers' incarceration. Most worried about there not being enough money to support the children; about how the children might be affected by witnessing their parents' suffering; and about the isolation and loneliness that they saw in their children during the separa-tion from the incarcerated parent, often exacerbated by a lack of other social supports.[11] More important, the detailed accounts that parents offered of family life in their qualitative interviews and longitudinal sur-veys highlighted fathers' dense and often essential contributions to their children's lives before the incarceration. Their stories expose the invisible social and economic losses that children suffer from the removal of fathers who, by some official accounts, were never there at all.

THE EXPERIENCE OF PARENT REMOVAL

The Erasure of Black Men's Reproductive Labor

Multi-site Family Study participants told us varied and complex stories of their relationships with their children. But many echoed with a single, painful theme: "being there" or "not being there." Rodney's story was one of these. A father of five who had served eighteen years in prison, he expressed deep pain and regret at having been incarcerated for much of his children's childhoods. In-person contact with his children during his long prison sentence was sparse. He especially cherished the photographs taken during his children's occasional visits, "because maybe I might see them three or four times this year and [then] might not see them for two years." For the duration of his term in prison, he viewed these visits as the best thing in his life. Staring at visiting-room snapshots in the long expanses between contact, he tracked his children's growth and development with a combination of love, awe, and overwhelming sorrow.

When a member of our research team asked Rodney after his release what it meant to be a good father, he answered, "Being there. Being present . . .*Always* being there for your kids. Never leaving them." Though Rodney worked hard to stay involved in his sons' lives while in prison, he observed that these efforts fell far short of what they needed from him: "It was like I was helpless. There was nothing I could do, and I am just constantly calling and writing and trying to—that ain't going to do it. They need somebody there." As he reflected on his parenting, his children, and how his time in prison affected their lives, he came back to this painful truth again and again: "They needed me there. They needed me there, plain and simple. . . . [My son] needed me and I wasn't there. And that did him bad."

The stark dichotomies of presence and absence that reverberate in parents' stories reflect an intimate awareness of the prevailing immediacy and concreteness of children's needs. They sum up the excruciating struggle—in some cases, the stark impossibility—of parents attempting to provide for such needs across a prison wall. They also expose a potent tension between the presumed rhetorical and official absence of many fathers of color from the domestic sphere and the hypersalience of their presence (and removal) for vulnerable children and households. The next two sections of this chapter bring together Multi-site Family Study data with other rigorous quantitative and qualitative research to illuminate the invisible losses of children when the criminal legal system summarily removes their parents from their lives and later redeposits them.

Material Deprivation

In the economically precarious households that bear the brunt of mass incarceration, the removal of an adult contributor can precipitate desperate material instability. When their partners and coparents became incarcerated, most of the 1,482 women whom we interviewed for the Multi-site Family Study worked full-time while parenting two to three young children alone. Their efforts earned a mean income of just $1,618 per month, such that even those who could find and sustain year-round employment lived in deep poverty by federal standards. (For women who were able to work steadily all year, earnings of $1,618 per month would result in an annual income of $19,416. In 2011, the year the Multi-site Family Study completed baseline enrollment, the federal poverty threshold for a family of four was $22,350.) Many women (41 percent) managed their parenting responsibilities without benefit of any paid leave from their employers. About one-third reported that they did not have housing of their own and were primarily staying with someone else.

Children of incarcerated parents are often unstably housed.[12] And interviews with children's mothers suggest that men's admission to prison, and sometimes also their release back into the community, can easily derail any housing stability the family had managed to achieve. The results can be catastrophic for children. Rigorous analysis of nationally representative data shows that a recent paternal incarceration roughly doubles children's risk of homelessness. Effects of fathers' incarceration on their children's homelessness risk occur via increases in mothers' material hardship and their isolation from formal and informal resources and declines in mothers' mental health.[13] In the context of acute material hardship, it also comes as no surprise that households of children of incarcerated fathers rely more heavily on public assistance and basic-need entitlement programs. Paternal incarceration prompts increased participation in Medicaid/State Children's Health Insurance Program, food stamps, and Temporary Assistance for Needy Families (TANF).[14]

The removal of one parent wreaks particular havoc for families living in already precarious financial situations. Qualitative interviews with Multi-site Family Study participants underscored how such households did not have the resources to sustain any additional blows to economic stability. As one father put it plainly, "It takes two to raise a family, especially in our situation. So, when I got incarcerated, she had nothing." Mothers, even those whose romantic relationships with their children's fathers had long since ended, made it clear that contributions from their children's fathers had been essential to their children's survival. Mothers and fathers alike dismissed the role of formal child support payments, often regarding them as being of limited value to the children. But fathers' more tangible (and nongovernment-mediated) contributions, such as buying clothes and diapers or paying utility bills in the child's home, were seen as critical. Fathers without access to money often contributed in other concrete ways—for example, caring for children during the daytime and keeping the mother's car running. Such contributions enabled mothers to balance a set of household and workforce obligations that would otherwise have been unmanageable. Indeed, many resident and nonresident fathers alike operated in the domestic economy in ways that were essential to material survival and highly salient to their partners and coparents—though they would not have surfaced in any official account of men's formal employment or child support participation. When fathers became incarcerated, they indicated, children's material well-being was severely affected by the abrupt disappearance of these concrete but unrecorded contributions.

Sadly for children, the material instability and hardship associated with a father's incarceration do not neatly end upon his release. Returning prisoners struggle for years, in many cases for the rest of their lives, with economic (in)stability (as detailed in chapter 3). As a result of economic hardship and family relationship disruption, formerly incarcerated parents make lower financial contributions to their households, and their partners face increased financial and emotional stress.[15] Families of former prisoners struggle disproportionately with meeting basic material needs such as food, housing, utilities, and medical care.[16] Among Multisite Family Study participants, the proportion of fathers who provided any form of material support for their children dropped substantially from pre- to postincarceration.[17] Qualitative interviews with mothers spelled out how the loss of the incarcerated parent's material contributions did not simply affect the household bottom line. Rather, it had consequences for the caregiving parent's physical and mental well-being that also affected the quality of care that her children received.

Losing a Parent (or Two)

When fathers are suddenly not there—whether owing to divorce, separation, military deployment, or some other cause—their children experience a range of serious challenges, from mental health symptoms to diminished engagement at school.[18] For children of incarcerated parents, this loss is often compounded by preexisting vulnerability and the traumatic circumstances under which fathers are taken away.[19] Children are routinely present for their parent's arrest. But parents are usually unable to communicate with them or protect them during the experience. Multi-site Family Study parents recounted numerous instances of arrest-related trauma to their children. One father, James, was haunted by the memory of his arrest and the fear of its lingering effects on his children: "It happened right in front of them. You know, the cops came in, you know, handcuffs and the whole nine. Kids were screaming. Yeah. That is something that I will never forget. And so, for the older one, I am sure that that clearly had some type of impact.... She was old enough to kind of know what was going on. And that is terrible. That makes me feel pretty bad." Although a precise estimate doesn't exist, studies suggest that at least a quarter of children witness their parent's arrest, and perhaps many more: depending on the study, researchers have found that 26 percent,[20] 43 percent,[21] and 80 percent[22] of children have been present when their parents were arrested. Children find their parents' encounters with law enforcement—which can involve breaking down the door of a home and the use of tasers, rubber bullets, and firearms—intensely frightening and traumatic. A young person working with San Francisco's Project WHAT!, a youth advocacy and empowerment project for children of incarcerated parents, offered this description of his father's arrest: "The cops started shooting rubber bullets at him. He was hit about four times, but didn't fall. When the cops started shooting, my brothers, my mom, and I dropped to the living room floor.... Then they shot him with Taser guns and that's when he fell."[23]

The violence and invasion of arrest often represents just the first of many traumatic encounters with criminal legal system personnel for children of incarcerated parents. One Multi-site Family Study mother expressed sorrow at having kept her children from seeing their father during most of his incarceration. She explained that the scenes of extreme physical subjection to correctional control that filled their visitation periods became too much:

> When the visit's over, you know, they stand the inmates up and put their handcuffs on and walk them out. [My son] flipped out to see his dad like that.... He's like "Come on, Daddy, we going home." He wanted him to come with him. Like, "Why he not coming?" And when he seen the police he

just—"Oh my God, Daddy?" He had a big old conniption fit. And I was embarrassed, 'cause I had two little babies in the car seat and he was like kicking and screaming. . . . So the visits started getting really hard for me. Even though I know it did [the father] good to see the kids, it was really hard for me afterwards to explain that to the boys or try to calm them down. So, after a while, we just agreed that we would cease the visits altogether.

As the pain of this mother's retelling suggests, children and fathers are not the only ones affected by the trauma of sudden, forcible, and repeated parent-child separation. Indeed, some of the most serious losses that children of incarcerated parents suffer are manifest in the relationship with the non-incarcerated parent. Quantitative research suggests that parental incarceration (overwhelmingly paternal incarceration) affects children primarily by reducing mothers' access to the material, social, and emotional resources they need for healthy parenting.[24] Among the Multi-site Family Study women who were left behind by a coparent's incarceration, most (62 percent) met diagnostic criteria for clinical depression during his prison stay. In qualitative interviews, these mothers described battling incapacitating sadness, depression, anger, and overwhelm at having been left to raise their children alone--often in poverty and sometimes also in physical danger.

Unlike fathers' suffering, to which children of incarcerated parents are usually exposed infrequently and for shorter periods, mothers' emotional pain is front and center in children's daily lives. Maternal depression, whether clinically diagnosed or not, powerfully shapes children's development and well-being.[25] For children of incarcerated parents, maternal mental health and mother-child interactions represent an important mechanism for the intergenerational transmission of incarceration-related harm. While this link has registered as a surprise among some researchers (including our team), it is plainly evident to parents themselves. In a qualitative interview conducted shortly after his release from prison, a Multi-site Family Study father explained forcefully to the study interviewer how urgent it was that he step back into providing material support for his children's mother, though they no longer had a romantic relationship and his own resources were scarce: "[If] she f-cked up, kids is f-cked up. I can't do that!"

Though never trivial, the sudden removal of a father reverberated differently for Multi-site Family Study children depending on their household circumstances—in particular, the division of domestic labor and material contributions between the parents prior to incarceration and the quality of the parent-child and parent-parent relationships. To be sure, even in families that were relatively stable before the incarceration, the imprisonment placed heavy material and emotional strains on the remaining parent that were then transferred to children. Mothers faced their own grief and loss and that of their children while engaged in a grinding and protracted battle to keep the family fed, clothed, and housed. Sandra, whose husband was admitted to prison while she was pregnant with their twin daughters, gave birth while he was still incarcerated. She spent his prison term bowled over by anger and grief and unable to parent her children in the ways she had hoped and planned:

INTERVIEWER: What was it like for you when [the father] was incarcerated?

SANDRA: Horrible. I felt like, just from him going to jail, like—I'm going to cry. Like, it was just so hard for me 'cause you depend on somebody for so much . . . for somebody just to come in, snatch him away without warning. . . . I couldn't work. Like my kids, they had like a really hard time adjusting to not seeing their father. And then for my daughters, I feel like they were robbed [because] they never got to meet their daddy. He was never able to be there.

Like many mothers in the study, Sandra found that it was not always possible to provide for her children's material and emotional needs while weathering her own incapacitating sense of overwhelm and despair.

Mothers also grappled with a fundamental tension: the imperative of meeting their children's intensified emotional needs during the incarceration (which required tremendous parental time and presence) against the financial pressure of earning enough money to support them alone (which often required long hours of work in low-wage jobs). For Natasha, who parented a three-year-old and a thirteen-year-old, awareness of her children's intense needs for love, attention, and reassurance landed bittersweetly: "Some children need to be loved. Like some of them can just maneuver out here and they fine and they might not be real touchy feely and all that. I don't have those kind of kids. I got—I have emotional kids that they don't just need you to tell them [you love them], they need to be shown. And I mean, I am sure all kids do, but you just have certain kids that are just—they need that. They need that extra."

Natasha's perceptions are borne out in child development research. Children who are securely attached to a parent or caregiver, who receive validation and coaching to help manage strong feelings, and whose parents and caregivers can manage their own emotions adequately may be protected against the negative consequences of parental incarceration.[26] Even as Natasha referenced acute awareness of her children's need for presence and emotional support, however, she described the three jobs she worked to fulfill her responsibility as their sole financial provider: "I got three jobs. My main job, I work at a hospital. My second main job, I work at a nursing home and then I work—in my third job I work through an agency. It is kind of good. I can set my schedule however I want to set it, on all my jobs. So, my primary [job], I work three twelves a week. But like I said, if I can work more hours, I do." An unrelenting work schedule appeared unexceptional among the mothers who participated in our study. Another mother described in detail the overwhelming financial strain she faced early in her children's father's incarceration, then proudly explained: "As for finances [now], I work sixty hours a week. This week I am working seventy between my three jobs. So we are fine." Despite the fact that the emotional and material care of their children was most mothers' overriding focus, it was unclear in these interviews how mothers could possibly cover all of their children's intense and competing needs during the father's incarceration.

For parents and households that enjoyed less stability before the incarceration, however, the loss of a father to prison can be even more catastrophic. Such was the case for Rodney's family. Rodney describes his children's mother as a good, kind person who suffered from a severe untreated addiction during his imprisonment:

> I had twin boys. . . . They was like five or six. And they had—they had basically almost starved to death. If it wasn't for the neighbors, somehow if the neighbors hadn't heard them—somehow the neighbors knew they was in there and called the police and the police broke the door down. Going in there and get my kids. They said there was no food in the house. It was feces around the house. It was crazy. She had left them there and they had been there at least a week by theirselves with no food or nothing.

In families like Rodney's, children faced extreme forms of hardship and neglect when their fathers were taken away. For such families, a father's imprisonment dealt a further destabilizing blow to mothers and children who were already highly vulnerable. At the same time, it eliminated a key figure who might otherwise have intervened to blunt children's hardship and protect their physical and emotional well-being.

Social Support and Social Exclusion

The dire straits that children of incarcerated parents and their caregivers face underscore the need for supports outside the family. But the need for outside support often goes unmet amid the stigma of conviction, a weak public safety net for poor families, and the social isolation and institutional alienation that these circumstances promote. As such, many children of incarcerated parents lack access to precisely the kinds of stabilizing social supports, beyond the nuclear family, that might otherwise mitigate the psychological effects of intrafamilial trauma. Children of incarcerated parents experience weakened informal social bonds and attenuated ties to formal institutions. Experiences and expectations of stigmatization around the criminalization of a parent keep children from being able to share fully about their experiences with potential peer and adult supports.[27] Children experience similar stigmatization and isolation in their relationships with authority figures, particularly those at school. Experimental research demonstrates that teachers expect less from children of incarcerated parents.[28] Teacher expectations powerfully affect students' educational achievement, a phenomenon known as the "Pygmalion Effect." Children's connectedness to school and school-based supports may be further eroded by adaptive system avoidance among parents who have suffered the sanctioning power of state institutions. Such avoidance systematically reduces parental involvement in education among justice-involved parents.[29]

The disruption of intra- and extrafamilial social ties affects children in subtler ways as well. Parent incarceration is tied to lingering experiences of social exclusion and social disengagement among children.[30] The essence of social exclusion lies at once in the direct harms of (objectively measurable) social deprivation and, equally, in what children take such deprivation to mean about themselves and the world. Qualitative and survey-based studies find that children, including children of incarcerated parents, track day-to-day experiences of social and material deprivation as indicators of their place in the broader social world.[31] For children of incarcerated parents, a lack of access to ordinary social activities or a lack of living conditions that children assess as being normative—for example, having "normal" day-to-day playtime with one's father or having a father present at birthdays and holidays—not only affects short-term well-being but also prompts children to form an image of themselves as missing out, isolated, and different from their peers.

In the context of looming social exclusion, social support from caring adults outside the immediate family can play a decisive role in supporting children's coping and resilience. During and after a parent's incarceration, the presence of grandparents, older siblings, teachers, and coaches help to support children's visions for the future and facilitate access to normalizing activities in the face of incarceration-related disruption.[32] For some children of incarcerated parents who manage to access external social connection and a sense of belonging, even relatively extreme adversities can be channeled into acts of positive resistance. For example, some Project WHAT! participants describe how the chance to contribute to the broader social world helped to build their sense of their own inner strength:

> Both my parents have been gone for a while. I lean on my little brothers for support. I look at them and they give me motivation to do something better. They see me and treat me like I brought them this far and it's just us, "The Three Musketeers." If I call either one of them, both of them will come running.[33]

> My parent's incarceration caused me to go into foster care. It also taught me that when you are at the bottom, you can't see anything but the top, which motivated me. It made me outgoing and positive.[34]

Despite the incredible resilience that many children demonstrate in the face of parental incarceration, parents and children alike carry a great deal of pain and fear around the possibility that children will never fully recover from the experience. For James, the father whose children bore traumatic witness to his last arrest, a poignant blending of hope and sorrow is evident when he speculates about how his children have been (and will be) affected by the experience. Aiming to end his story on a hopeful note, he suggests, "Kids are resilient. I mean, ultimately, I think they are young enough that, you know, as time progresses, it may completely go away." Then he adds, "Maybe not for the oldest." Like so many other parents affected by incarceration, James expresses a powerful faith in his children's resilience and their prospects for a positive future. But that faith is tempered, of necessity, by an understanding that the hoped-for future is uncertain at best.

The Pain and Uncertainty of Parental Reentry

Many children and parents await the return from prison with great eagerness and excitement. Fathers in the Multi-site Family Study often approached postprison parenting with renewed devotion, and some took on significant childcare responsibilities for younger children. For Rodney and other fathers like him, reentry from prison afforded a precious chance to finally "be there" for a younger child in the ways that he could not be for those who came of age during his imprisonment. Though Rodney and his youngest child's mother were no longer romantically involved when we interviewed them, they both suggest that Rodney's life after prison revolved completely around caring for his child. Though the child officially lived with her mother, both parents reported that Rodney cared for her from 6:30 a.m. to 8:00 p.m. most days: preparing all her meals, taking her swimming and for walks, playing with her at the neighborhood playground, and routinely feeding a group of local ducks they had befriended in their daily rounds.

Despite the potential sweetness and significance of a parent-child reunion, reentry does not typically dissipate the negative effects of parental imprisonment. In the best circumstances, children face formidable adjustment challenges during this period, including sudden changes in parental roles and routines. Many must also cope with the reality of a returned parent's diminished parenting capacity. The challenging personal circumstances common among returning prisoners—from traumatic stress and depression to a severe lack of basic resources like money, housing, and transportation—can present major barriers to healthy and reliable parenting involvement.

As a result, a parent's long-awaited return from prison can be a time of tremendous disappointment. Released fathers spend less time with their children, are less likely to live with their children, and contribute less financially to their children than they did before they were imprisoned.[35] Children may also be exposed to damaging forms of interaction between their parents during the reentry period. As we saw in chapter 4, reentry can be rife with struggle and conflict for romantic and coparenting couples. The severe economic strain that is almost universal among re-entrants and their households is correlated with forms of interparental conflict—particularly recurrent and poorly resolved conflict, aggressive behavior, and conflicts over children—that commonly lead to distress and other behavioral health problems among children.[36] Among parents in the Multi-site Family Study, these damaging forms of conflict and violence were extremely widespread, affecting about half of the study sample.[37]

The hopes and challenges of parent-child reunification are accompanied, for children, by the looming likelihood of losing the parent to prison again. Parents are no exception to the stark odds of rearrest and reincarceration, which see the majority of released prisoners returned to prison custody within thirty-six months of their release. This means that children typically live through the intensely hopeful and challenging postrelease period only to have the parent taken away again. For older children, who consciously remember and track prior traumas and disappointments, the possibility of losing the parent to prison again represents an especially fearful prospect. Perhaps for this reason, it was the older children in the Multi-site Family Study sample whose relationships with their incarcerated parents appeared to suffer the most.[38] One Multi-site Family Study father explained in detail how hard it had been to rebuild a relationship with his oldest child after he returned from his most recent time in prison: "You've got to earn their trust again. That was the hardest part right there, earning her trust. Earning my oldest daughter's trust, anyway. My other two, they flock to me because they—you know, they're still little. But my oldest, she think I was going to be back out here on that law ride again. But now she's coming around." Though the parent recounts his older child's "coming around" as a relative success, it is easy to imagine the redoubled devastation that looms behind the statistical likelihood that this father will again become incarcerated. The cyclical nature of the disruptions that children of incarcerated parents experience in their most important attachments inculcates a sense of perpetual insecurity, of losses at once lingering and imminent.

It is unsurprising, then, that parental imprisonment profoundly affects children's mental and emotional well-being and behavior. Children of incarcerated parents are more likely to experience childhood cognitive difficulties and attentional problems, to exhibit aggression and other externalizing behaviors, and to experience depression.[39] The work of sociologist Anna Haskins and others has demonstrated convincingly that these difficulties place children, disproportionately children of color, at a deep disadvantage in the primary functional activity of childhood: learning. Children of incarcerated parents are less well prepared for school and fare worse in the school environment. They tend to have poorer grades and lower lifetime educational attainment.[40]

Having an incarcerated father also exposes young people to greater physical harm. Children of incarcerated parents face a heightened risk of being neglected, physically abused, or sexually assaulted in childhood.[41] They are also more likely than their peers to experience a childhood traumatic brain injury and lifetime neurological difficulties.[42] Although all children of incarcerated parents are vulnerable to these negative outcomes, it seems that paternal (rather than maternal) incarceration is particularly impactful. And paternal incarceration appears the most damaging for children whose fathers lived with them before incarceration, who did not abuse their mothers, and who return to the child's home after incarceration—and for those whose fathers spend more of the childhood years in (or in and out of) prison.[43]

The material effects of parental imprisonment can also have long-lasting consequences for children's life trajectories.[44] Parental unemployment and low-paying employment, each widespread among returning prisoners, are associated with lower child educational attainment. And parental engagement in low-quality, high-strain jobs—the kinds of jobs that returning prisoners tend to be able to get—is associated with poorer child behavioral health.[45] Parents' experiences of poverty-related strain can also contribute to toxic stress among their children, a phenomenon with wide-ranging and often lifelong ramifications. Children whose parents are economically stressed experience chronic stimulation of the hypothalamic-pituitary-adrenocortical axis, which brings chronic cortisol secretion and immune activation. Problems in executive function (regulating emotional affect and impulsivity), endocrine system disruptions, and changes in gene expression result. Each of these physiological adaptations can bring serious interpersonal, physical, and behavioral health consequences over a lifetime.[46]

ADDING UP THE INTERGENERATIONAL PRICE OF INCARCERATION

The fact that parental incarceration disproportionately affects vulnerable and disadvantaged children is a troubling reality. It also presents challenges for researchers who aim to understand and quantify exactly how parental incarceration affects children. We must do so without experimental data that could truly isolate the effects of parental incarceration from other disadvantages. Tackling this challenge, sociologist Kristin Turney made creative use of data from the National Survey of Children's Health to examine the links between parental incarceration and child outcomes. Turney conducted her analysis under two different sets of assumptions. Her first set of models examined child well-being as a function of parental incarceration while adjusting for a variety of parent and child demographic and socioeconomic characteristics. In these models, parental incarceration made children more likely to experience poor overall physical health, as well as asthma, obesity, or activity limitations; depression, anxiety, behavioral problems, or developmental delays; and chronic school absence. Turney's second set of models estimated the effect of parental incarceration on child well-being using a more conservative strategy that adjusted not only for sociodemographic characteristics of parents and children but also for a wide array of other adverse circumstances in children's lives—circumstances that could have plausibly predated *or* resulted from parental incarceration. These included household material hardship, disrupted family structure, and poor mental health of mothers and other household members, each of which has been shown in other research to result from parental incarceration. Even with this extremely conservative approach, Turney found that parental incarceration predicted children's attention deficit disorders, learning disabilities, behavioral problems, speech and language problems, and developmental delays.[47] This work provides convincing evidence that parental imprisonment has wide-ranging negative effects on children, even beyond the effects of other disadvantaging circumstances in their lives.

Effects of parental incarceration on children can manifest as early as birth and continue for decades. Babies in the nationally representative Pregnancy Risk Assessment Monitoring System study whose fathers had been incarcerated were twice as likely to die in infancy as those whose fathers were not.[48] (These effects are concentrated among children whose fathers did not abuse their mothers prior to their incarceration, reinforcing the pivotal idea that effects of paternal incarceration on children occur largely through changes in mothers' well-being.) Other challenges, such as behavioral health conditions or the inability to complete formal education, emerge only as children grow older.[49] Compared to similarly disadvantaged children whose parents did not go to prison during their childhoods, children of incarcerated parents are significantly less likely to complete every major educational milestone. One of the most critical milestones of youth, in terms of its rippling effects on well-being over the life course, is completing high school. Examining data from the National Longitudinal Survey of Adolescent Health, researchers at the Florida State College of Criminal Justice found that children of incarcerated parents were fully one-third less likely than their peers to obtain a high school diploma. The effect of parental incarceration on high school completion held even when the research team matched children in the study on a very wide array of other factors that also could be expected to influence high school dropout rates: among them, household socioeconomic status, housing stability, neighborhood crime and safety factors, and parents' misuse of alcohol and other drugs.[50]

To understand how long the effects of parental incarceration might persist over a lifetime, the Florida State researchers also applied propensity score matching. They aimed to isolate the effects of parental incarceration over time, net of other forms of disadvantage, by comparing children of incarcerated parents with children of never-incarcerated parents who had similar demographic, family, social, economic, and neighborhood characteristics. Well into adulthood, children of incarcerated parents had poorer relationships, poorer behavioral health, and lower educational attainment and earnings than their peers.[51] Researchers at the French National Institute for Health and Medical Research looked even further along the life course in a landmark study of childhood adversity and mortality among more than fifteen thousand adults. They examined the effects of having a parent incarcerated or placed on probation or parole alongside effects of five other adverse childhood experiences (parental separation or divorce, placement in foster care, physical neglect, parental alcohol abuse, and parental mental illness) that are all highly correlated with parental incarceration.[52] Those who experienced these adversities in childhood had a sharply increased risk of dying young, between the ages of sixteen and fifty. For women, experiencing just one such adversity in childhood increased the risk of premature death by 66 percent; two or more adversities produced an increase of 80 percent. For men, exposure to two or more events increased the risk of premature death by 57 percent. Researchers found that the influence of parental incarceration and related adversities persisted, even after they adjusted for any differences in socioeconomic status, behavioral health, and body composition that had manifested by young adulthood.[53]

The material consequences of parental incarceration add up over a lifetime, as well. Extensive, rigorous research on the effects of education on earnings establishes that children's noncompletion of high school limits their access to economic resources for the rest of their lives. One recent study, led by researchers at the Social Security Administration, combined data on educational attainment and lifetime earnings from the Survey of Income and Program Participation and the Social Security Administration. The researchers applied logistic regression to assess the influence of high school completion on lifetime earnings while controlling for other sociodemographic and aptitude differences between young people that could independently affect both their lifetime earnings and the likelihood that they were able to complete high school. Their models suggested that men with less than a high school degree had median lifetime earnings of $1.13 million, compared to median lifetime earnings of $1.54 million among otherwise similar men who did have a high school degree (but no further formal education). For women, median lifetime earnings with less than a high school degree were $510,000, compared to $800,000 for similar women who did complete high school.[54] (The same study found that differences in lifetime earnings between those who did and did not attain a college degree were even steeper, but because of limitations in available survey data, the researchers could not isolate differences in college or graduate degree attainment. As a rigorous assessment of the effect of parental incarceration on the likelihood of completing college remains unavailable as of this writing, its economic consequences must be excluded from my estimates.)

Focusing on the lifetime earnings impact of high school completion offers a valuable starting point for comprehending the scale of economic damage visited on American children of incarcerated parents in the context of mass incarceration. The fact that children of incarcerated parents are a third less likely to complete high school than similar children of never-incarcerated parents indicates decisively that current and former prisoners are not the only ones condemned to poverty by incarceration. This work also calls grave attention to the potential role of parental incarceration in perpetuating deep, racialized economic inequality across generations.[55]

Using a life table method, criminologist Christopher Wildeman calculated the likelihood that a given American child would have one or both parents imprisoned at a given point in childhood. He determined that 2.2 to 2.4 percent of white children born in 1978 and 3.6 to 4.1 percent of white children born in 1990 experienced the incarceration of a parent by their fourteenth birthdays. In each of these cohorts, Black children experienced parental incarceration at dramatically higher rates than their white peers: 13.8 to 15.2 and 25.1 to 28.4 percent of those born in 1978 and 1990, respectively.[56] To understand how these rates of parental incarceration could affect the earnings of each group of children as they grow up, I first approximate the number of children in each birth cohort from 1980 to 2004 who were affected by parental incarceration during childhood by taking the lower bound of each of Wildeman's estimates of the race-specific rate of parental incarceration among children born that year. For the birth cohort years between Wildeman's first estimate (for the 1978 birth cohort) and his second estimate (for the 1990 birth cohort), I assume a linear increase from 1980 to 1990 and use the point along that linear trajectory as the rate for that year. For the birth cohort years after Wildeman's second estimate (1991–2002), I use the 1990 estimate as the rate for that year. I then apply these rates to the CDC's vital statistics on the number of Black and white babies born in each of those years, which yields an estimate of the number of children affected by parental incarceration in each birth cohort.

Next, I apply the National Center for Education Statistics (NCES) race- and gender-specific estimates of high school completion rates for each birth cohort as a proxy for the number of children of incarcerated parents who would have been expected to complete high school absent the influence of parental incarceration. Using the effect size estimated by the Florida State researchers, I multiply this number by 0.67 to generate the number of children of incarcerated parents who would be actually expected to complete high school; I then subtract the second number from the first to obtain the number of children in that birth cohort who likely would have completed high school if not for the incarceration of a parent. Finally, I multiply this number by the Social Security Administration's estimates for the gender-specific impact of high school completion on lifetime earnings.[57]

According to these estimates, the magnitude of high school noncompletion associated with parental incarceration would result in total lifetime earnings losses of $796 billion ($796,041,374,521) in 2020 dollars for American children born during the height of mass incarceration. Of these losses, the majority ($451,575,202,406) have accrued to Black children of incarcerated parents. Because of limitations in available quantitative data on children of incarcerated parents and simplifying assumptions made for estimation purposes, this figure is imprecise. It accounts for (notably large) gender differences in the lifetime economic value of high school completion, but it does not account for race-by-gender differences. Furthermore, in extending the rate of parental incarceration that Wildeman calculated for the 1990 birth cohort out through the 2004 birth cohort, I do not account for how the continuing, steep increase in the rate of adult incarceration (which did not begin to level off until 2008) affected children born from 1991 to 2004.

Its imprecision notwithstanding, the resulting figure of more than $796 billion represents a lower-bound estimate. Most of the limitations in my approach, including the data sources used and the calculations themselves, would tend to bias it downward. First, the numbers do not include harms to children of other racial identities besides Black and white. (Wildeman's life table analysis focused specifically on how parental incarceration might shape Black-white disparities in child outcomes. It omitted children of other racial identities, including Latinx and Native children, whom BJS statistics suggest were also at elevated risk of parental incarceration.) Second, it focuses only on children whose parents were incarcerated before the child's fourteenth birthday. (Parental incarceration during the teenage years can also impact children, but such effects are less well understood.) Third, my estimates use the lower bound of each of Wildeman's estimates for these calculations. Fourth, I focus on parental-incarceration-related disadvantage with regard to one educational milestone only (high school completion), although strong evidence exists that children of incarcerated parents are less likely to complete subsequent educational milestones as well—including college graduation—that exert an even bigger influence on lifetime earnings than high school completion.[58]

Finally, the general-population NCES high school completion rates, used here as a standard against which to compare the lesser completion rates expected of children of incarcerated parents (to estimate lost earnings due specifically to excess high school noncompletion among children of incarcerated parents), already reflect some underlying influence of parental incarceration. This is particularly true for general-population estimates that reflect the high school "pushout" of Black students (see chapter 2), which are likely substantially depressed by the up to 27 percent of those students who were children of incarcerated parents. If it were possible to compare the expected high school completion rates of children of incarcerated parents against those of a sample that included *only* children of nonincarcerated parents, the estimate of excess high school dropout because of parental incarceration (relative to the expected rate absent parental incarceration) would likely rise. Still, limitations notwithstanding, these estimates offer a meaningful floor for grasping the rough economic scale on which mass incarceration has defined the futures of children of incarcerated parents. In so doing, it has also contributed to the impoverishment of already-poor families and the entrenched racialized economic inequality that persists across multiple generations of American children.

REPAIRING HARM TO CHILDREN OF INCARCERATED PARENTS

Children's well-being is inseparable from that of their parents. This singular fact unites a wide body of research on the harms of parental incarceration for children. And it fundamentally undermines the legal and philosophical premise of imposing imprisonment as an individual punishment for convicted adults. One can only hope that moral and political momentum continues to gather for ending a form of punishment that massively and systematically injures those who have never committed a criminal act. Yet even in the best policy scenarios, millions of vulnerable children will continue to be newly touched by parental incarceration, and millions more will weather a parent's transition back from prison in the coming decades. A national effort to repair harms to children of incarcerated parents must not only make reparations for past damages but make earnest effort to mitigate future harm.

Repairing Material Damage

Children born in the era of mass incarceration will pay a ruinous material price for parental incarceration over the course of their lives. The calculations presented here suggest that children of Black parents targeted for mass imprisonment, even just the subset for whom we have reliable data on which to base these estimates, will suffer roughly $452 billion in long-term damages from being unable to complete high school. While Black children will pay the single highest price, children of incarcerated parents more broadly are expected to sustain at least $796 billion in lifetime economic harms. As mass incarceration has targeted individuals and families who were already severely economically disadvantaged, these costs have been exacted from those who can least afford them.

The youngest of the "children of the prison boom,"[59] who were born in 2002, entered adulthood in 2020. For them, any forward-looking efforts to mitigate the consequences of parental incarceration will come too late to reverse the cascading effects of toxic stress and social and material deprivation that many have already survived. But making material reparations to the now-grown children of incarcerated parents represents an opportunity for moral repair, as well as a chance to mitigate the reverbera-tions of this harm in future generations of children whom these children will parent. Cash-value reparations to Black children whose parents were affected by a racially targeted incarceration campaign should be distrib-uted at a level concomitant with their estimated losses in educational attainment. Such compensation could be offered through a variety of instruments at the choice of the recipient (as also discussed in preceding chapters). These could include tax credits; lump-sum, annual, or monthly cash-value transfers; interest-bearing trust funds; or grant-making funds that support a broad range of asset-building and life-sustaining endeavors.

Mitigating Harm to Future Children

As we work to build a system of justice that harms no one, immediate reforms are needed to minimize and mitigate harm to the children of pris-oners and former prisoners. As researchers and advocates for children of incarcerated parents have been arguing for decades,[60] the myriad correc-tional policies that continue to exacerbate children's pain and suffering during their parents' incarceration must be swiftly reversed.[61] More broadly, we must act to mitigate the development of toxic stress, prevent and reverse far-reaching social and material losses, and better support long-term hopes and aspirations among the children of the incarcerated.

REDUCING SOCIAL LOSS AND STRAIN

Urgent policy change is needed to ameliorate the deep social losses that children experience during and after a parent's incarceration. To cope with a criminal legal system that systematically and forcibly removes par-ents from their lives, children need support for healthy contact with their incarcerated parents, lessened exposure to the suffering of their nonincar-cerated parents and other caregivers, and aid in connecting with other forms of social support. Caregivers often invest substantial effort in main-taining parent-child contact during the incarceration but encounter a multitude of barriers, traumatic experiences, and minimal support when they attempt to do so. Their experiences point to a need for more humane law enforcement and correctional practices that limit trauma to children during arrest and prison visitation. Such measures should include, at a minimum, trauma-sensitive law enforcement and correctional officer protocols, the transfer of incarcerated parents to facilities near their home communities, child-friendly prison and jail visitation environments and visitor admission policies, support with visitor approval processes, transportation for visiting caregivers and children, access to free or rate-capped telephone calling from prisons, and integrated community support programs that serve both children and their caregivers during a parent's incarceration.[62] Though none of these measures can eliminate the fundamental harm to children of parental imprisonment, they could help to ameliorate the direct trauma associated with a parent's removal from the household or community, as well as children's detrimental exposure to the pain and suffering of their other parents and caregivers.

To help children process the loss and suffering to which they are exposed during and after a parent's incarceration, appropriate counseling should be made widely and freely available. Many families coping with incarceration and reentry do not have resources to coordinate, finance, and provide transportation for regular therapy visits for their children. Nor are therapeutic services tailored to the needs of children of incarcerated parents widely available in every affected community. Expanding the availability, capacity, and cultural and situational competence of counseling services in public schools could help to ensure that children have meaningful access to mental health care. Home-based parent-child therapy represents another important, promising approach to supporting children and their parents in healthy coping with the trauma of parental incarceration. Home-based parent-child treatment, designed and tested among low-income children with posttraumatic stress symptoms, has been shown to reduce children's emotional and behavioral symptoms while also bolstering caregiver responsiveness and improving caregiver-child relationships.[63] In addition, potential exists to expand the capacity of pediatricians, emergency room personnel, and other primary care providers to offer mental health screening, services, and referrals for children affected by incarceration.[64]

Children of incarcerated parents, like all children, need access to nonparental forms of social support. This need can go unmet because of the stigma of parental incarceration and children's associated social and insti-

tutional isolation. Efforts to address discriminatory and exclusionary
social attitudes toward people affected by incarceration, to develop institutional practices that are fully inclusive of children of incarcerated parents, and to provide enhanced social support (such as mentoring) could
help to address this gap. Young adult children of incarcerated parents,
now entering the workforce in burgeoning numbers, may be particularly
well suited to design and implement such efforts.[65]

ADDRESSING POVERTY AND HOUSING INSTABILITY

Limiting children's exposure to severe poverty and housing instability during and after parental incarceration is essential to their healthy development. This goal can be partly accomplished by addressing the collateral
consequences of incarceration for parents' workforce participation and
earnings (discussed in chapter 3) and eliminating cost-shifting from correctional and human services systems to prisoners' partners and coparents
(discussed in chapter 4). But additional support, specifically focused on
preventing homelessness and promoting housing stability, is also needed
for children affected by parental incarceration. First, the Department of
Housing and Urban Development (HUD), which has already encouraged
local housing authorities to revise their standards for excluding individuals or their families from subsidized housing on the basis of criminal
record, should prohibit such exclusions outright. Second, HUD's family-
unification housing vouchers show great potential for preventing incarceration-related household disruption and housing instability. The current
program, administered jointly in selected communities by local public
housing authorities and child welfare agencies, provides non-time-limited
rental assistance and supportive services to families of children whom
local child welfare systems identify as being in danger of out-of-home
placement or who are delayed in reunification with their families because
of inadequate housing. In a policy environment in which few homeless-
ness-related interventions have shown clear effectiveness,[66] HUD's reunification voucher program has demonstrated measurable reductions in
child maltreatment and improvements in housing stability among families
in the child welfare system.[67] Given the heavy overlap between child welfare and justice-involved populations and the urgent complex of housing-
and family-reunification-related needs that face children of incarcerated

parents, expanding eligibility to include all children affected by parental incarceration would be a logical extension of the program's original model and mission. Doing so could help stabilize children's households through incarceration and reentry and perhaps prevent two of the most severe known consequences of parental incarceration: child maltreatment and homelessness. Housing-focused peer support models developed for homeless parents, such as Circle of Parents,[68] could also be helpful for nonincarcerated parents and caregivers who are facing the common challenge of keeping children housed and nurtured while navigating another parent's incarceration.[69]

The extreme vulnerability of children of incarcerated parents highlights the broader issue of inadequate basic safety-net programs to protect all children from severe material hardship. Efforts to protect all children from poverty should be enriched and redoubled in the wake of mass incarceration. Full funding for the Children's Health Insurance Program, administered jointly by federal and state Medicaid agencies, should be restored. Critical food benefits offered through the Supplemental Nutrition Assistance Program (SNAP) and the Special Supplemental Nutrition Program for Women, Infants, and Children should be expanded, and streamlined state-administered eligibility and application processes—which had improved SNAP uptake among qualified families but were threatened and curtailed under the Trump administration[70]—should be reinstated. Finally, the Child and Dependent Care Credit should be increased or other tax-credit-based or direct-subsidy childcare assistance should be expanded for low-income parents and caregivers.

PREVENTING THE DEVELOPMENT OF TOXIC STRESS

The lifelong consequences of parental imprisonment occur when children do not receive adequate support for coping with trauma and adversity. Toxic stress, a recognized set of neurochemical, anatomical, and epigenetic changes that affect children whose coping mechanisms have been overwhelmed, mediates the relationship between the material and social losses that children of incarcerated parents experience and their long-term well-being.[71] Reviewing a formidable body of evidence on childhood toxic stress, the American Academy of Pediatrics concluded:

It is not adversity alone that predicts poor outcomes. It is the absence or insufficiency of protective relationships that reinforce healthy adaptations to stress, which, in the presence of significant adversity, leads to disruptive physiologic responses (i.e., toxic stress) that produce "biological memories" that increase the risk of health-threatening behaviors and frank disease later in life. . . . The prevention of long-term, adverse consequences is best achieved by the buffering protection afforded by stable, responsive relationships that help children develop a sense of safety, thereby facilitating the restoration of their stress response systems to baseline.[72]

The imperative of maintaining or restoring children's access to protective social buffering is nowhere more urgent than among children who face parental incarceration.

Supporting prosocial buffering for children without further burdening their parents and caregivers—like the young mother who told our study team that she was doing "fine" working sixty or seventy hours a week at three jobs while caring alone for high-need children—is a challenging prospect. But robust home visiting programs show significant promise for preventing toxic stress among children while alleviating (rather than increasing) their caregivers' burdens. Developed to support vulnerable parents before a child's birth and during early childhood, home visiting programs offer in-home support with parenting, navigating programs and services, and health and developmental screening and referral.[73] They work to alleviate external sources of household strain (such as poverty-related stressors) while supporting caregivers in meeting children's needs for emotional security and responsiveness.[74] Two of the best-tested home visiting models (Healthy Families America and the Nurse-Family Partnership program) show broad, consistent, replicable, and significant effects. They improve child health, development, and school readiness; decrease child maltreatment and family violence; boost maternal health; increase positive and responsive parenting; and bolster family economic well-being.[75] In so doing, home visiting programs may also support better outcomes in later childhood, such as high school graduation, that are known to be affected by parental incarceration. Home visiting programs should be offered in their robust, empirically tested form to the households of all children who experience a parent's incarceration in jail or prison.

SUPPORTING CHILDREN'S LONG-TERM ASPIRATIONS

Multistage educational supports should be extended to children of incarcerated parents to support their educational attainment and the associated opportunity to realize longer-term life goals.[76] Children of incarcerated parents who are more connected to school and family are better able to avoid negative repercussions for their own educational attainment.[77] Family-centered early intervention programs, which aim to support children's educational participation through secure connections at home and at school, could help to unlock the powerful resilience to which Project WHAT! and Multi-site Family Study participants attest in their most hopeful narratives. For example, Parent Corps trains teachers, behavioral health professionals, paraprofessionals, and parents in strategies for creating predictable, safe, and nurturing home and school environments in which trauma-exposed children can self-regulate and thrive. Developed and tested among parents and teachers of vulnerable preschool and kindergarten children, the program has shown sustained, positive effects on children's educational achievement and mental health.[78] Making such programs available to those who teach and parent children affected by incarceration could boost children's coping skills and educational engagement, both of which would position them to reach a broad range of life goals and aspirations.

Finally, given the increased risk of homelessness that children face during and after a parent's incarceration, and the inherently destabilizing nature of parents' transitions into and out of prison, promising strategies for educating homeless and highly mobile children might also hold potential for engaging children of incarcerated parents. Evidence suggests that early childhood education programs, outreach and education for school staff on meeting the needs of students in transition, and cross-school educational coordination can help affected children succeed even under very challenging circumstances, with school psychologists playing a key role in these efforts.[79] Institutions of secondary and higher education should also extend proactive admission and scholarship assistance to children affected by parental incarceration. Such supports could help promote high school and college completion among children of incarcerated parents, while helping to ensure that the next generation of scholarship on these and other social issues benefits from their intellectual leadership.

CONCLUSION

Accomplished activist Emani Davis spent most of her childhood with her father incarcerated. Davis went on to achieve national and international recognition for her advocacy on behalf of children of incarcerated parents. And she once commented candidly, "I look like the poster child of children of incarcerated parents. But I'm not okay." Her bare statement makes plain the dual weight of hope and pain that so many children of incarcerated parents carry for a lifetime.

Rodney, the father who mourned "not being there" for his sons during his incarceration, spoke with awe and respect about his own "poster child," who took over many parental responsibilities during Rodney's long incarceration: "He was the one who would lead [his siblings], like even when their mom was out smoking dope and not feeding them, he was going to go out and do what he got to do to make sure he feeds his siblings. They looked up to him." He recounts with deep gratitude how his other children managed to escape prison and graduate from high school, calling it a "miracle."

But Rodney's grief over what happened to the "poster child," the son who kept Rodney's other children from harm, was impossible to contain in the script of our research interview. Nor does it fit on this page. Late in his interview, Rodney describes how he called from prison to tell his son, then a senior in high school, that he would not be home in time for his graduation:

> I would always tell them, like, man, I will be home to see you graduate. This was even when they was young. Like, man, by the time you graduate, I will be there. I will see you walk that stage. So finally, that time came. It was 2008, which was the year that my twins would graduate. And I went to the parole board I think in January. . . .
>
> Long story short, they didn't let me out. They gave me four more years. So, I had to get on the phone, and I remember I called them and my son, the one that is in jail now, he was crying so bad. And he was like, he just kept, he said, "Dad, I don't care no more." I said, "What you mean?" He said, "I don't care. I don't care. Man, mommy out here on crack, you in there, you got to do four more. Man, I can't do this no more. I am done. I am done. It is over." . . . And he just spiraled down after that.
>
> Man, that probably was the first time I cried since my grandma died when I was like seventeen. You know what I am saying? Because I knew; I could hear it in his voice, and I knew it was going to get tricky. And I am in

jail, so I am seeing kids his age come in here every day. I have nightmares that my son was coming to the same jail I was in. I am talking about literally wake up and thinking that I heard his name or somebody was telling me, like, "Hey, your son just got off the bus." I would have these nightmares all the time.

Unfortunately, it did not take long for the nightmares to become reality. The state, which seemed notably absent during the years that Rodney's oldest child struggled alone to support himself and his siblings, arrived with swift and brutal efficiency to punish that child as soon as he collapsed under the burden. Late in our interview, tucked among softer references to "being there" (and not) for his sons and little anecdotes from his long days with his toddler, Rodney explained that his beloved oldest son had been sent away on a ten-year sentence before his own release from prison.

For those who have never experienced the imprisonment of a parent or of a child, $796 billion might seem an impossibly heavy representation of the burden that children of incarcerated parents have carried. But for a father who listened helplessly over a prison telephone to the moment when his child's strength gave out beneath it, no figure can begin to express that weight.

6 "Systematic Deconstruction"

THE COLLECTIVE EFFECTS OF MASS INCARCERATION

Gifted and intensely driven, Joseph T. Jones Jr. makes it difficult to imagine any ending to his story other than the one he has achieved: adviser to two presidential administrations, founding president of an influential nonprofit, and die-hard family man. Yet Jones arrived at this destination by a long and hazard-ridden road. His six decades in Baltimore encompass at least as many incarnations. He has been a kid with an absent father, an adolescent struggling with a heroin addiction, a young adult cycling through jail and prison, a father of three with a knack for inspiring other dads, and a fifty-year-old recent college graduate. Today, he is a relentless innovator in the human services space and the visionary leader behind the Center for Urban Families' work to build a Baltimore, and a nation, beyond mass incarceration.

After Freddie Gray was killed by police in 2015, the Center for Urban Families became ground zero for weeks of civil unrest in Baltimore. Amid the fierce and unrelenting mass protest, a state of emergency was declared and National Guard troops were deployed. The neighborhood where the center is located was scorched by the confrontation. Jones, who has grown up, lived, and worked under many of the same conditions that surrounded Freddie Gray and his neighbors, cannot pretend surprise at the ferocious outcry against the killing. He has witnessed firsthand the catastrophic effects of Baltimore's "zero tolerance" criminal justice regime and the systematic removal and long-term incapacitation of Black men it has brought about: "It's almost a systematic deconstruction. It's what you'd do if you wanted to destroy a population completely but just didn't want to kill them. You'd create a set of circumstances that people just could not overcome, an American apparatus that keeps people in that place.... Mass incarceration has depleted talent and optimism in communities to the point where you can have a Freddie Gray situation. Folks have been segregated and isolated in [impoverished] communities and they're trapped where they can't get out."[1]

Forming a true picture of mass incarceration's effects on racial inequality in America requires that we look first at the historic transformation it has effected in urban Black communities like the one where Freddie Gray lived and died. Such communities have been subjected to a four-decade campaign of state force, unmatched in its reach or its violent intensity. This chapter considers mass incarceration as a form of collective, political violence. It assesses the systemic influence of that violence on the economic well-being, physical health, and political power of Black communities and its consequences for racial inequality and population health in the nation as a whole.

MASS INCARCERATION AS COLLECTIVE VIOLENCE

Trauma scholar Kaethe Weingarten, who has spent her career studying the effects of violence on victims and witnesses, observes that the violence of the state has a uniquely damaging effect. Weingarten argues that such political violence is distinguished from other forms of aggression by its group-based deployment and by the fact that either the perpetrator or the victim group (and often both) view it as being "intended to influence power relations" between them.[2] She suggests that violence carried out under these circumstances has lingering and devastating repercussions for the well-being and collective functioning of targeted communities. Whether this is a useful lens for understanding the ramifications of mass incarceration depends, of course, on whether we consider mass incarceration to be "group-based violence" and whether we perceive it as having been "intended" to diminish the power of the communities targeted.

There is no mistaking that contemporary regimes of law enforcement, detention, and imprisonment in the United States involve the massive use of violence. Armed government personnel, including police, sheriffs, and jail officers, constitute the front line of mass incarceration. Such personnel regularly use physical force in the course of policing, arresting, and detaining people who have not been convicted of crimes. Even when not immediately deadly, subjection to such force often comes with devastating consequences, including suicide.[3] Indeed, the threat and use of force is so pervasive that many residents of urban Black communities have been trained by experience to expect violent treatment from police.[4] For members of these communities, even those who have not been personally singled out for arrest or prosecution, weaponized government surveillance and the constant threat of violence are a fact of life.[5]

For those who are personally arrested and sentenced, however, a more intensive complex of violent encounters awaits. Prisoners experience high rates of physical and sexual violence while incarcerated. While official statistics on physical assault victimization in prisons are lacking, both peer-to-peer violence and the authoritarian violence necessary to enforce complete physical control by correctional officers are recognized as endemic to prisons everywhere.[6] Though considerable intra- and international variation exists in the conditions of confinement in state and federal correctional systems, punishment scholar Leonidas Cheliotis argues that "the inherently violent nature of the experience for those subjected to it" is ubiquitous and unmistakable.[7]

The group-based nature of mass incarceration–era violence is also unmistakable. Black Americans are disproportionately targeted for policing and punishment at every potential point of justice system contact and at every stage in processing. Urban communities of color, and individual Black men within them, also bear a disproportionate share of law enforcement–related physical assault.[8] Indeed, the phenomenon we call "mass incarceration" is so sharply and precisely directed at Black men that French sociologist Loïc Wacquant famously pointed out that the term (with its implication of breadth) is a misnomer. Rather, a discrete number of urban communities of color have been subjected to hyperincarceration and, as in other major historical examples of political violence, have faced not simply the use of physical force by state personnel but the systematic, physical removal and enduring social dislocation of their members. Much critical work on mass incarceration focuses heavily on its historic scale: the fact that currently the United States incarcerates its residents at a rate eight times its historical average.[9] But this stunning scale can also be a distraction. As Weingarten concludes from her research on other forms of state violence, it is the "purposes, not the scale of the destruction or the horror" that distinguish political violence and underlie its profound collective consequences.[10]

The blunt political rhetoric surrounding the advent of mass incarceration made its purpose abundantly clear. Though Richard Nixon's most infamous contribution to mass incarceration is the War on Drugs that launched under his presidency, Nixon's expressed intention to criminalize communities of color to undermine their political power was documented even before he took office. Discussing a campaign advertisement with a staffer, Nixon communicated his approval like this: "It hits it right on the nose. It's all about law and order and the damn Negro–Puerto Rican groups out there."[11] One of the most authoritative and enlightening accounts of the intentions behind the hypercarceral drug war that Nixon would launch once he gained office comes from an interview with former Nixon domestic-affairs aide John Ehrlichman. After the administration ended, Ehrlichman explained plainly to a reporter that the president's "war" was conceived as a strategy to disrupt and undermine the political power of the communities of color that Nixon and colleagues saw as political enemies:

> You want to know what this was really all about? The Nixon campaign in 1968, and the Nixon White House after that, had two enemies: the antiwar left and Black people. You understand what I'm saying? We knew we couldn't make it illegal to be either against the war or Black, but by getting the public to associate the hippies with marijuana and Blacks with heroin, and then criminalizing both heavily, we could disrupt those communities. We could arrest their leaders, raid their homes, break up their meetings, and vilify them night after night on the evening news.[12]

Reviewing an enormous body of evidence on patterns of criminalized activity and government responses to it across the 1970s, 1980s, and

1990s, sociologists Sara Wakefield and Christopher Uggen conclude definitively that neither the precipitous rise in overall incarceration rates nor the racial disproportionality in incarceration can be attributed to differences in rates of criminalized activity. Rather, the evidence points to the fact that increasing deployment of policing and incarceration against Black Americans was (and is) an "intensely political" strategy.[13]

The repressive policing of Black communities and the mass removal of Black men did effectively counter the powerful momentum for racial and economic justice that had built up during the Lyndon Johnson era, a period that saw the passage of the Civil Rights Act and the Voting Rights Act and comprehensive antipoverty programs.[14] Hyperincarceration succeeded in rolling back the threatening political power of the Black communities at which Nixon's government had taken aim.[15] In the years that followed, the disenfranchisement of prisoners and those with felony records removed as many as one in four Black men from voting eligibility in some states—a change that appears to have successfully altered the result of several presidential elections.[16] Even more significant, it may have also attenuated the democratic participation of those left behind in targeted communities.[17] Together, these phenomena effectively buttressed an American "racial caste system" that activists and voters in Black communities had been effectively challenging prior to mass incarceration.[18]

UNDERSTANDING THE COLLECTIVE IMPRINT OF MASS INCARCERATION

A Legacy of Collective Violence

Collective violence, by its very nature, harms entire communities. In her pathbreaking writings about the legacy of state violence among the Lakota and other Native North American tribes, Maria Yellow Horse Brave Heart explains that histories of "genocide, oppression, and racism" produce a "historical trauma response" that affects the community as a whole, even those who did not experience the harm firsthand. The trauma and grief resulting from "cross-generational collective losses" are not individual, affective experiences; they ripple across generations and throughout entire communities.[19] In Native communities that have survived forced relocation and massacre, Brave Heart argues, contemporary exposures to violence activate and reinforce the lingering, collective experiences of historical harm.

Brave Heart's historical trauma framework has been borne out in extensive research with survivors of collective violence and their descendants: Native children forcibly separated from their parents and subjected to physical abuse and captivity at Indian boarding schools, combat veterans exposed to wartime trauma, and those targeted for collective violence in occupied territories.[20] Studies that measure biomarkers of stress and trauma find that group-based violence precipitates a common set of physiological and epigenetic changes. Such changes manifest even among members of the community who were not directly subjected to the violence. Effects continue to register into the next generations, including among children born after the collective violence has come to an end.[21] Studies with communities targeted for attempted genocide, terrorism, and other forms of collective violence show that children of survivors exhibit altered cortisol patterns resembling those of their parents.[22] Another biomarker common among trauma survivors, methylation of the *FKBP5* gene, is evident not only among Holocaust survivors but also their children.[23] Alterations to cortisol and *FKBP5* methylation are, in turn, associated with serious physical and mental health conditions, including diabetes, depression, and PTSD. These conditions, which are disproportionately prevalent among groups targeted for discrimination and collective violence, appear to arise as part of a chronic physiological stress response activated by trauma exposure.[24]

In urban Black communities targeted for mass incarceration, the large-scale, forcible removal of Black men from economic, political, and social life ripples through affected neighborhoods and changes the nation as a whole.[25] Residents of targeted communities in the United States evidence symptoms similar to those documented in research with other survivors of collective violence;[26] that is, "the psychological and emotional consequences of the trauma experience are transmitted to subsequent generations through physiological, environmental and social pathways resulting in an intergenerational cycle of trauma response."[27] Evidence on the intergenerational transmission of trauma suggests that these collective effects are long-lasting, extending even beyond an individual lifetime.

The spillover of unresolved trauma, particularly in family relationships, means that the effects of collective violence on a community could persist for multiple generations if left unaddressed. Research on the community- and national-level consequences of mass incarceration suggests that it has, indeed, contributed to broad and persistent legacies of trauma and disadvantage. As we have seen, the repercussive effects of mass incarceration for criminalized youth, prisoners and former prisoners, and their families are often plain, devastating, and life-altering. But their effects on the myriad urban communities that have weathered decades of hyperincarceration have been "death by a thousand little cuts."[28] Extensive evidence suggests that the collective and cumulative harms of mass incarceration are much more than the sum of their parts. They depress the overall economic well-being and physical health of Black communities in America and exacerbate the disparities that divide those communities from the rest of the nation.

Economic Damage to Black Communities

Reflecting on the collective economic effect of mass incarceration in Baltimore neighborhoods, Joe Jones offers a historical observation. Throughout the final six decades of slavery, he explains, Maryland was home to a "mix of freed Africans and folks who were still in slavery." During this period, "there was little accumulation of wealth among the freed Africans because they were using what they had to buy family members out of slavery." His observation offers historical context and also a potent analogy for the economic plight of mass incarceration–era Baltimore and the nation as a whole. Across the country, many urban Black communities have carried a dual burden: the inherited, unremediated economic effects of enslavement and legal segregation and the contemporary economic spillover effects of hyperincarceration. In such communities, even now, surplus income is an exception rather than a rule, government help (particularly for adult men) is both meager and scarce, and mutual aid is a necessity of survival. The resources required to support incapacitated community members, including those incapacitated by the criminal legal system, often come from other severely impoverished households in the same community. At the community level, then, mass incarceration has not simply meant the lost economic contributions of the many individuals who have been removed and then returned in an economically incapacitated condition. The quietly privatized task of supporting such individuals' survival during and after imprisonment has actively drained the marginal financial resources that nonincarcerated individuals in their communities might have otherwise managed to use for their own advancement and well-being.

The collective burden of mass incarceration–era cost shifting alone could have a dramatic negative impact on a community's economic well-being. But the social consequences of concentrated incarceration and reentry inflict further economic damage. As Joe Jones explains, the systematic removal of young Black men in Baltimore "deprives our community of strong community members, deprives children of strong fathers, deprives our labor force of talent, deprives our educational system of individuals who would have studied and developed themselves and gone on to do great things." Quantitative research in other American cities bears Jones out. When a high proportion of young adult men are removed and returned in a rapidly cycling manner, as they have been in the context of mass incarceration, communities miss out on largely unheralded but crucial social functions that young men would otherwise serve in their networks. Their presence plays an indispensable role in collective economic survival by helping community members connect to employment and other economic resources beyond their immediate familial and social circles. In their absence, low-income communities become more and more alienated from external resources.[29]

In addition, mass incarceration undermines educational opportunities for young people in neighborhoods with high rates of incarceration—and undermines the collective future economic prospects that educational opportunities can bring. Whether or not their own families are directly affected, students who attend schools with high rates of parental incarceration have significantly lower lifetime educational attainment than similar students at schools with low rates of parental incarceration. In fact, children of nonincarcerated parents who attend schools with elevated school-level rates of parental incarceration are just about as likely to complete college as children of incarcerated parents who attend schools with low school-level rates of parental incarceration. The many students for whom these two adverse conditions converge—that is, those whose parents have been incarcerated and who also attend a school with high rates of parental incarceration—are one-quarter as likely to complete college as those who face neither adversity.[30]

What happens to Black Americans who have no familial, social, or neighborhood connections to former prisoners or their children? Though mass incarceration has made this situation more the exception than the norm,[31] wholesale criminalization has eroded the foundations of economic participation even among individuals whose own lives remain wholly untouched by incarceration. The association of Blackness with drug use and criminality, which Nixon's government intentionally cultivated with its War on Drugs, has extended itself well into the twenty-first century.[32] Mass incarceration has helped to reformulate and extend the many other forms of vilification of Blackness that predated it.[33] The powerful racist association between Blackness and criminality represents a major cultural accomplishment of the mass incarceration era. This association harms all Black Americans, regardless of their own contact with the criminal legal system or even their familial or geographic proximity to those involved with that system.

Today, racialized perceptions of criminality profoundly curtail economic opportunity in Black communities. Teachers and childcare providers regard their Black students with suspicion as early as preschool. When researchers at Yale's Child Study Center asked early childhood educators to watch a group of preschool-aged children for "behavior that could become a potential challenge," eye-tracking technology showed that the educators most often trained their gazes on Black boys.[34] Observational studies in prekindergarten and elementary school settings show that teachers both watch for and outwardly communicate the "badness" of Black male students and are more likely to escalate their disciplinary actions with Black male students than with their peers, even in preschool.[35] Educators' perceptions of and interactions with students, of course, shape how youth see themselves and how they perform academically.[36] The negative content of official academic records that teachers construct for their Black male students helps to prime them for further punishment and criminalization rather than prepare them for educational advancement.[37]

Leading an organization that works to remedy the collective deficits in educational priming and preparation that have resulted from racial criminalization, Joe Jones notes that reversing educational damage sustained by Black communities over multiple generations is no trivial undertaking: "It's motivating a person to believe that they deserve to be in society and there are opportunities if they work really hard. Then it's the academic and hard skills acquisition. And you're asking them to do that now as adults who have all kinds of barriers, as opposed to as a little person nurtured by adults and who benefited from uninterrupted educational participation and is prepared for youth employment and who goes from there." The systematic, collective deprivation of adequate educational preparation for Black residents, and the high prevalence of felony records that accompanies it, has citywide consequences as well. It prevents cities like Baltimore, whose workforce has been heavily impacted by racial criminalization, from fully benefiting from the periods of economic growth that might otherwise offer the chance to reduce poverty and improve residents' quality of life: "When you come back down to communities right now where you have a robust economy and employers are dying for workers, we're in a really good place, close to full employment, and there aren't enough workers to fill jobs—and part of the reason is that jobs require skills beyond those that folks who have been involved in the criminal legal system have, or involve roles that they are prohibited from filling due to their records."

In the workforce, Black candidates are systematically disadvantaged by the stigma of presumed criminality—again, regardless of their individual or familial connections to the criminal legal system. In the context of widespread, racially targeted policing and prosecution of Black individuals, it comes as no surprise that employers maintain demonstrable racial biases about the potential criminality of applicants. The implementation of "Ban the Box" policies in some jurisdictions, which restrict employers from collecting conviction information on initial job applications, created the opportunity for a natural experiment to better understand how information about an applicant's race and conviction history are used in hiring decisions. Building on Devah Pager's landmark study of racialized employment discrimination against those who disclose having a conviction history,[38] researchers at the University of Chicago created and submitted fifteen thousand experimental job applications to assess hiring practices among New York and New Jersey employers before and after "Ban the Box" went into effect. Prior to the ban, they found, applicants who indicated that they did not have a criminal record were 62 percent more likely to be considered than those who did, and white applicants were 7 percent more likely to be called back than Black applicants. After "Ban the Box" went into effect, however, employers' responses to applicant race changed dramatically. Racial discrimination spiked: when employers could no longer ask about conviction histories on the job application, white applicants became 45 percent more likely to be called back than similarly qualified Black applicants.[39] These findings suggest that employers shifted from discriminating on the basis of stated criminal record to using race as a proxy for criminality.

Incarceration-related discrimination and the racialized stigma that emanates from it shapes labor market practices and broader economies. In this way, mass incarceration has helped to consolidate racialized economic inequality on a national scale. The widespread, intensive, and racially targeted use of incarceration exacerbates racial disparities in earnings at the national level.[40] According to Wakefield and Uggen, the scale, distribution, and effects of imprisonment in the era of mass incarceration have brought the prison alongside the educational system and the labor market as one of the country's chief institutions of economic stratification: "Sociologists have long understood inequality with reference to the stratifying institutions that sort people into more or less advantaged social categories. . . . These institutions both reflect and create inequality by differentially conferring access and opportunity across social groups. . . . Like other stratifying institutions, the prison both reflects pre-existing disparities and acts as an independent cause generating future disparities."[41] The population-level racial disparities that imprisonment exacerbates are wide and persistent. American households with a white "head of household" (as designated by the Census Bureau) have a median income 65 percent higher than do households with a Black "head of household."[42] These income disparities add up across generations, such that racial disparities in assets are even starker. The median net worth of white households is $141,900, while the median net worth of Black households is $11,000. The share that Black Americans hold in the country's wealth has increased very little since the Emancipation Proclamation.[43]

Damage to the Collective Health of Black Communities

Hyperincarceration has damaged the collective health of Americans in ways that far exceed the damage evident among individuals touched by imprisonment or even their own families and communities. The effects of mass incarceration on the physical well-being of Black Americans are so profound as to resemble a "new eugenics."[44] This scholarly characterization eerily echoes the analysis that Joe Jones offers from direct lived experience when he states that mass incarceration is "what you'd do if you wanted to destroy a population completely but just didn't want to kill them." The intense concentration of incarceration's negative effects in Black communities and the massive rate and scale of incarceration nationwide have combined to measurably widen national disparities between Black and white Americans' physical health in an era that politely eschews official racial discrimination.

Regardless of one's own involvement with the law, living in a neighborhood that is targeted for intensive policing and incarceration confers risk for a number of cognitive, physical, and behavioral health problems.[45] Children who grow up in highly incarcerated neighborhoods experience greater cognitive difficulties—including difficulties with reading comprehension, math problem-solving, and memory and concentration—regardless of whether their own parents become incarcerated.[46] Individuals living in urban neighborhoods with higher incarceration rates experience significantly higher rates of asthma.[47] Residents of highly incarcerated neighborhoods are also two to three times more likely to experience current or lifetime behavioral health problems, including clinical depression and anxiety disorders. Even when researchers control for a variety of other individual- and neighborhood-level characteristics that could influence behavioral health risk, these effects persist.[48]

In the nation as a whole, hyperincarceration worsens racial disparities in cognitive, behavioral, and physical health. Mass incarceration has driven up Black-white disparities in children's externalizing problems (such as aggression) by as much as 26 percent and widened racial disparities in children's internalizing problems (such as depression) by as much as 45 percent. The heightened risk of cognitive challenges among children of incarcerated parents accounts for up to 15 percent of the Black-white gap in school achievement observed at age nine.[49] Children who struggle with early cognitive and behavioral health difficulties are poised for a lifetime of disadvantage. Teachers' ratings of kindergarteners' prosociality, for example, predict their adult success and well-being across a broad set of life domains, including "education, employment, criminal activity, substance use, and mental health."[50] For this reason, the chasm between Black and white children's well-being has stark consequences for the possibility of equal opportunity in America.

Economic damage appears to account for much of the impact of mass incarceration on community and population health. The harsh poverty to which many former prisoners, their families, and their neighborhoods are condemned is strongly correlated with poorer physical and mental health and a shorter lifespan.[51] Social factors may be significant mediators as well. High neighborhood incarceration rates, for example, alter sexual partnership patterns and sexual risk taking.[52] These disrupted modes of intimate relating appear, in turn, to lead to elevated rates of sexually transmitted infections in heavily incarcerated neighborhoods.[53]

Decades of hyperpolicing and hyperincarceration of young Black men may also shape social norms in ways that promote racial disparities in gun-related injury and mortality. Many scholars have suggested that the practices of surveillance and removal that have accompanied mass incarceration in Black communities actually promote, rather than protect against, violence.[54] As Joe Jones observes:

> In my peer group, there was a badge of honor associated with having survived the criminal justice system and coming back to the community. . . . You went in and survived it and if you didn't have that experience, you were almost the oddball, if you couldn't say you were able to go to jail and come home. . . . If the majority of people in your family and social network have an experience, the children begin to matriculate toward that experience as well, and it's hard to turn it around. . . . Now you have an issue with the saturation of the community with guns and weapons we never saw in our communities before. It's almost now a badge of honor if you can take a bullet and survive. Those are the unattended and not-well-known things that happen in communities that people struggle to understand. And people who are involved in it struggle to fight their way out of it.

As a result, the National Medical Association (NMA) has declared the aggressive policing and overuse of imprisonment characteristic of the mass incarceration era as a major public health threat for Black Americans. The NMA argues that current criminal legal system tactics in urban communities of color promote a racialized "epidemic" of violent injury in such communities.[55]

Hyperincarceration's damaging effects on physical health and well-being in Black communities and on national health disparities are undeniable. But isolating these effects presents methodological challenges for researchers. At the individual level, preexisting disadvantages like socioeconomic status and behavioral health conditions put individuals at heightened risk for incarceration; incarceration, in turn, exacerbates socioeconomic disadvantage and behavioral health difficulties. As such, distinguishing cause and effect in the observed relationships between incarceration and other disadvantages is difficult. The potential bidirectionality of these relationships at the individual level makes pinpointing the link between community- and national-level incarceration rates and negative health outcomes more challenging. The challenge facing researchers is heightened by the fact that experimental data on the imposition of incarceration are very rare. Furthermore, most available nonexperimental data do not allow researchers to match or adjust against a suitably comprehensive set of observed characteristics, nor do they permit controlling for unobserved characteristics using successive waves of longitudinal information.[56] Yet theoretical work on social stratification and inequality in the United States suggests that researchers should not be looking for cleanly unidirectional pathways from incarceration to disadvantage—for example, expecting that imprisonment unilaterally creates Black-white disparities in health or earnings.[57]

Scholars have probably just begun to uncover the complex relationships among hyperincarceration, racial disparities, and disease epidemiology in the United States. We know that different rates of incarceration contribute to racial and geographic health disparities in asthma, human immunodeficiency virus (HIV), midlife health status, and disability.[58] State-level racial health disparities in HIV incidence are heavily explained by the rates at which a state incarcerates its residents.[59] In international comparative research, increases in a nation's rate of incarceration correlate directly with increases in the national rate of tuberculosis infection.[60] Given its individual-level sequelae (including posttraumatic stress and depression), it is also likely that mass imprisonment shapes the community epidemiology of stress-related conditions and accompanying racial disparities in their prevalence.[61] More research is needed to fully understand how mass incarceration may influence the population distribution of stress-related conditions, which include many of the most prevalent and impactful diseases faced by the American population—for example, behavioral health conditions, diabetes, and cardiovascular disease.

The cumulative impact of hyperincarceration on racial disparities in physical health and well-being is stark. In Baltimore, for example, residents of the low-income, predominantly Black neighborhoods that have been targeted for incarceration can expect to survive an average of twenty fewer years than those who live in the city's affluent, predominantly white neighborhoods. The same is true in Chicago, Philadelphia, and other American cities that have invested decades in the harsh and targeted policing of already vulnerable communities.[62]

Nationally, too, the effects are staggering. Mass incarceration has measurably impeded America's progress with regard to two of the most important indicators of population health in the world: infant mortality and life expectancy.[63] Christopher Wildeman's investigation of this phenomenon began with the observation that infant mortality had not declined nearly as much in the United States over recent decades as it had in other wealthy democracies. According to Rice and colleagues' estimates, Black children remain more than twice as likely to die in infancy as white children.[64] Wildeman explains:

> The American infant mortality rate is an outlier relative to other longstanding democracies, as illustrated by the fact that it exceeds that of all other similar nations by at least 30 percent and that absolute and relative declines in the American infant mortality rate have been smaller than those of other similar nations over the last 15 years.... The American infant mortality rate even increased in 2002. Second, the Black-White gap in the infant mortality rate has stopped decreasing since the 1990s and remains substantial.[65]

Indeed, high infant mortality, and wide racial disparities in infant mortality, have persisted in the United States even as each has been the focus of major public health intervention efforts.[66]

Wildeman used data from the Pregnancy Risk Assessment Monitoring System to examine America's apparent demographic aberrations in more depth. He found that the strong link between parental incarceration and infant mortality has had far-reaching consequences for the nation's overall infant mortality. If the incarceration rate had plateaued at the already-high rate it had attained by 1990, the infant mortality rate would have been almost 4 percent lower in 2003, the last year included in Wildeman's analysis. In the context of the hyperincarceration of Black parents (but not white parents), parental incarceration has tended to increase Black infant mortality (but not white infant mortality). Thus, disparities in infant mortality have risen in proportion to the rise of incarceration itself, such that every increase of one standard deviation in the incarceration rate is associated with a stunning 0.34 standard deviation increase in the racial disparity in infant mortality. Wildeman's state-level analysis found that, had incarceration remained at 1990 rates, Black infant mortality would have been 7 percent lower. (There was no similar association for the white infant mortality rate.)[67] The effects of mass incarceration on life expectancy, another crucial measure of population health, appear equally devastating. If incarceration rates in the United States had remained at their mid-1980s level, overall life expectancy at birth in the United States would have increased 51 percent more from 1983 to 2005 than it actually did.[68]

ADDING UP THE COMMUNITY AND COLLECTIVE HARMS OF MASS INCARCERATION IN AMERICA

Prison, as an institution, has come to define life and death in America. Around the world, incarceration rates are closely tied to key indicators of population health. But compared to other wealthy democracies, America's incarceration rates exert a stronger detrimental influence on the well-being of its people. The origins of this stronger effect remain unknown: more limited government safety-net programs, poorer conditions of imprisonment, or the fact that imprisonment is particularly harmful when used widely are all possible explanations.[69] When the population-level harms of mass incarceration are fully accounted for, however, one thing is clear: mass incarceration does not simply drive a wide range of specific racial health disparities *within* the United States. It contributes in

significant ways to overall national trends in life and death and to disparities between the United States and other countries of similar wealth.

From a birds-eye view, even the known, profound harms of mass incarceration in the lives of individuals and families are less pernicious than its
community and collective ones. Joe Jones, who came of age on the leading
edge of mass incarceration, has registered each of them firsthand. He
argues that the system of aggressive policing and imprisonment that began
in his early youth has produced an interrelated set of harms to public services, community infrastructure, and quality of life that affect everyone.
Jones uses Baltimore as an example of this point: "We have structural inequalities and deterioration in our educational infrastructure, and our
housing stock is one of the worst in the country. It reverberates. There's
also the impact it has on health care. . . . People in [our] communities
don't engage systems easily. People are hesitant to engage systems, so they
wait until they have an acute issue and present in an ER. . . . So the operating budgets of our hospitals have been astronomical, because they're deal-
ing with a population that doesn't access preventive health care."

Over the course of almost a half century, the pervasive harms of mass
incarceration have locked into place with one another, coming to define
almost every aspect of public and private life in Baltimore. Though the
damaging effects of mass incarceration operate synergistically at the local
community level, these local dynamics are broadly replicated. As Jones
explains, "This is a set of issues that impacts urban communities across
the country." In fact, other scholars have described very similar processes
in Chicago,[70] Detroit,[71] Oakland, Philadelphia, San Francisco, Seattle,
St. Louis, and Washington, DC.[72] Extend this scene across many of the
nation's urban centers—which were home to 81 percent of Americans as
of the 2010 census[73]—and it is easy to imagine how profoundly the age of
mass incarceration may have shaped life in America.

We know that the overuse of incarceration has meant that Americans
born over the last four decades, whether they had direct contact with the
criminal legal system or not, were more likely to die in infancy and are living shorter lives overall.[74] To understand just how much life has been lost
as a result, we can compare Wildeman's estimates of what infant mortality
and life expectancy at birth would have looked like without mass incarceration (that is, if incarceration rates had stayed at their 1980 level)

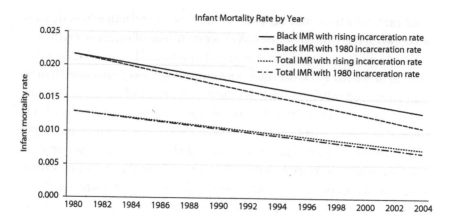

Figure 3. Infant Mortality Rate by Year, 1980–2004. Image preparation by Justin Landwehr.

against his figures for infant mortality and life expectancy at birth given actual incarceration rates. We then multiply the difference by the number of births in 2004 (the birth cohort on which he focuses) to estimate the number of mass incarceration–related infant deaths that occurred in that birth cohort and the number of years of life that those born in that year lost owing to mass incarceration. Next, we can extrapolate rough estimates for mass incarceration–related infant mortality in other birth cohorts by creating point estimates from two straight lines drawn between Wildeman's paired 1980 and 2004 estimates and comparing the difference between them for each of the intervening birth years. According to this calculation, mass incarceration was associated with 24,896 more infant deaths in America from 1981 to 2004 (fig. 3). As the graph illustrates, these mass incarceration–related deaths were distributed very unevenly by race. Black children experienced an estimated 68 percent (or 17,010) of the incarceration-related infant deaths that occurred during this time period.

Sadly, the heightened risks of premature death associated with mass incarceration do not end in infancy. Life expectancy at birth, which takes into account both infant mortality and later mortality, has improved markedly less in the United States than it would have without mass incarceration. Calculations using Wildeman's estimates indicate that Americans born from 1981 to 2004 will collectively lose a total of 14,937,839 years of life related to mass incarceration. Again, Black Americans carry a disproportionate share of the incarceration-related mortality burden. The share of lost life-years among Black Americans born in those years is 6,185,423, or 41 percent.

Mass incarceration has produced, and will continue to produce, a great loss of life. It has claimed lives even among individuals who never set foot inside a prison. These lost lives and years of life are priceless; no amount of money could adequately compensate the loss. In considering reparations for mass incarceration, however, we would be remiss to ignore this harm. Governments and other public institutions, in weighing potential investments in life-saving interventions (whether in health care or environmental protection), are regularly forced to assign a value to human life. The current Value of a Statistical Life set by the federal government is $7.4 million in 2006 dollars.[75] Adjusted to 2020 dollars, it is equivalent to $9.6 million. The figure represents the mean monetary amount that members of the public would agree is reasonable to invest to save a single life. By this measure, avoiding the scale of infant death that was associated with mass incarceration over the years 1981 to 2004 would have been worth $238,803,339,860 (including $163,157,094,865 associated with avoiding Black infant mortality) to the American public. This monumentally meaningful reduction would have been possible if we had refused to escalate rates of incarceration beyond the 1980 level.

Governments and health insurers around the world have also assigned various values to the gain or loss of a year of human life or the equivalent of a year of life in improved life quality. Such values are typically expressed in terms of the willingness to pay for one quality-adjusted life year (QALY). But estimates vary widely, depending on the study population and estimation technique. Swedish economists, aiming to identify a more normative value for practical use, reviewed twenty-four studies from around the world (primarily the United States and Europe) on the willingness to pay for a QALY. Standardizing each estimate to 2010 euros, they found a mean value of €74,159 (or $117,565 in 2020 US dollars).[76] Multiplying this figure by the number of years of lost life expectancy associated with mass incarceration for the 1981 to 2004 birth cohorts, we obtain a value of $1,756,172,669,613. Reflecting the starkly uneven racial distribution of incarceration-related premature mortality, this figure includes $727,191,572,689 for lost life expectancy among Black Americans.

Beginning to add up the community and collective harms of mass incarceration also calls attention to what we don't know—that is, to what extent mass incarceration has also conferred collective benefits, at least for certain Americans. Its decidedly detrimental effects on our national health aside, it is quite possible that large segments of the white and non-Black populations have gained from the massive political and economic incapacitation of Black Americans. By systematically depressing the educational attainment of Black youth; removing Black men from the labor market in huge numbers; and diverting the time and material resources of partners, mothers, and whole communities to the four-alarm fire of supporting incarcerated and formerly incarcerated people, mass incarceration may have artificially advantaged non-Black Americans in the labor market, the housing market, and other domains. We can't yet calculate the size of these likely benefits from the information we have, but the task of accounting transparently for the national consequences of mass incarceration will remain incomplete until we do.

In considering the other limitations of the figures presented in this chapter, it is important to note that Wildeman's original estimates of infant mortality and life expectancy at birth in 2004 using 1980 and 2004 incarceration rates were made by pooling state-level data and weighting all states equally. When the CDC generates national estimates, it weights states by population. As a result, Wildeman's estimates of life expectancy at birth are slightly lower than those prepared by the CDC for the same years. This difference introduces some potential imprecision; however, because my calculation hinges on comparing Wildeman's two estimates to one another and extending them retrospectively (rather than triangulating between Wildeman's figures and the CDC's), the difference is of relatively limited consequence for this purpose.

One must also bear in mind that the phenomena these two figures represent are not mutually exclusive; life expectancy at birth takes into account infant mortality and mortality in later childhood and adulthood. In addition, they assume that infant mortality rate and life expectancy at birth both changed in a linear fashion over the period 1981 to 2004, when in fact those rates changed unevenly. Perhaps most important, the figures for infant mortality represent lives already lost that could have been saved had the United States not engaged in its mass incarceration "experiment." But estimates of lost life expectancy at birth are (by definition) projections based on the assumption that mortality-related factors in effect at the time of a person's birth will exert a similar influence throughout the lifetime. This assumption is flawed for many mass incarceration–era birth cohorts, as rates of incarceration rose very steeply for several more years before their peak in 2009, when they began to slowly decline. Given the disproportionate share of premature mortality that occurs in the early childhood years, even if the incarceration rate were to decline steeply from this point forward, the lost years of life calculated here for the 1981 to 2004 birth cohorts likely would remain an underestimate. In addition, the monetary value assigned to each individual lost year is likely an underestimate, as I have used the mean value produced by the Swedish research team despite that team's finding that QALY values tend to be higher for changes in life expectancy compared to changes in quality of life alone. Finally, like most estimates in this book, these figures make the aspirational assumption that individuals who are now coming of age are the last Americans to be harmed by mass incarceration. Whether this last assumption holds, or whether the figures presented in this book will balloon with harms yet to come, is a question that will be decided by our commitment to reparative action.

REPAIRING THE COUNTRY: SYSTEMATIC RECONSTRUCTION

Mass incarceration is the most sustained, far-reaching, and deadly form of political violence carried out in the United States since the beginning of the twentieth century. It has impoverished and foreshortened the lives of individuals convicted of crime, punished their families and children, destroyed public life in targeted neighborhoods and cities, and taken many years off our lives. Though broad in its reach, the damage of mass incarceration has been heavily concentrated among Black Americans and also among the most economically vulnerable of us. The system of punitive exclusion that produced that damage serves at once to exacerbate racial and economic stratification and exclusion and also to mask it.[77]

National recovery and reconstruction are urgent. The evidence presented in this chapter highlights mass incarceration's potent recipe for collective damage. It combines the intensive intervention of hyperpolicing and hyperincarceration in targeted urban areas, and specifically against men of color within those areas, with the vast continental scale on which that intensity has been replicated. Joe Jones weighs the challenge of counteracting harms that are "deep and systemic across the country" with the gravity and the determination of a person who has devoted many decades to facing them. He argues persuasively that, to counter the nationwide consequences of mass incarceration and move beyond it, we must harness the synergistic effects within and across local communities that made it so damaging in the first place.

Acknowledging that this is a monumental task with little precedent to guide it, Jones nevertheless sees a pivotal opportunity to "knit together" the kinds of advocacy and policy transformation efforts at the local and state levels that could produce a massive, nationwide shift. Neither cynical nor naive, he holds a clear conviction that a recovery is possible alongside the hard-won understanding that it will come neither easily nor from small, isolated efforts. Rather, our reconstructive effort must match the scale and comprehensiveness of the "systematic deconstruction" that has preceded it.

Doing so will require targeted and strategic support for local institutions in all neighborhoods that have been put under siege by the force of the state. It will require investment in damaged municipal infrastructures in the cities where those communities are located. It will also require broad, federal efforts to reverse the stratifying effects of the prison on racialized economic inequality and health disparities nationwide. Daunting as these imperatives may be, they are critical to the health and well-being of our nation.

By the widely agreed-upon metrics used by governments and health care institutions, the calculations presented in this chapter indicate that the magnitude of lost human life associated with the current punishment regime would merit an investment of at least $890 billion to reverse. What we have learned from years of quantitative research on mass incarceration's community and collective harms aligns closely with the lived expertise of a community leader who has spent a lifetime overcoming them. Each point to the same strategy for bringing them to an end: we must mobilize America's vast resources to address the intra- and inter-community dynamics that have destroyed neighborhoods around the country and take concerted federal action to reverse nationwide inequities in physical health and economic well-being. Though necessarily broad, such efforts must focus particular attention on the economic and health status of Black Americans and on the low-income, urban communities of color that have formed the epicenters of this catastrophe.

The work of rebuilding should begin in local communities, especially in schools. Reversing the central role that schools in hyperincarcerated neighborhoods play in perpetuating intergenerational disadvantage and criminalization is critical.[78] Public education funding structures that reproduce inequality will continue to work systematically against the future prospects of youth in overincarcerated, undersupported communities. We must remake the current public education funding model that uses public resources to fund expensive, life-enhancing educations for children of privilege and cut-rate, criminalizing school experiences for poor children of color.

Law and education scholars suggest that allocating widely disparate funding to local schools on the basis of local property tax revenues, though it is standard practice in most US states, violates the promise of equal opportunity in the federal constitution.[79] Several state supreme courts (including those of Connecticut and Vermont) have ruled that it violates their state constitutions on this basis. Rather than addressing the basic injustice of such funding practices, many states and school districts have created additional mechanisms that further divert public dollars away from students in impoverished communities for the benefit of students in wealthy communities. Charter schools and the movement toward public school privatization are cause for particular concern in communities affected by incarceration. With few exceptions, educational privatization deepens the problems of racial and socioeconomic isolation and educational disparities among students that have been promoted by mass incarceration.[80] Rather than allow further privatization and the atomization that accompanies it, states can restructure public school funding to ensure equitable public education to all children.[81] Local school systems can opt for proven equity-promoting measures, such as universal prekindergarten education programs, that have enduring effects on school engagement and achievement for vulnerable students.[82] Evidence-based preschool education practices, implemented in the context of Head Start programs, have produced sustained positive effects on children's later classroom participation, social skills, and relationships with teachers and peers.[83] Such programs should be made available to all children in neighborhoods with high rates of incarceration.

High school completion initiatives in schools with high rates of parent incarceration could also help reverse the local effects of mass incarceration. Recognizing the crucial role of high school completion in students' long-term health and well-being, the CDC carried out a massive 2015 review of research on the effectiveness of programs designed to promote high school diploma attainment. They found strong evidence for a broad menu of strategies (including "vocational training, alternative schooling, social–emotional skills training, college-oriented programming, mentoring and counseling, supplemental academic services, school and class restructuring, multiservice packages, attendance monitoring and contingencies, community service, and case management") that were very successful at increasing high school graduation in school communities with high proportions of low-income and racial minority families.[84] These are the same communities that have been targeted for overincarceration and whose recovery must be supported. Multiservice packages, developed to support school engagement among students who are navigating challenges or instabilities at home, could be particularly valuable given the destabilizing effects of incarceration in such communities.[85] One model, the Cluster Plan for Dropout Prevention, brings together teams of school staff and community service providers—for example, a school services specialist, an attendance monitor, school administrators, an addiction specialist, and a child welfare case manager. The team initiates services with students in middle school, advocates for them with their teachers, and implements plans to address any underlying barriers that are affecting their educational participation or standing in the way of their achievement.[86] Expanding the availability of such programs in hyperincarcerated neighborhoods could help all young people to realize their full educational potential; build a foundation for realizing later-life goals; and support their physical, emotional, and material well-being over a lifetime.

Schools in hyperincarcerated communities can also work to repair parents' and family members' engagement with the public school system to counter the erosion of community trust in public systems.[87] Levels of family engagement in schools strongly influence students' rates of high school completion or dropout.[88] Local schools have a unique opportunity to position themselves as a practical resource for community members, particularly in high-incarceration communities, where material strain is a fact of life and even modest forms of material support can be meaningful. Robust before- and after-school programs and concrete assistance, such as school supplies, uniforms, and subsidized meal programs, have become increasingly scarce as more school systems become privatized. A renewed emphasis on such concrete supports could help to rebuild school engagement in communities that have otherwise been conditioned, by life in a punitive era, to minimize contact with institutions.

Although schools play a focal role in the distribution of advantage and disadvantage in urban communities and society at large, other community institutions contribute as well—for better and worse. Addressing the housing and health care infrastructure deterioration that has accompanied mass incarceration is critical to stemming the disadvantaging effects that such deficiencies have on entire communities. Hospitals and health care facilities that face chronic financial strain and accompanying staffing shortages tend to provide low-quality patient care.[89] Community-based primary health care approaches developed with and for members of heavily incarcerated communities offer one promising approach for beginning to rebuild the health care infrastructure. The Transitions Clinic model, for example, leverages Federally Qualified Health Center funding (made available through Section 330 of the Public Health Service Act) to deliver primary care in communities affected by incarceration that are federally designated as "underserved."[90] This model could be extended to include intensive, culturally and situationally responsive community mental health services, given the disproportionate behavioral health burden that heavily incarcerated communities bear.[91] Adequately funded, culturally competent health care providers not only deliver better-quality care; they create a trusted interface for connecting members of resource-alienated communities with other services. Randomized trials show that leveraging community health care infrastructures to simultaneously address social determinants of health, such as poverty and material strain, can significantly improve community members' ability to access employment, childcare, fuel assistance, and other critical resources.[92]

Spatial disparities in the availability and affordability of urban housing play a similarly critical role in distributing access to "place-based opportunities" for residents.[93] Poor-quality housing stock in hyperincarcerated communities must be addressed, such that residents who choose to can stay and thrive in the places where they have personal history and social ties. One of the widely touted interventions to address community-level resource deprivation involves supporting residents to obtain housing in higher-opportunity neighborhoods.[94] But such initiatives, since they focus on helping individual families leave rather than on improving housing options and living conditions within their neighborhoods, are inherently limited in their transformative scale. No matter how effective they are, they improve outcomes only for a small number of individuals within a community rather than for the community as a whole. Furthermore, dispersal-oriented programs like these fail to account for people's own residential preferences, including the enduring social and historical value that many disadvantaged neighborhoods have to their residents.

Community-level housing interventions can work to affirm the underlying social value of neighborhoods devastated by incarceration while addressing the "spatial inequality of opportunity" perpetuated by poor housing stock and physical isolation from living-wage jobs.[95] Improvements in housing infrastructure and affordability should be accompanied by economic and community development initiatives that bring better jobs to these communities and help their residents access the educational opportunities required to qualify for them. As housing researchers Arthur Acolin and Susan Wachter explain:

> Local- and state-level initiatives and public-private partnerships will need to be adopted, as will public and private financing initiatives. This strategic framework will require providing new funding not only for expanded housing assistance, but also for bringing opportunity, through economic and community development, to places left behind. This development should include initiatives to promote job formation by state and regional actors . . . to improve access to education . . . and to provide skill training. . . . These initiatives pursue more-inclusive growth by acting on the labor markets and by finding ways to increase educational attainments for a broader range of children.[96]

Legal scholar Mehrsa Baradaran, whose work focuses on wealth and inequality, advocates persuasively for a community revitalization strategy that she contends would address the localized poverty, and deep racial wealth disparities, to which mass incarceration has contributed. The proposal, dubbed the Twenty-First Century Homestead Act, involves federal financing to make vacant housing stock in resource-alienated urban neighborhoods available to low-income individuals while building local job availability through the creation of federally funded health care, long-term care and childcare facilities, and community and technical colleges in the targeted areas.[97] Distinct from prior resettlement programs that separate low-income individuals from their communities or revitalization initiatives that have heavily profited real estate investors, Baradaran's model would build the value that neighborhoods hold for low-income residents while addressing their isolation from critical resources and positioning them to collectively benefit from the full social and economic participation of their members.

To date, the vision of community-wide, intersectoral collaboration to reconnect neighborhoods to resources and opportunities has remained more aspiration than reality. The Center for Urban Families, which focuses on rebuilding family, community, and opportunity within neighborhoods affected by mass incarceration, represents a remarkable exception. The center, founded by Joe Jones, operates a tightly connected suite of programs to strengthen and repair family relationships, create new educational opportunities (including adult skill training for those disconnected from schooling and the workforce by mass incarceration), and develop connections to high-quality employment. Mobilizing a combination of public- and private-sector partnerships, the center has helped to bring hundreds of "felon-friendly" jobs to Baltimore neighborhoods and to reconnect more than twenty-six thousand community members to the social and economic fabric of their communities. Community-level recovery efforts like these should be funded in all communities affected by incarceration at a level concomitant with the documented damages such communities have sustained.

Federal funding for recovery from mass incarceration should be used to support community-based reconstruction at a massive scale. It can and must address the persistent, interlinked racial inequities in population health and economic well-being that mass incarceration has helped to perpetuate.[98] Though long regarded as a fact of life in the United States, intergenerational, racialized poverty could be significantly corrected with a robust national antipoverty campaign. Important historical models exist, including Roosevelt's New Deal and Johnson's War on Poverty. But the United States has yet to carry out a national antipoverty initiative to its completion—that is, eradicating poverty and eliminating (rather than covertly protecting) racial disparities in income and assets.

A universal baby bond program, such as the one proposed by Senator Cory Booker in the American Opportunity Accounts Act, represents a powerful tool for addressing enduring racialized wealth inequality.[99] As Booker envisions it, the program would create an interest-bearing seed savings account for every child in the United States at the time of birth. The account would be supplemented with sliding-scale annual federal contributions for families at the lower end of the income spectrum until the child reaches age eighteen, at which time the funds could be redeemed for education or other asset-building purposes. Using data from the Panel Study of Income Dynamics, poverty scholar Naomi Zewde ran simulation models to assess the effect of a potential baby bond program. Her models demonstrate that a baby bond initiative that uses family wealth (rather than income, as in the current legislative proposal) to determine the size of annual supplemental contributions would substantially reduce Black-white wealth disparities while also narrowing the overall gap between the richest and poorest Americans. In particular, an asset-scaled bond initiative would dramatically reduce the current 1:16 asset disparity that divides young Black Americans and young white Americans to 1:1.4. Zewde further notes that the cost of such a program to the federal government is comparable to that of other basic welfare programs, such as SNAP, and "less than the annual tax revenues lost to the preferential treatment of capital gains and dividend income."[100]

Compelling proposals for federal efforts confronting racialized poverty have also been advanced by Mehrsa Baradaran and Marian Wright Edelman. Baradaran's proposal centers on a portfolio of housing finance programs that would facilitate Black home ownership (including shared equity mortgages, a down payment assistance fund, and New Deal–style mortgage underwriting program), as well as universal day care.[101] Edelman argues for a nine-point federal initiative to eliminate child poverty. Her vision includes a minimum-wage increase, a transitional jobs program, increased SNAP benefits, child support pass-through allowances for SNAP and TANF recipients, expanded access to childcare subsidies and low-income housing vouchers, and antipoverty tax credits (including making the child tax credit fully refundable, increasing the Child and Dependent Care Credit, and expanding the Earned Income Tax Credit). Researchers at the Urban Institute assessed the potential impact of Edelman's suite of proposals by applying microsimulation models to census data on a large, representative sample of American households from 2010. They found that this package of policies, if applied together, would reduce the number of children living in poverty by 60 percent.[102] The reduction would be achieved for an annual investment of approximately $77 billion, which Edelman notes could be diverted from a variety of sources. "For the nearly $1.5 trillion projected costs of the [F35 fighter jet] program, the nation could reduce child poverty by 60 percent for 19 years."[103] As the estimates presented earlier in this chapter suggest, the figure also represents a small fraction of the human price that communities of color have paid for mass incarceration.

CONCLUSION

Had Joseph T. Jones Jr. not come of age just as the American government began a massive campaign of political violence against communities like his, he might have lived an entirely different life. Born in a different decade or even on a different side of Baltimore, a young person of Jones's will and intellectual ability would likely have found an easier and more direct route into the community leadership and national influence he eventually achieved: early labeling as a gifted student, a well-supported and high-achieving educational experience, a series of increasingly prestigious jobs laid out like stepping stones. But his path to leadership, like the eroded infrastructure of Baltimore's low-income neighborhoods, was not smooth or well-paved. One could say Jones was a product of the community where he grew up and that the community where he grew up was a product of a time that has since become known as the era of mass incarceration.

In one sense, it's true: mass incarceration has catastrophically reshaped the communities it targeted, and those disadvantaging community circumstances have been manifested in the human lives lived out (or fore-shortened) within them. As citizens and residents of this country, we must be prepared to openly acknowledge the extent of the destruction carried out with our tax dollars if we are to begin to repair it. As social scientists, we must avoid perpetuating the expectation that people born into deci-mated urban communities all over America will somehow pull hard enough on their own bootstraps to defy gravity.

Even with that shift in perspective, however, we may still miss more than half the story. If Jones and his city are any indication, the very mech-anisms of interdependence that the "war" on Black Americans capitalized on for its terrible success—the deep connection between individual fates and the fates of urban neighborhoods, the ways that the fates of those neighborhoods are tied to the direction of the nation—hold the key to repair and reconstruction. Over the course of a lifetime, and particularly in the last twenty years of his leadership at the Center for Urban Families, Jones has reshaped the city that shaped him through relentlessly success-ful policy advocacy, social program design, ambitious partnership build-ing, and workforce development. The fates of neighborhoods and the fates of individuals are indeed inseparable, and no person born in a different decade or even on a different side of Baltimore could have been as tena-cious or as effective in this work of transformation. No outsider could have begun to know how it would even be possible.

Like other forms of political violence that have exerted intergenera-tional effects, mass incarceration both requires and produces an intergen-erational resistance. Standing on the shoulders of the first generation of hyperincarcerated Americans—people like Jones—the Movement for Black Lives has risen up from all the scattered ground zeros of mass incar-ceration. And the fates of these neighborhoods will drive the direction of the nation from here. As Jones explains, the intensely targeted, intensely destructive nature of mass incarceration in certain communities and its far-reaching national effects can also be its undoing:

> Baltimore is unique, but this is also a set of issues that impacts urban com-munities across the country. Some of what has happened [here] with mass incarceration has happened in Oakland, Chicago, St. Louis, and across the southern United States. One of the ways we have "benefited"—and I do not mean to say we have actually benefited in any way, but one of the redeeming

things about this, especially with the evolution of social media, is that we have so much more information and can show some of the exploitation that has happened as a result of mass incarceration and a more enlightened population of young people. . . . You've got now this group of young, academically prepared activists who have more access to truthful information about the African American experience who are pushing the system, pushing policy, and now I don't think we can ever remain where we are. I don't think we can ever go back.

The queer youth of color at the vanguard of the Movement for Black Lives affirm this truth with their voices and bodies. Challenging the violent state repression with which many have lived their whole lives, their advocacy has so transformed the state and national policy environment that countless mainstream political candidates have been forced to take a position on their platform. Ceasing and reversing the harms of mass incarceration is the first item on the agenda.

> We demand an end to the criminalization, incarceration, and killing of our people:
> Divest from surveillance, policing, mass criminalization, incarceration and deportation.
> Invest in making communities stronger and safer through quality, affordable housing, living wage employment, public transportation, education, and health care that includes voluntary, harm reduction and patient-driven, community-based mental health and substance abuse treatment.
> Invest in community-based transformative violence prevention and intervention strategies that offer support for criminalized populations.
> Uncouple access to services, care, and support from the criminal punishment system.
> Provide reparations to survivors of police violence and their families, and to survivors of prison, detention and deportation violence, and their families.[104]

The youth of Baltimore's Mondawmin Mall; of Oakland's flatlands; of Ferguson, Missouri; and of countless other American communities ground up in the machinery of mass incarceration have mounted a more ferocious and transformative resistance than anyone in communities left untroubled by mass incarceration could have possibly imagined. Incarceration's deadly community and collective harms may require as many decades to reverse as they took to create. Doing so may cost as many government resources as we have previously invested in extreme forms of punishment. Expecting that the work will be easy does not serve us. But the bold and transformative vision coming out of urban communities at the epicenter of the carceral catastrophe surely affirms that there is no going back and no remaining where we are.

7 Dreaming an America beyond Mass Incarceration

> If America does not use her vast resources of wealth to end poverty and make it possible for all of God's children to have the basic necessities of life, she too will go to hell.
>
> Martin Luther King Jr., "Speech to Striking Sanitation Workers"

It has long been clear that the United States has the resources and infrastructure to end racialized poverty entirely.[1] Presidents from Lyndon Johnson to Barack Obama have lifted up eliminating poverty as a pressing and achievable national goal. Johnson famously characterized it as something that "the richest nation on Earth can afford."[2] Yet many Americans have come to view true equal opportunity as an impossible dream,[3] even as one presidential administration after another finds ways to sustain the exorbitant costs of the tough-on-crime political agenda and many other stunningly expensive endeavors that have little human value.[4]

The false foreclosure of equal opportunity in America and our ongoing acceptance of racialized poverty as an irremediable fact of life are the saddest inheritances of the mass incarceration era. The deployment of the criminal legal system as a political weapon against Black communities has played a pivotal role in deepening racial wealth inequality. The subterranean force of mass incarceration, running counter to the bold efforts of millions of ordinary people, activists, and policy makers, has created the false appearance that intergenerational poverty and racial inequality are intractable problems. This chapter brings together the evidence and calculations presented throughout this book to lay out the cumulative, historical impact of mass incarceration on racialized economic injustice in the United States. I will argue that the costs and harms of mass incarceration have kept real racial and economic justice out of reach during a time when it is otherwise a reasonable and attainable goal. Imagining what an America not under the perpetual influence of racial terrorism would look like, the chapter concludes by suggesting how we might apply the three basic pillars of transitional justice—"truth-telling, restitution or reparation, and reform of abusive state institutions"—to bring that new country into being.[5]

THE NATION MASS INCARCERATION HAS MADE

Since the end of the American Revolution in 1783 and the advent of the United States of America, some part of this country has always been in shackles. As Michelle Alexander famously observed, the number of Black men living under the control of the criminal legal system in contemporary America well exceeds the number who were held captive in slavery before the Civil War.[6] That sustaining captivity on such a massive scale has enormous costs and consequences is the subject of a growing consensus among many researchers and policy experts, from the National Academies of Sciences to the Council on State Governments.[7] But we seldom grasp just how much the America we know has been shaped by these practices, nor do we pause to consider what might become possible—perhaps for the first time in American history—if we chose to reverse both the policies of mass incarceration and their far-reaching consequences.

The public policies that made mass incarceration a reality have lost the support of the American public and many elected representatives on each side of the congressional aisle.[8] Yet their actual undoing remains just that: undone. At the state and federal levels, handling this neglected task would pave the way for more effective, efficient strategies in many other areas where suffering and disparity have appeared unresponsive to public effort.

Despite extraordinarily high levels of health and health care–related spending in the United States, for example, Americans live shorter lives than residents of similarly wealthy nations and lag far behind on many important measures of health and well-being.[9] The National Academies of Sciences notes that, even as some health disparities gradually narrow, disparities have persisted or widened with regard to infant mortality, HIV, and cardiovascular disease.[10] What seems to distinguish these consequential events and conditions from others is the fact that their prevalence and distribution have been profoundly shaped by mass incarceration.

Efforts to achieve health equity and a higher quality of life for all Americans are likely to be ineffective (or at least highly inefficient) for as long as our health care and public health systems fight an uphill battle against the influence of a harmful criminal legal system. We must begin to critically assess our dueling policy approach to many social ills, which mixes support with punishment. By taking this approach, we risk undermining potentially supportive human services and public health initiatives with corrosive criminal legal system intervention. How many of the promising or evidence-based approaches currently being implemented by health and human services systems would better realize their intended outcomes without interference from a hyperpunitive machinery? It is an imminently answerable question.

WHY CAN'T WE JUST MOVE ON?

If we wish to know what is truly possible in America, we must put the work of transitional justice at the top of the national agenda. Worldwide, a multitude of countries have achieved meaningful recovery from periods of mass racial violence, injustice, and atrocity. Their experiences point to three essential tasks of transitional justice: telling the truth about what has happened, reforming public institutions affected by injustice, and making concrete amends to those who have been harmed.[11] When these tasks are addressed, it suggests, nations can actually move on from histories of political violence. When they are neglected, the legacies of those horrors can persist indefinitely.

Facing the insidious, long-range effects of mass incarceration on so many areas of American life is a grim prospect, to be sure. Beneath it, however, lies an opportunity. The evidence reviewed in this book suggests that ongoing, and sometimes widening, disparities in health and economic well-being are neither impossibly nor mysteriously entrenched.

Rather, the public investments we have made to address these and other social issues affecting vulnerable, low-income Americans—such as through Head Start programs, workforce opportunity programs, public health initiatives, and more—may be working at cross purposes with detrimental criminal legal interventions that target those same communities. Expending public funds on criminal legal system practices that measurably erode economic stability and well-being in vulnerable families while dedicating other funding streams to try to economically stabilize and support them seems to be a losing proposition for everyone.[12] The research evidence summarized in this book suggests that desisting from the criminal legal system practices that constitute mass incarceration would end much suffering and avert many deaths. It would also remove the barriers that such practices have silently set against our efforts to achieve public health, maximize human potential, and guarantee equal opportunity.

History and common sense each suggest that simply desisting from destruction will not restore things to a pre-harmed state. This truth is plain in *Black Reconstruction*, W. E. B. Du Bois's authoritative history of the post–Civil War period in America. His scrupulously researched account depicts relentless efforts by freed Black Americans to build futures for themselves, their families, and communities while fighting for full political and economic participation: "They restored the lost crops; they established schools; they gave votes to the poor whites; they established democracy; and they even saved a pittance of land and capital out of their still slave-bound wage."[13] Even these heroic efforts, accounts of which require many hundreds of pages in Du Bois's tome, came nowhere close to righting the brutally subordinate economic and political position of Black communities. The public policies that had made legal enslavement possible no longer stood, but the underlying system on which they had rested remained and, with it, the starkly unequal distribution of power and resources that allowed former enslavers (and others who benefited from maintaining a steeply pitched economic playing field) to crush the opportunity Reconstruction had presented for racial and economic progress. Instead of enduring progress, this period ultimately saw a successful push "back toward slavery."[14]

Moving the country beyond slavery, Du Bois argued, would have demanded more than the Herculean capabilities that Black Americans applied to the task. It called for a full-fledged, national recovery and reconstruction effort—one not exclusively reliant on the striving of those who had been harmed under the preceding regime but driven by the initiative and commitment of the many who had benefited from it. Such an effort, of course, was never undertaken.

This tale of missed opportunity for repair and the perpetual state of racial and economic injustice to which it condemned us has endured well beyond slavery and Reconstruction. It has repeated itself with the coming and going of Jim Crow–era legal segregation and its quieter but equally impactful successor, an epoch of legal economic exclusion characterized by redlining and other forms of discrimination in banking and housing.[15] It goes like this: The harmfulness of a particular set of institutional policies becomes widely evident; the offending policies are eventually reformed but with little attempt at repairing the damage already done; and the legacy of economic and political exclusion and disadvantage left in their wake creates the fertile ground on which yet another set of harmful policies can be planted in its place.[16] That sequence forms the plot of the quintessential American ghost story.

Now is the time to make mass incarceration the final chapter in that story. Compared to the generations before us, who left other epochs of racist harm unaddressed, we have much richer information to drive the work of repair. The harms of mass incarceration have been meticulously documented. Transitional justice research has gleaned valuable insight, from a multitude of international contexts, on strategies for repairing similar harms. And incisive scholarship on the aftermath of earlier periods of unreconstructed racial harm in America makes the stakes of transitional justice abundantly clear to us in a way that they may not have been to our predecessors.

Transitional justice scholars argue convincingly for truth-telling as a first step in any project of national recovery from racist collective violence. One of the well-documented, if paradoxical, realities of such violence is that members of the racial group that initiated the harm tend to be deeply isolated from awareness of its effects.[17] Awareness-raising efforts, like those that accompanied the Civil Liberties Act of 1988 (which initiated redress for the internment of Japanese Americans during World War II), can help to build a basic, factual understanding of mass incarceration in

communities that have been shielded from both the reality and the consequences of the punishment period. The evidence assembled in this book,
which is itself intended to offer such an understanding, suggests five major
harms of which all Americans must be made aware:

1. Children of color have been criminalized and deprived of many of the
   essentials of a healthy childhood.

2. Individuals who have served their legally imposed sentences—
   disproportionately Black men—have been saddled with harsh,
   extralegal punishments in the form of enduring physical, social, and
   economic deprivation and debility.

3. The oversized apparatus of punishment has been sustained in part by
   the uncompensated and heavily coerced labor and resources of adult
   family members of prisoners, disproportionately women of color.

4. The children of incarcerated parents have lost not only a parent's presence but pivotal, early forms of social and educational opportunity and
   support.

5. Urban communities that represent the geographic epicenters of mass
   incarceration have sustained critical damage to almost every important
   local institution, and America's physical and economic well-being has
   been eroded by ongoing disparity and injustice.

Of course, our understanding of these harms will never be complete. As
Clint Smith puts it, "I realize that I do not yet have all the words to discuss
a crime that is still unfolding."[18] But it is time to reckon with what we do
know of the harm and begin to put it to rest.

RECKONING WITH THE TRUE HARMS OF
MASS INCARCERATION

To comprehend the scope of mass incarceration's harms requires contend-
ing, first, with its direct costs. In 2016, according to the Obama White
House, these totaled a steep $270 billion per year, or 1.4 percent of the
gross domestic product[19] (a cost equal to $296 billion in 2020 dollars). It
also demands that we account for the host of complex, indirect costs borne
by targeted children, families, and neighborhoods, as well as members of
the tax-paying public. Research capable of rigorously quantifying all the

ways that large-scale imprisonment has influenced the health and well-being of Americans on a national scale remains incomplete. And we still know very little about how non-Black Americans may have gained under this policy regime. Still, the information we have today shows definitively that mass incarceration shapes the conditions of life in America for all of us, even those who never enter a prison. And it indicates that the tremendous direct costs of mass incarceration to the general public are greatly overshadowed by the indirect costs to Black Americans that have been estimated in the preceding chapters.

Examining early experiences of the criminal legal system among American young people, we find evidence that youth of color have been targeted for policing and pushed out of mainstream institutions by government agencies focused heavily on criminalization and punishment. For young people who have come of age in the era of mass incarceration, the resulting racially disproportionate disconnection from education and employment in youth and young adulthood is associated with personal and public damages totaling approximately $6.09 trillion ($6,085,783,435,849) in 2020 dollars. Fully $4.31 trillion ($4,307,612,644,035) of these damages are associated with the systematic disconnection of Black youth.

For those convicted of a crime and incarcerated as adults, the material and psychological fallout from that experience tends to linger far beyond the term of incarceration. Adults who have ever been in prison remain severely disadvantaged in multiple arenas, particularly the formal economy. Over the course of their lifetimes, the ever-incarcerated men who are alive today will amass a total earnings deficit of roughly $2.04 trillion ($2,042,797,121,141) compared to similar adult men who were never incarcerated. Of this total deficit, greater than half ($1,073,285,607,447) represents wages lost to formerly incarcerated Black men.

Adults who experience a close family member's incarceration, overwhelmingly the partners and mothers of incarcerated men, bear the displaced costs of jailing, imprisonment, and community reintegration. Mass-scale incarceration and release, carried out in the absence of a functioning public safety net, has created enormous, uncompensated and invisible work that women are coerced into performing on behalf of their family members and the state. The inflation-adjusted value of women's investments in maintaining family relationships with prisoners and helping them reintegrate after release is likely at least $299 billion ($298,507,728,919). Such labor, and the multidimensional social and economic losses and strains that accompany it, take a heavy toll on women's health, placing them at elevated risk for cardiovascular disease, depression, and other conditions. The health care and lost productivity costs of excess stroke, heart attack, and major depression events attributable to experiences of partner, coparent, and other family member incarceration among adult women are approximately $1.97 trillion ($1,968,735,208,326). Of the total $2.27 trillion in physical and material costs and consequences borne by women with incarcerated family members, approximately $433 billion ($433,627,754,703) is associated with the excess burden of incarceration in Black communities.

Children of incarcerated parents experience steep material and interpersonal losses and strains. These harms accumulate during the parent's imprisonment and continue to reverberate on their return to the community and family. Even after reaching adulthood, individuals who weathered a parent's incarceration as minors tend to experience lower-quality interpersonal relationships, lower educational attainment, lower earnings, poorer behavioral health, and a higher risk of dying young than similar individuals whose parents were not incarcerated during their childhoods. The economic value of children's lost educational attainment alone (associated with children of incarcerated parents' elevated likelihood of leaving high school prematurely) totals about $796 billion ($796,041,374,521) among those born from 1978 to 2002. Well over half of this figure ($451,575,202,406) represents the value of the high school degrees not attained by Black children of incarcerated parents.

Finally, the racially and economically marginalized communities from which incarcerated individuals are drawn, and to which they return after release, have endured a set of harms and hardships far greater than the sum of their parts. Neighborhoods with a high proportion of resident involvement with the criminal legal system—the ones that geographers infamously dubbed "million dollar blocks" based on the costs of imprisoning their residents[20]—have seen the gradual erosion of their formal institutions and informal, social network resources. At the same time, the sweeping criminalization of Blackness that was integral to Nixon's War on Drugs (and the decades of racially targeted crime policies that have ensued) shapes the lives of all Black Americans, whether they have personally dealt with the criminal legal system or not. Combined, these community- and population-level dynamics contribute to wide national disparities in health and access to economic resources. The chasm between Black and white Americans' physical and material well-being is most starkly evident with regard to infant mortality, a tragedy twice as likely to befall Black children as white.[21] Among infants born from 1980 to 2004, mass incarceration elevated the death rate by a magnitude that public entities would generally be willing to expend $239 billion ($238,803,339,860) to prevent. Most of this figure ($163,157,094,865) represents avoidable deaths among Black infants. (To be clear, assigning any economic value to these lost lives is impossible. But neither can we afford to omit them in grappling with the damage.) Mass incarceration also diminished population-level life expectancy for Americans born from 1981 to 2004 by a degree that government actors would generally value at $1.76 trillion ($1,756,172,669,613). This figure includes $727 billion ($727,191,572,689) associated with lost life expectancy among Black Americans.

Together, the damages that can be reasonably estimated from current evidence total a staggering $13.19 trillion ($13,186,840,878,229). The estimate, of course, is far from perfect. I have attempted, using the social scientific research we have in hand as of this writing, to make as complete an accounting as possible; to lay out my calculations plainly, specifying their shortcomings and simplifications; and to note the limitations of the underlying data on which my approximations are based. But several additional, overarching limitations should be emphasized. First, despite growing research attention, quantitative data from rigorously designed and executed studies of individual, family, neighborhood, and national-level effects of mass incarceration are lacking.[22] In limiting my estimates of collateral costs to those for which solid evidence exists—not just evidence on the connection between mass incarceration and a given harm but on the incidence or magnitude of that harm and on its economic value—I have made only a partial account. Second, the costs of direct and indirect exposure to criminalization and incarceration accrue over entire lifetimes, and many are transmitted intergenerationally as well. Where possible, I have attempted to account for these perpetually compounding costs, but the temporal span of most estimates is limited by available data: depending on the nature of each calculation and the data on which it was based, in some cases I could only account for costs in a partial set of birth cohorts or among those Americans who are still living.

What we know for certain is that Black Americans have paid handsomely for the harsh policies born under Presidents Johnson and Nixon and expanded by almost every administration, and at every level of government, in the years since.[23] Although proponents of these tough-on-crime policies would suggest that their consequences are worthwhile if they succeed in reducing crime, a preponderance of evidence indicates that any returns on the carceral investment are grossly diminished by its overuse.[24] And even the limited set of consequences enumerated in the preceding pages is large enough to be meaningful on a macroeconomic scale. Given what can come of leaving such damage unaddressed, it will serve us far better to act now than to let the known costs and damages of mass incarceration continue to compound while we await a perfect understanding.[25]

ENVISIONING A FULL-SCALE RECONSTRUCTION

The next step in achieving transitional justice for mass incarceration is to reclaim and repurpose the public institutions whose functioning has been distorted by the punitive era. Such institutions have been used inappropriately (and often unwittingly) to serve the interests of white political and economic dominance and bent to the tasks of surveillance, criminalization, punishment, and exclusion. Schools and social services agencies must be revitalized, and law enforcement and correctional infrastructures must be eliminated or entirely reimagined. Just as the harms of mass incarceration have taken shape at many social levels—shaping the individual lives of criminalized youth and adults, their families, their neighborhoods and communities, and the nation as a whole—so, too, must reparative efforts target multiple domains. Synthesizing the more detailed proposals assembled in each of the preceding chapters, this section offers starting points for the work of institutional transformation.

The work of institutional repair and rebuilding should be guided by an overarching grasp of the reconstruction project. Repair efforts, if they are to succeed, must be concomitant with the scale of the damage done. The analyses presented in this book have put the economic value of that damage at approximately $13.2 trillion over the roughly four-decade heyday of mass incarceration. The portion of these damages that was imposed on Black individuals, families and communities should be allocated to compensatory, cash-value restitution to all affected Black Americans as part of the restitution project outlined in the following section of this chapter. The remaining $6.03 trillion ($6,030,391,002,084) in known damages represents a useful funding target for the work of transforming public institutions and building or rebuilding local, collective endeavors that advance the social and economic power of all individuals and communities that have been harmed and burdened by mass incarceration. Funding for this work would ideally roll out over two decades, beginning immediately and continuing through the acute period of mass decarceration that lies ahead. Reappropriating the operating expenses of our current correctional systems over that time span would cover the full cost of this transformative investment.

To redress harms to youth of color in communities targeted for heavy policing and incarceration will involve reclaiming the opportunities from which they have been systematically excluded and replacing the mass incarceration–era "youth control complex" with a "youth support complex" that allows young people to make mistakes, furnishes chances to build positive educational and workforce credentials, and connects them with supportive adults who believe in their potential.[26] (This goal, and specific policy strategies for achieving it, are discussed in more detail in chapter 2.) Opportunity Youth Collaboratives, already under way in some cities, represent one promising approach for connecting government agencies that bring access to needed resources with community-based organizations that are trusted by youth of color in order to create a community-wide youth support system. Full-time, wraparound youth leadership programs for young people who are struggling are also critical. Scaling up Youth Build, a successful full-time program developed by urban young people of color working on behalf of their own communities, would support opportunities for youth to develop practical skills, leadership capabilities, and cultural and community pride. In schools, punitive and exclusionary discipline practices must be replaced by actively welcoming environments staffed with people who come from young people's communities and understand their experiences. Making school-based mental health services for trauma widely and readily accessible to all students and instituting restorative justice-based approaches to school rule enforcement are equally critical. Finally, young people's contributions to the future of their communities, which may well take the form of protest (particularly for youth who have previously been silenced and excluded by mainstream institutions) should be met with support and genuine responsiveness from the systems they dare to confront and transform.

To redress harms to adults who have been incarcerated, we must rework the state, municipal, and community infrastructures that have enabled perpetual punishment of former prisoners. Public institutions must also be better supported to receive and integrate the many Americans who will join the ranks of the formerly incarcerated in the coming period of mass decarceration. (This goal, and potential policy strategies for achieving it, are discussed in more detail in chapter 3.) Guided by a "grounded preventive justice" model, we can also begin to make the use of imprisonment obsolete through effective preventive design of public institutions and spaces, a strong social safety net, and safe refuge for those affected by violence.[27] Individuals who have spent time in prison environments deserve robust support for individual recovery and reintegration into family, community, and work. To succeed at these tasks, health and human services systems will require the expertise of those who have lived through imprisonment and its aftermath themselves. Existing mechanisms for selecting and funding postprison reintegration programs, such as the Second Chance Act infrastructure in the Bureau of Justice Assistance, might serve this purpose effectively—particularly to the extent they can incorporate the leadership of directly affected individuals and can be funded at a level reflecting the scale of their charge. Universal prisoner reentry programs should support every former prisoner in a process of individual recovery and personal transformation. This includes support to cope psychologically with the experiences of imprisonment and release, maintain or repair relationships and social support networks, and connect to meaningful postprison opportunities, whether educational, vocational, professional, creative, or entrepreneurial. Interventions must also be designed to confront and transform the damaging, discriminatory, and stigmatizing encounters that greet many former prisoners (especially those who are Black men) when they interface with social institutions. Existing infrastructures in other sectors, such as the Veterans Administration and the public health system, could be transformed and expanded to serve former prisoners through the decarcerative transition.

To redress the harms sustained by adult family members of current and former prisoners, disproportionately women of color, all forms of cost-shifting from departments of correction and human services agencies onto prisoners' families must be eliminated. (This goal, and potential policy strategies for achieving it, are discussed in more detail in chapter 4.) This includes an immediate end to charging the incarcerated for necessities such as food, clothing, toiletries, and means of communication with the outside world (such as telephone calls or video visiting). It also means an immediate end to the imposition of legal fines and fees during and immediately after incarceration, which cannot reasonably be paid by prisoners or recent releasees without incomes, and are generally transferred to family members. An adequate social safety net for incarcerated and reentering individuals will also help to end the silent privatization of prisoner reintegration support and the coercive extraction of uncompensated labor and other resources from women. In the meantime, the grandmothers, mothers, partners, coparents, and other family members of current and former prisoners need direct supports to lighten the physical, emotional, and material burdens they have carried. This should include supports for maintaining (or regaining) physical and mental health, healthy interpersonal relationships, and stable housing. It should also include the support to pursue personal dreams that have been sacrificed to the imperative of ensuring a family member's survival through and after imprisonment. With few existing models for such an endeavor, there is a crucial need to engage the leadership of prisoners' family members themselves in designing and testing new approaches. With their guidance, support structures developed for military families could also be adapted and extended to ensure that families affected by incarceration have access to health care, affordable options for maintaining healthy and safe relationships with their loved ones, free or subsidized housing and childcare, and equitable opportunities for pursuing their own personal development.

To redress harms to children of incarcerated parents will require comprehensive intervention during and long after parental incarceration.

Support is needed to address toxic stress, repair social losses, address poverty and housing instability, and support educational engagement and retention. (These goals, and potential policy strategies for achieving them, are discussed in more detail in chapter 5.) The reality of harm transfer from incarcerated parents to their children means that noncarceral, preventive justice approaches that minimize psychological harm to parents and ameliorate the material damages they sustain are critical in preventing harm to children. Children's stress coping could be further supported by home visiting programs, home-based parent-child therapy, trauma-informed school counseling services, and other mental health approaches that avoid placing additional burden on their caregivers. To minimize children's social losses, existing barriers to family contact could be replaced with active practical supports (e.g., transportation assistance) and robust individual and family mental health services to support healthy interactions and healthy coping with the challenging emotions that such situations precipitate for children and their parents. Housing instability might be addressed through an adaptation of HUD's current family-unification housing voucher program and housing peer support models that have proven helpful for other vulnerable families with children. Finally, family-centered early intervention programs and affirmative admission and scholarship assistance for children of incarcerated parents could help to promote the future intellectual and civic leadership of a new generation of individuals with powerful, firsthand insights on our public systems.

Rebuilding the neighborhoods and cities hardest hit by mass incarceration will require intensively targeted recovery efforts in every affected locale. (These goals, and potential policy strategies for achieving them, are discussed in more detail in chapter 6.) We must reverse the damage to formal and informal local infrastructures through strategies that address geographic resource isolation and reflect and harness the pivotal role of schools in deepening or ameliorating socioeconomic stratification. This transformation could begin with equitable school funding policies that ensure an equal (or greater) public investment in the education of children in hyperincarcerated neighborhoods as in affluent neighborhoods. It could also include universal prekindergarten education programs, high school completion initiatives, and community engagement initiatives that are specifically tailored to repair damaged relationships between formal institutions and communities targeted for mass surveillance and criminalization. Health services infrastructures in such communities could be strengthened by adapting existing, federally subsidized primary care models to deliver local, culturally competent care for those who have been chronically overpunished and underserved. Revitalized health and social services infrastructures at the local level could help to address social determinants of health by connecting community members to other resources and services and ensuring that trauma-responsive behavioral health services are made freely available to everyone who needs them.

At the national level, we must end racialized poverty and reverse its tragic effects on infant mortality rates and life expectancy. This work could begin with a robust and comprehensive federal initiative designed to eliminate racial economic inequality (also discussed in more detail in chapter 6). Building on the successes and the failures of earlier federal antipoverty campaigns, including the New Deal and War on Poverty, such an initiative should be designed to center the urgent needs of Black children and families who have been disproportionately criminalized and impoverished by mass incarceration. Universal baby bonds represent a highly promising means for addressing intergenerational racialized poverty and promoting equal opportunity for all children.[28] If issued to every child in the United States at birth and supplemented with annual federal contributions inversely proportionate to family wealth, baby bonds could dramatically reduce poverty and racial wealth disparities while costing less than the value of current capital gains and dividend income tax breaks given to the wealthiest Americans.[29] Marian Wright Edelman's multipronged proposal for eliminating child poverty—to increase the minimum wage, institute a transitional jobs program, increase food stamp benefits, create a child support pass-through allowance for households receiving food stamps or TANF, broaden the availability of childcare and housing vouchers for low-income families, and modify the tax code to help low-income families keep more of their earnings—represents another potent starting point.[30] Though legally race neutral, such policies would decisively reverse the deep racial disparities in physical and economic well-being that mass incarceration has perpetuated.

FROM RETRIBUTIVE TO (RE)DISTRIBUTIVE JUSTICE

Rebuilding and remaking formal and informal institutions in the wake of mass incarceration will benefit all Americans. Still, recognizing that mass incarceration was used as an instrument of racial persecution and repression, the reparations project must also make direct amends to Black Americans. Official recognition and apology for the harms caused by agencies at multiple levels of government should be accompanied by material reparations. Cash-value restitution, an undertaking for which there is ample international and even national precedent, is essential to truly redress the documented racist origins, and highly racialized consequences, of this policy regime. The vast extralegal damages that Black prisoners, their children and families, and their communities have suffered—which total at least $7.16 trillion based on the subset of damages estimated in this book—should be made right through a carefully executed program of financial restitution.

Monetary reparations proposals date back to the 1700s in the United States, as we saw in chapter 1. Historically, most such proposals have focused on compensating Black Americans for harms suffered under slavery and in the Reconstruction years.[31] More recently, however, monetary reparations proposals have also included calls to redress the economic harms of Jim Crow, legal segregation, and housing-related discrimination.[32]

Opposition to these proposals often centers on either the perceived temporal remoteness and contemporary irrelevance of the harms (particularly for members of the white American public asked to consider reparations for enslavement) or on expressions of skepticism over how they could be reasonably distributed. In considering monetary reparations for mass incarceration, however, objections related to its temporal remoteness are obviated by the continued existence of most of the policy and procedural infrastructure that drives it. Objections related to the contemporary irrelevance of harms arising from these policies are thoroughly addressed by scientific evidence that a great many living Americans, young and old, have been harmed by mass incarceration and that its ill effects will continue to accumulate in the population for at least several more decades.

In any program of monetary compensation, including reparations for mass incarceration, the approach to identifying recipients and the mechanisms by which they will be compensated deserve earnest and thorough consideration. A primary concern with the distribution of reparations is how to identify those affected. For past harms, such as enslavement, incomplete public and genealogical records make this task more laborious and burdensome (though far from impossible) for the average descendant of an affected person. In this regard, however, reparations for mass incarceration present much less of a challenge. Prison records maintained by federal and state correctional systems (and centrally by the Bureau of Justice Statistics through the National Corrections Reporting Program) provide an authoritative record of those who have served time in adult prison facilities. Birth certificates, marriage licenses, and prison visiting records could begin to identify the parents, partners, and coparents of those who have been imprisoned.

To help locate formerly incarcerated individuals and their children or adult family members for purposes of making reparations, correctional records might be linked by federal government staff within the United States Census Bureau's Center for Administrative Records Research and Applications secure data environment. Those data support linking to a broad array of other government databases, including benefits data (e.g., Supplemental Security Income, TANF, Medicaid, and Veterans' Administration benefits); employment and unemployment information; information collected by the American Community Survey and decennial Census; and data from public housing, rental assistance, and subsidized mortgage programs.[33] Identifying heavily affected neighborhoods and cities for purposes of distributing community-level reparations is also highly feasible—and much less complex. Criminal justice data mapping resources, including the Justice Atlas and the Justice Mapping Center (developed by the spatial scientists who coined "million dollar blocks") are publicly available. These resources contain detailed data on prison admissions, releases, and other measures of intensity of criminal legal system involvement by geographic area over time.

Once affected individuals and communities have been identified for compensation, strategies and vehicles for the distribution of reparations should be considered with care. Economist Sandy Darity and colleagues, in assessing the potential economic effects of reparations for slavery and Jim Crow, contend that both the approach to monetary reparations and the relative economic position of payment recipients at the time of the distribution shapes the longer-term effects of restitution. If payments are distributed to a population of lower-income and lower-wealth individuals in a manner that encourages funds to be rapidly disposed of on goods and services, the distribution can create a meaningful economic stimulus—but the biggest boon will ultimately be reaped by those who own the productive capacity for those goods and services at the time of distribution.[34] More liquid forms of cash-value transfer (such as a onetime, lump-sum check) are therefore less effective for redressing deficits in the relative economic position of reparations recipients over the long term. Darity proposes several alternative mechanisms to help ensure that reparations payments have the intended longer-term corrective effect on the economic status of those who receive them. Reparations could be used to create a publicly administered fund from which eligible individuals would seek grants for asset-building endeavors such as education, home purchase, or small business start-up. Alternatively, the amount of the entitlement could be provided directly to each eligible individual in the form of a voucher that could be redeemed for expenses related to these asset-building activities. A third and more flexible option (from the recipient perspective) is the creation of interest-bearing trust funds for eligible individuals from which the interest may be used for any purpose, while preserving the principal as a longer-term asset.[35]

Direct cash-value compensation could be augmented by other, enduring forms of reparatory aid to individuals. Such supports could build on existing federal scholarship and work subsidy program infrastructures. Supplemental aid in such a form could help to support reparations recipients in making long-term investments in their own desired futures. For example, a national tuition repayment program for formerly incarcerated individuals, their partners, and children could be modeled on the Montgomery GI Bill, which provided for up to thirty-six months of educational support to American military veterans, redeemable within fifteen years of military discharge. A subsidized employment program for the formerly incarcerated and their family members could be modeled on the AmeriCorps VISTA program, which provides a living allowance and educational stipend to young Americans for a year of full-time work in a public agency or nonprofit organization. (The VISTA stipend structure, which is designed to support recent college graduates with no dependents or other familial obligations, would require significant adjustment to be appropriate to this purpose.)

Finally, in the context of a universal baby-bond program, supplemental bond contributions could be issued to all minor children of incarcerated parents. For those who are younger at the time of issuance, compensatory bond contributions could be redeemed for a variety of stabilizing and asset-building purposes or left to build value during early adulthood—ultimately helping to counterbalance earnings losses that accumulate over the life course. For adult children of incarcerated parents, the receipt and maturation of such a bond could still be economically and personally meaningful. For example, matured bonds might furnish the retirement funds that an individual was unable to save during a lifetime of under-compensated work. In addition, some of the same strategies considered for reparations to former prisoners—a government-administered fund or asset-building vouchers in an amount concomitant with expected earnings losses—could be used to transfer resources to their children as well. These efforts could help to ensure that today's "children of the prison boom"[36] are the last generation to experience its full devastation.

WHAT DIFFERENCE WOULD IT MAKE?

As Toni Morrison writes in *Beloved,* "This is not a story to pass on." Like Morrison's leading ghost, the reality of mass incarceration (and the centuries-long sequence of racial atrocities of which it is a part) has endured whether we speak of it or not. But would making reparations now for the harm of mass incarceration really make a difference in the broader state of racial and economic justice in America?

Perhaps the most meaningful index of racialized poverty and systematic economic disadvantage in America is the Black-white wealth gap, which has widened throughout the heyday of mass incarceration. Data from the Federal Reserve Board's Survey of Consumer Finance indicate that over the thirty-year period from 1983 to 2013, the wealth of the typical white household (operationalized in this study to exclude durable goods) rose 14 percent. During this same period, the wealth of the typical

Black household diminished by 75 percent.[37] We will never know what the racial wealth gap might have looked like today had we opted for a supportive and transformative (rather than punitive) approach to the social problems that faced America in the 1960s and 1970s. Yet it behooves us to ask how the current racial wealth gap would change if the economic damages that mass incarceration has inflicted on Black households were repaired.

To address this question, we can look to the total value of the wealth difference between Black and white family households. Federal reserve data indicate that the mean wealth of an American household in 2019 was $748,800, including mean wealth of $983,400 for white households and mean wealth of $142,500 for Black households.[38] (Although median wealth is sometimes discussed when examining the economic well-being of a typical household, mean wealth better accounts for the large share of wealth owned by white families at the uppermost extreme of the economic spectrum. Thus, it is a more meaningful measure of racial wealth disparities.)[39] According to the most recent census, there are 9,948,000 Black family households in the United States.[40] Together, the wealth of these households totals roughly $1,417,590,000,000. The difference between this figure and the total wealth that Black households would have, if it were equal to that held by white households, is approximately $8.37 trillion ($8,365,273,200,000). Summing the economic value of the subset of damages to Black individuals, families, and communities that could be quantified in the preceding chapters yields a total of $7.16 trillion ($7,156,449,876,145). Returning these damages to Black households and communities affected by mass incarceration would close 86 percent of the wealth gap that divides Black families from their white counterparts.

CONCLUSION

In the winter of 1856, Margaret Garner, the real person on whom Toni Morrison based *Beloved*, escaped the Kentucky plantation where she was enslaved with her four children and several other Black households. She and her family members were hunted by US Marshals, who found them barricaded in the home of a free Black comrade just over the Ohio River.

As the home was being raided, the real Margaret Garner killed her toddler to prevent the child from being recaptured. The rest of the family was returned by force to their former enslaver in Kentucky. They were resold, in quick succession, to other slaveholders in Louisiana and Mississippi. One of their surviving children was killed in a drowning accident during one of these forced moves, and Garner herself died in Mississippi of typhoid fever in 1858.[41]

But Morrison's novel ends differently. In it, Garner and her three other children survive the attempt at recapture and make a home in a small community on the outskirts of an Ohio town. The child she killed lives on, too. Her ghost, "Beloved," emerges one day from the stream behind the family's little settlement, moves in, and stays to haunt the home and community. Eventually, as the book's final passage recounts, the lost child's persistent, ghostly presence is simply part of the surroundings:

> This is not a story to pass on.
> Down by the streams in back of 124 her footprints come and go, come and go. They are so familiar. Should a child, an adult place his feet in them, they will fit. Take them out and they disappear again as though nobody ever walked there.
> By and by all trace is gone, and what is forgotten is not only the footprints but the water too and what is down there. The rest is weather. Not the breath of the disremembered and unaccounted for, but wind in the eaves, or spring ice thawing too quickly. Just weather.[42]

In Morrison's powerful telling, the ghost of Margaret Garner's child and the unspeakable, unreconstructed harms of enslavement that brought her into being never disappear. They are a force of nature in the little town, like the cold wind that penetrates its houses or the shattering crack that a sudden thaw makes on the river. Indistinguishable from the winter harshness, the haunting eventually becomes an unchallengeable part of the difficult environment in which the surviving must make their lives.

This is not a story to pass on. Now, as we have before, America has an opportunity to rebuild and recover from the misuse of our public systems and infrastructures for repressive ends. Effecting this transformation will be no trivial undertaking; neither was the era of mass incarceration that brought us here, nor any of the earlier campaigns of racial terrorism that laid the groundwork for this one. Yet the evidence brought forth in this book suggests that investing the ingenuity and resources to effect a true reconstruction from these damages could be more transformative and more fruitful than we have previously recognized.

A precise understanding of how mass incarceration has shaped the country we know—an America of gaping racial disparities, gendered harm, and persistently unequal opportunities for children—is also the best window we have into the other America that is possible. Should we undertake the long-deferred repairs to which this understanding compels us, and begin responding to social ills in ways that do not themselves inflict damage, we might glimpse a new version of ourselves: a people whose collective functioning, for the first time in our history, does not require the shackling of any human being. Ending poverty and ensuring that all children have the necessities of life are just the beginning of what we might do together.

Appendix

The qualitative research and structural equation modeling included in this book were carried out using deidentified, secondary data from the Multi-site Family Study on Incarceration, Parenting and Partnering. This appendix describes the purpose and design of that study, as well as its data-collection approach, analytic methods, and sample characteristics. (Methods for calculating the economic value of the harms described in each chapter of the book, which are specific to the body of evidence on which each focuses, have been detailed in the "Adding Up" section of each chapter.)

MULTI-SITE FAMILY STUDY PURPOSE AND DESIGN

The Multi-site Family Study was conducted from 2006 to 2016 by a small team of researchers, including the author, at the nonprofit policy research institute RTI International. The study was supported by the United States Department of Health and Human Services through the federal Office of the Assistant Secretary for Planning and Evaluation (which conducts policy research, planning and coordination on behalf of the department) and the Office of Family Assistance (which administers Temporary Assistance to Needy Families and other social welfare programs). The study was funded to determine whether a set of federal demonstration programs intended to strengthen family relationships among returning prisoners and their partners succeeded in fostering relationship stability, improving child well-being, and supporting desistance. Generally speaking, they did not.[1] But the project generated the most comprehensive longitudinal data ever collected on returning prisoners and their families.

The Multi-site Family Study recruited 1,991 incarcerated men and 1,482 of their female-identified intimate or coparenting partners. Incarcerated men were recruited from state prison facilities in five states where the federal demonstration programs that the study was evaluating were delivered: New York, New Jersey, Indiana, Ohio, and Minnesota. To be eligible, men had to be capable of consenting to and completing the study interviews in English and to self-identify as being in a committed intimate or coparenting relationship with a female partner. (Based on the federal Defense of Marriage Act, which had not yet been struck down by the courts at the time these programs were implemented, programs were understood to be limited to different-sex couples consisting of an incarcerated man and his female partner or coparent.) On completing the baseline interview, each male interviewee was asked to refer the study team to his intimate or coparenting partner. Female partners were contacted separately, invited to participate in the study, and typically interviewed in community settings. Each couple member was interviewed separately at nine, eighteen, and thirty-four months after baseline (with thirty-four-month interviews limited to the couples in the two states that contributed the largest sample, Indiana and Ohio). By that time, most male partners had been released from prison into the community. Near the conclusion of the longitudinal surveys, couples in which the male partner was approaching release or had been recently released and who were living near eight selected metropolitan areas were invited to participate in in-depth qualitative interviews.

DATA COLLECTION

Experienced field interviewers with specialized training in collecting data in correctional settings conducted each of the computerized, longitudinal interviews in private rooms within state prisons and local jails or in private community settings. Interviews began with computer-assisted personal interviewing, in which interviewers asked questions out loud to respondents and entered their answers electronically in a computerized survey instrument. To maximize confidentiality and candor, interviewers then assisted respondents in switching into audio computer-assisted self-interviewing (ACASI) mode to answer more sensitive questions, including those about the couple relationship and about any criminalized behaviors. ACASI allowed respondents to read each survey question on the screen while it was read aloud through headphones and select their answers on the laptop in privacy. The survey module containing these sensitive items, which was embedded in the middle of the instrument, was automatically locked as soon as it was completed by the respondent, such that interviewers could not access the respondent's answers. Interviewers explained the computerized privacy and confidentiality protections to participants and also informed them during the informed consent process that their answers were protected from subpoena or other use by law enforcement agencies under a federal Certificate of Confidentiality obtained from the United States Department of Health and Human Services. The survey captured extensive data on couple and parenting relationships in the context of criminal legal system involvement, with a particular focus on the incarceration during which participants were enrolled in the study and any reentry process that took place during their study follow-up period. Response rates were generally at or above 75 percent for each interview wave.

In-depth qualitative data were collected from a subsample of 167 respondents. This subsample was limited to couples who lived within thirty minutes of the outer boundaries of one of eight metropolitan areas in Indiana, Ohio, and New York (where most of the study sample lived) and in which the male partner was released from incarceration between May 2012 and December 2015. Members of each couple were interviewed separately; the other member of the couple was not permitted to be in the same building at the time of the interview. During the ninety-minute qualitative interviews, the author and other members of the research team talked with participants about their family structure, living arrangements, and household economic stability, including whether or how these had changed because of the incarceration; the nature and quality of their relationships with their intimate partners, coparents, and children; whether and how the incarceration had shaped their intimate and coparenting relationships; whether and how being imprisoned had affected the male partner's mind-set or ways of relating; their perspectives on gender roles and on healthy and unhealthy intimate relationships; their expectations and experiences of intimate and coparenting relationships, employment, finances, and informal supports after the male partner's return from prison; and the influence of institutional policies and formal and informal supports on these relationships. Interviewers also referred to a respondent profile summarizing selected survey responses that had been provided by the interview participant over the course of the study, including reports of their partnership and parenting status and of partner violence. For study couples in which the male partner had not yet been released from prison at the time the qualitative study was fielded, each partner was invited to complete one in-depth qualitative interview shortly before his release and another shortly after his release. For couples in which the male partner had already been released from prison, each partner was invited to complete a single interview. All qualitative interviews were audio recorded. A professional transcriptionist prepared deidentified verbatim transcripts, and recordings were subsequently destroyed. Deidentified transcripts were then subject to an additional deidentification step in which a trained member of the research team reviewed each transcript to remove any remaining information that could be used to deductively identify a study participant (e.g., mention of a respondent's place of employment). Such information was systematically redacted from every transcript to produce a qualitative file suitable for public use.

All Multi-site Family Study data-collection protocols were reviewed and approved by the Office for Human Research Protections in the United States Department of Health and Human Services (DHHS) and by an Institutional Review Board maintained by RTI International. A federal

Certificate of Confidentiality was obtained from the DHHS Office for Human Research Protections, which protects the data from subpoena or other law enforcement use. All data were deidentified before being made publicly available through the Inter-university Consortium for Political and Social Research at the University of Michigan.[2] The analyses conducted for this book, which used exclusively deidentified data, were exempted from IRB review because they did not constitute research with human subjects as defined by the *United States Code of Federal Regulations* (45 CFR 46, 102).

ANALYTIC METHODS

The qualitative analyses reported in chapters 2 through 6 were guided by an initial qualitative codebook, developed with guidance from the original Multi-site Family Study research team, that included deductive codes based on prior literature and the original study research questions. Transcripts were coded in ATLAS.ti. Queries were run in ATLAS.ti by the author using Boolean language to identify text data related to how direct and indirect experiences with the criminal legal system shaped childhood, postprison reentry experiences, and the experiences of women with an incarcerated or reentering partner or coparent. Query results were reviewed to identify themes, generating a spreadsheet of themes and the text passages that substantiated them. The strongest identified themes were elaborated in analytic memos and later developed into full text.

The structural equation models reported in chapter 2 used longitudinal survey data from reentering men and their partners. All available waves of data were included. Structural equation models were constructed in Stata 15.1 using survey reports of criminal legal system exposure, behavioral health, interpersonal style, couple conflict dynamics, and men's physical partner violence perpetration. Three dimensions of men's criminal legal system exposure were measured with self-report items: childhood criminal legal system exposure (including age at first arrest, number of parents, parent figures, or grandparents arrested, and number of stays in juvenile detention); lifetime criminal legal system exposure (including lifetime number of arrests, convictions, and adult prison or jail incarcerations); and conditions of the most recent confinement (including duration, number of transfers, and days spent in solitary confinement). Behavioral health items captured men's self-reported posttraumatic stress symptoms and alcohol and drug problems. Posttraumatic stress was captured using a composite based on the four-item Primary Care PTSD Screen and two individual items on fearfulness and preoccupation.[3] For all three variables, higher values indicated worse symptoms. Self-reported alcohol and other drug problems were measured with two composites based on the CAGE five-item problem drinking questionnaire and four-item problem drug use questionnaire and a single item indicating how often the respondent experienced anger problems when drinking or using drugs.[4] For all three items, higher values indicated greater problems. Two dimensions of men's interpersonal style were measured with self-report items. Reactivity was measured using three Likert-type items (such as, "You often respond quickly and emotionally when something happens") and noncooperativeness was measured with three Likert-type items (such as, "People involved with you have to learn how to do things your way"). For each of the variables, higher values indicated greater reactivity or noncooperativeness. Couple conflict dynamics were measured using five self-reported items that captured how often the couple was able to manage conflict in nondestructive ways (for example, maintaining a sense of humor when arguing, not letting small issues escalate), with higher values indicating healthier conflicts. Men's physical violence perpetration with their study partners was measured using items on physical violence from the Revised Conflict Tactics Scale.[5]

In addition, the analysis of mass incarceration's community and collective harms to Black Americans, presented in chapter 6, was heavily informed by a telephone interview with Joseph T. Jones Jr. All quotations from Jones are taken from that interview, which was conducted by the author in 2018 for the expressed purpose of informing the analysis presented in this book.

SAMPLE CHARACTERISTICS

The characteristics of the Multi-site Family Study qualitative sample, on whom most of the work in the book focuses, are presented in Table 1.

Table 1   Characteristics of Multi-site Family Study Qualitative Sample

	Men (n = 83)	Women (n = 84)
Age at study enrollment (mean)	33.7 years	32.6 years
Race/Ethnicity		
Black	65%	66%
White	28%	25%
Hispanic/Latinx	07%	06%
Another race*	10%	02%
Multiracial	04%	04%
Relationship with survey partner		
Married	25%	18%
In an intimate relationship	71%	70%
In a coparenting relationship only	04%	12%
Relationship duration (mean)	9.1 years	7.9 years
Parenting/Coparenting characteristics		
Number of children (mean)	2.3	2.3
Number of coparents (mean)	3.1	2.2
Coparent any children w/survey partner	90%	93%
History of criminal legal system involvement		
Age at first arrest (mean)	17.0 years	N/A
Number of lifetime arrests (mean)	13.2	1.7
Prior adult incarcerations (mean)	5.3	N/A
Time served at study enrollment (median)	2.5 years	N/A
Current incarceration term (median)	6.0 years	N/A

* "Another race" included American Indian or Alaska Native, Native Hawaiian or other Pacific Islander, Asian, or self-description by the respondent as "some other race."

Typical participants were in their early thirties. About two-thirds of participants were Black (65 percent of men and 66 percent of women), one-quarter were white (28 percent of men and 25 percent of women), and 6 to 7 percent were Latinx. The remainder identified with another racial or ethnic group or reported a multiracial identity. Most were in long-term, intimate or coparenting relationships with one another and reported an average relationship duration of eight to nine years. They typically had two or more children together, and each usually also had at least one child whom they coparented with another adult besides their study partner. At the time of enrollment in the study, all men were incarcerated in state prison, and most had extensive experience with the criminal legal system, averaging thirteen lifetime arrests and six prior incarcerations. Most women in the study had also had some direct contact with the criminal legal system, though less extensive; they reported an average of two lifetime arrests.

Notes

CHAPTER 1. DISREMEMBERED AND
UNACCOUNTED FOR

1. Michelle Alexander, *The New Jim Crow: Mass Incarceration in the Age of Colorblindness* (New York: New Press, 2010); Michelle Alexander, "The New Jim Crow," *Ohio State Journal of Criminal Law* 9, no. 1 (2011): 7; Elizabeth Hinton, *From the War on Poverty to the War on Crime: The Making of Mass Incarceration in America* (Cambridge, MA: Harvard University Press, 2016).

2. Andrew Valls, "Racial Justice as Transitional Justice," *Polity* 36, no. 1 (2003): 53–71.

3. Elizabeth Hinton and DeAnza Cook, "The Mass Criminalization of Black Americans: A Historical Overview," *Annual Review of Criminology* 4, no. 1 (2021): 27, https://doi.org/10.1146/annurev-criminol-060520-033306.

4. Nazgol Ghandnoosh, "U.S. Prison Decline: Insufficient to Undo Mass Incarceration," Sentencing Project, May 19, 2020, www.sentencingproject.org/publications/u-s-prison-decline-insufficient-undo-mass-incarceration; Magnus Lofstrom and Steven Raphael, "Incarceration and Crime: Evidence from California's Public Safety Realignment Reform," *ANNALS of the American Academy of Political and Social Science* 664, no. 1 (2016):196–220, https://doi.org/10.1177/0002716215599732; Marc Mauer and Nazgol Ghandnoosh, "Can We Wait 88 Years to End Mass Incarceration?," *Huffington Post*, Dec. 6, 2017, www.huffpost.com/entry/88-years-mass-incarceration_b_4474132?guccounter=1.

5. Mauer and Ghandnoosh, "Can We Wait?"

6. Council on State Governments, *Confined and Costly* (Washington, DC: CSG Justice Center, June 2019), https://csgjusticecenter.org/publications/confined-costly; Lofstrom and Raphael, "Incarceration and Crime"; National Institute of Justice, "State Responses to Mass Incarceration," *Office of Justice Programs* (Washington DC: Department of Justice, 2011), www.ojp.gov/library/publications/state-responses-mass-incarceration-panel-discussion-2011-nij-conference.

7. Natasha A. Frost and Todd R. Clear, "Understanding Mass Incarceration as a Grand Social Experiment," *Studies in Law, Politics, and Society* 47 (2009): 159.

8. David Garland, *Mass Imprisonment: Social Causes and Consequences* (London: Sage, 2001).

9. Loïc Wacquant, "Deadly Symbiosis: When Ghetto and Prison Meet and Mesh," *Punishment and Society* 3, no. 1 (2001): 96.

10. Wendy Sawyer and Peter Wagner, "Mass Incarceration: The Whole Pie 2020," Prison Policy Initiative, March 24, 2020, www.prisonpolicy.org/reports/pie2020.html; Wendy Sawyer, "Artist Collaboration: Visualizing 10.6 Million Jail Admissions Each Year," Prison Policy Initiative, March 22, 2018, www.prisonpolicy.org/blog/2018/03/22/chalabi.

11. Equal Justice Initiative, *United States Still Has Highest Incarceration Rate in the World* (Montgomery, AL: Equal Justice Initiative, 2019), https://eji.org/news/united-states-still-has-highest-incarceration-rate-world.

12. Danielle Kaeble and Mary Cowhig, "Correctional Populations in the United States, 2016," US Department of Justice, Bulletin, April 2018, 14.

13. Matthew Friedman, "Just Facts: As Many Americans Have Criminal Records as College Diplomas," Brennan Center for Justice, Nov. 17, 2015.

14. Sarah K. S. Shannon et al., "The Growth, Scope, and Spatial Distribution of People with Felony Records in the United States, 1948–2010," *Demography* 54, no. 5 (2017): 1795–1818, https://doi.org/10.1007/s13524-017-0611-1.

15. Jerrett Jones, "Examining the Relationship between Paternal Incarceration, Maternal Stress, and Harsh Parenting," Fragile Families Working Paper WP13–03-FF, 2013, 37.

16. National Academies of Sciences, Engineering and Medicine, *The Effects of Incarceration and Reentry on Community Health and Well-Being: Proceedings of a Workshop* (Washington, DC: National Academies Press, 2020), https://doi.org/10.17226/25471; Todd R. Clear, "The Effects of High Imprisonment Rates on Communities," *Crime and Justice* 37, no. 1 (2008): 97–132; Bruce Western, Becky Pettit, and Josh Guetzkow, "Black Economic Progress in the Era of Mass Imprisonment," in *Invisible Punishment: The Collateral Consequences of Mass Imprisonment,* ed. Marc Mauer and Meda Chesney-Lind (New York: New Press, 2002), 165–80; Jeremy Travis, Bruce Western, and F. Stevens Redburn, eds., *The Growth of Incarceration in the United States: Exploring Causes and Consequences* (Washington, DC: National Academies Press, 2014); Christopher Wildeman and Emily A. Wang, "Mass Incarceration, Public Health, and Widening

Inequality in the USA," *The Lancet* 389, no. 10077 (2017): 1464–74, https://doi .org/10.1016/S0140-6736(17)30259-3; Kathryn M. Nowotny and Anastasiia Kuptsevych-Timmer, "Health and Justice: Framing Incarceration as a Social Determinant of Health for Black Men in the United States," *Sociology Compass* 12, no. 3 (2018): e12566, https://doi.org/10.1111/soc4.12566; Anna R. Haskins, "Unintended Consequences: Effects of Paternal Incarceration on Child School Readiness and Later Special Education Placement," *Sociological Science* 1, no. 11 (2014): 141–58, https://doi.org/10.15195/v1.a11; Anna R. Haskins and Wade C. Jacobsen, "Schools as Surveilling Institutions? Paternal Incarceration, System Avoidance, and Parental Involvement in Schooling," *American Sociological Review* 82, no. 4 (2017): 175–83; Tasseli McKay et al., *Holding On: Family and Fatherhood during Incarceration and Reentry* (Oakland: University of California Press, 2019); Anne M. Nurse, *Fatherhood Arrested: Parenting from within the Juvenile Justice System* (Nashville: Vanderbilt University Press, 2002); Sara Wakefield, "Accentuating the Positive or Eliminating the Negative? Paternal Incarceration and Caregiver-Child Relationship Quality," *Journal of Criminal Law & Criminology* 104, no. 4 (2015): 905.

17. Christopher Wildeman, "Incarceration and Population Health in Wealthy Democracies," *Criminology* 54, no. 2 (2016): 360–82, http://dx.doi.org.proxy.lib .duke.edu/10.1111/1745-9125.12107.

18. Clear, "Effects of High Imprisonment Rates"; Mark L. Hatzenbuehler et al., "The Collateral Damage of Mass Incarceration: Risk of Psychiatric Morbidity among Nonincarcerated Residents of High-Incarceration Neighborhoods," *American Journal of Public Health* 105, no. 1 (2015): 138–43, https://doi .org/10.2105/AJPH.2014.302184; Maria R. Khan et al., "Dissolution of Primary Intimate Relationships during Incarceration and Implications for Post-Release HIV Transmission," *Journal of Urban Health* 88, no. 2 (2011): 365–75; David S. Kirk, "A Natural Experiment of the Consequences of Concentrating Former Prisoners in the Same Neighborhoods," *Proceedings of the National Academy of Sciences* 112, no. 22 (2015): 6943–48.

19. Megan Comfort, "Punishment beyond the Legal Offender," *Annual Review of Law and Social Science* 3, no. 1 (2007): 271–96.

20. Hinton and Cook, "Mass Criminalization"; Etienne G. Krug et al., "The World Report on Violence and Health," *The Lancet* 360, no. 9339 (2002): 1083–88; Kaethe Weingarten, "Witnessing the Effects of Political Violence in Families: Mechanisms of Intergenerational Transmission and Clinical Interventions," *Journal of Marital and Family Therapy* 30, no. 1 (2004): 45–59.

21. Scott W. Phillips, "Myths, Militarism and the Police Patrol Rifle," *Policing & Society* 26, no. 2 (2016): 185–96, https://doi.org/10.1080/10439463.2014.92 2088; Geoff Ward, "Living Histories of White Supremacist Policing: Towards Transformative Justice," *Du Bois Review: Social Science Research on Race* 15, no. 1 (2018): 167–84; Raja Staggers-Hakim, "The Nation's Unprotected Children and

the Ghost of Mike Brown, or the Impact of National Police Killings on the Health and Social Development of African American Boys," *Journal of Human Behavior in the Social Environment* 26, nos. 3–4 (2016): 390–99, https://doi.org/10.10 80/10911359.2015.1132864.

22. Alexander, *The New Jim Crow;* Hinton, *From the War on Poverty;* Bryan Stevenson, "Keynote Address by Mr. Bryan Stevenson," *DePaul Law Review* 53, no. 4 (2004): https://via.library.depaul.edu/cgi/viewcontent.cgi?article=1484& context=law-review.

23. See, e.g., Becky Pettit, *Invisible Men: Mass Incarceration and the Myth of Black Progress* (New York: Russell Sage, 2012); and Bruce Western and Katherine Beckett, "How Unregulated Is the U.S. Labor Market? The Penal System as a Labor Market Institution," *American Journal of Sociology* 104, no. 4 (1999): 1030–60, https://doi.org/10.1086/210135.

24. Pilar Hernández, "Trauma in War and Political Persecution: Expanding the Concept," *American Journal of Orthopsychiatry* 72, no. 1 (2002): 17; Cindy A. Sousa, "Political Violence, Collective Functioning and Health: A Review of the Literature," *Medicine, Conflict, and Survival* 29, no. 3 (2013): 169–97; Weingarten, "Witnessing the Effects of Political Violence."

25. Catherine Burnette, "Historical Oppression and Intimate Partner Violence Experienced by Indigenous Women in the United States: Understanding Connections," *Social Service Review* 89, no. 3 (2015): 531–63, https://doi .org/10.1086/683336; Maria Yellow Horse Brave Heart, "Wakiksuyapi: Carrying the Historical Trauma of the Lakota," *Tulane Studies in Social Welfare* 21, no. 22 (2000): 245–66; Maria Yellow Horse Brave Heart et al., "Historical Trauma among Indigenous Peoples of the Americas: Concepts, Research, and Clinical Considerations," *Journal of Psychoactive Drugs* 43, no. 4 (2011): 282–90.

26. Toni Morrison, *Beloved* (New York, NY: Alfred A. Knopf, 1987), 275.

27. Morrison, 1.

28. Clint Smith, *How the Word Is Passed: A Reckoning with the History of Slavery across America* (New York: Little, Brown, 2021), 268–69.

29. United Nations Secretary-General, *United Nations Approach to Transitional Justice: Guidance Note of the Secretary-General,* March 2010, 3.

30. Desmond S. King and Jennifer M. Page, "Towards Transitional Justice? Black Reparations and the End of Mass Incarceration," *Ethnic and Racial Studies* 41, no. 4 (2018): 739–58, https://doi.org/10.1080/01419870.2018.1381341.

31. Nanci Adler, *Understanding the Age of Transitional Justice: Crimes, Courts, Commissions, and Chronicling* (New Brunswick, NJ: Rutgers University Press, 2018), Goodson Law Library https://find.library.duke.edu/catalog /DUKE008366828; Paige Arthur, "How 'Transitions' Reshaped Human Rights: A Conceptual History of Transitional Justice," *Human Rights Quarterly* 31, no. 2 (2009): 325, https://doi.org/10.1353/hrq.0.0069; David C. Gray, "A No-Excuse Approach to Transitional Justice: Reparations as Tools of Extraordinary

Justice," *Washington University Law Review* 87, no. 5 (2010): 1043–1104; Uğur Ümit Üngör and Nanci Adler, "Indonesia in the Global Context of Genocide and Transitional Justice," *Journal of Genocide Research* 19, no. 4 (2017): 10.

32. Joanna Pozen, Richard Neugebauer, and Joseph Ntaganira, "Assessing the Rwanda Experiment: Popular Perceptions of Gacaca in Its Final Phase," *International Journal of Transitional Justice* 8, no. 1 (2014): 31–52, https://doi.org/10.1093/ijtj/ijt029.

33. Samar El-Masri, Tammy Lambert, and Joanna R. Quinn, eds., *Transitional Justice in Comparative Perspective: Preconditions for Success* (Cham: Springer, 2020), https://find.library.duke.edu/catalog/DUKE009594582.

34. Hugo van der Merwe and Brinton Lykes, "Idealists, Opportunists and Activists: Who Drives Transitional Justice?," *International Journal of Transitional Justice* 12, no.3 (2018): 381, https://doi.org/10.1093/ijtj/ijy022.

35. Cyanne E. Loyle, "Transitional Justice and Political Order in Rwanda," *Ethnic and Racial Studies* 41, no. 4 (2018): 663–80, https://doi.org/10.1080/014 19870.2017.1366537; Pozen, Neugebauer, and Ntaganira, "Assessing the Rwanda Experiment"; Susan Thomson, "The Darker Side of Transitional Justice: The Power Dynamics behind Rwanda's Gacaca Courts," *Africa* 81, no. 3 (2011): 373–90.

36. Matthew Evans, "A Future without Forgiveness: Beyond Reconciliation in Transitional Justice," *International Politics* 55, no. 5 (2018): 678–92, https://doi.org/10.1057/s41311-017-0091-3.

37. Joanna R. Quinn, "Tractionless Transitional Justice in Uganda: The Potential for Thin Sympathetic Interventions as Ameliorating Factor," in *Transitional Justice in Comparative Perspective: Preconditions for Success*, ed. Samar El-Masri, Tammy Lambert, and Joanna R. Quinn (Cham: Springer, 2020), 19–48.

38. Quinn, 20.

39. El-Masri, Lambert, and Quinn, *Transitional Justice*, 219.

40. Vesla M. Weaver, Andrew Papachristos, and Michael Zanger-Tishler, "The Great Decoupling: The Disconnection between Criminal Offending and Experience of Arrest across Two Cohorts," *RSF: The Russell Sage Foundation Journal of the Social Sciences* 5, no. 1 (2019): 89–123, https://doi.org/10.7758/RSF .2019.5.1.05.

41. Heather Ann Thompson, "The Racial History of Criminal Justice in America," *Du Bois Review: Social Science Research on Race* 16, no. 1 (2020): 221–41, https://doi.org/10.1017/S1742058X19000183.

42. M. Brinton Lykes and Hugo van der Merwe, "Exploring/Expanding the Reach of Transitional Justice," *International Journal of Transitional Justice* 11, no. 3 (2017): 374, https://doi.org/10.1093/ijtj/ijx026.

43. James Gump, "Unveiling the Third Force: Toward Transitional Justice in the USA and South Africa, 1973-1994," *Safundi* 15, no. 1 (2014): 75–100.

44. King and Page, "Towards Transitional Justice?," 740.

45. Adam Serwer, "The Fight over the 1619 Project Is Not about the Facts," *The Atlantic,* Dec. 23, 2019, www.theatlantic.com/ideas/archive/2019/12 /historians-clash-1619-project/604093.

46. Courtney M. Bonam et al., "Ignoring History, Denying Racism: Mounting Evidence for the Marley Hypothesis and Epistemologies of Ignorance," *Social Psychological and Personality Science* 10, no. 2 (2019): 257–65, https:// doi.org/10.1177/1948550617751583; Jessica C. Nelson, Glenn Adams, and Phia S. Salter, "The Marley Hypothesis: Denial of Racism Reflects Ignorance of History," *Psychological Science* 24, no. 2 (2013): 213–18, https://doi.org/10.1177 /0956797612451466.

47. Reflective Democracy Campaign, *Reflective Democracy Research Findings,* 2017, https://wholeads.us/wp-content/uploads/2019/04/2017-report-corrected-4.2019.pdf.

48. Timothy L. O'Brien, "Arresting Confidence: Mass Incarceration and Black-White Differences in Perceptions of Legal Authorities," *Social Science Quarterly* 101, no. 5 (2020): 1905–19, https://doi.org/10.1111/ssqu.12842; Joe Soss and Vesla Weaver, "Police Are Our Government: Politics, Political Science, and the Policing of Race-Class Subjugated Communities," *Annual Review of Political Science* 20, no. 1 (2017): 565–91, https://doi.org/10.1146/annurev-polisci-060415-093825; Vesla M. Weaver and Amanda Geller, "De-policing America's Youth: Disrupting Criminal Justice Policy Feedbacks That Distort Power and Derail Prospects," *ANNALS of the American Academy of Political and Social Science* 685, no. 1 (2019): 190–226, https://doi.org/10.1177/0002716219871899.

49. Katherine Beckett and Bruce Western, "Governing Social Marginality: Welfare, Incarceration, and the Transformation of State Policy," *Punishment & Society* 3, no. 1 (2001): 43–59, https://doi.org/10.1177/14624740122228249; Craig Haney, "The Psychological Impact of Incarceration: Implications for Post-prison Adjustment," in *Prisoners Once Removed: The Impact of Incarceration and Reentry on Children, Families, and Communities,* ed. Jeremy Travis and Michelle Waul (Washington, DC: Urban Institute, 2003), 33–66; Jeffrey Kling, "Incarceration Length, Employment, and Earnings," *American Economic Review* 96, no. 3 (2006): 863–76; Michael Massoglia and William Alex Pridemore, "Incarceration and Health," *Annual Review of Sociology* 41, no. 1 (2015): 291–310, https://doi .org/10.1146/annurev-soc-073014-112326; Christopher Uggen, Jeff Manza, and Melissa Thompson, "Citizenship, Democracy, and the Civic Reintegration of Criminal Offenders," *Annals of the American Academy of Political and Social Science* 605, no. 1 (2006): 281–310, https://doi.org/10.1177/0002716206286898; Bruce Western and Christopher Wildeman, "Punishment, Inequality, and the Future of Mass Incarceration," *University of Kansas Law Review* 57, no. 4 (2008): 851–78.

50. Lawrence D. Bobo and Victor Thompson, "Racialized Mass Incarceration: Poverty, Prejudice, and Punishment," in *Doing Race: 21 Essays for the 21st Century,* ed. Hazel R. Markus and Paula Moya (New York: Norton, 2010), 322–55.

51. Joyce A. Arditti, "Families and Incarceration: An Ecological Approach," *Families in Society: Journal of Contemporary Social Services* 86, no. 2 (2005): 251–60; Holly Foster and John Hagan, "Incarceration and Intergenerational Social Exclusion," *Social Problems* 54, no. 4 (2007): 399–433; Amanda Geller et al., "Beyond Absenteeism: Father Incarceration and Child Development," *Demography* 49, no. 1 (2012): 49–76; Creasie F. Hairston, *Focus on Children with Incarcerated Parents: An Overview of the Research Literature* (Baltimore: Annie E. Casey Foundation, 2008); Haskins, "Unintended Consequences"; Anna R. Haskins, "Paternal Incarceration and Child-Reported Behavioral Functioning at Age 9," *Social Science Research* 52 (2015): 18–33, https://doi.org/10.1016/j.ssresearch.2015.01.001; Wakefield, "Accentuating the Positive"; Christopher Wildeman, "Parental Incarceration, Child Homelessness, and the Invisible Consequences of Mass Imprisonment," *ANNALS of the American Academy of Political and Social Science* 651, no. 1 (2014): 74–96.

52. Robert J. Sampson and Charles Loeffler, "Punishment's Place: The Local Concentration of Mass Incarceration," *Daedalus: The Journal of the American Academy of Arts & Sciences* 139, no. 3 (2010): 20–31.

53. Marion Daniel Bennett, "So Much Trouble on My Mind: African American Males Coping with Mental Health Issues and Racism," *Urban Social Work* 4, no. 2 (2020): 152–72, https://doi.org/10.1891/USW-D-19-00005; Clear, "Effects of High Imprisonment Rates"; Hatzenbuehler et al., "Collateral Damage"; Khan et al., "Dissolution"; Kirk, "Natural Experiment"; Joscha Legewie and Jeffrey Fagan, "Aggressive Policing and the Educational Performance of Minority Youth," *American Sociological Review* 84, no. 2 (2019): 220–47, https://doi.org/10.1177/0003122419826020.

54. Bobo and Thompson, "Racialized Mass Incarceration"; Hinton and Cook, "Mass Criminalization."

55. Haskins and Jacobsen, "Schools as Surveilling Institutions?"; Sara Wakefield and Christopher Wildeman, *Children of the Prison Boom: Mass Incarceration and the Future of American Inequality* (London: Oxford University Press, 2014); Bruce Western and Christopher Wildeman, "The Black Family and Mass Incarceration," *Annals of the American Academy of Political and Social Science* 621, no. 1 (2009): 221–42; Christopher Wildeman and Christopher Muller, "Mass Imprisonment and Inequality in Health and Family Life," *Annual Review of Law and Social Science* 8, no. 1 (2012): 11–30.

56. Tracey Meares, "Policing and Procedural Justice: Shaping Citizens' Identities to Increase Democratic Participation," *Northwestern University Law Review* 111, no. 6 (2017): 1525; Weaver and Geller, "De-policing America's Youth"; Vesla M. Weaver and Amy E. Lerman, "Political Consequences of the Carceral State," *American Political Science Review* 104, no. 4 (2010): 817–33, https://doi.org/10.1017/S0003055410000456.

57. William A. Darity Jr. and A. Kirsten Mullen, *From Here to Equality: Reparations for Black Americans in the Twenty-First Century* (Chapel Hill: University of North Carolina Press, 2020), 478–80.

58. Sarah Esther Lageson, *Digital Punishment: Privacy, Stigma, and the Harms of Data-Driven Criminal Justice* (New York: Oxford University Press, 2020).

59. Gray, "A No-Excuse Approach," 1095.

60. Alfred L. Brophy, "Reconsidering Reparations," *Indiana Law Journal* 81, no. 3 (2006): 811.

61. Gray, "A No-Excuse Approach"; Darity and Mullen, *From Here to Equality,* 445–46.

62. Gray, "A No-Excuse Approach," 1050–51.

63. Michael T. Martin and Marilyn Yaquinto, eds., *Redress for Historical Injustices in the United States: On Reparations for Slavery, Jim Crow, and Their Legacies* (Durham, NC: Duke University Press, 2007), 3, https://find.library. duke.edu/catalog/DUKE003876909; James Bolner, "Toward a Theory of Racial Reparations," in *Redress for Historical Injustices in the United States: On Reparations for Slavery, Jim Crow, and Their Legacies,* ed. Michael Martin and Marilyn Yaquinto (Durham, NC: Duke University Press, 2007), 132.

64. Martin and Yaquinto, *Redress for Historical Injustices;* William Darity, "Forty Acres and a Mule in the 21st Century," *Social Science Quarterly* 89, no. 3 (2008): 656–64; King and Page, "Towards Transitional Justice?"

65. Valls, "Racial Justice"; Gray, "A No-Excuse Approach."

66. Darity, "Forty Acres"; Martin and Yaquinto, *Redress for Historical Injustices.*

67. Toni Morrison, *Beloved* (New York: Vintage, 2007), 7.

68. Wildeman, "Incarceration and Population Health."

69. Robinson Randall, *The Debt: What America Owes to Blacks* (New York: Dutton, 2000), 8.

70. William A. Darity, "How Obama Failed Black Americans," *The Atlantic,* Dec. 22, 2016, www.theatlantic.com/politics/archive/2016/12/how-barack-obama-failed-black-americans/511358.

71. Peter Dixon, "Analysis | U.S. Cities and States Are Discussing Reparations for Black Americans. Here's What's Key," *Washington Post,* August 24, 2020, www.washingtonpost.com/politics/2020/08/24/us-cities-states-are-discussing-reparations-black-americans-heres-whats-key.

72. Boris I. Bittker, *The Case for Black Reparations* (New York: Vintage, 1973); Ta-Nehisi Coates, "The Case for Reparations," *The Atlantic,* June 15, 2014, 54–71; Ta-Nehisi Coates, "The Case for Considering Reparations," *The Atlantic,* Jan. 27, 2016; Darity and Mullen, *From Here to Equality;* Darity, "Forty Acres"; Martin and Yaquinto, *Redress for Historical Injustices.*

73. King and Page, "Towards Transitional Justice?"; Ta-Nehisi Coates, "The Black Family in the Age of Mass Incarceration," *The Atlantic,* Oct. 2015, www.theatlantic.com/magazine/archive/2015/10/the-black-family-in-the-age-of-mass-incarceration/403246.

74. Bruce Western, *Homeward: Life in the Year after Prison* (New York: Russell Sage, 2018); Susanne Karstedt, Hollie Nyseth Brehm, and Laura C. Frizzell, "Genocide, Mass Atrocity, and Theories of Crime: Unlocking Criminology's Potential," *Annual Review of Criminology* 4, no. 1 (2021): 75–97, https://doi.org/10.1146/annurev-criminol-061020-022050; Patrick Sharkey, "The Long Reach of Violence: A Broader Perspective on Data, Theory, and Evidence on the Prevalence and Consequences of Exposure to Violence," *Annual Review of Criminology* 1, no. 1 (2018): 85–102, https://doi.org/10.1146/annurev-criminol-032317-092316.

75. Travis, Western, and Redburn, "Growth of Incarceration"; Jeffrey D. Morenoff and Sam Norris, "Measuring Costs and Benefits of Incarceration" (unpublished Congressional Briefing presented at Cost and Effect: Measuring the Impact of Incarceration on Individuals, Neighborhoods, and Society, Washington, DC, 2019); John Schmitt, Kris Warner, and Sarika Gupta, *The High Budgetary Cost of Incarceration* (Washington, DC: Center for Economic and Policy Research, 2010), 19; Robert J. Sampson, "The Incarceration Ledger: Toward a New Era in Assessing Societal Consequences," *Criminology and Public Policy* 10, no. 3 (2011): 819–28.

76. Lily George et al., eds., *Neo-colonial Injustice and the Mass Imprisonment of Indigenous Women* (New York: Palgrave Macmillan, 2020), https://doi.org/10.1007/978-3-030-44567-6; Tanya Golash-Boza, "The Parallels between Mass Incarceration and Mass Deportation: An Intersectional Analysis of State Repression," *Journal of World-Systems Research* 22, no. 2 (2016): 484–509, https://doi.org/10.5195/jwsr.2016.616; Benjamin Madley, "California's First Mass Incarceration System: Franciscan Missions, California Indians, and Penal Servitude, 1769–1836," *Pacific Historical Review* 88, no. 1 (2019): 14.

77. Larry Greenfeld and Steven Smith, *American Indians and Crime* (Washington, DC: US Department of Justice, 1999), 51; Becky Pettit and Carmen Gutierrez, "Mass Incarceration and Racial Inequality," *American Journal of Economics and Sociology* 77, nos. 3–4 (2018): 1153–82, https://doi.org/10.1111/ajes.12241.

78. Sarah Eppler-Epstein et al., *The Alarming Lack of Data on Latinos in the Criminal Justice System* (Washington DC: Urban Institute, 2016), http://urbn.is/cjdata.

79. John H. Laub and Robert J. Sampson, "Turning Points in the Life Course: Why Change Matters to the Study of Crime," *Criminology* 31, no. 3 (1993): 301–25; Evelyn J. Patterson and Christopher Wildeman, "Mass Imprisonment and the Life Course Revisited: Cumulative Years Spent Imprisoned and Marked for Working-Age Black and White Men," *Social Science Research* 53 (2015): 325–37, https://doi.org/10.1016/j.ssresearch.2015.06.011; Becky Pettit and Bruce Western, "Mass Imprisonment and the Life Course: Race and Class Inequality in U.S. Incarceration," *American Sociological Review* 69 (2004): 151–69; Megan C. Kurlychek and Brian D. Johnson, "Cumulative Disadvantage in the American Criminal Justice

System," *Annual Review of Criminology* 2, no. 1 (2019): 291–319, https://doi
.org/10.1146/annurev-criminol-011518-024815; Pamela K. Lattimore, Debbie
Dawes, and Kelle Barrick, *Desistance from Crime over the Life Course* (Washington, DC: US Department of Justice, 2018), 35, https://www.ncjrs.gov/pdffiles1
/nij/grants/252080.pdf.

80. Morrison, *Beloved*, 66.

CHAPTER 2. "INSTITUTIONALIZED"

1. David S. Kirk and Sara Wakefield, "Collateral Consequences of Punishment: A Critical Review and Path Forward," *Annual Review of Criminology*
1, no. 1 (2018): 171–94, https://doi.org/10.1146/annurev-criminol-032317-092045.

2. Anupa Bir and Christine Lindquist, "Multi-site Family Study on Incarceration, Parenting and Partnering, 2008–2014 [5 States]," (Ann Arbor, MI: Inter-university Consortium for Political and Social Research [distributor] [ICPSR],
Nov. 17, 2017).

3. Karen P. Bennett-Haron et al., *Understanding, Dismantling, and Disrupting the Prison-to-School Pipeline* (Lanham, MD: Lexington Books, 2017); Nancy
A. Heitzeg, "Education or Incarceration: Zero Tolerance Policies and the School
to Prison Pipeline," *Forum on Public Policy Online*, no. 2 (2009): https://
eric.ed.gov/?id=EJ870076; Johanna Wald and Daniel J. Losen, "Defining and
Redirecting a School-to-Prison Pipeline," *New Directions for Youth Development*, no. 99 (2003): 9–15, https://doi.org/10.1002/yd.51; Catherine Y. Kim, Daniel J. Losen, and Damon T. Hewitt, *The School-to-Prison Pipeline* (New York:
New York University Press, 2010).

4. Weaver and Geller, "De-policing America's Youth," 201.

5. Kristin Henning, "Criminalizing Normal Adolescent Behavior in Communities of Color: The Role of Prosecutors in Juvenile Justice Reform," *Cornell Law
Review* 98, no. 2 (2012): 387.

6. Gwen Prowse, Vesla M. Weaver, and Tracey L. Meares, "The State from
Below: Distorted Responsiveness in Policed Communities," *Urban Affairs
Review* 56, no. 5 (2020): 1423–71, https://doi.org/10.1177/1078087419844831.

7. Amy E. Lerman and Vesla M. Weaver, *Arresting Citizenship: The Democratic Consequences of American Crime Control* (Chicago: University of Chicago
Press, 2014).

8. Hinton, *From the War on Poverty*.

9. Linda K. Mancillas, *Presidents and Mass Incarceration: Choices at the Top,
Repercussions at the Bottom* (Santa Barbara: Praeger, 2018); Mark Mauer, "Why
Are Tough on Crime Policies So Popular?," *Stanford Law & Policy Review* 11, no.
1 (1999): 9–22.

10. Elizabeth Hinton, "Creating Crime: The Rise and Impact of National Juvenile Delinquency Programs in Black Urban Neighborhoods," *Journal of Urban History* 41, no. 5 (2015): 808-24; Heather Schoenfeld, *Building the Prison State: Race and the Politics of Mass Incarceration* (Chicago: University of Chicago Press, 2018).

11. Ta-Nehisi Coates, *Between the World and Me* (New York: Spiegel & Grau, 2015).

12. Vesla M. Weaver, "More Security May Actually Make Us Feel Less Secure," *Proceedings of the National Academy of Sciences—PNAS* 115, no. 39 (2018): 9649-51, https://doi.org/10.1073/pnas.1813014115.

13. Wildeman, "Parental Incarceration, Child Homelessness."

14. Kameron J. Sheats et al., "Violence-Related Disparities Experienced by Black Youth and Young Adults: Opportunities for Prevention," *American Journal of Preventive Medicine* 55, no. 4 (2018): 462-69, https://doi.org/10.1016/j.amepre.2018.05.017; Gopal K. Singh et al., "All-Cause and Cause-Specific Mortality among US Youth: Socioeconomic and Rural-Urban Disparities and International Patterns," *Journal of Urban Health* 90, no. 3 (2012): 388-405, https://doi.org/10.1007/s11524-012-9744-0; Gopal K. Singh and Michael D. Kogan, "Widening Socioeconomic Disparities in US Childhood Mortality, 1969-2000," *American Journal of Public Health* 97, no. 9 (2007): 1658-65, https://doi.org/10.2105/AJPH.2006.087320.

15. Jessica Wolpaw Reyes, "Environmental Policy as Social Policy? The Impact of Childhood Lead Exposure on Crime," *B.E. Journal of Economic Analysis & Policy* 7, no. 1 (2007): 51, https://doi.org/10.2202/1935-1682.1796.

16. Kevin Drum, "A Very Brief History of Super-Predators," *Mother Jones*, March 3, 2016, www.motherjones.com/kevin-drum/2016/03/very-brief-history-super-predators; Gerald Markowitz, "The Childhood Lead Poisoning Epidemic in Historical Perspective," *Endeavour* 40, no. 2 (2016): 93-101, https://doi.org/10.1016/j.endeavour.2016.03.006.

17. John Dilulio, "The Coming of the Super-Predators," *Weekly Standard*, Nov. 27, 1995, 3-4 www.weeklystandard.com/john-j-dilulio-jr/the-coming-of-the-super-predators.

18. Drum, "A Very Brief History."

19. Hillary Clinton, "1996: Hillary Clinton on 'Superpredators' (C-SPAN)," YouTube video, 1:07, www.youtube.com/watch?v=j0uCrA7ePno.

20. K. Babe Howell, "The Costs of Broken Windows Policing: Twenty Years and Counting," *Cardozo Law Review* 37 no. 3 (2015): 1059-74; Tracey Meares, "Broken Windows, Neighborhoods, and the Legitimacy of Law Enforcement or Why I Fell in and out of Love with Zimbardo," *Journal of Research in Crime and Delinquency* 52, no. 4 (2015): 609-25, https://doi.org/10.1177/0022427815583911; Ana Muniz, "Maintaining Racial Boundaries: Criminalization, Neighborhood Context, and the Origins of Gang Injunctions," *Social Problems* 61, no. 2 (2014): 216-36, https://doi.org/10.1525/sp.2014.12095; Tom R. Tyler, Jonathan Jackson,

and Avital Mentovich, "The Consequences of Being an Object of Suspicion: Potential Pitfalls of Proactive Police Contact," *Journal of Empirical Legal Studies* 12, no. 4 (2015): 602–36, https://doi.org/10.1111/jels.12086; David Weisburd et al., "Proactive Policing: A Summary of the Report of the National Academies of Sciences, Engineering, and Medicine," *Asian Journal of Criminology* 14, no. 2 (2019): 145–77, https://doi.org/10.1007/s11417-019-09284-1.

21. Rory Kramer and Brianna Remster, "Stop, Frisk, and Assault? Racial Disparities in Police Use of Force during Investigatory Stops," *Law & Society Review* 52, no. 4 (2018): 960–93, https://doi.org/10.1111/lasr.12366.

22. Victor M. Rios, *Punished: Policing the Lives of Black and Latino Boys* (New York: New York University Press, 2011), 16.

23. Andrea L. Dennis, "Decriminalizing Childhood," *Fordham Urban Law Journal* 45, no. 1 (2017): 1; Kristin Henning, "The Challenge of Race and Crime in a Free Society: The Racial Divide in Fifty Years of Juvenile Justice Reform," *George Washington Law Review* 86, no. 6 (2018): 1604; Weaver and Geller, "De-policing America's Youth."

24. Vern Kenneth Baxter and Peter Marina, "Cultural Meaning and Hip-Hop Fashion in the African-American Male Youth Subculture of New Orleans," *Journal of Youth Studies* 11, no. 2 (2008): 93–113, https://doi.org/10.1080/13676260701800761; Erin M. Kerrison, Jennifer Cobbina, and Kimberly Bender, "'Your Pants Won't Save You': Why Black Youth Challenge Race-Based Police Surveillance and the Demands of Black Respectability Politics," *Race and Justice* 8, no. 1 (2018), 7–26.

25. Weaver and Geller, "De-policing America's Youth"; Tracey L. Meares, "The Law and Social Science of Stop and Frisk," *Annual Review of Law and Social Science* 10, no. 1 (2014): 335–52, https://doi.org/10.1146/annurev-lawsocsci-102612-134043.

26. Michael Pinard, *Poor, Black and "Wanted": Criminal Justice in Ferguson and Baltimore*, Digital Commons@UM Carey Law, July 2015, 5.

27. Lauren Nichol Gase et al., "Understanding Racial and Ethnic Disparities in Arrest: The Role of Individual, Home, School, and Community Characteristics," *Race and Social Problems* 8, no. 4 (2016): 296–312, https://doi.org/10.1007/s12552-016-9183-8; Weaver, Papachristos, and Zanger-Tishler, "The Great Decoupling."

28. Pinard, *Poor, Black and "Wanted*," 864.

29. Pinard.

30. Rios, *Punished*, 5.

31. Susan A. Bandes et al., "The Mismeasure of Terry Stops: Assessing the Psychological and Emotional Harms of Stop and Frisk to Individuals and Communities," *Behavioral Sciences & the Law* 37, no. 2 (2019): 176–94, https://doi.org/10.1002/bsl.2401.

32. Rios, *Punished*, 58.

33. Henning, "Criminalizing Normal Adolescent Behavior"; Prowse, Weaver, and Meares, "The State from Below."

34. Henry F. Fradella and Michael D. White, "Reforming Stop-and-Frisk," *Criminology, Criminal Justice, Law & Society* 18, no. 3 (2017): 45–64; Meares, "Broken Windows"; Weisburd et al., "Proactive Policing."

35. Weaver and Lerman, "Political Consequences."

36. Jordan E. DeVylder et al., "Elevated Prevalence of Suicide Attempts among Victims of Police Violence in the USA," *Journal of Urban Health* 94, no. 5 (2017): 629–36; Jordan E. DeVylder et al., "Association of Exposure to Police Violence with Prevalence of Mental Health Symptoms among Urban Residents in the United States," *JAMA Network Open* 1, no. 7 (2018): e184945.

37. David S. Kirk and Robert J. Sampson, "Juvenile Arrest and Collateral Educational Damage in the Transition to Adulthood," *Sociology of Education* 86, no. 1 (2013): 36–62; Michelle Maroto and Bryan L. Sykes, "The Varying Effects of Incarceration, Conviction, and Arrest on Wealth Outcomes among Young Adults," *Social Problems* 67, no. 4 (2020): 698–718, https://doi.org/10.1093/socpro/spz023.

38. A. A. Sewell and Kevin A. Jefferson, "Collateral Damage: The Health Effects of Invasive Police Encounters in New York City," *Journal of Urban Health: Bulletin of the New York Academy of Medicine* 93 Suppl 1.S1 (2016): 42–67, https://doi.org/10.1007/s11524-015-0016-7; Juan Del Toro et al., "The Criminogenic and Psychological Effects of Police Stops on Adolescent Black and Latino Boys," *Proceedings of the National Academy of Sciences—PNAS* 116, no. 17 (2019): 8261–68, https://doi.org/10.1073/pnas.1808976116; A. A. Sewell, Kevin A. Jefferson, and Hedwig Lee, "Living under Surveillance: Gender, Psychological Distress, and Stop-Question-and-Frisk Policing in New York City," *Social Science & Medicine* 159 (2016): 1–13, https://doi.org/10.1016/j.socscimed.2016.04.024; Kristin Turney, "Depressive Symptoms among Adolescents Exposed to Personal and Vicarious Police Contact," *Society and Mental Society and Mental Health* 11, no. 2 (2021): 113–33.

39. Legewie and Fagan, "Aggressive Policing."

40. Del Toro et al., "Criminogenic and Psychological Effects."

41. Victor M. Rios, *Human Targets: Schools, Police, and the Criminalization of Latino Youth* (Chicago: University of Chicago Press, 2017); Carla Shedd, *Unequal City: Race, Schools, and Perceptions of Injustice* (New York: Russell Sage, 2015); Lizbet Simmons, *The Prison School: Educational Inequality and School Discipline in the Age of Mass Incarceration* (Oakland: University of California Press, 2017).

42. Heitzeg, "Education or Incarceration"; David M. Ramey, "Recent Developments in School Social Control," *Sociology Compass* 14, no. 2 (2019): e12743, https://doi.org/10.1111/soc4.12743; Simmons, *The Prison School*.

43. Pamela Fenning and Jennifer Rose, "Overrepresentation of African American Students in Exclusionary Discipline: The Role of School Policy,"

Urban Education 42, no. 6 (2007): 536–59, https://doi.org/10.1177 /0042085907305039; Kathleen Nolan, *Police in the Hallways: Discipline in an Urban High School* (Minneapolis: University of Minnesota Press, 2011), http:// ebookcentral.proquest.com/lib/duke/detail.action?docID=784156.

44. L. Musu-Gillette et al., *Indicators of School Crime and Safety: 2017* (NCES 2018–036/NCJ 251413) (Washington, DC: National Center for Education Statistics, US Department of Education, and Bureau of Justice Statistics, Office of Justice Programs, US Department of Justice, 2018), https://nces.ed.gov /pubs2018/2018036.pdf; Lauren Musu-Gillette et al., *Indicators of School Crime and Safety: 2016* (Washington, DC: National Center for Educational Statistics, US Department of Education, and Bureau of Justice Statistics, Office of Justice Programs, US Department of Justice, 2017), https://nces.ed.gov/pubs2017 /2017064.pdf.

45. Emily G. Owens, "Testing the School-to-Prison Pipeline," *Journal of Policy Analysis and Management* 36, no. 1 (2016): 11–37, https://doi.org/10.1002 /pam.21954; Christina Pigott, Ami E. Stearns, and David N. Khey, "School Resource Officers and the School to Prison Pipeline: Discovering Trends of Expulsions in Public Schools," *American Journal of Criminal Justice* 43, no. 1 (2018): 120–38, http://dx.doi.org.proxy.lib.duke.edu/10.1007/s12103-017-9412-8; Matthew T. Theriot, "School Resource Officers and the Criminalization of Student Behavior," *Journal of Criminal Justice* 37, no. 3 (2009): 280–87.

46. Emily K. Weisburst, "Patrolling Public Schools: The Impact of Funding for School Police on Student Discipline and Long-Term Education Outcomes," *Journal of Policy Analysis and Management* 38, no. 2 (2019): 338–65, https:// doi.org/10.1002/pam.22116.

47. Nolan, *Police in the Hallways*.

48. NASRO, "School Resource Officers: Frequently Asked Questions," National Association of School Resource Officers (Hoover, AL: NASRO, 2018), https://nasro.org/faq.

49. Weisburst, "Patrolling Public Schools."

50. Christopher A. Mallett, "The School-to-Prison Pipeline: A Critical Review of the Punitive Paradigm Shift," *Child and Adolescent Social Work Journal* 33, no. 1 (2016): 15–24.

51. Tianna Hill and Yecenia Casiano, "Issue Brief 57: From Suspension to Support in the Early Grades" (Farmington, CT: Child Health and Development Institute, 2017), www.chdi.org/index.php/publications/issue-briefs/issue-brief-57-suspension-support-early-grades; J. Michael Murphy et al., "Scope, Scale, and Dose of the World's Largest School-Based Mental Health Programs," *Harvard Review of Psychiatry* 25, no. 5 (2017): 218–28, https://doi.org/10.1097 /HRP.0000000000000149.

52. Mallett, "The School-to-Prison Pipeline."

53. Allison Ann Payne and Kelly Welch, "How School and Education Impact the Development of Criminal and Antisocial Behavior," in *The Development of Criminal and Antisocial Behavior,* ed. Julien Morizot and Lila Kazemian (Cham: Springer, 2015), 237–51, https://doi.org/10.1007/978-3-319-08720-7_15.

54. Henning, "Criminalizing Normal Adolescent Behavior"; Aaron Kupchik and Torin Monahan, "The New American School: Preparation for Post-Industrial Discipline," *British Journal of Sociology of Education* 27, no. 5 (2006): 617–31, https://doi.org/10.1080/01425690600958816; Mallett, "The School-to-Prison Pipeline"; Sean Nicholson-Crotty, Zachary Birchmeier, and David Valentine, "Exploring the Impact of School Discipline on Racial Disproportion in the Juvenile Justice System," *Social Science Quarterly* 90, no. 4 (2009): 1003–18, https://doi.org/10.1111/j.1540-6237.2009.00674.x; Owens, "Testing the School-to-Prison Pipeline."

55. Abigail Novak, "The Association between Experiences of Exclusionary Discipline and Justice System Contact: A Systematic Review," *Aggression and Violent Behavior* 40 (2018): 73–82.

56. Tracey L. Shollenberger, "Racial Disparities in School Suspension and Subsequent Outcomes," in *Closing the School Discipline Gap: Equitable Remedies for Excessive Exclusion,* ed. Daniel J. Losen (New York: Teachers College Press, 2015), 31–44.

57. Yolanda Anyon et al., "The Persistent Effect of Race and the Promise of Alternatives to Suspension in School Discipline Outcomes," *Children and Youth Services Review* 44 (2014): 379–86, https://doi.org/10.1016/j.childyouth.2014.06.025; Matthew L. Mizel et al., "To Educate or to Incarcerate: Factors in Disproportionality in School Discipline," *Children and Youth Services Review* 70 (2016): 102–11, https://doi.org/10.1016/j.childyouth.2016.09.009; Anthony A. Peguero et al., "Punishing the Children of Immigrants: Race, Ethnicity, Generational Status, Student Misbehavior, and School Discipline," *Journal of Immigrant & Refugee Studies* 13, no. 2 (2015): 200–220, https://doi.org/10.1080/15562948.2014.951136; Michael Rocque and Ray Paternoster, "Understanding the Antecedents of the 'School-to-Jail' Link: The Relationship between Race and School Discipline," *Journal of Criminal Law and Criminology* 101, no. 2 (2011): 633–65; Russell J. Skiba et al., "Race Is Not Neutral: A National Investigation of African American and Latino Disproportionality in School Discipline," *School Psychology Review* 40, no. 1 (2011): 85–107.

58. Kelly Welch and Allison Ann Payne, "Racial Threat and Punitive School Discipline," *Social Problems* 57, no. 1 (2010): 29.

59. Myles Moody, "From Under-Diagnoses to Over-Representation: Black Children, ADHD, and the School-to-Prison Pipeline," *Journal of African American Studies* 20, no. 2 (2016): 152–63.

60. Nolan, *Police in the Hallways;* Marvin J. Berlowitz, Rinda Frye, and Kelli M. Jette, "Bullying and Zero-Tolerance Policies: The School to Prison Pipeline," *Multicultural Learning and Teaching* 12, no. 1 (2017): 7–25.

61. Anyon et al., "Persistent Effect of Race"; Welch and Payne, "Racial Threat."

62. Welch and Payne, "Racial Threat," 41.

63. Mallett, "The School-to-Prison Pipeline"; Simmons, *The Prison School;* Russell J. Skiba, Mariella I. Arredondo, and Natasha T. Williams, "More Than a Metaphor: The Contribution of Exclusionary Discipline to a School-to-Prison Pipeline," *Equity & Excellence in Education* 47, no. 4 (2014): 546–64, https://doi .org/10.1080/10665684.2014.958965; Welch and Payne, "Racial Threat."

64. Georgia B. Calhoun et al., "Parental Monitoring and Perceptions Related to Juvenile Offenders Who Fight and Carry Weapons," *Journal of Family Violence* 30, no. 5 (2015): 643–50, http://dx.doi.org.proxy.lib.duke.edu/10.1007 /s10896-015-9682-1; Victor M. Rios, "The Hyper-Criminalization of Black and Latino Male Youth in the Era of Mass Incarceration," *Souls: A Critical Journal of Black Politics, Culture, and Society* 8, no. 2 (2006): 40–54.

65. Linda A. Teplin et al., *Violent Death in Delinquent Youth after Detention* (US Department of Justice, 2015); Kramer and Remster, "Stop, Frisk, and Assault?"

66. Kerrison, Cobbina, and Bender, "'Your Pants Won't Save You,'" 12, 13.

67. Hinton, "Creating Crime."

68. Rios, *Punished.*

69. Rios, 44.

70. National Research Council and Institute of Medicine, *Juvenile Crime, Juvenile Justice* (Washington, DC: National Academies Press, 2001), https:// www.nap.edu/catalog/9747/juvenile-crime-juvenile-justice.

71. National Research Council, *Reforming Juvenile Justice: A Developmental Approach* (Washington, DC: National Academies Press, 2013), https://doi .org/10.17226/14685.

72. Henning, "Criminalizing Normal Adolescent Behavior," 383.

73. John Dilulio, "My Black Crime Problem, and Ours," *City Journal* (Spring 1996): www.city-journal.org/html/my-black-crime-problem-and-ours-11773 .html; Vincent Schiraldi quotes Dilulio in Vincent Schiraldi, "Will the Real John Dilulio Please Stand Up," *Washington Post,* Feb. 5, 2001; see also Patrick McCarthy, Vincent N. Schiraldi, and Miriam Shark, *The Future of Youth Justice: A Community Based Alternative to the Youth Prison Model* (Cambridge, MA: Harvard Kennedy School of Government, 2016), www.hks.harvard.edu/centers/wiener /programs/criminaljustice/research-publications/executive-sessions/executive- session-on-community-corrections.

74. Alfred Blumstein, Jacqueline Cohen, and Daniel Nagin, *Deterrence and Incapacitation : Estimating the Effects of Criminal Sanctions on Crime Rates*

(Washington: National Academy of Sciences, 1978), https://trove.nla.gov.au/version/13493907.

75. Melissa Sickmund, Anthony Sladky, and Wei Kang, "Easy Access to Juvenile Court Statistics: 1985–2011" (Washington, DC: Office of Juvenile Justice and Delinquency Prevention, 2014).

76. Wendy Sawyer, *Youth Confinement: The Whole Pie 2019* (Northampton, MA: Prison Policy Initiative, 2019), www.prisonpolicy.org/reports/youth2019.html.

77. Patrick Griffin et al., "Trying Juveniles as Adults: An Analysis of State Transfer Laws and Reporting" (Washington, DC: US Department of Justice, 2011).

78. H. Mitchell Caldwell, "Reeling in Gang Prosecution: Seeking a Balance in Gang Prosecution," *University of Pennsylvania Journal of Law and Social Change* 18, no. 4 (2015): 35.

79. Rebecca K. Helm et al., "Too Young to Plead? Risk, Rationality, and Plea Bargaining's Innocence Problem in Adolescents," *Psychology, Public Policy, and Law* 24, no. 2 (2018): 180–91, https://doi.org/10.1037/law0000156; Laurel LaMontagne, "Children under Pressure: The Problem of Juvenile False Confessions and Potential Solutions," *Western State University Law Review* 41, no. 1 (2013): 29; Allison D. Redlich, "The Susceptibility of Juveniles to False Confessions and False Guilty Pleas," *Rutgers Law Review* 62, no. 4 (2009): 943; Christine S. Scott-Hayward, "Explaining Juvenile False Confessions: Adolescent Development and Policy Interrogation," *Law & Psychology Review* 31 (2007): 53.

80. Erika N. Fountain and Jennifer L. Woolard, "How Defense Attorneys Consult with Juvenile Clients about Plea Bargains," *Psychology, Public Policy, and Law* 24, no. 2 (2018): 192–203, https://doi.org/10.1037/law0000158.

81. Helm et al., "Too Young to Plead?"

82. Tina M. Zottoli et al., "Plea Discounts, Time Pressures, and False-Guilty Pleas in Youth and Adults Who Pleaded Guilty to Felonies in New York City," *Psychology, Public Policy, and Law* 22, no. 3 (2016): 250.

83. Amanda NeMoyer et al., "Attorney Perspectives on Juvenile and Adult Clients' Competence to Plead Guilty," *Psychology, Public Policy, and Law* 24, no. 2 (2018): 171.

84. National Research Council and Institute of Medicine, *Juvenile Crime, Juvenile Justice.*

85. Joshua C. Cochran and Daniel P. Mears, "Race, Ethnic, and Gender Divides in Juvenile Court Sanctioning and Rehabilitative Intervention," *Journal of Research in Crime and Delinquency* 52, no. 2 (2015): 181–212.

86. John R. Mills, Anna Dorn, and Amelia Hritz, *Juvenile Life without Parole in Law and Practice: The End of Superpredator Era Sentencing* (Rochester, NY: Social Science Research Network, 2015), https://papers.ssrn.com/abstract=2663834.

87. Carly B. Dierkhising et al., "Trauma Histories among Justice-Involved Youth: Findings from the National Child Traumatic Stress Network," *European Journal of Psychotraumatology* 4, no. 1 (2013): 20274. https://doi.org/10.3402/ejpt.v4i0.20274.

88. Julian D. Ford et al., "Poly-Victimization and Risk of Posttraumatic, Depressive, and Substance Use Disorders and Involvement in Delinquency in a National Sample of Adolescents," *Journal of Adolescent Health* 46, no. 6 (2010): 545–52.

89. Jeffrey D. Burke, Edward P. Mulvey, and Carol A. Schubert, "Prevalence of Mental Health Problems and Service Use among First-Time Juvenile Offenders," *Journal of Child and Family Studies* 24, no.12 (2015): 3774–81, https://doi.org/10.1007/s10826-015-0185-8; Linda A. Teplin et al., "Psychiatric Disorders in Youth in Juvenile Detention," *Archives of General Psychiatry* 59, no. 12 (2002): 1133–43; Gail A. Wasserman et al., "The Voice DISC-IV with Incarcerated Male Youths: Prevalence of Disorder," *Journal of the American Academy of Child & Adolescent Psychiatry* 41, no. 3 (2002): 314–21; Gail A. Wasserman, Susan J. Ko, and Larkin S. McReynolds, "Assessing the Mental Health Status of Youth in Juvenile Justice Settings," *Juvenile Justice Bulletin*, August 2004.

90. Machteld Hoeve et al., "The Association between Childhood Maltreatment, Mental Health Problems, and Aggression in Justice-Involved Boys," *Aggressive Behavior* 41, no. 5 (2015): 488–501, https://doi.org/10.1002/ab.21586.

91. Jennifer A. Rosenblatt, Abram Rosenblatt, and Edward E. Biggs, "Criminal Behavior and Emotional Disorder: Comparing Youth Served by the Mental Health and Juvenile Justice Systems," *Journal of Behavioral Health Services & Research* 27, no. 2 (2000): 227–37; Sarah M. Manchak et al., "The Influence of Co-occurring Mental Health and Substance Use Problems on the Effectiveness of Juvenile Drug Courts," *Criminal Justice Policy Review* 27, no. 3 (2016): 247–64, https://doi.org/10.1177/0887403414564464.

92. Maryann Davis et al., "Longitudinal Patterns of Offending during the Transition to Adulthood in Youth from the Mental Health System," *Journal of Behavioral Health Services & Research* 31, no. 4 (2004): 351–66, https://doi.org/10.1007/BF02287689.

93. John Robst, Mary Armstrong, and Norin Dollard, "The Association between Type of Out-of-Home Mental Health Treatment and Juvenile Justice Recidivism for Youth with Trauma Exposure," *Criminal Behaviour and Mental Health* 27, no. 5 (2017): 501–13, https://doi.org/10.1002/cbm.2024.

94. Karen M. Abram et al., "Comorbidity and Continuity of Psychiatric Disorders in Youth after Detention: A Prospective Longitudinal Study," *JAMA Psychiatry* 72, no.1 (2015): 84–93, https://doi.org/10.1001/jamapsychiatry.2014.1375; Burke, Mulvey, and Schubert, "Prevalence of Mental Health Problems."

95. Burke, Mulvey, and Schubert, "Prevalence of Mental Health Problems."

96. Abram et al., "Comorbidity and Continuity."

97. Ignatius A. Samuel, "Utilization of Mental Health Services among African-American Male Adolescents Released from Juvenile Detention: Examining Reasons for Within-Group Disparities in Help-Seeking Behaviors," *Child and Adolescent Social Work Journal* 32, no. 1 (2015): 33–43, https://doi.org/10.1007 /s10560-014-0357-1.

98. Thomas W. Wojciechowski, "Racial Disparities in Community Mental Health Service Use among Juvenile Offenders," *Journal of Racial and Ethnic Health Disparities* 6, no. 2 (2019): 393–400, https://doi.org/10.1007/s40615-018-00536-x.

99. David J. Jones, "Primary Prevention and Health Outcomes: Treatment of Residential Lead-Based Paint Hazards and the Prevalence of Childhood Lead Poisoning," *Journal of Urban Economics* 71, no. 1 (2012): 151–64, https://doi .org/10.1016/j.jue.2011.06.002.

100. Anna Aizer and Janet Currie, *Lead and Juvenile Delinquency: New Evidence from Linked Birth, School and Juvenile Detention Records* (Cambridge: National Bureau of Economic Research, 2017), https://doi.org/10.3386/w23392; Hans Grönqvist, J. Peter Nilsson, and Per-Olof Robling, "Early Lead Exposure and Outcomes in Adulthood" (working paper, 2017); Philip J. Landrigan et al., "Environmental Pollutants and Disease in American Children: Estimates of Morbidity, Mortality, and Costs for Lead Poisoning, Asthma, Cancer, and Developmental Disabilities," *Environmental Health Perspectives* 110, no. 7 (2002): 721–28.

101. CDC, "Childhood Lead Poisoning Prevention," National Center for Environmental Health, Dec. 22, 2021, www.cdc.gov/nceh/lead/default.htm.

102. Jaime Raymond, "Childhood Blood Lead Levels in Children Aged 5 Years—United States, 2009–2014," *Morbidity and Mortality Weekly Reports: Surveillance Summaries* 66, no. 3 (2017): 1–7, https://doi.org/10.15585/mmwr .ss6603a1.

103. Olivier Boucher et al., "Response Inhibition and Error Monitoring during a Visual Go/No-Go Task in Inuit Children Exposed to Lead, Polychlorinated Biphenyls, and Methylmercury," *Environmental Health Perspectives* 120, no. 4 (2012): 608–15, https://doi.org/10.1289/ehp.1103828; Shuangxing Hou et al., "A Clinical Study of the Effects of Lead Poisoning on the Intelligence and Neurobehavioral Abilities of Children," *Theoretical Biology & Medical Modelling* 10, no. 1 (2013): 13, https://doi.org/10.1186/1742-4682-10-13.

104. Rick Nevin, "Understanding International Crime Trends: The Legacy of Preschool Lead Exposure," *Environmental Research* 104, no. 3 (2007): 315–36; Robert J. Sampson and Alix S. Winter, "Poisoned Development: Assessing Childhood Lead Exposure as a Cause of Crime in a Birth Cohort Followed through Adolescence," *Criminology* 56, no. 2 (2018): 269–301, https://doi.org/10.1111/1745-9125.12171; Paul B. Stretesky and Michael J. Lynch, "The Relationship between Lead and Crime," *Journal of Health and Social Behavior* 45, no. 2 (2004): 214–29,

https://doi.org/10.1177/002214650404500207; Paul B. Stretesky and Michael J. Lynch, "The Relationship between Lead Exposure and Homicide," *Archives of Pediatrics & Adolescent Medicine* 155, no. 5 (2001): 579–82.

105. Howard W. Mielke and Sammy Zahran, "The Urban Rise and Fall of Air Lead (Pb) and the Latent Surge and Retreat of Societal Violence," *Environment International* 43 (2012): 48–55, https://doi.org/10.1016/j.envint.2012.03.005.

106. Aizer and Currie, *Lead and Juvenile Delinquency;* Stretesky and Lynch, "Lead and Crime."

107. Landrigan et al., "Environmental Pollutants."

108. Clive R. Belfield, Henry M. Levin, and Rachel Rosen, *The Economic Value of Opportunity Youth* (Washington, DC: Corporation for National and Community Service, 2012); Martha Ross and Nicole Prchal Svajlenka, "Employment and Disconnection among Teens and Young Adults: The Role of Place, Race, and Education," *Brookings,* May 24, 2016, www.brookings.edu/research/employment-and-disconnection-among-teens-and-young-adults-the-role-of-place-race-and-education.

109. Belfield, Levin, and Rosen, *Economic Value.*

110. Henning, "Criminalizing Normal Adolescent Behavior"; Henning, "The Challenge of Race and Crime in a Free Society: The Racial Divide in Fifty Years of Juvenile Justice Reform"; Novak, "Association between Experiences."

111. Ross and Svajlenka, "Employment and Disconnection."

112. Erin Horvat and James Davis, "Schools as Sites for Transformation: Exploring the Contribution of Habitus," *Youth & Society* 42, no. 1 (2010): 142–70, https://doi.org/10.1177/0044118X09358846; Rios, *Punished;* Shepherd Zeldin et al., "Youth-Adult Partnership and Youth Civic Development: Cross-National Analyses for Scholars and Field Professionals," *Youth & Society* 49, no. 7 (2017): 851–78, https://doi.org/10.1177/0044118X15595153.

113. William Darity Jr. and Dania Frank, "The Economics of Reparations," *American Economic Review* 93, no. 2 (2003): 326–29, https://doi.org/10.1257/000282803321947281.

114. Darity and Mullen, *From Here to Equality,* 490.

115. John M. Bridgeland, Erin S. Ingram, and Matthew Atwell, *A Bridge to Reconnection: A Plan for Reconnecting One Million Opportunity Youth Each Year through Federal Funding Streams* (Washington, DC: Civic Enterprises, 2016), 28.

116. M. Anne Visser, "Beyond Labor Markets and Schools: Community-Based Youth Serving Organizations and the Integration of Puerto Rican and Dominican Disconnected Youth in New York City," *Centro Journal* 30, no. 1 (2018): 4–31.

117. Maria Veronica Svetaz et al., "A Community Based Participatory Research (CBPR) Journey Bringing Culture and Family to the Center of an Intervention to Promote Positive Youth Development and Reproductive Health: The Encuentro

Project," *Journal of Adolescent Health* 58, no. 2 (2016): S5, https://doi.org/10.1016/j.jadohealth.2015.10.026; Zeldin et al., "Youth-Adult Partnership."

118. YouthBuild, "YouthBuild," 2018, www.youthbuild.org.

119. Rios, "Hyper-Criminalization," 44.

120. Peter Frumkin et al., "Inside National Service: AmeriCorps' Impact on Participants," *Journal of Policy Analysis and Management* 28, no. 3 (2009): 394–416; Peter Z. Schochet, John Burghardt, and Sheena McConnell, "Does Job Corps Work? Impact Findings from the National Job Corps Study," *American Economic Review* 98, no. 5 (2008): 1864–86, https://doi.org/10.1257/aer.98.5.1864.

121. Andrew Wiegand et al., *Adapting to Local Context: Findings from the Youthbuild Evaluation Implementation Study*, MDRC/ERIC, Feb. 2015, https://eric.ed.gov/?id=ED558510.

122. Cynthia Miller et al., *Building a Future: Interim Impact Findings from the YouthBuild Evaluation*, MDRC/ERIC, Nov. 2016, https://eric.ed.gov/?id=ED571142.

123. YouthBuild, "YouthBuild."

124. Dan Bloom, *Programs and Policies to Assist High School Dropouts in the Transition to Adulthood* (Washington, DC: MDRC, 2010), https://files.eric.ed.gov/fulltext/EJ883080.pdf.

125. Horvat and Davis, "Schools as Sites for Transformation," 143, 158, 167.

126. Anna J. Egalite, Brian Kisida, and Marcus A. Winters, "Representation in the Classroom: The Effect of Own-Race Teachers on Student Achievement," *Economics of Education Review* 45 (2015): 44–52; Alena Friedrich et al., "Pygmalion Effects in the Classroom: Teacher Expectancy Effects on Students' Math Achievement," *Contemporary Educational Psychology* 41 (2015): 1–12, https://doi.org/10.1016/j.cedpsych.2014.10.006; Seth Gershenson, Stephen B. Holt, and Nicholas W. Papageorge, "Who Believes in Me? The Effect of Student-Teacher Demographic Match on Teacher Expectations," *Economics of Education Review* 52 (2016): 209–24; Hana Turner, Christine M. Rubie-Davies, and Melinda Webber, "Teacher Expectations, Ethnicity and the Achievement Gap," *New Zealand Journal of Educational Studies* 50, no. 1 (2015): 55–69.

127. Davido Dupree, Tirzah R. Spencer, and Margaret Beale Spencer, "Stigma, Stereotypes and Resilience Identities: The Relationship between Identity Processes and Resilience Processes among Black American Adolescents," in *Youth Resilience and Culture* (Dordrecht: Springer, 2015), 117–29, https://doi.org/10.1007/978-94-017-9415-2_9; Shawn C. T. Jones and Enrique W. Neblett, "Racial-Ethnic Protective Factors and Mechanisms in Psychosocial Prevention and Intervention Programs for Black Youth," *Clinical Child and Family Psychology Review* 19, no. 2 (2016): 134–61, https://doi.org/10.1007/s10567-016-0201-6; Catherine Panter-Brick, "Culture and Resilience: Next Steps for Theory and Practice," in *Youth Resilience and Culture* (Dordrecht: Springer, 2015), 233–44, https://doi.org/10.1007/978-94-017-9415-2_17.

128. Satyasree Upadhyayula et al., "The Association of Ethnic Pride with Health and Social Outcomes among Young Black and Latino Men after Release from Jail," *Youth & Society* 49, no. 8 (2017): 1057–76.

129. Joanna L. Williams and Nancy L. Deutsch, "Beyond Between-Group Differences: Considering Race, Ethnicity, and Culture in Research on Positive Youth Development Programs," *Applied Developmental Science* 20, no. 3 (2016): 203–13, https://doi.org/10.1080/10888691.2015.1113880.

130. Lisa Wexler et al., "Preliminary Evaluation of a School-Based Youth Leadership and Prevention Program in Rural Alaska Native Communities," *School Mental Health* 9, no. 2 (2017): 172–83, https://doi.org/10.1007/s12310-016-9203-2.

131. BreAnna L. Davis et al., "Racial Socialization, Private Regard, and Behavior Problems in African American Youth: Global Self-Esteem as a Mediator," *Journal of Child and Family Studies* 26, no. 3 (2017): 709–20, https://doi.org/10.1007/s10826-016-0601-8; Cheryl Grills et al., "Culture, Racial Socialization, and Positive African American Youth Development," *Journal of Black Psychology* 42, no. 4 (2016): 343–73, https://doi.org/10.1177/0095798415578004.

132. Kimberly Hoagwood and Holly D. Erwin, "Effectiveness of School-Based Mental Health Services for Children: A 10-Year Research Review," *Journal of Child and Family Studies* 6, no. 4 (1997): 435–51, https://doi.org/10.1023/A:1025045412689; Amanda L. Sanchez et al., "The Effectiveness of School-Based Mental Health Services for Elementary-Aged Children: A Meta-Analysis," *Journal of the American Academy of Child & Adolescent Psychiatry* 57, no. 3 (2018): 153–65, https://doi.org/10.1016/j.jaac.2017.11.022.

133. Emily J. Aron and Jeff Q. Bostic, "Because That's Where the Kids Are: Willie Sutton's First-Grade Teacher on Why She Taught School," *Journal of the American Academy of Child & Adolescent Psychiatry* 57, no. 3 (2018): 141–42, https://doi.org/10.1016/j.jaac.2018.01.001.

134. Sanchez et al., "Effectiveness of School-Based Mental Health Services."

135. Lisa H. Jaycox et al., "Support for Students Exposed to Trauma: A Pilot Study," *School Mental Health* 1, no. 2 (2009): 49–60, https://doi.org/10.1007/s12310-009-9007-8; Meg Walkley and Tory L. Cox, "Building Trauma-Informed Schools and Communities," *Children & Schools* 35, no. 2 (2013): 123–26, https://doi.org/10.1093/cs/cdt007.

136. Jessica R. Goodkind, Marianna D. LaNoue, and Jaime Milford, "Adaptation and Implementation of Cognitive Behavioral Intervention for Trauma in Schools with American Indian Youth," *Journal of Clinical Child & Adolescent Psychology* 39, no. 6 (2010): 858–72, https://doi.org/10.1080/15374416.2010.517166.

137. Martha Frias-Armenta et al., "Restorative Justice: A Model of School Violence Prevention," *Science Journal of Education* 6, no. 1 (2018): 39–45; Mara Schiff, "Dignity, Disparity and Desistance: Effective Restorative Justice Strate-

gies to Plug the 'School-to-Prison Pipeline,'" UCLA: The Civil Rights Project, Jan. 2013, https://escholarship.org/uc/item/6kw7w8s8; Anita Wadhwa, *Restorative Justice in Urban Schools: Disrupting the School-to-Prison Pipeline* (New York: Routledge, 2015).

138. Russell J. Skiba and Daniel J. Losen, "From Reaction to Prevention: Turning the Page on School Discipline," *American Educator* 39, no. 4 (2016): 4.

139. Jason Langberg and Angela Ciolfi, "Busting the School-to-Prison Pipeline," *Education Digest* 82, no. 5 (2017): 42–47.

140. Rios, *Punished,* 170.

141. Visser, "Beyond Labor Markets and Schools."

142. Noah E. Borrero et al., "School as a Context for 'Othering' Youth and Promoting Cultural Assets," *Teachers College Record* 114, no. 2 (2012): 1–37; Visser, "Beyond Labor Markets and Schools."

143. Nolan, *Police in the Hallways;* Borrero et al., "School as a Context."

144. Elan C. Hope and Margaret Beale Spencer, "Civic Engagement as an Adaptive Coping Response to Conditions of Inequality: An Application of Phenomenological Variant of Ecological Systems Theory (PVEST)," in *Handbook on Positive Development of Minority Children and Youth,* ed. Natasha J. Cabrera and Birgit Leyendecker (Cham: Springer, 2017), 421–35, https://doi.org/10.1007/978-3-319-43645-6_25.

145. James Sloam, "New Voice, Less Equal: The Civic and Political Engagement of Young People in the United States and Europe," *Comparative Political Studies* 47, no. 5 (2014): 665, https://doi.org/10.1177/0010414012453441.

146. Pinard, *Poor, Black and "Wanted,"* 863.

147. Kerrison, Cobbina, and Bender, "'Your Pants Won't Save You'"; Rios, *Punished.*

148. Charleston Area Convention and Visitor's Bureau, "Explore Charleston," 2018, www.charlestoncvb.com.

149. Eugene Scott, "Black Lives Matter Protesters Confront Hillary Clinton at a Fundraiser," *CNNPolitics,* Feb. 25, 2016, www.cnn.com/2016/02/25/politics/hillary-clinton-black-lives-matter-whichhillary/index.html.

CHAPTER 3. "MORE THAN A SHELL"

1. Gil Batle, "Hatched in Prison," 2016, www.gilbatle.com/hatched-in-prison.

2. Matthew R. Durose, Alexia D. Cooper, and Howard N. Snyder, *Recidivism of Prisoners Released in 30 States in 2005: Patterns from 2005 to 2010* (Washington, DC: US Department of Justice, 2014); Christy A. Visher and Jeremy Travis, "Life on the Outside: Returning Home after Incarceration," *Prison Journal* 91, no. .3_suppl (2011): 102S–19S.

3. Loïc Wacquant, "Prisoner Reentry as Myth and Ceremony," *Dialectical Anthropology* 34, no. 4 (2010): 605–20, https://doi.org/10.1007/s10624-010-9215-5.

4. Reuben Jonathan Miller, *Halfway Home: Race, Punishment, and the After-life of Mass Incarceration* (New York: Little, Brown, 2021), https://find.library .duke.edu/catalog/DUKE009852438.

5. Tasseli McKay et al., "Family Life before and during Incarceration," *Journal of Offender Rehabilitation* 57, no. 2 (2018): 96–114, https://doi.org/10.1080 /10509674.2018.1441209.

6. Loïc Wacquant, "The Curious Eclipse of Prison Ethnography in the Age of Mass Incarceration," *Ethnography* 3, no. 4 (2002): 371–97.

7. Steven Shavell, "A Simple Model of Optimal Deterrence and Incapacita-tion," NBER Working Paper Series, Working Paper 20747, National Bureau of Economic Research, Cambridge, MA, Dec. 2014, https://doi.org/10.3386 /w20747.

8. Wildeman and Wang, "Mass Incarceration," 1466.

9. Christopher Wildeman, Maria D. Fitzpatrick, and Alyssa W. Goldman, "Conditions of Confinement in American Prisons and Jails," *Annual Review of Law and Social Science* 14, no. 1 (2018): 29–47, https://doi.org/10.1146 /annurev-lawsocsci-101317-031025.

10. Terry A. Kupers, *Solitary* (Berkeley: University of California Press, 2017), www.ucpress.edu/book/9780520292239/solitary; Travis, Western, and Red-burn, "Growth of Incarceration"; Wildeman and Wang, "Mass Incarceration."

11. Craig Haney, "Restricting the Use of Solitary Confinement," *Annual Review of Criminology* 1, no. 1 (2018): 285–310, https://doi.org/10.1146/annurev-criminol-032317-092326; Terry A. Kupers, "Trauma and Its Sequelae in Male Prisoners: Effects of Confinement, Overcrowding, and Diminished Services," *American Journal of Orthopsychiatry* 66, no. 2 (1996): 189–96; Kupers, *Solitary.*

12. Alessandro De Giorgi, "Back to Nothing: Prisoner Reentry and Neoliberal Neglect," *Social Justice* 44, no. 1 (2017): 83–120.

13. Miller, *Halfway Home.*

14. Western, *Homeward.*

15. Massoglia and Pridemore, "Incarceration and Health"; Wildeman and Wang, "Mass Incarceration."

16. I. A. Binswanger et al., "Release from Prison: A High Risk of Death for Former Inmates," *New England Journal of Medicine* 356, no. 2 (2007): 157–65.

17. E. A. Wang et al., "Incarceration, Incident Hypertension, and Access to Health Care: Findings from the Coronary Artery Risk Development in Young Adults (CARDIA) Study," *Archives of Internal Medicine* 169, no. 7 (2009): 687–93.

18. Christopher Wildeman, Kristin Turney, and Jason Schnittker, "The Hedonic Consequences of Punishment Revisited," *Journal of Criminal Law & Criminology* 104, no. 1 (2014): 133; Wildeman and Wang, "Mass Incarceration"; Jason Schnittker, Michael Massoglia, and Christopher Uggen, "Out and Down: Incarceration and Psychiatric Disorders," *Journal of Health and Social Behavior* 53, no. 4 (2012): 448–64, https://doi.org/10.1177/0022146512453928; Kristin Turney, Hedwig Lee, and Megan Comfort, "Discrimination and Psychological Distress among Recently Released Male Prisoners," *American Journal of Men's Health* 7, no. 6 (2013): 482–93.

19. Miller, *Halfway Home*.

20. Christy Visher, Jennifer Yahner, and Nancy La Vigne, *Life after Prison: Tracking the Experiences of Male Prisoners Returning to Chicago, Cleveland, and Houston* (Washington, DC: Urban Institute, Justice Policy Center, 2010).

21. Danielle Wallace et al., "Examining the Role of Familial Support during Prison and after Release on Post-Incarceration Mental Health," *International Journal of Offender Therapy and Comparative Criminology* 60, no. 1 (2016): 3–20, https://doi.org/10.1177/0306624X14548023.

22. Khan et al., "Dissolution"; Thomas J. Mowen and Christy A. Visher, "Changing the Ties That Bind," *Criminology & Public Policy* 15, no. 2 (2016): 503–28.

23. Robert Apel et al., "Collateral Effects of Incarceration: Effects on Marriage and Divorce," *Journal of Quantitative Criminology* 26 (2010): 269–300; Leonard Lopoo and Bruce Western, "Incarceration and the Formation and Stability of Marital Unions," *Journal of Marriage and Family* 67, no. 3 (2005): 721–34.

24. Adrian Cherney and Robin Fitzgerald, "Finding and Keeping a Job: The Value and Meaning of Employment for Parolees," *International Journal of Offender Therapy and Comparative Criminology* 60, no. 1 (2016): 21–37, https://doi.org/10.1177/0306624X14548858.

25. Sarah Lageson and Christopher Uggen, "How Work Affects Crime—and Crime Affects Work—over the Life Course," in *Handbook of Life-Course Criminology*, ed. Chris L. Gibson and Marvin D. Krohn (New York: Springer, 2013), 201–12; Christy A. Visher, Sara A. Debus-Sherrill, and Jennifer Yahner, "Employment after Prison: A Longitudinal Study of Former Prisoners," *Justice Quarterly* 28, no. 5 (2011): 698–718.

26. Catrina Palmer and Johnna Christian, "Work Matters: Formerly Incarcerated Men's Resiliency in Reentry," *Equality, Diversity and Inclusion* 38, no. 5 (2019): 583–98, https://doi.org/10.1108/EDI-10-2018-0177.

27. Dina R. Rose and Todd R. Clear, "Incarceration, Social Capital, and Crime: Examining the Unintended Consequences of Incarceration," *Criminology* 36, no. 3 (1998): 441–79.

28. Shawn D. Bushway, Michael A. Stoll, and David Weiman, eds., *Barriers to Reentry? The Labor Market for Released Prisoners in Post-Industrial America* (New York: Russell Sage, 2007).

29. Sarah Esther Lageson, Mike Vuolo, and Christopher Uggen, "Legal Ambiguity in Managerial Assessments of Criminal Records," *Law & Social Inquiry* 40, no. 1 (2015): 175–204, https://doi.org/10.1111/lsi.12066; Christopher Uggen et al., "The Edge of Stigma: An Experimental Audit of the Effects of Low-Level Criminal Records on Employment," *Criminology* 52, no. 4 (2014): 627–54, https://doi.org/10.1111/1745-9125.12051.

30. Devah Pager and Lincoln Quillian, "Walking the Talk? What Employers Say versus What They Do," *American Sociological Review* 70, no. 3 (2005): 355–80.

31. Devah Pager, "The Mark of a Criminal Record," *American Journal of Sociology* 108, no. 5 (2003): 937–75.

32. Robert Brame et al., "Cumulative Prevalence of Arrest from Ages 8 to 23 in a National Sample," *Pediatrics* 129, no. 1 (2012): 21–27; Devah Pager, *Marked: Race, Crime, and Finding Work in an Era of Mass Incarceration* (Chicago: University of Chicago Press, 2007); Devah Pager, Bruce Western, and Naomi Sugie, "Sequencing Disadvantage: Barriers to Employment Facing Young Black and White Men with Criminal Records," *ANNALS of the American Academy of Political and Social Science* 623, no. 1 (2009): 195–213.

33. Priya Baskaran, "Respect the Hustle: Necessity Entrepreneurship, Returning Citizens, and Social Enterprise Strategies," *Maryland Law Review* 78 (2018): 323; Amy P. Meek, "Street Vendors, Taxicabs, and Exclusion Zones: The Impact of Collateral Consequences of Criminal Convictions at the Local Level," *Ohio State Law Journal* 75, no. 1 (2014): 1.

34. Visher, Yahner, and La Vigne, *Life after Prison.*

35. Bruce Western, "The Impact of Incarceration on Wage Mobility and Inequality," *American Sociological Review* 67, no. 4 (2002): 526–46, http://dx.doi.org.proxy.lib.duke.edu/10.2307/3088944; Bruce Western, Jeffrey R. Kling, and David F. Weiman, "The Labor Market Consequences of Incarceration," *NCCD News* 47, no. 3 (2001): 410–27.

36. Mary Pattillo, David Weiman, and Bruce Western, *Imprisoning America: The Social Effects of Mass Incarceration* (New York: Russell Sage, 2004); Bruce Western and Becky Pettit, "Incarceration and Social Inequality," *Daedalus: The Journal of the American Academy of Arts & Sciences* 139, no. 3 (2010): 8–19.

37. Travis, Western, and Redburn, "Growth of Incarceration," 258.

38. Khaing Zaw, Darrick Hamilton, and William Darity, "Race, Wealth and Incarceration: Results from the National Longitudinal Survey of Youth," *Race and Social Problems* 8, no. 1 (2016): 103–15.

39. Visher and Travis, "Life on the Outside," 1124.

40. Pamela K. Lattimore et al., "Prisoner Reentry Services: What Worked for SVORI Evaluation Participants," Washington, DC: National Institute of Justice, 2012.

41. C. Visher et al., "Evaluating the Long-Term Effects of Prisoner Reentry Services on Recidivism: What Types of Services Matter?," *Justice Quarterly* 34, no. 1 (2017): 136–65.

42. Prowse, Weaver, and Meares, "The State from Below," 1442.

43. Kirk and Wakefield, "Collateral Consequences of Punishment."

44. Charles E. Lewis Jr, Irwin Garfinkel, and Qin Gao, "Incarceration and Unwed Fathers in Fragile Families," *Journal of Sociology & Social Welfare* 34, no. 3 (2007): 77.

45. Amanda Geller, Irwin Garfinkel, and Bruce Western, "The Effects of Incarceration on Employment and Wages: An Analysis of the Fragile Families Survey," Center for Research on Child Wellbeing, Working Papers 932, Princeton University, School of Public and International Affairs, Center for Research on Child Wellbeing (2006), 1.

46. Western, "The Impact of Incarceration."

47. Thomas P. Bonczar, *Prevalence of Imprisonment in the U.S. Population, 1974-2001* (Washington, DC: US Department of Justice, 2003).

48. Visher and Travis, "Life on the Outside"; Philip Taylor, "Age and Work: International Perspectives," *Social Policy and Society* 3, no. 2 (2004): 163–70, https://doi.org/10.1017/S1474746403001623.

49. John Gramlich, "The Gap between the Number of Blacks and Whites in Prison Is Shrinking," Pew Research Center, April 30, 2019, www.pewresearch.org/fact-tank/2018/01/12/shrinking-gap-between-number-of-blacks-and-whites-in-prison.

50. Darity and Mullen, *From Here to Equality.*

51. Sharon Yamato, "Civil Liberties Act of 1988," in *Densho Encyclopedia* (Seattle, WA: Densho, 2020), http://encyclopedia.densho.org/Civil_Liberties_Act_of_1988.

52. Shannon et al., "Growth, Scope, and Spatial Distribution."

53. Pamela K. Lattimore, Beth M. Huebner, and Faye S. Taxman, *Handbook on Moving Corrections and Sentencing Forward: Building on the Record* (Abingdon, UK: Routledge, 2020).

54. Pager, *Marked.*

55. Lageson and Uggen, "How Work Affects Crime."

56. James M. Quane, William Julius Wilson, and Jackelyn Hwang, "Black Men and the Struggle for Work: Social and Economic Barriers Persist," *Education Next* 15, no. 2 (2015): 22–30.

57. Kevin T. Schnepel, "Economics of Incarceration," *Australian Economic Review* 49, no. 4 (2016): 515–23; Arne L. Kalleberg and Steven P. Vallas, eds., *Precarious Work* (Bingley: Emerald Group, 2017).

58. Travis, Western, and Redburn, "Growth of Incarceration"; Mowen and Visher, "Changing the Ties."

59. Raelene M. Leach, Teresa Burgess, and Chris Holmwood, "Could Recidivism in Prisoners Be Linked to Traumatic Grief? A Review of the Evidence," *International Journal of Prisoner Health* 4, no. 2 (2008): 104–19.

60. Gareth Hopkin et al., "Interventions at the Transition from Prison to the Community for Prisoners with Mental Illness: A Systematic Review," *Administration and Policy in Mental Health and Mental Health Services Research* 45, no. 4 (2018): 623–34.

61. Michelle S. Phelps, "Mass Probation from Micro to Macro: Tracing the Expansion and Consequences of Community Supervision," *Annual Review of Criminology* 3, no. 1 (2020); Miller, *Halfway Home.*

62. Allegra McLeod, "Prison Abolition and Grounded Justice," *Georgetown Law Faculty Publications and Other Works,* Scholarly Commons (2015): https:// scholarship.law.georgetown.edu/facpub/1490.

63. R. Feinberg and Tasseli McKay, "Connecting Older Prison Reentrants to Health Coverage and Public Benefits: Miami-Dade County's Criminal Mental Health Project" (Research Triangle Park, NC: RTI International, 2018), www .rti.org/publication/miami-dade-county%E2%80%99s-criminal-mental-health-project/fulltext.pdf.

64. Turney, Lee, and Comfort, "Discrimination and Psychological Distress."

65. Amanda Agan and Sonja Starr, "Ban the Box, Criminal Records, and Racial Discrimination: A Field Experiment," *Quarterly Journal of Economics* 133, no. 1 (2018): 191–235; Pager, *Marked;* Uggen et al., "The Edge of Stigma."

66. Jennifer Hickes Lundquist, Devah Pager, and Eiko Strader, "Does a Criminal Past Predict Worker Performance? Evidence from One of America's Largest Employers," *Social Forces* 96, no. 3 (2018): 1039–68.

67. Agan and Starr, "Ban the Box"; Jennifer L. Doleac and Benjamin Hansen, "Does 'Ban the Box' Help or Hurt Low-Skilled Workers? Statistical Discrimination and Employment Outcomes When Criminal Histories Are Hidden," NBER Working Paper Series, Working Paper 22469, National Bureau of Economic Research, Cambridge, MA, July 2016, https://doi.org/10.3386 /w22469.

68. Jennifer Bronson, Laura M. Maruschak, and Marcus Berzofsky, "Disabilities among Prison and Jail Inmates, 2011–12" (Washington, DC: US Department of Justice Bureau of Justice Statistics, 2015).

69. McLeod, "Prison Abolition," 1161.

70. Maya Angelou, "Caged Bird," in *Shaker, Why Don't You Sing?* (New York: Random House, 1983).

71. CBS News, "Gil Batle," 2015.

CHAPTER 4. "I ALWAYS PUT THE BURDEN ON HER SHOULDERS"

1. Gina Clayton et al., *The Political Isolation and Resistance of Women with Incarcerated Loved Ones* (Oakland, CA: Essie Justice Group, 2018), 67.

2. Megan Comfort, "'Papa's House': The Prison as Domestic and Social Satellite," *Ethnography* 3, no. 4 (2002): 470.

3. Alyse Emdur, *Prison Landscapes* (London: Four Corners, 2013), www.alyseemdur.com/4_Prison%20Landscapes/index.php.

4. Donald Clemmer, *The Prison Community* (New York: Holt, Rinehart and Winston, 1958).

5. Megan Comfort, *Doing Time Together: Love and Family in the Shadow of the Prison* (Chicago: University of Chicago Press, 2008).

6. Adrienne Roberts, *Gendered States of Punishment and Welfare : Feminist Political Economy, Primitive Accumulation and the Law* (London: Routledge, 2016), 93, https://doi.org/10.4324/9781315542362.

7. Jennifer Bronson and E. Ann Carson, *Prisoners in 2017* (Washington, DC: US Department of Justice, 2019), www.bjs.gov/content/pub/pdf/p17.pdf.

8. Peter K. Enns et al., "What Percentage of Americans Have Ever Had a Family Member Incarcerated? Evidence from the Family History of Incarceration Survey (FamHIS)," *Socius* 5 (2019): https://doi.org/10.1177/2378023119829332; Christopher Wildeman and Hedwig Lee, "Women's Health in the Era of Mass Incarceration," *Annual Review of Sociology* 47, no. 1 (2021): 543-65, https://doi.org/10.1146/annurev-soc-081320-113303.

9. Silvia Federici, *Revolution at Point Zero: Housework, Reproduction, and Feminist Struggle* (London: PM Press, 2012).

10. Bonczar, *Prevalence of Imprisonment.*

11. Wendy Sawyer, *The Gender Divide: Tracking Women's State Prison Growth* (Northampton, MA: Prison Policy Initiative, 2018), www.prisonpolicy.org/reports/women_overtime.html.

12. Creasie Finney Hairston, "Family Ties during Imprisonment: Important to Whom and for What?," *Journal of Sociology and Social Welfare* 18, no. 1 (1991): 85-104; Creasie Finney Hairston and William Oliver, "Women's Experiences with Men's Incarceration and Reentry," in *Women and Girls in the Criminal Justice System,* ed. Russ Immarigeon (Kingston, NJ: Civic Research Institute, 2011), 48-1-5, www.civicresearchinstitute.com/toc/WGB2TOC.pdf; Creasie Finney Hairston, "Family Ties during Imprisonment: Do They Influence Future Criminal Activity?," *Federal Probation* 52, no. 1 (1988): 48-52; Laura T. Fishman, *Women at the Wall: A Study of Prisoners' Wives Doing Time on the Outside* (Albany: State University of New York Press, 1990).

13. Christopher Wildeman, "Imprisonment and (Inequality in) Population Health," *Social Science Research* 41, no. 1 (2012): 74-91.

14. Saneta deVuono-Powell et al., *Who Pays? The True Cost of Incarceration on Families* (Oakland, CA: Ella Baker Center, Forward Together, Research Action Design, 2015), http://ellabakercenter.org/who-pays-the-true-cost-of-incarceration-on-families.

15. Jeff Christian, Johnna Mellow, and Shenique Thomas, "Social and Economic Implications of Family Connections to Prisoners," *Journal of Criminal Justice* 34, no. 4 (2006): 443–52; Johnna Christian, "Riding the Bus: Barriers to Prison Visitation and Family Management Strategies," *Journal of Contemporary Criminal Justice* 21, no. 1 (2005): 31–48; Clayton et al., *Political Isolation and Resistance;* Megan Comfort, et al., "The Costs of Incarceration for Families of Prisoners," *International Review of the Red Cross* 98, no. 903 (2017): 1–16; deVuono-Powell et al., *Who Pays?*

16. Drew Kukorowski, "The Price to Call Home: State-Sanctioned Monopolization in the Prison Phone Industry" (Northampton, MA: Prison Policy Initiative, 2012).

17. Olga Grinstead et al., "The Financial Cost of Maintaining Relationships with Incarcerated African American Men: A Survey of Women Prison Visitors," *Journal of African-American Men* 6, no. 1 (2001): 59–70.

18. deVuono-Powell et al., *Who Pays?*

19. Amanda Geller, Irwin Garfinkel, and Bruce Western, "Paternal Incarceration and Support for Children in Fragile Families," *Demography* 48, no. 1 (2011): 25–47.

20. Ofira Schwartz-Soicher, Amanda Geller, and Irwin Garfinkel, "The Effect of Paternal Incarceration on Material Hardship," *Social Service Review* 85, no. 3 (2011): 447–73; Amanda Geller and Allyson Walker Franklin, "Paternal Incarceration and the Housing Security of Urban Mothers," *Journal of Marriage and Family* 76, no. 2 (2014): 411–27.

21. Lopoo and Western, "Incarceration"; Michael Massoglia, Brianna Remster, and Ryan D. King, "Stigma or Separation? Understanding the Incarceration-Divorce Relationship," *Social Forces* 90, no. 1 (2011): 133–55, https://doi.org/10.1093/sf/90.1.133; Kristin Turney, "Hopelessly Devoted? Relationship Quality during and after Incarceration," *Journal of Marriage and Family* 77, no. 2 (2015): 480–95, https://doi.org/10.1111/jomf.12174; Khan et al., "Dissolution."

22. Clayton et al., *Political Isolation and Resistance,* 48.

23. Enns et al., "What Percentage of Americans."

24. Wildeman and Lee, "Women's Health."

25. Hedwig Lee et al., "Racial Inequalities in Connectedness to Imprisoned Individuals in the United States," *Du Bois Review: Social Science Research on Race* 12, no. 2 (2015): 269–82.

26. Hedwig Lee and Christopher Wildeman, "Things Fall Apart: Health Consequences of Mass Imprisonment for African American Women," *Review of*

Black Political Economy 40, no. 1 (2013): 41, https://doi.org/10.1007/s12114-011-9112-4.

27. Angela Bruns and Hedwig Lee, "Partner Incarceration and Women's Substance Use," *Journal of Marriage and Family* 82, no. 4 (2020): 1178–96, https://doi.org/10.1111/jomf.12659.

28. Wacquant, "Prisoner Reentry"; Noah D. Zatz, "Get to Work or Go to Jail: State Violence and the Racialized Production of Precarious Work," *Law & Social Inquiry* 45, no. 2 (2020): 304–38, https://doi.org/10.1017/lsi.2019.56.

29. Matthew DelSesto, "Contested Theories of Prison Labor Practice," *Sociology Compass* 15, no. 7 (2021), https://doi.org/10.1111/soc4.12888.

30. Beth E. Richie, "The Social Impact of Mass Incarceration on Women," in *Invisible Punishment: The Collateral Consequences of Mass Imprisonment*, ed. Marc Mauer and Meda Chesney-Lind (New York: New Press, 2011), 146.

31. Comfort, *Doing Time Together;* Clayton et al., *Political Isolation and Resistance;* deVuono-Powell et al., *Who Pays?*

32. Comfort, *Doing Time Together*, 159.

33. Comfort, 108.

34. Megan Comfort, "'A Twenty-Hour-a-Day Job': The Impact of Frequent Low-Level Criminal Justice Involvement on Family Life," *ANNALS of the American Academy of Political and Social Science* 665, no. 1 (2016): 71, https://doi.org/10.1177/0002716215625038.

35. Federici, *Revolution at Point Zero*, 16.

36. Arlie Hochschild and Anne Machung, *The Second Shift: Working Families and the Revolution at Home* (New York: Penguin, 2012).

37. Ashley Provencher and James M. Conway, "Health Effects of Family Member Incarceration in the United States: A Meta-Analysis and Cost Study," *Children and Youth Services Review* 103 (2019): 87–99, https://doi.org/10.1016/j.childyouth.2019.05.029; Wildeman and Lee, "Women's Health."

38. Christopher Wildeman, Alyssa W. Goldman, and Hedwig Lee, "Health Consequences of Family Member Incarceration for Adults in the Household," *Public Health Reports* 134, no. 1_suppl (2019): 15S–21S, https://doi.org/10.1177/0033354918807974.

39. Kerry M. Green et al., "Impact of Adult Sons' Incarceration on African American Mothers' Psychological Distress," *Journal of Marriage and Family* 68, no. 2 (2006): 430–41.

40. Christopher Wildeman, Jason Schnittker, and Kristin Turney, "Despair by Association? The Mental Health of Mothers with Children by Recently Incarcerated Fathers," *American Sociological Review* 77, no. 2 (2012): 216–43.

41. Christopher Wildeman, Hedwig Lee, and Megan Comfort, "A New Vulnerable Population? The Health of the Female Romantic Partners of Recently Released Male Prisoners," *Women's Health Issues* 26, no. 3 (2013): 335–40.

42. Bruns and Lee, "Partner Incarceration."

43. Catherine Sirois, "The Strain of Sons' Incarceration on Mothers' Health," *Social Science & Medicine* 264 (2020): 113264.

44. Lee and Wildeman, "Things Fall Apart."

45. Hedwig Lee et al., "A Heavy Burden: The Cardiovascular Health Conse- quences of Having a Family Member Incarcerated," *American Journal of Public Health* 104, no. 3 (2014): 421–27.

46. Wildeman and Lee, "Women's Health"; Maria R, Khan et al., "Incarcera- tion, Sex with an STI- or HIV-Infected Partner, and Infection with an STI or HIV in Bushwick, Brooklyn, NY: A Social Network Perspective," *American Jour- nal of Public Health* 101, no. 6 (2011): 11.

47. Tasseli McKay et al., "Intimate Partner Violence in Couples Navigating Incarceration and Reentry," *Journal of Offender Rehabilitation* 57, no. 5 (2018): 273–93, https://doi.org/10.1080/10509674.2018.1487897.

48. Megan Comfort et al., "Partnerships after Prison: Couple Relationships during Reentry," *Journal of Offender Rehabilitation* 57, no. 2 (2018): 188–205, https://doi.org/10.1080/10509674.2018.1441208.

49. Hairston and Oliver, , "Women's Experiences"; William Oliver and Creasie Finney Hairston, "Intimate Partner Violence during the Transition from Prison to the Community: Perspectives of Incarcerated African American Men," *Jour- nal of Aggression, Maltreatment & Trauma* 16, no. 3 (2008): 258–76, https://doi .org/10.1080/10926770801925577.

50. Richie, "Social Impact," 147.

51. E. Ann Carson and Joseph Mulako-Wangota, *Count of Total Releases* (Washington, DC: US Department of Justice, 2020), https://www.bjs.gov/index .cfm?ty=nps.

52. Valerie A. Clark and Grant Duwe, "Distance Matters: Examining the Fac- tors That Impact Prisoner Visitation in Minnesota," *Criminal Justice and Behavior* 44, no. 2 (2017): 184–204, https://doi.org/10.1177/0093854816667416.

53. Mimi Cantwell, *Prisoners in 1978*, National Prison Statistics Program (Washington, DC: US Department of Justice, 1979), www.bjs.gov/content/pub /pdf/psfi78.pdf; E. Ann Carson, *Prisoners in 2018* (Washington, DC: US Depart- ment of Justice, 2020), www.bjs.gov/index.cfm?ty=pbdetail&iid=6846.

54. John Roman et al., *Impact and Cost Benefit Analysis of the Maryland Reentry Partnership Initiative* (Washington, DC: Urban Institute, Justice Policy Center, 2007), http://webarchive.urban.org/UploadedPDF/311421_Maryland_ Reentry.pdf.

55. Carson and Mulako-Wangota, *Count of Total Releases.*

56. Lee et al., "A Heavy Burden."

57. Enns et al., "What Percentage of Americans."

58. Dalia Giedrimiene and Rachel King, "Abstract 207: Burden of Cardiovas- cular Disease (CVD) on Economic Cost. Comparison of Outcomes in US and

Europe," *Circulation: Cardiovascular Quality and Outcomes* 10, no. suppl_3 (March 2017): x, https://doi.org/10.1161/circoutcomes.10.suppl_3.207.

59. Evelyn Bromet et al., "Cross-National Epidemiology of DSM-IV Major Depressive Episode," *BMC Medicine* 9, no. 1 (2011): 90, https://doi.org/10.1186/1741-7015-9-90; Enns et al., "What Percentage of Americans."

60. Wildeman, Schnittker, and Turney, "Despair by Association?"

61. Gordon Parker et al., "Costs of the Principal Mood Disorders: A Study of Comparative Direct and Indirect Costs Incurred by Those with Bipolar I, Bipolar II and Unipolar Disorders," *Journal of Affective Disorders* 149, no. 1 (2012): 46–55, https://doi.org/10.1016/j.jad.2012.10.002.

62. Katherine Beckett, "The Politics, Promise, and Peril of Criminal Justice Reform in the Context of Mass Incarceration," *Annual Review of Criminology* 1, no. 1 (2018): 235–59, https://doi.org/10.1146/annurev-criminol-032317-092458.

63. Council on State Governments. *Confined and Costly.*

64. United States Department of Agriculture, "USDA Proposes to Close SNAP Automatic Eligibility Loophole," press release, July 23, 2019 www.usda.gov/media/press-releases/2019/07/23/usda-proposes-close-snap-automatic-eligibility-loophole.

65. Springboard to Opportunities, "Magnolia Mother's Trust," 2020 http://springboardto.org/index.php/page/the-magnolia-mothers-trust.

66. Elaine Maag, Donald Marron, and Erin Huffer, *Expanding the Earned Income Tax Credit: The Economic Security Project's Cost-of-Living Refund* (Washington, DC: Urban Institute, 2019), www.taxpolicycenter.org/publications/expanding-earned-income-tax-credit-economic-security-projects-cost-living-refund.

67. Clayton et al., *Political Isolation and Resistance,* 83–85.

CHAPTER 5. "THEY NEEDED ME THERE"

1. Sesame Street, "Little Children, Big Challenges: Incarceration," YouTube video, June 12, 2013, www.youtube.com/watch?v=QvMm7t29oeM.

2. David Murphey and P. Mae Cooper, *Parents behind Bars: What Happens to Their Children?* (Washington, DC: Child Trends, October 2015), www.childtrends.org/publications/parents-behind-bars-what-happens-to-their-children.

3. Kristin Turney, "Adverse Childhood Experiences among Children of Incarcerated Parents," *Children and Youth Services Review* 89 (2018): 218–25, https://doi.org/10.1016/j.childyouth.2018.04.033.

4. Christopher Wildeman, "Paternal Imprisonment, the Prison Boom, and the Concentration of Childhood Disadvantage," *Demography* 46 (2009): 265–80.

5. Gordon B. Dahl and Lance Lochner, "The Impact of Family Income on Child Achievement: Evidence from the Earned Income Tax Credit," *American Economic Review* 102, no. 5 (2012): 1927–56; Elizabeth Thomson, Thomas L. Hanson, and Sara S. McLanahan, "Family Structure and Child Well-Being: Economic Resources vs. Parental Behaviors," *Social Forces* 73, no. 1 (1994): 221–42; Robert C. Whitaker, Shannon M. Phillips, and Sean M. Orzol, "Food Insecurity and the Risks of Depression and Anxiety in Mothers and Behavior Problems in Their Preschool-Aged Children," *Pediatrics* 118, no. 3 (2006): e859–68.

6. Gresham Sykes, *The Society of Captives: A Study of a Maximum Security Prison* (Princeton, NJ: Princeton University Press, 1958).

7. Nicola Lacey, *Penal Theory and Penal Practice: A Communitarian Approach* (Cullompton, UK: Willan, 2003), 178.

8. Caroline Lanskey et al., "Prisoners' Families, Penal Power, and the Referred Pains of Imprisonment," in *Prisons, Punishment, and the Family: Towards a New Sociology of Punishment?*, ed. Rachel Condry and Peter Scharff Smith (Oxford: Oxford University Press, 2018).

9. Megan Comfort, "Doing Time Together: Love and Family in the Shadow of the Prison"; Michel Foucault and Arlette Farge, *Le désordre des familles* (Paris: Gallimard, 2014).

10. Rachel Condry and Peter Scharff Smith, eds., *Prisons, Punishment, and the Family: Towards a New Sociology of Punishment?* (Oxford: Oxford University Press, 2018).

11. Megan L. Comfort et al., *Parenting and Partnership When Fathers Return from Prison: Findings from Qualitative Analysis* (Washington, DC: ASPE Research Brief, 2016); Christine H. Lindquist et al., "The Experiences of Families during a Father's Incarceration: Descriptive Findings from Baseline Data Collection for the Multi-Site Family Study on Incarceration, Parenting and Partnering" (Washington, DC: US Department of Health and Human Services, 2015).

12. Amanda Geller and Marah A. Curtis, "A Sort of Homecoming: Incarceration and the Housing Security of Urban Men," *Social Science Research* 40, no. 4 (2011): 1196–1213; Amanda Geller and Allyson Walker Franklin, "Paternal Incarceration and the Housing Security of Urban Mothers," *Journal of Marriage and Family* 76, no. 2 (2014): 411–12.

13. Wildeman, "Parental Incarceration, Child Homelessness."

14. Naomi Sugie, "Punishment and Welfare: Paternal Incarceration and Families' Receipt of Public Assistance," *Social Forces* 90, no. 4 (2012): 1403–27.

15. John M. Halushka, "The Runaround: Punishment, Welfare, and Poverty Survival after Prison." *Social Problems* 67, no. 2 (2020): 233–50; Sheri Pruitt Walker, "The Effects of the Incarceration of Fathers on the Health and Wellbeing of Mothers and Children" (PhD diss., University of Maryland, College Park, 2011).

16. Schwartz-Soicher, Geller, and Garfinkel, "Effect of Paternal Incarceration."

17. McKay et al., "'Always Having Hope': Father-Child Relationships after Reentry from Prison," *Journal of Offender Rehabilitation* 57, no. 2 (2018): 162–87.

18. Amato, "Research on Divorce: Continuing Trends and New Developments," *Journal of Marriage and Family* 72, no. 3 (2010): 650–66; Flouri, Narayannan, and Midouhas, "The Cross-Lagged Relationship between Father Absence and Child Problem Behaviour in the Early Years," *Child: Care, Health, and Development* 41, no. 6 (2015): 1090–97; McLanahan, Tach, and Schneider, "The Causal Effects of Father Absence," *Annual Review of Sociology* 39, no. 1 (2013): 399–427.

19. Helene Oldrup and Signe Frederiksen, "Are the Children of Prisoners Socially Excluded?," in *Prisons, Punishment, and the Family: Towards a New Sociology of Punishment?*, ed. Rachel Condry and Peter Scharff Smith (Oxford: Oxford University Press, 2018), 102.

20. Al M. Best et al., "Relationship Processes and Resilience in Children with Incarcerated Parents: Abstract," *Monographs of the Society for Research in Child Development* 78, no.3 (2013): vii.

21. Project WHAT, *We're Here and Talking* (Oakland, CA: Community Works West, 2016).

22. C. J. Kampfner, "Post-traumatic Stress Reactions in Children of Imprisoned Mothers," in *Children of Incarcerated Parents*, ed. K. Gabel & D. Johnston (New York: Lexington Books, 1995), 89–100.

23. Project WHAT, 10.

24. Wakefield, "Accentuating the Positive"; Wildeman, Schnittker, and Turney, "Despair by Association?"; Wildeman, "Parental Incarceration, Child Homelessness.",

25. Kerry Bell, Karen Bloor, and Catherine Hewitt, "How Do Undiagnosed Symptoms of Maternal Psychological Distress during the Postnatal Period Affect Child Developmental Outcomes?," *Maternal and Child Health Journal* 23, no. 9 (2019): 1187–95, https://doi.org/10.1007/s10995-019-02749-w.

26. Best et al., "Relationship Processes"; Zeman et al., "Maternal Incarceration, Children's Psychological Adjustment, and the Mediating Role of Emotion Regulation," *Journal of Abnormal Child Psychology* 46, no. 2 (2018): 223–36.

27. Susan M. Dennison and Kirsten L. Besemer, "Missing and Missing Out: Social Exclusion in Children with an Incarcerated Parent," in *Prisons, Punishment, and the Family: Towards a New Sociology of Punishment?*, ed. Rachel Condry and Peter Scharff Smith (Oxford: Oxford University Press, 2018); Oldrup and Frederiksen, "Children of Prisoners."

28. Danielle H. Dallaire, Anne Ciccone, and Laura C. Wilson, "Teachers' Experiences with and Expectations of Children with Incarcerated Parents," *Journal of Applied Developmental Psychology* 31, no. 4 (2010): 281–90, https://doi.org/10.1016/j.appdev.2010.04.001.

29. Haskins and Jacobsen, "Schools as Surveilling Institutions?"

30. Foster and Hagan, "Incarceration and Intergenerational Social Exclusion."

31. Dennison and Besemer, "Missing and Missing Out"; Kirsten L. Besemer and Susan Dennison, "Intergenerational Social Exclusion in Prisoners' Families," in *The Palgrave Handbook of Prison and the Family,* ed. Marie Hutton and Dominique Moran (Cham: Springer, 2019), 479–501, https://doi.org/10.1007/978-3-030-12744-2_23; Oldrup and Frederiksen, "Children of Prisoners."

32. Luther, "Examining Social Support among Adult Children of Incarcerated Parents," *Family Relations* 64, no. 4 (2015): 505–18.

33. Project WHAT, 18.

34. Project WHAT, 13.

35. McKay et al., "Family Life."

36. Acquah et al., *Inter-parental Conflict and Outcomes for Children in the Contexts of Poverty and Economic Pressure* (London: Early Intervention Foundation, 2017).

37. McKay et al., "Intimate Partner Violence."

38. McKay et al., "'Always Having Hope.'"

39. Johnson et al., "Ever-Increasing Levels of Parental Incarceration and the Consequences for Children"; Sara Wakefield and Christopher Wildeman, "Mass Imprisonment and Racial Disparities in Childhood Behavioral Problems" *Criminology & Public Policy* 10, no. 3 (2011): 793–817; Wildeman, "Paternal Incarceration and Children's Physically Aggressive Behaviors."

40. Haskins, "Unintended Consequences"; Haskins, "Paternal Incarceration and Child-Reported Behavioral Functioning"; Anna R. Haskins, "Beyond Boys' Bad Behavior: Paternal Incarceration and Cognitive Development in Middle Childhood" *Social Forces* 95, no. 2 (2016): 861–92, https://doi.org/10.1093/sf/sow066; Foster and Hagan, "The Mass Incarceration of Parents in America: Issues of Race/Ethnicity, Collateral Damage to Children, and Prisoner Reentry," *ANNALS of the American Academy of Political and Social Science* 623, no.1 (2009): 179–94; John Hagan and Holly Foster, "Children of the American Prison Generation: Student and School Spillover Effects of Incarcerating Mothers" *Law & Society Review* 46, no. 1 (2012): 37–69. https://doi.org/10.1111/j.1540-5893.2012.00472.x; Haskins, "Unintended Consequences"; Anna R. Haskins, "Paternal Incarceration and Children's Schooling Contexts: Intersecting Inequalities of Educational Opportunity" *Annals of the American Academy of Political and Social Science* 674, no. 1 (2017): 134–62, https://doi.org/10.1177/0002716217732011; Turney and Haskins, "Falling Behind? Children's Early Grade Retention after Paternal Incarceration."

41. Foster and Hagan, "Incarceration and Intergenerational Social Exclusion."

42. Brewer-Smyth, Pohlig, and Bucurescu, "Female Children with Incarcerated Adult Family Members at Risk for Lifelong Neurological Decline."

43. Swisher and Shaw-Smith, "Paternal Incarceration and Adolescent Well-Being: Life Course Contingencies and Other Moderators"; Christopher Wildeman, "Imprisonment and Infant Mortality" *Social Problems* 59, no. 2 (2012): 228–57; Yaros et al., "Child Well-Being When Fathers Return from Prison."

44. J. M. Pascoe et al., "Mediators and Adverse Effects of Child Poverty in the United States," *Pediatrics* 137, no. 4 (2016): e20160340, https://doi.org/10.1542/peds.2016-0340; Hirokazu Yoshikawa, J. Lawrence Aber, and William R. Beardslee, "The Effects of Poverty on the Mental, Emotional, and Behavioral Health of Children and Youth: Implications for Prevention," *American Psychologist* 67, no. 4 (2012): 272–84, https://doi.org/10.1037/a0028015.

45. Yoshikawa, Aber, and Beardslee, "Effects of Poverty."

46. Pascoe et al., "Mediators and Adverse Effects."

47. Turney, "Stress Proliferation across Generations? Examining the Relationship between Parental Incarceration and Childhood Health."

48. Wildeman, "Imprisonment and Infant Mortality."

49. Myriam Forster et al., "The Role of Familial Incarceration and Ethnic Identity in Suicidal Ideation and Suicide Attempt: Findings from a Longitudinal Study of Latinx Young Adults in California," *American Journal of Community Psychology* 64, no. 1–2 (2019): 191–201, https://doi.org/10.1002/ajcp.12332; Holly Foster and John Hagan, "Maternal and Paternal Imprisonment and Children's Social Exclusion in Young Adulthood," *Journal of Criminal Law & Criminology* 105, no. 2 (2015): 387–429; Daniel P. Mears and Sonja E. Siennick, "Young Adult Outcomes and the Life-Course Penalties of Parental Incarceration," *Journal of Research in Crime and Delinquency* 53, no. 1 (2016): 3–35.

50. Mears and Siennick, "Young Adult Outcomes."

51. Mears and Siennick.

52. Bruns and Lee, "Partner Incarceration"; Kristin Turney, "The Consequences of Paternal Incarceration for Maternal Neglect and Harsh Parenting," *Social Forces* 92, no. 4 (2014): 1607–36; Kristin Turney and Christopher Wildeman, "Adverse Childhood Experiences among Children Placed in and Adopted from Foster Care: Evidence from a Nationally Representative Survey," *Child Abuse & Neglect* 64 (2017): 117–29, https://doi.org/10.1016/j.chiabu.2016.12.009; Wakefield, "Accentuating the Positive."

53. Michelle Kelly-Irving et al., "Adverse Childhood Experiences and Premature All-Cause Mortality," *European Journal of Epidemiology* 28, no. 9 (2013): 721–34, https://doi.org/10.1007/s10654-013-9832-9.

54. Christopher R. Tamborini, ChangHwan Kim, and Arthur Sakamoto, "Education and Lifetime Earnings in the United States," *Demography* 52, no. 4 (2015): 1383–1407, https://doi.org/10.1007/s13524-015-0407-0.

55. Wakefield and Wildeman, *Children of the Prison Boom.*

56. Wildeman, "Paternal Imprisonment."

57. Tamborini, Kim, and Sakamoto, "Education and Lifetime Earnings."

58. Tamborini, Kim, and Sakamoto.

59. Wakefield and Wildeman, *Children of the Prison Boom*.

60. Creasie Finney Hairston, *Fathers in Prison and Their Children: Visiting Policy Guidelines* (University of Illinois at Chicago: Jane Addams Center for Social Policy and Research; Jane Addams College of Social Work, 1996).

61. Sylvia A. Harvey, *The Shadow System: Mass Incarceration and the American Family* (New York: Bold Type Books, 2020), https://go.exlibris.link /Bk2v0r0P.

62. Hairston, *Fathers in Prison;* Megan Comfort et al., "Taking Children into Account: Addressing Intergenerational Effects of Parental Incarceration," *Criminology & Public Policy* 10, no. 3 (2011): 839–50; Tasseli McKay et al., "If Family Matters: Supporting Family Relationships during Incarceration and Reentry," *Criminology & Public Policy* 15, no. 2 (2016): 529–42.

63. Joanna R. Love and Robert A. Fox, "Home-Based Parent Child Therapy for Young Traumatized Children Living In Poverty: A Randomized Controlled Trial," *Journal of Child & Adolescent Trauma* 12, no. 1 (2019): 73–83, https://doi .org/10.1007/s40653-017-0170-z.

64. Elizabeth S. Barnert and Paul J. Chung, "Responding to Parental Incarceration as a Priority Pediatric Health Issue," *Pediatrics* 142, no. 3 (2018): https:// doi.org/10.1542/peds.2018-1923.

65. Susan D. Phillips and Trevor Gates, "A Conceptual Framework for Understanding the Stigmatization of Children of Incarcerated Parents," *Journal of Child and Family Studies* 20, no. 3 (2011): 286–94.

66. Ellen L. Bassuk et al., "The Effectiveness of Housing Interventions and Housing and Service Interventions on Ending Family Homelessness: A Systematic Review," *American Journal of Orthopsychiatry* 84, no. 5 (2014): 457–74, https://doi.org/10.1037/ort0000020; Ellen L. Bassuk, Jacqueline A. Hart, and Effy Donovan, "Resetting Policies to End Family Homelessness," *Annual Review of Public Health* 41, no. 1 (2020): 247–63, https://doi.org/10.1146/annurev-publhealth-040119-094256.

67. Michael Pergamit, Mary Cunningham, and Devlin Hanson, "The Impact of Family Unification Housing Vouchers on Child Welfare Outcomes," *American Journal of Community Psychology* 60, nos. 1–2 (2017): 103–13, https://doi .org/10.1002/ajcp.12136.

68. Mary E. Haskett et al., "Feasibility, Acceptability, and Effects of a Peer Support Group to Prevent Child Maltreatment among Parents Experiencing Homelessness," *Children and Youth Services Review* 73 (2017): 187–96, https:// doi.org/10.1016/j.childyouth.2016.12.012.

69. Creasie Finney Hairston, *Children with Parents in Prison: Child Welfare Policy, Program, and Practice Issues* (New York: Routledge, 2017); Creasie Finney Hairston and Patricia W. Lockett, "Parents in Prison: New Directions for Social Services," *Social Work with Groups* 32, no. 2 (1987): 162–64.

70. United States Department of Agriculture, "USDA Proposes to Close SNAP."

71. Pascoe et al., "Mediators and Adverse Effects."

72. Andrew S. Garner et al., "Early Childhood Adversity, Toxic Stress, and the Role of the Pediatrician: Translating Developmental Science into Lifelong Health," *Pediatrics* 129, no. 1 (2012): e225, https://doi.org/10.1542/peds.2011-2662.

73. Charles Michalopoulos et al., *The Mother and Infant Home Visiting Program Evaluation: Early Findings on the Maternal, Infant, and Early Childhood Home Visiting Program*. OPRE Report 2015-11 (Washington, DC: US Department of Health and Human Services, 2015).

74. Laurie S. Abbott and Lynn T. Elliott, "Eliminating Health Disparities through Action on the Social Determinants of Health: A Systematic Review of Home Visiting in the United States, 2005–2015," *Public Health Nursing* 34, no. 1 (2017): 2–30; Sarah A. Avellar and Lauren H. Supplee, "Effectiveness of Home Visiting in Improving Child Health and Reducing Child Maltreatment," *Pediatrics* 132, Supplement 2 (2013): S90–99; Lauren E. Stargel, Rebecca C. Fauth, and M. Ann Easterbrooks, "Home Visiting Program Impacts on Reducing Homelessness among Young Mothers," *Journal of Social Distress and the Homeless* 27, no. 1 (2018): 89–92.

75. Emily Sama-Miller et al., *Home Visiting Programs: Reviewing Evidence of Effectiveness* (Washington, DC: US Department of Health and Human Services, 2017).

76. Susan Aud, Mary Ann Fox, and Angelina KewalRamani, *Status and Trends in the Education of Racial and Ethnic Groups*, NCES 2010-015 (Washington, DC: US Department of Education, 2010).

77. Emily B. Nichols, Ann B. Loper, and J. Patrick Meyer, "Promoting Educational Resiliency in Youth with Incarcerated Parents: The Impact of Parental Incarceration, School Characteristics, and Connectedness on School Outcomes," *Journal of Youth and Adolescence* 45, no. 6 (2016): 1090–1109, https://doi.org/10.1007/s10964-015-0337-6.

78. Laurie Miller Brotman et al., "Effects of ParentCorps in Prekindergarten on Child Mental Health and Academic Performance: Follow-up of a Randomized Clinical Trial through 8 Years of Age," *JAMA Pediatrics* 170, no. 12 (2016): 1149–55.

79. Ann S. Masten et al., "Educating Homeless and Highly Mobile Students: Implications of Research on Risk and Resilience," *School Psychology Review* 44, no. 3 (2015): 315–30.

CHAPTER 6. "SYSTEMATIC DECONSTRUCTION"

1. Joseph T. Jones Jr., interview by author, January 2018. All subsequent quotations attributed to Jones are from this interview.

2. Weingarten, "Witnessing the Effects," 52.

3. DeVylder et al., "Elevated Prevalence of Suicide."

4. Matthew Desmond, Andrew V. Papachristos, and David S. Kirk, "Evidence of the Effect of Police Violence on Citizen Crime Reporting," *American Sociological Review* 85, no. 1 (2020): 184–90, https://doi.org/10.1177/0003122419895979.

5. Kerrison, Cobbina, and Bender, "'Your Pants Won't Save You.'"

6. Baz Dreisinger, *Incarceration Nations* (New York: Other Press, 2016); Carol Martin and Kimmet Edgar, "The Social Context of Prison Violence," *Criminal Justice Matters* 42, no. 1 (2000): 24–25, https://doi.org/10.1080/09627250008552883; Lara Stemple and Ilan H. Meyer, "The Sexual Victimization of Men in America: New Data Challenge Old Assumptions," *American Journal of Public Health* 104, no. 6 (2014): e19–26, https://doi.org/10.2105/ajph.2014.301946.

7. Leonidas K Cheliotis, "Our Violence and Theirs: Comparing Prison Realities," *South Atlantic Quarterly* 113, no. 3 (2014): 443.

8. Paul Butler, *Chokehold: Policing Black Men* (New York: New Press, 2017); William Terrill and Michael D. Reisig, "Neighborhood Context and Police Use of Force," *Journal of Research in Crime and Delinquency* 40, no. 3 (2016): 291–321, https://doi.org/10.1177/0022427803253800.

9. Western and Pettit, "Incarceration and Social Inequality."

10. Weingarten, "Witnessing the Effects," 7.

11. Vesla M. Weaver, "Frontlash: Race and the Development of Punitive Crime Policy," *Studies in American Political Development* 21, no. 2 (2007): 259, https://doi.org/10.1017/S0898588X07000211.

12. Ehrlichman is quoted in Dan Baum, "Legalize It All," *Harper's Magazine*, April 1, 2016, 22.

13. Sara Wakefield and Christopher Uggen, "Incarceration and Stratification," *Annual Review of Sociology* 36, no. 1 (2010): 392, https://doi.org/10.1146/annurev.soc.012809.102551; see also David Jacobs and Ronald E. Helms, "Toward a Political Model of Incarceration: A Time-Series Examination of Multiple Explanations for Prison Admission Rates," *American Journal of Sociology* 102, no. 2 (1996): 323–57, https://doi.org/10.1086/230949.

14. Hinton, *From the War on Poverty*.

15. Kramer and Remster, "Stop, Frisk, and Assault?"

16. Jeff Manza and Christopher Uggen, *Locked Out: Felon Disenfranchisement and American Democracy* (New York: Oxford University Press, 2006).

17. Weaver and Lerman, "Political Consequences."

18. Alexander, *The New Jim Crow*.

19. Maria Yellow Horse Brave Heart et al., "Wicasa Was'aka: Restoring the Traditional Strength of American Indian Boys and Men," *American Journal of Public Health* 102, Suppl. 2 (2012): S178, https://doi.org/10.2105/AJPH.2011.300511; Brave Heart, "Wakiksuyapi."

20. Ian G. Barron and Ghassan Abdallah, "Intergenerational Trauma in the Occupied Palestinian Territories: Effect on Children and Promotion of Healing," *Journal of Child & Adolescent Trauma* 8, no. 2 (2015): 103–10; Amy Bombay, Kimberly Matheson, and Hymie Anisman, "The Intergenerational Effects of Indian Residential Schools: Implications for the Concept of Historical Trauma," *Transcultural Psychiatry* 51, no. 3 (2014): 320–38; Rachel Dekel and Hadass Goldblatt, "Is There Intergenerational Transmission of Trauma? The Case of Combat Veterans' Children," *American Journal of Orthopsychiatry* 78, no. 3 (2008): 281–89, https://doi.org/10.1037/a0013955.

21. Jutta Lindert et al., "Psychopathology of Children of Genocide Survivors: A Systematic Review on the Impact of Genocide on Their Children's Psychopathology from Five Countries," *International Journal of Epidemiology* 46, no. 1 (2017): 246–57, https://doi.org/10.1093/ije/dyw161; Vanja Vukojevic et al., "Epigenetic Modification of the Glucocorticoid Receptor Gene Is Linked to Traumatic Memory and Post-Traumatic Stress Disorder Risk in Genocide Survivors," *Journal of Neuroscience* 34, no. 31 (2014): 10274–84, https://doi.org/10.1523/jneurosci.1526-14.2014.

22. Rachel Yehuda and Linda M. Bierer, "Transgenerational Transmission of Cortisol and PTSD Risk," *Progress in Brain Research* 167 (2007): 121–35.

23. Rachel Yehuda et al., "Holocaust Exposure Induced Intergenerational Effects on FKBP5 Methylation," *Biological Psychiatry* 80, no. 5 (2016): 372–80.

24. Brave Heart et al., "Historical Trauma."

25. Western and Pettit, "Incarceration and Social Inequality"; Dorothy Roberts, "The Social and Moral Cost of Mass Incarceration in African American Communities," *Stanford Law Review* 56, no. 5 (2004): 1271–1305.

26. Katherine P. Theall et al., "Association between Neighborhood Violence and Biological Stress in Children," *JAMA Pediatrics* 171, no. 1 (2017): 53–60, https://doi.org/10.1001/jamapediatrics.2016.2321.

27. Michelle Sotero, "A Conceptual Model of Historical Trauma: Implications for Public Health Practice and Research," *Journal of Health Disparities Research and Practice* 1, no. 1 (2006): 95.

28. Sampson and Loeffler, "Punishment's Place"; Todd R. Clear, *Imprisoning Communities: How Mass Incarceration Makes Disadvantaged Neighborhoods Worse* (Oxford: Oxford University Press, 2009), 94.

29. Clear, "Effects of High Imprisonment Rates."

30. John Hagan and Holly Foster, "Children of the American Prison Generation: Student and School Spillover Effects of Incarcerating Mothers," *Law & Society Review* 46, no. 1 (2012): 37–69, https://doi.org/10.1111/j.1540-5893.2012.00472.x.

31. Wildeman and Wang, "Mass Incarceration."

32. Mancillas, *Presidents and Mass Incarceration*.

33. Alexander, *The New Jim Crow*; CalvinJohn Smiley and David Fakunle, "From 'Brute' to 'Thug': The Demonization and Criminalization of Unarmed

Black Male Victims in America," *Journal of Human Behavior in the Social Environment* 26, nos. 3–4 (2016): 350–66, https://doi.org/10.1080/10911359.2015.1 129256.

34. Walter S. Gilliam et al., *Do Early Educators' Implicit Biases Regarding Sex and Race Relate to Behavior Expectations and Recommendations of Preschool Expulsions and Suspensions?*, Yale University Child Study Center, Sept. 28, 2016, 6.

35. Jason T. Downer et al., "Teacher-Child Racial/Ethnic Match within Pre-Kindergarten Classrooms and Children's Early School Adjustment," *Early Childhood Research Quarterly* 37, no. 4 (2016): 26–38, https://doi.org/10.1016/j. ecresq.2016.02.007.

36. Friedrich et al., "Pygmalion Effects."

37. Lynette Parker, "Schools and the No-Prison Phenomenon: Anti-Blackness and Secondary Policing in the Black Lives Matter Era," *Journal of Educational Controversy* 12, no. 1 (2017): 11.

38. Pager, *Marked*.

39. Agan and Starr, "Ban the Box."

40. Bruce Western, *Punishment and Inequality in America* (New York: Russell Sage, 2006).

41. Wakefield and Uggen, "Incarceration and Stratification," 388–89.

42. Pew Research Center, *On Views of Race and Inequality, Blacks and Whites Are Worlds Apart* (Washington, DC: Pew Research Center, 2016), www .pewsocialtrends.org/2016/06/27/on-views-of-race-and-inequality-blacks-and-whites-are-worlds-apart.

43. Mehrsa Baradaran, *The Color of Money: Black Banks and the Racial Wealth Gap* (Cambridge: Belknap, 2017); Mehrsa Baradaran, "No Justice. No Peace: Underlying the Nationwide Protests for Black Lives Is the Racial Wealth Gap," American Prospect, June 17, 2020, https://prospect.org/civil-rights/no-justice-no-peace-fix-the-racial-wealth-gap.

44. James Oleson, "The New Eugenics: Black Hyper-Incarceration and Human Abatement," *Social Sciences (Basel)* 5, no. 4 (2016): 66, https://doi .org/10.3390/socsci5040066.

45. Sampson and Loeffler, "Punishment's Place"; Wildeman and Wang, "Mass Incarceration."

46. Anna R. Haskins and Erin J. McCauley, "Casualties of Context? Risk of Cognitive, Behavioral and Physical Health Difficulties among Children Living in High-Incarceration Neighborhoods," *Journal of Public Health* 27, no. 2 (2019): 175–83, https://doi.org/10.1007/s10389-018-0942-4.

47. Joseph W. Frank et al., "Neighborhood Incarceration Rate and Asthma Prevalence in New York City: A Multilevel Approach," *American Journal of Public Health* 103, no. 5 (2013): e38–44.

48. Hatzenbuehler et al., "Collateral Damage."

49. Haskins, "Beyond Boys' Bad Behavior."

50. Damon E. Jones, Mark Greenberg, and Max Crowley, "Early Social-Emotional Functioning and Public Health: The Relationship between Kindergarten Social Competence and Future Wellness," *American Journal of Public Health* 105, no. 11 (2015): 2283, https://doi.org/10.2105/ajph.2015.302630.

51. Raj Chetty et al., "The Association between Income and Life Expectancy in the United States, 2001–2014," *JAMA: Journal of the American Medical Association* 315, no. 16 (2016): 1750–66, https://doi.org/10.1001/jama.2016.4226; Johannes Haushofer and Ernst Fehr, "On the Psychology of Poverty," *Science (American Association for the Advancement of Science)* 344, no. 6186 (2014): 862–67, https://doi.org/10.1126/science.1232491.

52. Maria R. Khan, William C. Miller, et al., "Timing and Duration of Incarceration and High-Risk Sexual Partnerships among African Americans in North Carolina," *Annals of Epidemiology* 18, no. 5 (2008): 403–10, https://doi.org/10.1016/j.annepidem.2007.12.003; Andrea K. Knittel et al., "Incarceration and Sexual Risk: Examining the Relationship between Men's Involvement in the Criminal Justice System and Risky Sexual Behavior," *AIDS and Behavior* 17, no. 8 (2013): 2703–14, https://doi.org/10.1007/s10461-013-0421-4.

53. Susan M. Rogers et al., "Incarceration, High-Risk Sexual Partnerships and Sexually Transmitted Infections in an Urban Population," *Sexually Transmitted Infections* 88, no. 1 (2012): 63–68, https://doi.org/10.1136/sextrans-2011-050280.

54. Clear, "Effects of High Imprisonment Rates"; Robert D. Crutchfield and Gregory A. Weeks, "The Effects of Mass Incarceration on Communities of Color," *Issues in Science and Technology* 32, no. 1 (2015): 109; Rios, *Punished.*

55. Eva Frazer et al., "The Violence Epidemic in the African American Community: A Call by the National Medical Association for Comprehensive Reform," *Journal of the National Medical Association* 110, no. 1 (2018): 4–15, https://doi.org/10.1016/j.jnma.2017.08.009.

56. Wildeman and Muller, "Mass Imprisonment and Inequality."

57. Wakefield and Uggen, "Incarceration and Stratification."

58. Wildeman and Wang, "Mass Incarceration."

59. Rucker C. Johnson and Steven Raphael, "The Effects of Male Incarceration Dynamics on Acquired Immune Deficiency Syndrome Infection Rates among African American Women and Men," *Journal of Law and Economics* 52, no. 2 (2009): 251–93.

60. David Stuckler et al., "Mass Incarceration Can Explain Population Increases in TB and Multidrug-Resistant TB in European and Central Asian Countries," *Proceedings of the National Academy of Sciences—PNAS* 105, no. 36 (2008): 13280–85, https://doi.org/10.1073/pnas.0801200105.

61. Hatzenbuehler et al., "Collateral Damage"; Jason Schnittker, Michael Massoglia, and Christopher Uggen, "Incarceration and the Health of the African

American Community," *Dubois Review* 8, no. 1 (2011): 133–41; Wildeman and Wang, "Mass Incarceration."

62. Center on Society and Health, "Mapping Life Expectancy" (Richmond: Virginia Commonwealth University, 2016).

63. Christopher Wildeman, Alyssa W. Goldman, and Kristin Turney, "Parental Incarceration and Child Health in the United States," *Epidemiologic Reviews* 40, no. 1 (2018): 146–56.

64. Whitney S. Rice et al., "Disparities in Infant Mortality by Race among Hispanic and Non-Hispanic Infants," *Maternal and Child Health Journal* 21, no. 7 (2017): 1581–88, https://doi.org/10.1007/s10995-017-2290-3.

65. Wildeman, "Imprisonment and Infant Mortality," 224.

66. CDC, "Infant Mortality: What Is CDC Doing?," 2020 www.cdc.gov /reproductivehealth/maternalinfanthealth/infantmortality-cdcdoing.htm.

67. Wildeman, "Imprisonment and Infant Mortality."

68. Wildeman and Wang, "Mass Incarceration."

69. Wildeman, "Incarceration and Population Health."

70. Robert J. Sampson, *Great American City* (Chicago: University of Chicago Press, 2012).

71. Heather Ann Thompson, "Unmaking the Motor City in the Age of Mass Incarceration," *Journal of Law in Society* 15, no. 1 (2013): 41.

72. Crutchfield and Weeks, "Effects of Mass Incarceration."

73. Lisa Lambert, "More Americans Move to Cities in Past Decade-Census," Reuters, March 26, 2012, www.reuters.com/article/usa-cities-population-idUSL2E8EQ5AJ20120326.

74. Wildeman, "Imprisonment and (Inequality in) Population Health."

75. Environmental Protection Agency, "Mortality Risk Valuation," Nov. 20, 2020, www.epa.gov/environmental-economics/mortality-risk-valuation.

76. Linda Ryen and Mikael Svensson, "The Willingness to Pay for a Quality Adjusted Life Year: A Review of the Empirical Literature," *Health Economics* 24, no. 10 (2015): 1289–1301 https://doi.org/10.1002/hec.3085.

77. Becky Pettit and Bryan L. Sykes, "Civil Rights Legislation and Legalized Exclusion: Mass Incarceration and the Masking of Inequality," *Sociological Forum* 30, no. S1 (2015): 589–611, https://doi.org/10.1111/socf.12179.

78. Anna R. Haskins, "Paternal Incarceration and Children's Schooling Contexts: Intersecting Inequalities of Educational Opportunity," *Annals of the American Academy of Political and Social Science* 674, no. 1 (2017): 134–62, https://doi.org/10.1177/0002716217732011; Foster and Hagan, "Maternal and Paternal Imprisonment."

79. Marta Tienda, "Thirteenth Annual Brown Lecture in Education Research: Public Education and the Social Contract: Restoring the Promise in an Age of Diversity and Division," *Educational Researcher* 46, no. 6 (2017): 271–83, https://doi.org/10.3102/0013189X17725499.

80. Robert Bifulco and Helen F. Ladd, "School Choice, Racial Segregation, and Test-Score Gaps: Evidence from North Carolina's Charter School Program," *Journal of Policy Analysis and Management* 26, no. 1 (2007): 31–56; Erica Frankenberg, Genevieve Siegel-Hawley, and Jia Wang, "Choice without Equity: Charter School Segregation," *Education Policy Analysis Archives/Archivos Analíticos de Políticas Educativas* 19 (2011); Gary Orfield and Erica Frankenberg, "Increasingly Segregated and Unequal Schools as Courts Reverse Policy," *Educational Administration Quarterly* 50, no. 5 (2014): 718–34, https://doi.org/10.1177/0013161x14548942.

81. Mehrsa Baradaran, "Closing the Racial Wealth Gap," *NYU Law Review* 95 (2020): 57–80.

82. Deborah Phillips, William Gormley, and Sara Anderson, "The Effects of Tulsa's CAP Head Start Program on Middle-School Academic Outcomes and Progress," *Developmental Psychology* 52, no. 8 (2016): 1247–61, https://doi.org/10.1037/dev0000151.

83. Karen L. Bierman et al., "Enriching Preschool Classrooms and Home Visits with Evidence-Based Programming: Sustained Benefits for Low-Income Children," *Journal of Child Psychology and Psychiatry* 58, no. 2 (2017): 129–37.

84. Robert A. Hahn et al., "Programs to Increase High School Completion: A Community Guide Systematic Health Equity Review," *American Journal of Preventive Medicine* 48, no. 5 (2015): 599–608.

85. Clear, *Imprisoning Communities*.

86. Hahn et al., "Programs"; Robert J. Rossi, *Evaluation of Projects Funded by the School Dropout Demonstration Assistance Program: Final Evaluation Report*, vol. 1, *Findings and Recommendations* (Washington, DC: US Department of Education, 1995).

87. Haskins and Jacobsen, "Schools as Surveilling Institutions?"

88. Meghan Ecker-Lyster and Christopher Niileksela, "Keeping Students on Track to Graduate: A Synthesis of School Dropout Trends, Prevention, and Intervention Initiatives," *Journal of At-Risk Issues* 19, no. 2 (2016): 24–31.

89. Linda H. Aiken, Sean P. Clarke, and Douglas M. Sloane, "Hospital Staffing, Organization, and Quality of Care: Cross-National Findings," *Nursing Outlook* 50, no. 5 (2002): 187–94, https://doi.org/10.1067/mno.2002.126696.

90. Aaron D. Fox et al., "Health Outcomes and Retention in Care Following Release from Prison for Patients of an Urban Post-Incarceration Transitions Clinic," *Journal of Health Care for the Poor and Underserved* 25, no. 3 (2014): 1139–52, https://doi.org/10.1353/hpu.2014.0139; Shira Shavit et al., "Transitions Clinic Network: Challenges and Lessons in Primary Care for People Released from Prison," *Health Affairs* 36, no. 6 (2017): 1006–15, https://doi.org/10.1377/hlthaff.2017.0089; Emily A. Wang et al., "Transitions Clinic: Creating a Community-Based Model of Health Care for Recently Released California Prisoners," *Public Health Reports* 125, no. 2 (2010): 171–77, https://doi.org/10.1177/003335491012500205.

91. Hatzenbuehler et al., "Collateral Damage."

92. Arvin Garg et al., "Addressing Social Determinants of Health at Well Child Care Visits: A Cluster RCT," *Pediatrics (Evanston)* 135, no. 2 (2015): e296–304, https://doi.org/10.1542/peds.2014-2888.

93. Arthur Acolin and Susan Wachter, "Opportunity and Housing Access," *Cityscape* 19, no. 1 (2017): 145.

94. Quynh C. Nguyen et al., "The Effects of a Housing Mobility Experiment on Participants' Residential Environments," *Housing Policy Debate* 27, no. 3 (2017): 419.

95. Acolin and Wachter, "Opportunity and Housing Access," 135.

96. Acolin and Wachter, 145.

97. Mehrsa Baradaran, *A Homestead Act for the 21st Century*, Great Democracy Initiative, May 2019, 32, https://rooseveltinstitute.org/wp-content/uploads/2021/08/GDI_Homestead-Act-21C_201905.pdf.

98. Mary Bassett and Sandro Galea, "Reparations as a Public Health Priority—A Strategy for Ending Black-White Health Disparities," *New England Journal of Medicine* 383 (2020): 2101–3.

99. Darrick Hamilton and William Darity, "Can 'Baby Bonds' Eliminate the Racial Wealth Gap in Putative Post-Racial America?," *Review of Black Political Economy* 37, nos. 3–4 (2010): 207–16, https://doi.org/10.1007/s12114-010-9063-1.

100. Naomi Zewde, "Universal Baby Bonds Reduce Black-White Wealth Inequality, Progressively Raise Net Worth of All Young Adults," *Review of Black PoliticalEconomy* 47, no. 1 (2020): 17, https://doi.org/10.1177/0034644619885321.

101. Baradaran, "Closing the Racial Wealth Gap."

102. Linda Giannarelli et al., *Reducing Child Poverty in the US*, Urban Institute, Jan. 2015, www.urban.org/research/publication/reducing-child-poverty-us.

103. Children's Defense Fund, "How to Cut Child Poverty by 60 Percent Right Now," Jan. 28, 2015, www.childrensdefense.org/2015/how-to-cut-child-poverty-by-60-percent-right-now.

104. Movement for Black Lives, "Vision for Black Lives," M4BL, 2020, https://m4bl.org/policy-platforms.

CHAPTER 7. DREAMING AN AMERICA BEYOND MASS INCARCERATION

1. Peter B. Edelman, *So Rich, so Poor: Why It's so Hard to End Poverty in America* (New York: New Press, 2012).

2. Lyndon Johnson, "War on Poverty" (Washington, DC, 1964); Barack Obama, "Remarks by the President on Sustainable Development Goals," speech delivered at the United Nations, New York, Sept. 27, 2015, https://obamawhitehouse.archives.gov/the-press-office/2015/09/27/remarks-president-sustainable-development-goals.

3. Thomas Suh Lauder and David Lauter, "Views on Poverty: 1985 and Today," *Los Angeles Times*, August 14, 2016, www.latimes.com/projects/la-na-pol-poverty-poll-interactive.

4. Mancillas, *Presidents and Mass Incarceration*.

5. Arthur, "How 'Transitions' Reshaped Human Rights," 325.

6. Alexander, "The New Jim Crow," 9.

7. M. Clement, M. Schwarzfeld, and M. Thompson, *The National Summit on Justice Reinvestment and Public Safety* (New York: Council of State Governments Justice Center, 2011); Travis, Western, and Redburn, "Growth of Incarceration."

8. Michael Tonry, "Remodeling American Sentencing: A Ten-Step Blueprint for Moving Past Mass Incarceration," *Criminology & Public Policy* 13, no. 4 (2014): 503-33, https://doi.org/10.1111/1745-9133.12097.

9. Haidong Wang et al., "Global, Regional, and National Levels of Neonatal, Infant, and under-5 Mortality during 1990-2013: A Systematic Analysis for the Global Burden of Disease Study 2013," *The Lancet (British Edition)* 384, no. 9947 (2014): 957-79, https://doi.org/10.1016/S0140-6736(14)60497-9.

10. James N. Weinstein et al., eds., *Communities in Action: Pathways to Health Equity*, Committee on Community-Based Solutions to Promote Health Equity in the United States (Washington, DC: National Academies Press, 2017), https://doi.org/10.17226/24624.

11. Arthur, "How 'Transitions' Reshaped Human Rights."

12. Tasseli E. McKay et al., *Holding On: Fatherhood and Family during and after Incarceration* (Berkeley: University of California Press, 2019).

13. William Edward Burghardt Du Bois, *Black Reconstruction in America: An Essay toward a History of the Part Which Black Folk Played in the Attempt to Reconstruct Democracy in America, 1860-1880* (Oxford: Oxford University Press, 1935), 633.

14. Du Bois, 131.

15. Coates, "The Case for Reparations"; Darity and Mullen, *From Here to Equality*.

16. Alexander, *The New Jim Crow*.

17. Quinn, "Tractionless Transitional Justice," 20.

18. Smith, , *How the Word Is Passed*, 289.

19. White House Council of Economic Advisors, *Economic Perspectives on Incarceration and the Criminal Justice System* (Washington, DC: Office of the Press Secretary, April 23, 2016), https://obamawhitehouse.archives.gov/the-press-office/2016/04/23/cea-report-economic-perspectives-incarceration-and-criminal-justice.

20. Eric Cadora and Laura Kurgan, "The Crime in Criminal Data," *Architecture: The AIA Journal* 95, no. 10 (2006): 52-53.

21. Rice et al., "Disparities in Infant Mortality."

22. Kirk and Wakefield, "Collateral Consequences of Punishment."

23. Hinton, *From the War on Poverty;* Tonry, "Remodeling American Sentencing."

24. Kirk and Wakefield, "Collateral Consequences of Punishment"; Sampson, "The Incarceration Ledger."

25. Christopher Wildeman, "Is It Better to Sit on Our Hands or Just Dive In: Cultivating Family-Friendly Criminal Justice Policy in the Contemporary Era," *Criminology and Public Policy* 15, no. 2 (2016): 497.

26. Rios, *Punished.*

27. McLeod, "Prison Abolition."

28. Hamilton and Darity, "Can 'Baby Bonds' Eliminate."

29. Zewde, "Universal Baby Bonds."

30. Marian Wright Edelman, foreword to *Ending Child Poverty Now,* Children's Defense Fund, 2019, www.childrensdefense.org/wp-content/uploads/2019/04/Ending-Child-Poverty-2019.pdf.

31. Bittker, *Case for Black Reparations.*

32. Coates, "The Case for Reparations"; Darity and Frank, "The Economics of Reparations"; Darity and Mullen, *From Here to Equality.*

33. E. Ann Carson, "Linking Administrative BJS Data: Better Understanding of Prisoners' Personal Histories by Linking the National Corrections Reporting Program (NCRP) and CARRA Data," Proceedings of the 2015 Federal Committee on Statistical Methodology (FCSM) Research Conference, Washington, DC, Dec. 1–3, 2015, https://nces.ed.gov/fcsm/pdf/A1_Carson_2015FCSM.pdf.

34. Darity, William A., Jr., Bidisha Lahiri, and Dania V. Frank, "Reparations for African-Americans as a Transfer Problem: A Cautionary Tale," *Review of Development Economics* 14, no. 2 (2010): 248–61, https://doi.org/10.1111/j.1467-9361.2010.00550.x.

35. Darity and Mullen, *From Here to Equality.*

36. Wakefield and Wildeman, *Children of the Prison Boom.*

37. Dedrick Asante-Muhammad et al., *The Road to Zero Wealth: How the Racial Wealth Divide Is Hollowing Out America's Middle Class,* Institute for Policy Studies/Prosperity Now, Sept. 2017, https://prosperitynow.org/files/PDFs/road_to_zero_wealth.pdf.

38. Neal Bhutta et al., *Disparities in Wealth by Race and Ethnicity in the 2019 Survey of Consumer Finances* (Washington, DC: Federal Reserve, 2020), www.federalreserve.gov/econres/notes/feds-notes/disparities-in-wealth-by-race-and-ethnicity-in-the-2019-survey-of-consumer-finances-20200928.htm; Neil Bhutta et al., "Changes in U.S. Family Finances from 2016 to 2019: Evidence from the Survey of Consumer Finances," *Federal Reserve Bulletin* 106, no. 5 (Sept. 2020): 42.

39. Darity and Mullen, *From Here to Equality.*

40. Census Bureau, *America's Families and Living Arrangements: 2020* (Washington, DC: United States Census Bureau, 2020), www.census.gov/data /tables/2020/demo/families/cps-2020.html.

41. Ohio History Central, "Margaret Garner," www.ohiohistorycentral.org/w /Margaret_Garner.

42. Morrison, *Beloved*, 275.

APPENDIX

1. Christine Lindquist et al., "The Multisite Family Study on Incarceration, Partnering, and Parenting: Program Impacts," *Journal of Offender Rehabilitation* 57, no. 2 (2018): 115–43, https://doi.org/10.1080/10509674.2018.1441211.

2. Bir and Lindquist, "Multi-site Family Study."

3. Annabel Prins et al., "The Primary Care PTSD Screen (PC-PTSD): Development and Operating Characteristics," *Primary Care Psychiatry* 9, no. 1 (2004): 9–14, https://doi.org/10.1185/135525703125002360.

4. Demmie Mayfield, Gail McLeod, and Patricia Hall, "The CAGE Questionnaire: Validation of a New Alcoholism Screening Instrument," *American Journal of Psychiatry* 131, no. 10 (1974): 1121–23.

5. Murray A. Straus et al., "The Revised Conflict Tactics Scales (CTS2): Development and Preliminary Psychometric Data," *Journal of Family Issues* 17, no. 3 (1996): 283–316.

Bibliography

Abbott, Laurie S., and Lynn T. Elliott. "Eliminating Health Disparities through Action on the Social Determinants of Health: A Systematic Review of Home Visiting in the United States, 2005–2015." *Public Health Nursing* 34, no. 1 (2017): 2–30.

Abram, Karen M., Naomi A. Zwecker, Leah J. Welty, Jennifer A. Hershfield, Mina K. Dulcan, and Linda A. Teplin. "Comorbidity and Continuity of Psychiatric Disorders in Youth after Detention: A Prospective Longitudinal Study." *JAMA Psychiatry* 72, no. 1 (2015): 84–93. https://doi.org/10.1001/jamapsychiatry.2014.1375.

Acolin, Arthur, and Susan Wachter. "Opportunity and Housing Access." *Cityscape* 19, no. 1 (2017): 135–50.

Acquah, Daniel, Ruth Sellers, Laura Stock, and Gordon Harold. *Inter-parental Conflict and Outcomes for Children in the Contexts of Poverty and Economic Pressure.* London: Early Intervention Foundation, 2017.

Adler, Nanci. *Understanding the Age of Transitional Justice: Crimes, Courts, Commissions, and Chronicling.* New Brunswick, NJ: Rutgers University Press, 2018.

Agan, Amanda, and Sonja Starr. "Ban the Box, Criminal Records, and Racial Discrimination: A Field Experiment." *Quarterly Journal of Economics* 133, no. 1 (2018): 191–235.

Aiken, Linda H., Sean P. Clarke, and Douglas M. Sloane. "Hospital Staffing, Organization, and Quality of Care: Cross-National Findings." *Nursing*

Outlook 50, no. 5 (2002): 187–94. https://doi.org/10.1067/mno.2002 .126696.

Aizer, Anna, and Janet Currie. *Lead and Juvenile Delinquency: New Evidence from Linked Birth, School and Juvenile Detention Records.* Cambridge: National Bureau of Economic Research, May 2017. https://doi.org/10.3386 /w23392.

Alexander, Michelle. "The New Jim Crow." *Ohio State Journal of Criminal Law* 9, no. 1 (2011): 7–26.

———, *The New Jim Crow: Mass Incarceration in the Age of Colorblindness.* New York: New Press, 2010.

Amato, Paul. "Research on Divorce: Continuing Trends and New Developments." *Journal of Marriage and Family* 72, no. 3 (2010): 650–66.

Angelou, Maya. "Caged Bird." In *Shaker, Why Don't You Sing?* New York: Random House, 1983.

Anyon, Yolanda, Jeffrey M. Jenson, Inna Altschul, Jordan Farrar, Jeanette McQueen, Eldridge Greer, Barbara Downing, and John Simmons. "The Persistent Effect of Race and the Promise of Alternatives to Suspension in School Discipline Outcomes." *Children and Youth Services Review* 44 (2014): 379–86. https://doi.org/10.1016/j.childyouth.2014.06.025.

Apel, Robert, Arjan Blokland, Paul Nieuwbeerta, and Marieke van Schellen. "Collateral Effects of Incarceration: Effects on Marriage and Divorce." *Journal of Quantitative Criminology* 26 (2010): 269–300.

Arditti, Joyce A. "Families and Incarceration: An Ecological Approach." *Families in Society: Journal of Contemporary Social Services* 86, no. 2 (2005): 251–60.

Aron, Emily J., and Jeff Q. Bostic. "Because That's Where the Kids Are: Willie Sutton's First-Grade Teacher on Why She Taught School." *Journal of the American Academy of Child & Adolescent Psychiatry* 57, no. 3 (2018): 141–42. https://doi.org/10.1016/j.jaac.2018.01.001.

Arthur, Paige. "How 'Transitions' Reshaped Human Rights: A Conceptual History of Transitional Justice." *Human Rights Quarterly* 31, no. 2 (2009): 321–67. https://doi.org/10.1353/hrq.0.0069.

Asante-Muhammad, Dedrick, Chuck Collins, Josh Hoxie, and Emanuel Nieves. *The Road to Zero Wealth: How the Racial Wealth Divide Is Hollowing Out America's Middle Class.* Institute for Policy Studies/Prosperity Now, Sept. 2017. https://prosperitynow.org/files/PDFs/road_to_zero_wealth.pdf.

Aud, Susan, Mary Ann Fox, and Angelina KewalRamani. *Status and Trends in the Education of Racial and Ethnic Groups.* NCES 2010–015. Washington, DC: US Department of Education, 2010.

Avellar, Sarah A., and Lauren H. Supplee. "Effectiveness of Home Visiting in Improving Child Health and Reducing Child Maltreatment." *Pediatrics* 132, Supplement 2 (2013): S90–99.

Bandes, Susan A., Marie Pryor, Erin M. Kerrison, and Phillip Atiba Goff. "The Mismeasure of Terry Stops: Assessing the Psychological and Emotional Harms of Stop and Frisk to Individuals and Communities." *Behavioral Sciences & the Law* 37, no. 2 (2019): 176–94. https://doi.org/10.1002/bsl.2401.

Baradaran, Mehrsa. "Closing the Racial Wealth Gap." *New York University Law Review* 95 (2020): 57–80.

———. *The Color of Money: Black Banks and the Racial Wealth Gap.* Cambridge: Belknap, 2017.

———. *A Homestead Act for the 21st Century.* Great Democracy Initiative, May 2019. https://rooseveltinstitute.org/wp-content/uploads/2021/08/GDI_Homestead-Act-21C_201905.pdf.

———. "No Justice. No Peace: Underlying the Nationwide Protests for Black Lives Is the Racial Wealth Gap." American Prospect, June 17, 2020. https://prospect.org/civil-rights/no-justice-no-peace-fix-the-racial-wealth-gap.

Barnert, Elizabeth S., and Paul J. Chung. "Responding to Parental Incarceration as a Priority Pediatric Health Issue." *Pediatrics* 142, no. 3 (2018): e20181923. https://doi.org/10.1542/peds.2018-1923.

Barron, Ian G., and Ghassan Abdallah. "Intergenerational Trauma in the Occupied Palestinian Territories: Effect on Children and Promotion of Healing." *Journal of Child & Adolescent Trauma* 8, no. 2 (2015): 103–10.

Baskaran, Priya. "Respect the Hustle: Necessity Entrepreneurship, Returning Citizens, and Social Enterprise Strategies." *Maryland Law Review* 78 (2018): 323–81.

Bassett, Mary, and Sandro Galea. "Reparations as a Public Health Priority—A Strategy for Ending Black-White Health Disparities." *New England Journal of Medicine* 383, no. 22 (2020): 2101–3.

Bassuk, Ellen L., Carmela J. DeCandia, Alexander Tsertsvadze, and Molly K. Richard. "The Effectiveness of Housing Interventions and Housing and Service Interventions on Ending Family Homelessness: A Systematic Review." *American Journal of Orthopsychiatry* 84, no. 5 (2014): 457–74. https://doi.org/10.1037/ort0000020.

Bassuk, Ellen L., Jacqueline A. Hart, and Effy Donovan. "Resetting Policies to End Family Homelessness." *Annual Review of Public Health* 41, no. 1 (2020): 247–63. https://doi.org/10.1146/annurev-publhealth-040119-094256.

Batle, Gil. *Hatched in Prison* at Ricco Maresca. 2016. www.gilbatle.com/hatched-in-prison.

Baxter, Vern Kenneth, and Peter Marina. "Cultural Meaning and Hip-Hop Fashion in the African-American Male Youth Subculture of New Orleans." *Journal of Youth Studies* 11, no. 2 (2008): 93–113. https://doi.org/10.1080/13676260701800761.

Beckett, Katherine. "The Politics, Promise, and Peril of Criminal Justice Reform in the Context of Mass Incarceration." *Annual Review of*

Criminology 1, no. 1 (2018): 235–59. https://doi.org/10.1146/annurev-criminol-032317-092458.

Beckett, Katherine, and Bruce Western. "Governing Social Marginality: Welfare, Incarceration, and the Transformation of State Policy." *Punishment & Society* 3, no. 1 (2001): 43–59. https://doi.org/10.1177/14624740122228249.

Belfield, Clive R., Henry M. Levin, and Rachel Rosen. *The Economic Value of Opportunity Youth*. Washington, DC: Corporation for National and Community Service, 2012.

Bell, Kerry, Karen Bloor, and Catherine Hewitt. "How Do Undiagnosed Symptoms of Maternal Psychological Distress during the Postnatal Period Affect Child Developmental Outcomes?" *Maternal and Child Health Journal* 23, no. 9 (2019): 1187–95. https://doi.org/10.1007/s10995-019-02749-w.

Bennett, Marion Daniel. "So Much Trouble on My Mind: African American Males Coping with Mental Health Issues and Racism." *Urban Social Work* 4, no. 2 (2020): 152–72. https://doi.org/10.1891/USW-D-19-00005.

Bennett-Haron, Karen P., Arash Daneshzadeh, Kenneth J. Fasching-Varner, Lori Latrice Martin, and Roland Mitchell. *Understanding, Dismantling, and Disrupting the Prison-to-School Pipeline*. Lanham, MD: Lexington Books, 2017.

Berlowitz, Marvin J., Rinda Frye, and Kelli M. Jette. "Bullying and Zero-Tolerance Policies: The School to Prison Pipeline." *Multicultural Learning and Teaching* 12, no. 1 (2017): 7–25.

Besemer, Kirsten L., and Susan Dennison. "Intergenerational Social Exclusion in Prisoners' Families." In *The Palgrave Handbook of Prison and the Family*, edited by Marie Hutton and Dominique Moran, 479–501. Cham: Springer, 2019. https://doi.org/10.1007/978-3-030-12744-2_23.

Best, Al M., Burt Burraston, Dawn K. Cecil, Danielle H. Dallaire, J. Mark Eddy, Maria I. Kuznetsova, et al. "Relationship Processes and Resilience in Children with Incarcerated Parents." *Monographs of the Society for Research in Child Development* 78, no. 3 (2013). https://doi.org/10.1111/mono.12016.

Bhutta, Neil, Jesse Bricker, Andrew C. Chang, Lisa J. Dettling, Sarena Goodman, Kevin B. Moore, Sarah Reber, et al. "Changes in U.S. Family Finances from 2016 to 2019: Evidence from the Survey of Consumer Finances." *Federal Reserve Bulletin* 106, no. 5 (Sept. 2020).

Bhutta, Neal, Andrew Chang, Lisa Dettling, and Joanne Hsu. *Disparities in Wealth by Race and Ethnicity in the 2019 Survey of Consumer Finances*. Washington, DC: Federal Reserve, Sept. 28, 2020. www.federalreserve.gov/econres/notes/feds-notes/disparities-in-wealth-by-race-and-ethnicity-in-the-2019-survey-of-consumer-finances-20200928.htm.

Bierman, Karen L., Brenda S. Heinrichs, Janet A. Welsh, Robert L. Nix, and Scott D. Gest. "Enriching Preschool Classrooms and Home Visits with Evidence-Based Programming: Sustained Benefits for Low-Income

Children." *Journal of Child Psychology and Psychiatry* 58, no. 2 (2017): 129–37.

Bifulco, Robert, and Helen F. Ladd. "School Choice, Racial Segregation, and Test-Score Gaps: Evidence from North Carolina's Charter School Program." *Journal of Policy Analysis and Management* 26, no. 1 (2007): 31–56.

Binswanger, Ingrid A., Marc F. Stern, Richard A. Deyo, Patrick J. Heagerty, Allen Cheadle, J. G. Elmore, et al. "Release from Prison: A High Risk of Death for Former Inmates." *New England Journal of Medicine* 356, no. 2 (2007): 157–65.

Bir, Anupa, and Christine Lindquist. "Multi-site Family Study on Incarceration, Parenting and Partnering, 2008–2014 [5 States]." Ann Arbor, MI: Inter-university Consortium for Political and Social Research [distributor] (ICPSR), Nov. 17, 2017. https://doi.org/10.3886/ICPSR36639.v1.

Bittker, Boris I. *The Case for Black Reparations.* New York: Vintage, 1973.

Bloom, Dan. *Programs and Policies to Assist High School Dropouts in the Transition to Adulthood.* Washington, DC: MDRC, 2010. https://files.eric.ed.gov /fulltext/EJ883080.pdf.

Blumstein, Alfred, Jacqueline Cohen, and Daniel Nagin. "The Dynamics of a Homeostatic Punishment Process." *Journal of Criminal Law and Criminology* 67, no. 3 (1977): 317–34.

Bobo, Lawrence D., and Victor Thompson. "Racialized Mass Incarceration: Poverty, Prejudice, and Punishment." In *Doing Race: 21 Essays for the 21st Century*, edited by Hazel R. Markus and Paula Moya, 322–55. New York: Norton, 2010.

Bolner, James. "Toward a Theory of Racial Reparations." In *Redress for Historical Injustices in the United States: On Reparations for Slavery, Jim Crow, and Their Legacies*, edited by Michael Martin and Marilyn Yaquinto, 134–42. Durham, NC: Duke University Press, 2007.

Bombay, Amy, Kimberly Matheson, and Hymie Anisman. "The Intergenerational Effects of Indian Residential Schools: Implications for the Concept of Historical Trauma." *Transcultural Psychiatry* 51, no. 3 (2014): 320–38.

Bonam, Courtney M., Vinoadharen Nair Das, Brett R. Coleman, and Phia Salter. "Ignoring History, Denying Racism: Mounting Evidence for the Marley Hypothesis and Epistemologies of Ignorance." *Social Psychological and Personality Science* 10, no. 2 (2019): 257–65. https://doi.org/10.1177 /1948550617751583.

Bonczar, Thomas P. *Prevalence of Imprisonment in the U.S. Population, 1974–2001.* Washington, DC: US Department of Justice, 2003.

Borrero, Noah E., Christine J. Yeh, Crivir I. Cruz, and Jolene F. Suda. "School as a Context for 'Othering' Youth and Promoting Cultural Assets." *Teachers College Record* 114, no. 2 (2012): 1–37.

Boucher, Olivier, Matthew J. Burden, Gina Muckle, Dave Saint-Amour, Pierre Ayotte, Éric Dewailly, et al. "Response Inhibition and Error Monitoring during a Visual Go/No-Go Task in Inuit Children Exposed to Lead, Poly-chlorinated Biphenyls, and Methylmercury." *Environmental Health Perspectives* 120, no. 4 (2012): 608–15. https://doi.org/10.1289/ehp.1103828.

Brame, Robert, Michael G. Turner, Raymond Paternoster, and Shawn D. Bushway. "Cumulative Prevalence of Arrest from Ages 8 to 23 in a National Sample." *Pediatrics* 129, no. 1 (2012): 21–27.

Brave Heart, Maria Yellow Horse. "Wakiksuyapi: Carrying the Historical Trauma of the Lakota." *Tulane Studies in Social Welfare* 21, no. 22 (2000): 245–66.

Brave Heart, Maria Yellow Horse, Josephine Chase, Jennifer Elkins, and Deborah B. Altschul. "Historical Trauma among Indigenous Peoples of the Americas: Concepts, Research, and Clinical Considerations." *Journal of Psychoactive Drugs* 43, no. 4 (2011): 282–90.

Brave Heart, Maria Yellow Horse, Jennifer Elkins, Greg Tafoya, Doreen Bird, and Melina Salvador. "Wicasa Was'aka: Restoring the Traditional Strength of American Indian Boys and Men." *American Journal of Public Health* 102, Suppl 2 (2012): S177–83.Brewer-Smyth, Kathleen, Ryan T. Pohlig, and Gabriel Bucurescu. "Female Children with Incarcerated Adult Family Members at Risk for Lifelong Neurological Decline." *Health Care for Women International* 37, no. 7 (2016): 802–13. https://doi.org/10.1080/07399332.2016.1140768.

Bridgeland, John M, Erin S. Ingram, and Matthew Atwell. *A Bridge to Reconnection: A Plan for Reconnecting One Million Opportunity Youth Each Year through Federal Funding Streams.* Washington, DC: Civic Enterprises, 2016.

Bromet, Evelyn, Laura Helena Andrade, Irving Hwang, Nancy A. Sampson, Jordi Alonso, Giovanni de Girolamo, et al. "Cross-National Epidemiology of DSM-IV Major Depressive Episode." *BMC Medicine* 9, no. 1 (2011): 90. https://doi.org/10.1186/1741-7015-9-90.

Bronson, Jennifer, and E. Ann Carson. *Prisoners in 2017.* Washington, DC: US Department of Justice, 2019. https://www.bjs.gov/content/pub/pdf/p17.pdf.

Bronson, Jennifer, Laura M. Maruschak, and Marcus Berzofsky. "Disabilities among Prison and Jail Inmates, 2011–12." Washington, DC: US Department of Justice, 2015.

Brophy, Alfred L. "Reconsidering Reparations." *Indiana Law Journal* 81, no. 3 (2006): 811–50.

Brotman, Laurie Miller, Spring Dawson-McClure, Dimitra Kamboukos, Keng-Yen Huang, Esther J. Calzada, Keith Goldfeld, et al. "Effects of ParentCorps in Prekindergarten on Child Mental Health and Academic Performance: Follow-Up of a Randomized Clinical Trial through 8 Years of Age." *JAMA Pediatrics* 170, no. 12 (2016): 1149–55.

Bruns, Angela, and Hedwig Lee. Partner Incarceration and Women's Substance Use." *Journal of Marriage and Family* 82, no. 4 (2020): 1178–96. https://doi.org/10.1111/jomf.12659.

Burke, Jeffrey D., Edward P. Mulvey, and Carol A. Schubert. "Prevalence of Mental Health Problems and Service Use among First-Time Juvenile Offenders." *Journal of Child and Family Studies* 24, no. 12 (2015): 3774–81. https://doi.org/10.1007/s10826-015-0185-8.

Burnette, Catherine. "Historical Oppression and Intimate Partner Violence Experienced by Indigenous Women in the United States: Understanding Connections." *Social Service Review* 89, no. 3 (2015): 531–63. https://doi.org/10.1086/683336.

Bushway, Shawn D., Michael A. Stoll, and David Weiman, eds. *Barriers to Reentry? The Labor Market for Released Prisoners in Post-Industrial America*. New York: Russell Sage, 2007.

Butler, Paul. *Chokehold: Policing Black Men*. New York: New Press, 2017.

Cadora, Eric, and Laura Kurgan. "The Crime in Criminal Data." *Architecture: The AIA Journal; Washington* 95, no. 10 (2006): 52–53.

Caldwell, H. Mitchell. "Reeling In Gang Prosecution: Seeking a Balance in Gang Prosecution." *University of Pennsylvania Journal of Law and Social Change* 18, no. 4 (2015): 341–75.

Calhoun, Georgia B., Brian A. Glaser, Jon Peiper, and Brendan M. Carr. "Parental Monitoring and Perceptions Related to Juvenile Offenders Who Fight and Carry Weapons." *Journal of Family Violence; New York* 30, no. 5 (2015): 643–50. https://link.springer.com/article/10.1007%2Fs10896-015-9682-1.

Cantwell, Mimi. *Prisoners in 1978*. National Prison Statistics Program. Washington, DC: US Department of Justice, 1979. https://www.bjs.gov/content/pub/pdf/psfi78.pdf.

Carson, E. Ann. "Linking Administrative BJS Data: Better Understanding of Prisoners' Personal Histories by Linking the National Corrections Reporting Program (NCRP) and CARRA Data." Proceedings of the 2015 Federal Committee on Statistical Methodology (FCSM) Research Conference, Washington, DC, Dec. 1–3, 2015. https://nces.ed.gov/fcsm/pdf/A1_Carson_2015FCSM.pdf.

———, *Prisoners in 2018*. Washington, DC: US Department of Justice, April 2020. https://www.bjs.gov/index.cfm?ty=pbdetail&iid=6846.

Carson, E. Ann, and Joseph Mulako-Wangota. *Count of Total Releases*. Washington, DC: US Department of Justice, 2020. https://www.bjs.gov/index.cfm?ty=nps.

CBS News. "Gil Batle." Dec. 27, 2015. YouTube video. www.cbsnews.com/video/ex-cons-artistic-expression-hatched-on-ostrich-eggs/#x.

CDC. "Childhood Lead Poisoning Prevention." National Center for Environmental Health, Dec. 22, 2021. www.cdc.gov/nceh/lead/default.htm.

———. "Infant Mortality: What Is CDC Doing?" Sept. 30, 2020. www.cdc.gov/reproductivehealth/maternalinfanthealth/infantmortality-cdcdoing.htm.

Census Bureau. *America's Families and Living Arrangements: 2020.* Washington, DC: United States Census Bureau, 2020. www.census.gov/data/tables/2020/demo/families/cps-2020.html.

Center on Society and Health. "Mapping Life Expectancy." Richmond: Virginia Commonwealth University, 2016.

Charleston Area Convention and Visitor's Bureau. "Explore Charleston." 2018. www.charlestoncvb.com.

Cheliotis, Leonidas K. "Our Violence and Theirs: Comparing Prison Realities." *South Atlantic Quarterly* 113, no. 3 (2014): 443–46.

Cherney, Adrian, and Robin Fitzgerald. "Finding and Keeping a Job: The Value and Meaning of Employment for Parolees." *International Journal of Offender Therapy and Comparative Criminology* 60, no. 1 (2016): 21–37. https://doi.org/10.1177/0306624X14548858.

Chetty, Raj, Michael Stepner, Sarah Abraham, Shelby Lin, Benjamin Scuderi, Nicholas Turner, et al. "The Association between Income and Life Expectancy in the United States, 2001–2014." *JAMA: The Journal of the American Medical Association* 315, no. 16 (2016): 1750–66. https://doi.org/10.1001/jama.2016.4226.

Children's Defense Fund. "How to Cut Child Poverty by 60 Percent Right Now." Jan. 28, 2015. www.childrensdefense.org/2015/how-to-cut-child-poverty-by-60-percent-right-now.

Christian, Jeff, Johnna Mellow, and Shenique Thomas. "Social and Economic Implications of Family Connections to Prisoners." *Journal of Criminal Justice* 34, no. 4 (2006): 443–52.

Christian, Johnna. "Riding the Bus: Barriers to Prison Visitation and Family Management Strategies." *Journal of Contemporary Criminal Justice* 21, no. 1 (2005): 31–48.

Clark, Valerie A., and Grant Duwe. "Distance Matters: Examining the Factors That Impact Prisoner Visitation in Minnesota." *Criminal Justice and Behavior* 44, no. 2 (2017): 184–204. https://doi.org/10.1177/0093854816667416.

Clayton, Gina, Endria Richardson, Lily Mandlin, and Brit Tany Farr. *The Political Isolation and Resistance of Women with Incarcerated Loved Ones.* Oakland, CA: Essie Justice Group, 2018.

Clear, Todd R. "The Effects of High Imprisonment Rates on Communities." *Crime and Justice* 37, no. 1 (2008): 97–132.

———. *Imprisoning Communities: How Mass Incarceration Makes Disadvantaged Neighborhoods Worse.* Oxford: Oxford University Press, 2009.

Clement, M., M. Schwarzfeld, and M. Thompson. *The National Summit on Justice Reinvestment and Public Safety.* New York: Council of State Governments Justice Center, 2011.

Clemmer, Donald. *The Prison Community.* New York: Holt, Rinehart and Winston, 1958.

Coates, Ta-Nehisi. *Between the World and Me*. New York: Spiegel & Grau, 2015.

———. "The Black Family in the Age of Mass Incarceration." *The Atlantic*, Oct. 2015.www.theatlantic.com/magazine/archive/2015/10/the-black-family-in-the-age-of-mass-incarceration/403246.

———. "The Case for Considering Reparations." *The Atlantic*, Jan. 27, 2016. www.theatlantic.com/politics/archive/2016/01/tanehisi-coates-reparations /427041.

———, "The Case for Reparations." *The Atlantic*, June 15, 2014, 54–71.

Cochran, Joshua C., and Daniel P Mears. "Race, Ethnic, and Gender Divides in Juvenile Court Sanctioning and Rehabilitative Intervention." *Journal of Research in Crime and Delinquency* 52, no. 2 (2015): 181–212.

Comfort, Megan. *Doing Time Together: Love and Family in the Shadow of the Prison*. Chicago: University of Chicago Press, 2008.

———. "'Papa's House': The Prison as Domestic and Social Satellite." *Ethnography* 3, no. 4 (2002): 467–99.

———. "Punishment beyond the Legal Offender." *Annual Review of Law and Social Science* 3, no. 1 (2007): 271–96.

———. "'A Twenty-Hour-a-Day Job': The Impact of Frequent Low-Level Criminal Justice Involvement on Family Life." *ANNALS of the American Academy of Political and Social Science* 665, no. 1 (2016): 63–79. https://doi.org/10 .1177/0002716215625038.

Comfort, Megan, Kathleen E. Krieger, Justin G. Landwehr, Tasseli McKay, Christine H. Lindquist, Rose Feinberg, et al. "Partnerships after Prison: Couple Relationships during Reentry." *Journal of Offender Rehabilitation* 57, no. 2 (2018): 188–205. https://doi.org/10.1080/10509674.2018 .1441208.

Comfort, Megan, Tasseli McKay, Justin Landwehr, Erin Kennedy, Anupa Bir, and Christine Lindquist. "The Costs of Incarceration for Families of Prisoners." *International Review of the Red Cross* 98, no. 903 (2017): 1–16.

Comfort, Megan, Tasseli McKay, Justin Landwehr, Erin Kennedy, Christine Lindquist, and Anupa Bir. *Parenting and Partnership When Fathers Return from Prison: Findings from Qualitative Analysis*. Washington, DC: ASPE Research Brief, 2016.

Comfort, Megan, Anne Nurse, Tasseli McKay, and Katie Kramer. "Taking Children into Account: Addressing Intergenerational Effects of Parental Incarceration." *Criminology & Public Policy* 10, no. 3 (2011): 839–50.

Condry, Rachel, and Peter Scharff Smith, eds. *Prisons, Punishment, and the Family: Towards a New Sociology of Punishment?* Oxford: Oxford University Press, 2018.

Council on State Governments. *Confined and Costly*. Washington, DC: CSG Justice Center, June 2019. https://csgjusticecenter.org/publications /confined-costly.

Crutchfield, Robert D., and Gregory A. Weeks. "The Effects of Mass Incarceration on Communities of Color." *Issues in Science and Technology* 32, no. 1 (2015): 46–51.

Dahl, Gordon B., and Lance Lochner. "The Impact of Family Income on Child Achievement: Evidence from the Earned Income Tax Credit." *American Economic Review* 102, no.5 (2012): 1927–56.

Dallaire, Danielle H., Anne Ciccone, and Laura C. Wilson. "Teachers' Experiences with and Expectations of Children with Incarcerated Parents." *Journal of Applied Developmental Psychology* 31, no. 4 (2010): 281–90. https://doi.org/10.1016/j.appdev.2010.04.001.

Darity, William A., Jr. "Forty Acres and a Mule in the 21st Century." *Social Science Quarterly* 89, no. 3 (2008): 656–64.

———. "How Obama Failed Black Americans." *The Atlantic*, Dec. 22, 2016. www.theatlantic.com/politics/archive/2016/12/how-barack-obama-failed-black-americans/511358.

Darity, William [A.], Jr., and Dania [V.] Frank. "The Economics of Reparations." *American Economic Review* 93, no. 2 (2003): 326–29. https://doi.org/10.1257/000282803321947281.

Darity, William A., Jr., Bidisha Lahiri, and Dania V. Frank. "Reparations for African-Americans as a Transfer Problem: A Cautionary Tale." *Review of Development Economics* 14, no. 2 (2010): 248–61. https://doi.org/10.1111/j.1467-9361.2010.00550.x.

Darity, William A., Jr., and A. Kirsten Mullen. *From Here to Equality: Reparations for Black Americans in the Twenty-First Century*. Chapel Hill: University of North Carolina Press, 2020.

Davis, BreAnna L., Mia A. Smith-Bynum, Farzana T. Saleem, Tiffany Francois, and Sharon F. Lambert. "Racial Socialization, Private Regard, and Behavior Problems in African American Youth: Global Self-Esteem as a Mediator." *Journal of Child and Family Studies* 26, no. 3 (2017): 709–20. https://doi.org/10.1007/s10826-016-0601-8.

Davis, Maryann, Steven Banks, William Fisher, and Albert Grudzinskas. "Longitudinal Patterns of Offending during the Transition to Adulthood in Youth from the Mental Health System." *Journal of Behavioral Health Services & Research* 31, no. 4 (2004): 351–66. https://doi.org/10.1007/BF02287689.

De Giorgi, Alessandro. "Back to Nothing: Prisoner Reentry and Neoliberal Neglect." *Social Justice* 44, no. 1 (2017): 83–120.

Dekel, Rachel, and Hadass Goldblatt. "Is There Intergenerational Transmission of Trauma? The Case of Combat Veterans' Children." *American Journal of Orthopsychiatry* 78, no. 3 (2008): 281–89. https://doi.org/10.1037/a0013955.

DelSesto, Matthew. "Contested Theories of Prison Labor Practice." *Sociology Compass* 15, no. 7 (2021): https://doi.org/10.1111/soc4.12888.

Del Toro, Juan, Tracey Lloyd, Kim S. Buchanan, Summer Joi Robins, Lucy Zhang Bencharit, Meredith Gamson Smiedt, et al. "The Criminogenic and Psychological Effects of Police Stops on Adolescent Black and Latino Boys." *Proceedings of the National Academy of Sciences—PNAS* 116, no. 17 (2019): 8261–68. https://doi.org/10.1073/pnas.1808976116.

Dennis, Andrea L. "Decriminalizing Childhood." *Fordham Urban Law Journal* 45, no. 1 (2017): 1–44.

Dennison, Susan M., and Kirsten L. Besemer. "Missing and Missing Out: Social Exclusion in Children with an Incarcerated Parent." In Condry and Scharff Smith, *Prisons, Punishment, and the Family*, 87–101.

Desmond, Matthew, Andrew V. Papachristos, and David S. Kirk. "Evidence of the Effect of Police Violence on Citizen Crime Reporting." *American Sociological Review* 85, no. 1 (2020): 184–90. https://doi.org/10.1177/0003122419895979.

deVuono-Powell, Saneta, Chris Schweidler, Alicia Walters, and Azadeh Zohrabi. *Who Pays? The True Cost of Incarceration on Families.* Oakland, CA: Ella Baker Center, Forward Together, Research Action Design, 2015. http://ellabakercenter.org/who-pays-the-true-cost-of-incarceration-on-families.

DeVylder, Jordan E., Jodi J. Frey, Courtney D. Cogburn, Holly C. Wilcox, Tanya L. Sharpe, Hans Y. Oh, et al. "Elevated Prevalence of Suicide Attempts among Victims of Police Violence in the USA." *Journal of Urban Health* 94, no. 5 (2017): 629–36.

DeVylder, Jordan E., Hyun-Jin Jun, Lisa Fedina, Daniel Coleman, Deidre Anglin, Courtney Cogburn, et al. "Association of Exposure to Police Violence with Prevalence of Mental Health Symptoms among Urban Residents in the United States." *JAMA Network Open* 1, no. 7 (2018): e184945.

Dierkhising, Carly B., Susan J. Ko, Briana Woods-Jaeger, Ernestine C. Briggs, Robert Lee, and Robert S. Pynoos. "Trauma Histories among Justice-Involved Youth: Findings from the National Child Traumatic Stress Network." *European Journal of Psychotraumatology* 4, no. 1 (2013): 20274. https://doi.org/10.3402/ejpt.v4i0.20274.

Dilulio, John. "The Coming of the Super-Predators." *Weekly Standard,* Nov. 27, 1995. www.weeklystandard.com/john-j-dilulio-jr/the-coming-of-the-super-predators.

———. "My Black Crime Problem, and Ours." *City Journal* (Spring 1996): www.city-journal.org/html/my-black-crime-problem-and-ours-11773.html.

Dixon, Peter. "Analysis | U.S. Cities and States Are Discussing Reparations for Black Americans. Here's What's Key." *Washington Post,* August 24, 2020. www.washingtonpost.com/politics/2020/08/24/us-cities-states-are-discussing-reparations-black-americans-heres-whats-key.

Doleac, Jennifer L., and Benjamin Hansen. "Does 'Ban the Box' Help or Hurt Low-Skilled Workers? Statistical Discrimination and Employment Outcomes When Criminal Histories Are Hidden." NBER Working Paper Series, Working Paper 22469. National Bureau of Economic Research, Cambridge, MA, July 2016. https://doi.org/10.3386/w22469.

Downer, Jason T., Priscilla Goble, Sonya S. Myers, and Robert C. Pianta. "Teacher-Child Racial/Ethnic Match within Pre-kindergarten Classrooms and Children's Early School Adjustment." *Early Childhood Research Quarterly* 37, no. 4 (2016): 26–38. https://doi.org/10.1016/j.ecresq.2016.02.007.

Dreisinger, Baz. *Incarceration Nations.* New York: Other Press, 2016.

Drum, Kevin. "A Very Brief History of Super-Predators." *Mother Jones,* March 3, 2016. www.motherjones.com/kevin-drum/2016/03/very-brief-history-super-predators.

Du Bois, William Edward Burghardt. *Black Reconstruction in America: An Essay Toward a History of the Part Which Black Folk Played in the Attempt to Reconstruct Democracy in America, 1860–1880.* New York: Oxford University Press, 2007. Originally published 1935.

Dupree, Davido, Tirzah R. Spencer, and Margaret Beale Spencer. "Stigma, Stereotypes and Resilience Identities: The Relationship between Identity Processes and Resilience Processes among Black American Adolescents." In *Youth Resilience and Culture,* edited by Linda C. Theron, Linda Liebenberg, and Michael Ungar, 117–29. Dordrecht: Springer, 2015. https://doi.org/10.1007/978-94-017-9415-2_9.

Durose, Matthew R., Alexia D. Cooper, and Howard N. Snyder. *Recidivism of Prisoners Released in 30 States in 2005: Patterns from 2005 to 2010.* Washington, DC: US Department of Justice, 2014.

Ecker-Lyster, Meghan, and Christopher Niileksela. "Keeping Students on Track to Graduate: A Synthesis of School Dropout Trends, Prevention, and Intervention Initiatives." *Journal of At-Risk Issues* 19, no. 2 (2016): 24–31.

Edelman, Marian Wright. Foreword to *Ending Child Poverty Now.* Children's Defense Fund, 2019. www.childrensdefense.org/wp-content/uploads/2019/04/Ending-Child-Poverty-2019.pdf.

Edelman, Peter B. *So Rich, so Poor: Why It's so Hard to End Poverty in America.* New York: New Press, 2012.

Egalite, Anna J., Brian Kisida, and Marcus A. Winters. "Representation in the Classroom: The Effect of Own-Race Teachers on Student Achievement." *Economics of Education Review* 45 (2015): 44–52.

El-Masri, Samar, Tammy Lambert, and Joanna R. Quinn. *Transitional Justice in Comparative Perspective: Preconditions for Success.* Cham: Springer/Palgrave Macmillan, 2020.

Emdur, Alyse. *Prison Landscapes.* London: Four Corners Books, 2013. www.alyseemdur.com/4_Prison%20Landscapes/index.php.

Enns, Peter K., Youngmin Yi, Megan Comfort, Alyssa W. Goldman, Hedwig Lee, Christopher Muller, Sara Wakefield, Emily A. Wang, and Christopher

Wildeman. "What Percentage of Americans Have Ever Had a Family Member Incarcerated? Evidence from the Family History of Incarceration Survey (FamHIS)." *Socius* 5 (2019): https://doi.org/10.1177/2378023119829332.

Environmental Protection Agency. "Mortality Risk Valuation." Nov. 20, 2020. www.epa.gov/environmental-economics/mortality-risk-valuation.

Eppler-Epstein, Sarah, Annie Gurvis, Ryan King, John Wehman, Vivian Hou, Alexandra Tilsley, et al. *The Alarming Lack of Data on Latinos in the Criminal Justice System.* Washington, DC: Urban Institute, 2016. http://urbn.is/cjdata.

Equal Justice Initiative. *United States Still Has Highest Incarceration Rate in the World.* Montgomery: Equal Justice Initiative, 2019. https://eji.org/news/united-states-still-has-highest-incarceration-rate-world.

Evans, Matthew. "A Future without Forgiveness: Beyond Reconciliation in Transitional Justice." *International Politics* 55, no. 5 (2018): 678–92. https://doi.org/10.1057/s41311-017-0091-3.

Federici, Silvia. *Revolution at Point Zero: Housework, Reproduction, and Feminist Struggle.* London: PM Press, 2012.

Feinberg, Rose, and Tasseli McKay. "Connecting Older Prison Reentrants to Health Coverage and Public Benefits: Miami-Dade County's Criminal Mental Health Project." Research Triangle Park, NC: RTI International, 2018. www.rti.org/publication/miami-dade-county%E2%80%99s-criminal-mental-health-project/fulltext.pdf.

Fenning, Pamela, and Jennifer Rose. "Overrepresentation of African American Students in Exclusionary Discipline: The Role of School Policy." *Urban Education* 42, no. 6 (2007): 536–59. https://doi.org/10.1177/0042085907305039.

Fishman, Laura T. *Women at the Wall: A Study of Prisoners' Wives Doing Time on the Outside.* Albany: State University of New York Press, 1990.

Flouri, Eirini, Martina K. Narayannan, and Emily Midouhas. "The Cross-Lagged Relationship between Father Absence and Child Problem Behaviour in the Early Years." *Child: Care, Health, and Development* 41, no. 6 (2015): 1090–97.

Ford, Julian D., Jon D. Elhai, Daniel F. Connor, and B. Christopher Frueh. "Poly-victimization and Risk of Posttraumatic, Depressive, and Substance Use Disorders and Involvement in Delinquency in a National Sample of Adolescents." *Journal of Adolescent Health* 46, no. 6 (2010): 545–52.

Forster, Myriam, Laurel Davis, Timothy J. Grigsby, Christopher J. Rogers, Steven F. Vetrone, and Jennifer B. Unger. "The Role of Familial Incarceration and Ethnic Identity in Suicidal Ideation and Suicide Attempt: Findings from a Longitudinal Study of Latinx Young Adults in California." *American Journal of Community Psychology* 64, no. 1–2 (2019): 191–201. https://doi.org/10.1002/ajcp.12332.

Foster, Holly, and John Hagan. "Incarceration and Intergenerational Social Exclusion." *Social Problems* 54, no. 4 (2007): 399–433.

———. "Maternal and Paternal Imprisonment and Children's Social Exclusion in Young Adulthood." *Journal of Criminal Law & Criminology* 105, no. 2 (2015): 387–429.

———. "The Mass Incarceration of Parents in America: Issues of Race/Ethnicity, Collateral Damage to Children, and Prisoner Reentry." *ANNALS of the American Academy of Political and Social Science* 623, no. 1 (2009): 179–94.

Foucault, Michel, and Arlette Farge. *Le désordre des familles: Lettres de cachet des archives de la bastille au XVIIIe siècle.* Paris: Gallimard, 2014.

Fountain, Erika N., and Jennifer L. Woolard. "How Defense Attorneys Consult with Juvenile Clients about Plea Bargains." *Psychology, Public Policy, and Law* 24, no. 2 (2018): 192–203. https://doi.org/10.1037/law0000158.

Fox, Aaron D., Matthew R. Anderson, Gary Bartlett, John Valverde, Joanna L. Starrels, and Chinazo O. Cunningham. "Health Outcomes and Retention in Care Following Release from Prison for Patients of an Urban Post-Incarceration Transitions Clinic." *Journal of Health Care for the Poor and Underserved* 25, no. 3 (2014): 1139–52. https://doi.org/10.1353/hpu.2014.0139.

Fradella, Henry F., and Michael D. White. "Reforming Stop-and-Frisk." *Criminology, Criminal Justice, Law & Society* 18, no. 3 (2017): 45–64.

Frank, Joseph W., Clemens S. Hong, S. V. Subramanian, and Emily A. Wang. "Neighborhood Incarceration Rate and Asthma Prevalence in New York City: A Multilevel Approach." *American Journal of Public Health* 103, no. 5 (2013): e38–44.

Frankenberg, Erica, Genevieve Siegel-Hawley, and Jia Wang. "Choice without Equity: Charter School Segregation." *Education Policy Analysis Archives/ Archivos Analíticos de Políticas Educativas* 19, no. 0 (2011): 1.

Frazer, Eva, Roger A. Mitchell, LaQuandra S. Nesbitt, Mallory Williams, Edith P. Mitchell, Richard Allen Williams, et al. "The Violence Epidemic in the African American Community: A Call by the National Medical Association for Comprehensive Reform." *Journal of the National Medical Association* 110, no. 1 (2018): 4–15. https://doi.org/10.1016/j.jnma.2017.08.009.

Frias-Armenta, Martha, Juan Carlos Rodríguez-Macías, Víctor Corral-Verdugo, Joaquín Caso-Niebla, and Violeta García-Arizmendi. "Restorative Justice: A Model of School Violence Prevention." *Science Journal of Education* 6, no. 1 (2018): 39–45.

Friedman, Matthew. "Just Facts: As Many Americans Have Criminal Records as College Diplomas." Brennan Center for Justice, Nov. 17, 2015. www.brennancenter.org/our-work/analysis-opinion/just-facts-many-americans-have-criminal-records-college-diplomas.

Friedrich, Alena, Barbara Flunger, Benjamin Nagengast, Kathrin Jonkmann, and Ulrich Trautwein. "Pygmalion Effects in the Classroom: Teacher Expectancy Effects on Students' Math Achievement." *Contemporary*

Educational Psychology 41 (2015): 1–12. https://doi.org/10.1016/j.cedpsych
.2014.10.006.

Frost, Natasha A., and Todd R. Clear. "Understanding Mass Incarceration as a
Grand Social Experiment." *Studies in Law, Politics, and Society* 47 (2009):
159–91.

Frumkin, Peter, JoAnn Jastrzab, Margaret Vaaler, Adam Greeney, Robert T.
Grimm, Kevin Cramer, et al. "Inside National Service: AmeriCorps' Impact
on Participants." *Journal of Policy Analysis and Management* 28, no. 3
(2009): 394–416.

Garg, Arvin, Sarah Toy, Yorghos Tripodis, Michael Silverstein, and Elmer
Freeman. "Addressing Social Determinants of Health at Well Child Care
Visits: A Cluster RCT." *Pediatrics (Evanston)* 135, no. 2 (2015): e296–304.
https://doi.org/10.1542/peds.2014-2888.

Garland, David. *Mass Imprisonment: Social Causes and Consequences.*
London: Sage, 2001.

Garner, Andrew S., Jack P. Shonkoff, Benjamin S. Siegel, Mary I. Dobbins,
Marian F. Earls, Andrew S. Garner, et al. "Early Childhood Adversity, Toxic
Stress, and the Role of the Pediatrician: Translating Developmental Science
into Lifelong Health." *Pediatrics* 129, no. 1 (2012): e224. https://doi.org/10
.1542/peds.2011-2662.

Gase, Lauren Nichol, Beth A. Glenn, Louis M. Gomez, Tony Kuo, Moira Inkelas,
and Ninez A. Ponce. "Understanding Racial and Ethnic Disparities in Arrest:
The Role of Individual, Home, School, and Community Characteristics."
Race and Social Problems 8, no. 4 (2016): 296–312. https://doi.org/10.1007
/s12552-016-9183-8.

Geller, Amanda, Carey E. Cooper, Irwin Garfinkel, Ofira Schwartz-Soicher, and
Ronald B. Mincy. "Beyond Absenteeism: Father Incarceration and Child
Development." *Demography* 49, no. 1 (2012): 49–76.

Geller, Amanda, and Marah A. Curtis. "A Sort of Homecoming: Incarceration
and the Housing Security of Urban Men." *Social Science Research* 40, no. 4
(2011): 1196–1213.

Geller, Amanda, and Allyson Walker Franklin. "Paternal Incarceration and the
Housing Security of Urban Mothers." *Journal of Marriage and Family* 76,
no. 2 (2014): 411–27.

Geller, Amanda, Irwin Garfinkel, and Bruce Western. "The Effects of Incarceration on Employment and Wages: An Analysis of the Fragile Families Survey."
Center for Research on Child Wellbeing, Working Papers 932, Princeton
University, School of Public and International Affairs, Center for Research
on Child Wellbeing. 2006.

———. "Paternal Incarceration and Support for Children in Fragile Families."
Demography 48, no. 1 (2011): 25–47.

George, Lily, Adele N. Norris, Antje Deckert, and Juan Tauri, eds. *Neo-colonial Injustice and the Mass Imprisonment of Indigenous Women.* New York: Palgrave Macmillan, 2020. https://doi.org/10.1007/978-3-030-44567-6.

Gershenson, Seth, Stephen B. Holt, and Nicholas W. Papageorge. "Who Believes in Me? The Effect of Student-Teacher Demographic Match on Teacher Expectations." *Economics of Education Review* 52 (2016): 209–24.

Ghandnoosh, Nazgol. "U.S. Prison Decline: Insufficient to Undo Mass Incarceration." The Sentencing Project, May 19, 2020. www.sentencingproject.org/publications/u-s-prison-decline-insufficient-undo-mass-incarceration.

Giannarelli, Linda, Kye Lippold, Sarah Minton, and Laura Wheaton. *Reducing Child Poverty in the US.* Washington, DC: Urban Institute, Jan. 2015. www.urban.org/research/publication/reducing-child-poverty-us.

Giedrimiene, Dalia, and Rachel King. "Abstract 207: Burden of Cardiovascular Disease (CVD) on Economic Cost. Comparison of Outcomes in US and Europe." *Circulation: Cardiovascular Quality and Outcomes* 10, no. suppl_3 (March 2017): x. https://doi.org/10.1161/circoutcomes.10.suppl_3.207.

Gilliam, Walter S., Angela N. Maupin, Chin R. Reyes, Maria Accavitti, and Frederick Shic. *Do Early Educators' Implicit Biases Regarding Sex and Race Relate to Behavior Expectations and Recommendations of Preschool Expulsions and Suspensions?* Yale University Child Study Center, Sept. 28, 2016.

Golash-Boza, Tanya. "The Parallels between Mass Incarceration and Mass Deportation: An Intersectional Analysis of State Repression." *Journal of World-Systems Research* 22, no. 2 (2016): 484–509. https://doi.org/10.5195/jwsr.2016.616.

Goodkind, Jessica R., Marianna D. LaNoue, and Jaime Milford. "Adaptation and Implementation of Cognitive Behavioral Intervention for Trauma in Schools with American Indian Youth." *Journal of Clinical Child & Adolescent Psychology* 39, no. 6 (2010): 858–72. https://doi.org/10.1080/15374416.2010.517166.

Google Info. "Google Search Results for 'Charleston Plantation.'" 2018. www.google.com/search?q=charleston+plantation&rlz=1C1GCEA_enUS896US896&oq=charleston+plantation&aqs=chrome..69i57j0i512j0i457i512j46i175i199i512l2j0i512l5.3976j0j4&sourceid=chrome&ie=UTF-8.

Gramlich, John. "The Gap between the Number of Blacks and Whites in Prison Is Shrinking." Pew Research Center, April 30, 2019. www.pewresearch.org/fact-tank/2018/01/12/shrinking-gap-between-number-of-blacks-and-whites-in-prison.

Gray, David C. "A No-Excuse Approach to Transitional Justice: Reparations as Tools of Extraordinary Justice." *Washington University Law Review* 87, no. 5 (2010): 1043–1104.

Green, Kerry M., Margaret E. Ensminger, Judith A. Robertson, and Hee-Soon Juon. "Impact of Adult Sons' Incarceration on African American Mothers' Psychological Distress." *Journal of Marriage and Family* 68, no. 2 (2006): 430–41.

Greenfeld, Larry, and Steven Smith. *American Indians and Crime.* Washington, DC: US Department of Justice, 1999.

Griffin, Patrick, Sean Addie, Benjamin Adams, and Kathy Firestine. "Trying Juveniles as Adults: An Analysis of State Transfer Laws and Reporting." Washington, DC: US Department of Justice, 2011.

Grills, Cheryl, Deanna Cooke, Jason Douglas, Andrew Subica, Sandra Villanueva, and Brittani Hudson. "Culture, Racial Socialization, and Positive African American Youth Development." *Journal of Black Psychology* 42, no. 4 (2016): 343–73. https://doi.org/10.1177/0095798415578004.

Grinstead, Olga, Bonnie Faigeles, Carrie Bancroft, and Barry Zack. "The Financial Cost of Maintaining Relationships with Incarcerated African American Men: A Survey of Women Prison Visitors." *Journal of African-American Men* 6, no. 1 (2001): 59–70.

Grönqvist, Hans, J. Peter Nilsson, and Per-Olof Robling. "Early Lead Exposure and Outcomes in Adulthood." Working paper, 2017.

Gump, James. "Unveiling the Third Force: Toward Transitional Justice in the USA and South Africa, 1973–1994." *Safundi* 15, no. 1 (2014): 75–100.

Hagan, John, and Holly Foster. "Children of the American Prison Generation: Student and School Spillover Effects of Incarcerating Mothers." *Law & Society Review* 46, no. 1 (2012): 37–69. https://doi.org/10.1111/j.1540-5893.2012.00472.x.

Hahn, Robert A., John A. Knopf, Sandra Jo Wilson, Benedict I. Truman, Bobby Milstein, Robert L. Johnson, et al. "Programs to Increase High School Completion: A Community Guide Systematic Health Equity Review." *American Journal of Preventive Medicine* 48, no. 5 (2015): 599–608.

Hairston, Creasie Finney. "Family Ties during Imprisonment: Do They Influence Future Criminal Activity?" *Federal Probation* 52, no. 1 (1988): 48–52.

———. "Family Ties during Imprisonment: Important to Whom and for What?" *Journal of Sociology and Social Welfare* 18, no. 1 (1991): 85–104.

———. *Fathers in Prison and Their Children: Visiting Policy Guidelines.* University of Illinois at Chicago: Jane Addams Center for Social Policy and Research; Jane Addams College of Social Work, 1996.

———. *Focus on Children with Incarcerated Parents: An Overview of the Research Literature.* Baltimore: Annie E. Casey Foundation, 2008.

Hairston, Creasie Finney, and Patricia W. Lockett. "Parents in Prison: New Directions for Social Services." *Social Work with Groups* 32, no. 2 (1987): 162–64.

Hairston, Creasie Finney, and William Oliver. "Women's Experiences with Men's Incarceration and Reentry." In *Women and Girls in the Criminal Justice System,* edited by Russ Immarigeon, 48-1-5. Kingston, NJ: Civic Research Institute, 2011.

Hairston, Creasie Finney, and Cynthia Seymour, eds. *Children with Parents in Prison: Child Welfare Policy, Program, and Practice Issues.* New York: Routledge, 2017.

Halushka, John M. "The Runaround: Punishment, Welfare, and Poverty Survival after Prison." *Social Problems* 67, no. 2 (2020): 233-50.

Hamilton, Darrick, and William Darity. "Can 'Baby Bonds' Eliminate the Racial Wealth Gap in Putative Post-Racial America?" *Review of Black Political Economy* 37, nos. 3-4 (2010): 207-16. https://doi.org/10.1007/s12114-010-9063-1.

Haney, Craig. "The Psychological Impact of Incarceration: Implications for Postprison Adjustment." In *Prisoners Once Removed: The Impact of Incarceration and Reentry on Children, Families, and Communities,* edited by Jeremy Travis and Michelle Waul, 33-66. Washington, DC: Urban Institute, 2003.

———. "Restricting the Use of Solitary Confinement." *Annual Review of Criminology* 1, no. 1 (2018): 285-310. https://doi.org/10.1146/annurev-criminol-032317-092326.

Harvey, Sylvia A. *The Shadow System: Mass Incarceration and the American Family.* New York: Bold Type Books, 2020. https://go.exlibris.link/Bk2v0r0P.

Haskett, Mary E., Katherine C. Okoniewski, Jenna M. Armstrong, Sally Galanti, Evan Lowder, Jessica Loehman, et al. "Feasibility, Acceptability, and Effects of a Peer Support Group to Prevent Child Maltreatment among Parents Experiencing Homelessness." *Children and Youth Services Review* 73 (2017): 187-96. https://doi.org/10.1016/j.childyouth.2016.12.012.

Haskins, Anna R. "Beyond Boys' Bad Behavior: Paternal Incarceration and Cognitive Development in Middle Childhood." *Social Forces* 95, no. 2 (2016): 861-92. https://doi.org/10.1093/sf/sow066.

———. "Paternal Incarceration and Children's Schooling Contexts: Intersecting Inequalities of Educational Opportunity." *Annals of the American Academy of Political and Social Science* 674, no. 1 (2017): 134-62. https://doi.org/10.1177/0002716217732011.

———. "Paternal Incarceration and Child-Reported Behavioral Functioning at Age 9." *Social Science Research* 52 (2015): 18-33. https://doi.org/10.1016/j.ssresearch.2015.01.001.

———. "Unintended Consequences: Effects of Paternal Incarceration on Child School Readiness and Later Special Education Placement." *Sociological Science* 1, no. 11 (2014): 141-58. https://doi.org/10.15195/v1.a11.

Haskins, Anna R., and Wade C. Jacobsen. "Schools as Surveilling Institutions? Paternal Incarceration, System Avoidance, and Parental Involvement in Schooling." *American Sociological Review* 82, no. 4 (2017): 657–84.

Haskins, Anna R., and Erin J. McCauley. "Casualties of Context? Risk of Cognitive, Behavioral and Physical Health Difficulties among Children Living in High-Incarceration Neighborhoods." *Journal of Public Health* 27, no. 2 (2019): 175–83. https://doi.org/10.1007/s10389-018-0942-4.

Hatzenbuehler, Mark L., Katherine Keyes, Ava Hamilton, Monica Uddin, and Sandro Galea. "The Collateral Damage of Mass Incarceration: Risk of Psychiatric Morbidity among Nonincarcerated Residents of High-Incarceration Neighborhoods." *American Journal of Public Health* 105, no. 1 (2015): 138–43. https://doi.org/10.2105/AJPH.2014.302184.

Haushofer, Johannes, and Ernst Fehr. "On the Psychology of Poverty." *Science (American Association for the Advancement of Science)* 344, no. 6186 (2014): 862–67. https://doi.org/10.1126/science.1232491.

Heitzeg, Nancy A. "Education or Incarceration: Zero Tolerance Policies and the School to Prison Pipeline." *Forum on Public Policy Online* 2009, no. 2 (2009). https://eric.ed.gov/?id=EJ870076.

Helm, Rebecca K., Valerie F. Reyna, Allison A. Franz, and Rachel Z. Novick. "Too Young to Plead? Risk, Rationality, and Plea Bargaining's Innocence Problem in Adolescents." *Psychology, Public Policy, and Law* 24, no. 2 (2018): 180–91. https://doi.org/10.1037/law0000156.

Henning, Kristin. "The Challenge of Race and Crime in a Free Society: The Racial Divide in Fifty Years of Juvenile Justice Reform." *George Washington Law Review* 86, no. 6 (2018): 1604–66.

———. "Criminalizing Normal Adolescent Behavior in Communities of Color: The Role of Prosecutors in Juvenile Justice Reform." *Cornell Law Review* 98, no. 2 (2012): 383–462.

Hernández, Pilar. "Trauma in War and Political Persecution: Expanding the Concept." *American Journal of Orthopsychiatry* 72, no. 1 (2002): 16–25.

Hill, Tianna, and Yecenia Casiano. "Issue Brief 57: From Suspension to Support in the Early Grades." Farmington, CT: Child Health and Development Institute, 2017. www.chdi.org/index.php/publications/issue-briefs/issue-brief-57-suspension-support-early-grades.

Hinton, Elizabeth. "Creating Crime: The Rise and Impact of National Juvenile Delinquency Programs in Black Urban Neighborhoods." *Journal of Urban History* 41, no. 5 (2015): 808–24.

———. *From the War on Poverty to the War on Crime: The Making of Mass Incarceration in America.* (Cambridge, MA: Harvard University Press, 2016).

Hinton, Elizabeth, and DeAnza Cook. "The Mass Criminalization of Black Americans: A Historical Overview." *Annual Review of Criminology* 4, no. 1 (2021): 261–86. https://doi.org/10.1146/annurev-criminol-060520-033306.

Hoagwood, Kimberly, and Holly D. Erwin. "Effectiveness of School-Based Mental Health Services for Children: A 10-Year Research Review." *Journal of Child and Family Studies* 6, no. 4 (1997): 435–51. https://doi.org/10.1023/A:1025045412689.

Hochschild, Arlie, and Anne Machung. *The Second Shift: Working Families and the Revolution at Home.* New York: Penguin, 2012.

Hoeve, Machteld, Olivier F. Colins, Eva A. Mulder, Rolf Loeber, Geert Jan J. M. Stams, and Robert R. J. M. Vermeiren. "The Association between Childhood Maltreatment, Mental Health Problems, and Aggression in Justice-Involved Boys." *Aggressive Behavior* 41, no. 5 (2015): 488–501. https://doi.org/10.1002/ab.21586.

Hope, Elan C., and Margaret Beale Spencer. "Civic Engagement as an Adaptive Coping Response to Conditions of Inequality: An Application of Phenomenological Variant of Ecological Systems Theory (PVEST)." In *Handbook on Positive Development of Minority Children and Youth,* edited by Natasha J. Cabrera and Birgit Leyendecker, 421–35. Cham: Springer, 2017. https://doi.org/10.1007/978-3-319-43645-6_25.

Hopkin, Gareth, S. Evans-Lacko, Andrew Forrester, Jenny Shaw, and Graham Thornicroft. "Interventions at the Transition from Prison to the Community for Prisoners with Mental Illness: A Systematic Review." *Administration and Policy in Mental Health and Mental Health Services Research* 45, no. 4 (2018): 623–34.

Horvat, Erin, and James Davis. "Schools as Sites for Transformation: Exploring the Contribution of Habitus." *Youth & Society* 42, no. 1 (2010): 142–70. https://doi.org/10.1177/0044118X09358846.

Hou, Shuangxing, Lianfang Yuan, Pengpeng Jin, Bojun Ding, Na Qin, Li Li, et al. "A Clinical Study of the Effects of Lead Poisoning on the Intelligence and Neurobehavioral Abilities of Children." *Theoretical Biology & Medical Modelling* 10, no. 1 (2013): 13. https://doi.org/10.1186/1742-4682-10-13.

Howell, K. Babe. "The Costs of 'Broken Windows' Policing: Twenty Years and Counting." *Cardozo Law Review* 37, no. 3 (2015): 1059–74.

Institute of Medicine, and National Research Council. "Investing in the Health and Well-Being of Young Adults." Washington, DC: National Academies Press, 2014.

Jacobs, David, and Ronald E. Helms. "Toward a Political Model of Incarceration: A Time-Series Examination of Multiple Explanations for Prison Admission Rates." *American Journal of Sociology* 102, no. 2 (1996): 323–57. https://doi.org/10.1086/230949.

Jaycox, Lisa H., Audra K. Langley, Bradley D. Stein, Marleen Wong, Priya Sharma, Molly Scott, et al. "Support for Students Exposed to Trauma: A Pilot Study." *School Mental Health* 1, no. 2 (2009): 49–60. https://doi.org/10.1007/s12310-009-9007-8.

Johnson, Rucker C. "Ever-Increasing Levels of Parental Incarceration and the Consequences for Children." In *Do Prisons Make Us Safer? The Benefits and Costs of the Prison Boom*, edited by Steven Raphael and Michael A. Stoll, (2009): 177–206. New York.

Johnson, Rucker C., and Steven Raphael. "The Effects of Male Incarceration Dynamics on Acquired Immune Deficiency Syndrome Infection Rates among African American Women and Men." *Journal of Law and Economics* 52, no. 2 (2009): 251–93.

Jones, Damon E., Mark Greenberg, and Max Crowley. "Early Social-Emotional Functioning and Public Health: The Relationship between Kindergarten Social Competence and Future Wellness." *American Journal of Public Health (1971)* 105, no. 11 (2015): 2283–90. https://doi.org/10.2105/ajph.2015 .302630.

Jones, David J. "Primary Prevention and Health Outcomes: Treatment of Residential Lead-Based Paint Hazards and the Prevalence of Childhood Lead Poisoning." *Journal of Urban Economics* 71, no. 1 (2012): 151–64. https://doi .org/10.1016/j.jue.2011.06.002.

Jones, Jerrett. "Examining the Relationship between Paternal Incarceration, Maternal Stress, and Harsh Parenting." Fragile Families Working Paper WP13–03-FF, 2013. https://fragilefamilies.princeton.edu/sites/fragilefamilies /files/wp13-03-ff.pdf.

Jones, Shawn C. T., and Enrique W. Neblett. "Racial-Ethnic Protective Factors and Mechanisms in Psychosocial Prevention and Intervention Programs for Black Youth." *Clinical Child and Family Psychology Review* 19, no. 2 (2016): 134–61. https://doi.org/10.1007/s10567-016-0201-6.

Kaeble, Danielle, and Mary Cowhig. "Correctional Populations in the United States, 2016." US Department of Justice. April 2018, 14. https://bjs.ojp.gov /content/pub/pdf/cpus16.pdf.

Kalleberg, Arne L., and Steven P. Vallas, eds. *Precarious Work*. Bingley, UK: Emerald Group, 2018.

Kampfner, Christina Jose, Katherine Gabel, and Denise Johnston. "Post-Traumatic Stress Reactions in Children of Imprisoned Mothers." In *Children of Incarcerated Parents*, ed. Katherine Gabel and Denise Johnston (New York: Lexington Books, 1995), 89–100.

Karstedt, Susanne, Hollie Nyseth Brehm, and Laura C. Frizzell. "Genocide, Mass Atrocity, and Theories of Crime: Unlocking Criminology's Potential." *Annual Review of Criminology* 4, no. 1 (2021): 75–97. https://doi.org/10.1146 /annurev-criminol-061020-022050.

Kelly-Irving, Michelle, Benoit Lepage, Dominique Dedieu, Mel Bartley, David Blane, Pascale Grosclaude, et al. "Adverse Childhood Experiences and Premature All-Cause Mortality." *European Journal of Epidemiology* 28, no. 9 (2013): 721–34. https://doi.org/10.1007/s10654-013-9832-9.

Kerrison, Erin M., Jennifer Cobbina, and Kimberly Bender. "'Your Pants Won't Save You': Why Black Youth Challenge Race-Based Police Surveillance and the Demands of Black Respectability Politics." *Race and Justice* 8, no. 1 (2018): 7–26.

Khan, Maria R., Lindy Behrend, Adaora A. Adimora, Sharon S. Weir, Becky White, and David A. Wohl. "Dissolution of Primary Intimate Relationships during Incarceration and Implications for Post-Release HIV Transmission." *Journal of Urban Health* 88, no. 2 (2011): 365–75.

Khan, Maria R, Matthew W. Epperson, Pedro Mateu-Gelabert, Melissa Bolyard, Milagros Sandoval, and Samuel R. Friedman. "Incarceration, Sex with an STI- or HIV-Infected Partner, and Infection with an STI or HIV in Bushwick, Brooklyn, NY: A Social Network Perspective." *American Journal of Public Health* 101, no. 6 (2011): 1110–17.

Khan, Maria R., William C. Miller, Victor J. Schoenbach, Sharon S. Weir, Jay S. Kaufman, David A. Wohl, et al. "Timing and Duration of Incarceration and High-Risk Sexual Partnerships among African Americans in North Carolina." *Annals of Epidemiology* 18, no. 5 (2008): 403–10. https://doi.org/10.1016/j.annepidem.2007.12.003.

Kim, Catherine Y., Daniel J. Losen, and Damon T. Hewitt. *The School-to-Prison Pipeline.* New York: New York University Press, 2010.

King, Desmond S., and Jennifer M. Page. "Towards Transitional Justice? Black Reparations and the End of Mass Incarceration." *Ethnic and Racial Studies* 41, no. 4 (2018): 739–58. https://doi.org/10.1080/01419870.2018.1381341.

King, Martin Luther, Jr. "Speech to Striking Sanitation Workers." Memphis, TN, March 18, 1968. Martin Luther King, Jr., Research and Education Institute, Stanford University. Chapter 31: The Poor People's Campaign. https://kinginstitute.stanford.edu/king-papers/publications/autobiography-martin-luther-king-jr-contents/chapter-31-poor-peoples.

Kirk, David S. "A Natural Experiment of the Consequences of Concentrating Former Prisoners in the Same Neighborhoods." *Proceedings of the National Academy of Sciences* 112, no. 22 (2015): 6943–48.

Kirk, David S., and Robert J. Sampson. "Juvenile Arrest and Collateral Educational Damage in the Transition to Adulthood." *Sociology of Education* 86, no. 1 (2013): 36–62.

Kirk, David S., and Sara Wakefield. "Collateral Consequences of Punishment: A Critical Review and Path Forward." *Annual Review of Criminology* 1, no. 1 (2018): 171–94. https://doi.org/10.1146/annurev-criminol-032317-092045.

Kling, Jeffrey. "Incarceration Length, Employment, and Earnings." *American Economic Review* 96, no. 3 (2006): 863–76.

Knittel, Andrea K., Rachel C. Snow, Derek M. Griffith, and Jeffrey Morenoff. "Incarceration and Sexual Risk: Examining the Relationship between Men's Involvement in the Criminal Justice System and Risky Sexual Behavior."

AIDS and Behavior 17, no. 8 (2013): 2703–14. https://doi.org/10.1007/s10461-013-0421-4.

Kramer, Rory, and Brianna Remster. "Stop, Frisk, and Assault? Racial Disparities in Police Use of Force during Investigatory Stops." *Law & Society Review* 52, no. 4 (2018): 960–93. https://doi.org/10.1111/lasr.12366.

Krug, Etienne G., James A. Mercy, Linda L. Dahlberg, and Anthony B. Zwi. "The World Report on Violence and Health." *The Lancet* 360, no. 9339 (2002): 1083–88.

Kukorowski, Drew. "The Price to Call Home: State-Sanctioned Monopolization in the Prison Phone Industry." Northampton, MA: Prison Policy Initiative, 2012.

Kupchik, Aaron, and Torin Monahan. "The New American School: Preparation for Post-Industrial Discipline." *British Journal of Sociology of Education* 27, no. 5 (2006): 617–31. https://doi.org/10.1080/01425690600958816.

Kupers, Terry A. *Solitary.* Berkeley: University of California Press, 2017. https://www.ucpress.edu/book/9780520292239/solitary.

———. "Trauma and Its Sequelae in Male Prisoners: Effects of Confinement, Overcrowding, and Diminished Services." *American Journal of Orthopsychiatry* 66, no. 2 (1996): 189–96.

Kurlychek, Megan C., and Brian D. Johnson. "Cumulative Disadvantage in the American Criminal Justice System." *Annual Review of Criminology* 2, no. 1 (2019): 291–319. https://doi.org/10.1146/annurev-criminol-011518-024815.

Lacey, Nicola. *Penal Theory and Penal Practice: A Communitarian Approach.* Cullompton, UK: Willan, 2003.

Lageson, Sarah, and Christopher Uggen. "How Work Affects Crime—and Crime Affects Work—over the Life Course." In *Handbook of Life-Course Criminology,* edited by Chris L. Gibson and Marvin D. Krohn, 201–12. New York: Springer, 2013.

Lageson, Sarah Esther. *Digital Punishment: Privacy, Stigma, and the Harms of Data-Driven Criminal Justice.* New York: Oxford University Press, 2020.

Lageson, Sarah Esther, Mike Vuolo, and Christopher Uggen. "Legal Ambiguity in Managerial Assessments of Criminal Records." *Law & Social Inquiry* 40, no. 1 (2015): 175–204. https://doi.org/10.1111/lsi.12066.

Lambert, Lisa. "More Americans Move to Cities in Past Decade-Census." Reuters, March 26, 2012. www.reuters.com/article/usa-cities-population-idUSL2E8EQ5AJ20120326.

LaMontagne, Laurel. "Children under Pressure: The Problem of Juvenile False Confessions and Potential Solutions." *Western State University Law Review* 41, no. 1 (2013): 29–56.

Landrigan, Philip J., Clyde B. Schechter, Jeffrey M. Lipton, Marianne C. Fahs, and Joel Schwartz. "Environmental Pollutants and Disease in American Children: Estimates of Morbidity, Mortality, and Costs for Lead Poisoning,

Asthma, Cancer, and Developmental Disabilities." *Environmental Health Perspectives* 110, no. 7 (2002): 721–28.

Langberg, Jason, and Angela Ciolfi. "Busting the School-to-Prison Pipeline." *Education Digest* 82, no. 5 (2017): 42–47.

Lanskey, Caroline, Friedrich Lösel, Lucy Markson, and Karen Souza. "Prisoners' Families, Penal Power, and the Referred Pains of Imprisonment." In Condry and Scharff Smith, *Prisons, Punishment, and the Family,* 181–95.

Lattimore, Pamela K., Kelle Barrick, Alexander Cowell, Debbie Dawes, Danielle Steffey, Stephen Tueller, et al. "Prisoner Reentry Services: What Worked for SVORI Evaluation Participants." Washington, DC: National Institute of Justice, 2012.

Lattimore, Pamela K., Debbie Dawes, and Kelle Barrick. *Desistance from Crime over the Life Course.* Washington, DC: US Department of Justice, 2018. https://www.ncjrs.gov/pdffiles1/nij/grants/252080.pdf.

Lattimore, Pamela K., Beth M. Huebner, and Faye S. Taxman. *Handbook on Moving Corrections and Sentencing Forward: Building on the Record.* Abingdon, UK: Routledge, 2020.

Laub, John H., and Robert J. Sampson. "Turning Points in the Life Course: Why Change Matters to the Study of Crime." *Criminology* 31, no. 3 (1993): 301–25.

Lauder, Thomas Suh, and David Lauter. "Views on Poverty: 1985 and Today." *Los Angeles Times,* August 14, 2016. www.latimes.com/projects/la-na-pol-poverty-poll-interactive.

Leach, Raelene M., Teresa Burgess, and Chris Holmwood. "Could Recidivism in Prisoners Be Linked to Traumatic Grief? A Review of the Evidence." *International Journal of Prisoner Health* 4, no. 2 (2008): 104–19.

Lee, Hedwig, Tyler McCormick, Margaret T. Hicken, and Christopher Wildeman. "Racial Inequalities in Connectedness to Imprisoned Individuals in the United States." *Du Bois Review: Social Science Research on Race* 12, no. 2 (2015): 269–82.

Lee, Hedwig, and Christopher Wildeman. "Things Fall Apart: Health Consequences of Mass Imprisonment for African American Women." *Review of Black Political Economy* 40, no. 1 (2013): 39–52. https://doi.org/10.1007/s12114-011-9112-4.

Lee, Hedwig, Christopher Wildeman, Emily A. Wang, Niki Matusko, and James S. Jackson. "A Heavy Burden: The Cardiovascular Health Consequences of Having a Family Member Incarcerated." *American Journal of Public Health* 104, no. 3 (2014): 421–27.

Legewie, Joscha, and Jeffrey Fagan. "Aggressive Policing and the Educational Performance of Minority Youth." *American Sociological Review* 84, no. 2 (2019): 220–47. https://doi.org/10.1177/0003122419826020.

Lerman, Amy E., and Vesla M. Weaver. *Arresting Citizenship: The Democratic Consequences of American Crime Control.* Chicago: University of Chicago Press, 2014.

Lewis Jr, Charles E., Irwin Garfinkel, and Qin Gao. "Incarceration and Unwed Fathers in Fragile Families." *Journal of Sociology & Social Welfare* 34, no. 3 (2007): 77–94.

Lindert, Jutta, Haim Y. Knobler, Ichiro Kawachi, Paul A. Bain, Moshe Z. Abramowitz, Charlotte McKee, et al. "Psychopathology of Children of Genocide Survivors: A Systematic Review on the Impact of Genocide on Their Children's Psychopathology from Five Countries." *International Journal of Epidemiology* 46, no. 1 (2017): 246–57. https://doi.org/10.1093/ije/dyw161.

Lindquist, Christine H., Tasseli McKay, Anupa Bir, and Danielle Steffey. "The Experiences of Families during a Father's Incarceration: Descriptive Findings from Baseline Data Collection for the Multi-site Family Study on Incarceration, Parenting and Partnering." Washington, DC: US Department of Health and Human Services, 2015.

Lindquist, Christine, Danielle Steffey, Stephen Tueller, Tasseli McKay, Megan Comfort, and Anupa Bir. "The Multisite Family Study on Incarceration, Partnering, and Parenting: Program Impacts." *Journal of Offender Rehabilitation* 57, no. 2 (2018): 115–43. https://doi.org/10.1080/10509674.2018.1441211.

Lofstrom, Magnus, and Steven Raphael. "Incarceration and Crime: Evidence from California's Public Safety Realignment Reform." *ANNALS of the American Academy of Political and Social Science* 664, no. 1 (2016): 196–220. https://doi.org/10.1177/0002716215599732.

Lopoo, Leonard, and Bruce Western. "Incarceration and the Formation and Stability of Marital Unions." *Journal of Marriage and Family* 67, no. 3 (2005): 721–34.

Love, Joanna R., and Robert A. Fox. "Home-Based Parent Child Therapy for Young Traumatized Children Living in Poverty: A Randomized Controlled Trial." *Journal of Child & Adolescent Trauma* 12, no. 1 (2019): 73–83. https://doi.org/10.1007/s40653-017-0170-z.

Loyle, Cyanne E. "Transitional Justice and Political Order in Rwanda." *Ethnic and Racial Studies* 41, no. 4 (2018): 663–80. https://doi.org/10.1080/01419870.2017.1366537.

Lundquist, Jennifer Hickes, Devah Pager, and Eiko Strader. "Does a Criminal Past Predict Worker Performance? Evidence from One of America's Largest Employers." *Social Forces* 96, no. 3 (2018): 1039–68.

Luther, Kate. "Examining Social Support among Adult Children of Incarcerated Parents." *Family Relations* 64, no. 4 (2015): 505–18.

Lykes, M. Brinton, and Hugo van der Merwe. "Exploring/Expanding the Reach of Transitional Justice." *International Journal of Transitional Justice* 11, no. 3 (2017): 371–77. https://doi.org/10.1093/ijtj/ijx026.

Maag, Elaine, Donald Marron, and Erin Huffer. *Expanding the Earned Income Tax Credit: The Economic Security Project's Cost-of-Living Refund.* Washington, DC: Urban Institute, June 10, 2019. www.taxpolicycenter.org/publications /expanding-earned-income-tax-credit-economic-security-projects-cost-living-refund.

Madley, Benjamin. "California's First Mass Incarceration System: Franciscan Missions, California Indians, and Penal Servitude, 1769–1836." *Pacific Historical Review* 88, no. 1 (2019): 14–47.

Mallett, Christopher A. "The School-to-Prison Pipeline: A Critical Review of the Punitive Paradigm Shift." *Child and Adolescent Social Work Journal* 33, no. 1 (2016): 15–24.

Manchak, Sarah M., Carrie Coen Sullivan, Myrinda Schweitzer, and Christopher J. Sullivan. "The Influence of Co-occurring Mental Health and Substance Use Problems on the Effectiveness of Juvenile Drug Courts." *Criminal Justice Policy Review* 27, no. 3 (2016): 247–64. https://doi.org/10.1177 /0887403414564464.

Mancillas, Linda K. *Presidents and Mass Incarceration: Choices at the Top, Repercussions at the Bottom.* Santa Barbara: Praeger, 2018.

Manza, Jeff, and Christopher Uggen. *Locked Out: Felon Disenfranchisement and American Democracy.* New York: Oxford University Press, 2006.

Markowitz, Gerald. "The Childhood Lead Poisoning Epidemic in Historical Perspective." *Endeavour* 40, no. 2 (2016): 93–101. https://doi.org/10.1016 /j.endeavour.2016.03.006.

Maroto, Michelle, and Bryan L. Sykes. "The Varying Effects of Incarceration, Conviction, and Arrest on Wealth Outcomes among Young Adults." *Social Problems* 67, no. 4 (2020): 698–718. https://doi.org/10.1093/socpro/spz023.

Martin, Carol, and Kimmet Edgar. "The Social Context of Prison Violence." *Criminal Justice Matters* 42, no. 1 (2000): 24–25. https://doi.org/10 .1080/09627250008552883.

Martin, Michael T., and Marilyn Yaquinto. *Redress for Historical Injustices in the United States: On Reparations for Slavery, Jim Crow, and Their Legacies.* Durham, NC: Duke University Press, 2007. https://find.library.duke.edu /catalog/DUKE003876909.

Massoglia, Michael, and William Alex Pridemore. "Incarceration and Health." *Annual Review of Sociology* 41, no. 1 (2015): 291–310. https://doi.org/10.1146 /annurev-soc-073014-112326.

Massoglia, Michael, Brianna Remster, and Ryan D. King. "Stigma or Separation? Understanding the Incarceration-Divorce Relationship." *Social Forces* 90, no. 1 (2011): 133–55. https://doi.org/10.1093/sf/90.1.133.

Masten, Ann S., Aria E. Fiat, Madelyn H. Labella, and Ryan A. Strack. "Educating Homeless and Highly Mobile Students: Implications of Research on Risk and Resilience." *School Psychology Review* 44, no. 3 (2015): 315–30.

Mauer, Marc. "Why Are Tough on Crime Policies So Popular?" *Stanford Law & Policy Review* 11, no. 1 (1999): 9–22.

Mauer, Marc, and Nazgol Ghandnoosh. "Can We Wait 88 Years to End Mass Incarceration?" *Huffington Post*, Dec. 6, 2017. www.huffpost.com/entry/88-years-mass-incarceration_b_4474132?guccounter=1.

Mayfield, Demmie, Gail McLeod, and Patricia Hall. "The CAGE Questionnaire: Validation of a New Alcoholism Screening Instrument." *American Journal of Psychiatry* 131, no. 10 (1974): 1121–23.

McCarthy, Patrick, Vincent N. Schiraldi, and Miriam Shark. *The Future of Youth Justice: A Community Based Alternative to the Youth Prison Model.* Cambridge, MA: Harvard Kennedy School of Government, Oct. 2016. www.hks.harvard.edu/centers/wiener/programs/criminaljustice/research-publications/executive-sessions/executive-session-on-community-corrections.

McKay, Tasseli, Megan Comfort, Christine Lindquist, and Anupa Bir. *Holding on: Family and Fatherhood during Incarceration and Reentry.* Oakland: University of California Press, 2019.

———. "If Family Matters: Supporting Family Relationships during Incarceration and Reentry." *Criminology & Public Policy* 15, no. 2 (2016): 529–42.

McKay, Tasseli, Rose Feinberg, Justin Landwehr, Julianne Payne, Megan Comfort, Christine Lindquist, Erin Kennedy, and Anupa Bir. "'Always Having Hope': Father–Child Relationships after Reentry from Prison." *Journal of Offender Rehabilitation* 57, no. 2 (2018): 162–87. https://doi.org/10.1080/10509674.2018.1441206.

McKay, Tasseli, Justin Landwehr, Christine Lindquist, Rose Feinberg, Megan Comfort, Julia Cohen, et al. "Intimate Partner Violence in Couples Navigating Incarceration and Reentry." *Journal of Offender Rehabilitation* 57, no. 5 (2018): 273–93. https://doi.org/10.1080/10509674.2018.1487897.

McKay, Tasseli, Christine Lindquist, Rose Feinberg, Danielle Steffey, Justin Landwehr, and Anupa Bir. "Family Life before and during Incarceration." *Journal of Offender Rehabilitation* 57, no. 2 (2018): 96–114. https://doi.org/10.1080/10509674.2018.1441209.

McLanahan, Sara, Laura Tach, and Daniel Schneider. "The Causal Effects of Father Absence." *Annual Review of Sociology* 39, no. 1 (2013): 399–427.

McLeod, Allegra. "Prison Abolition and Grounded Justice." *Georgetown Law Faculty Publications and Other Works* (2015): 1490. https://scholarship.law.georgetown.edu/facpub/1490.

Meares, Tracey. "Broken Windows, Neighborhoods, and the Legitimacy of Law Enforcement or Why I Fell in and out of Love with Zimbardo." *Journal of Research in Crime and Delinquency* 52, no. 4 (2015): 609–25. https://doi.org/10.1177/0022427815583911.

———. "Policing and Procedural Justice: Shaping Citizens' Identities to Increase Democratic Participation." *Northwestern University Law Review* 111, no. 6 (2017): 1525–35.

Meares, Tracey L. "The Law and Social Science of Stop and Frisk." *Annual Review of Law and Social Science* 10, no. 1 (2014): 335–52. https://doi.org/10.1146/annurev-lawsocsci-102612-134043.

Mears, Daniel P., and Sonja E. Siennick. "Young Adult Outcomes and the Life-Course Penalties of Parental Incarceration." *Journal of Research in Crime and Delinquency* 53, no. 1 (2016): 3–35.

Meek, Amy P. "Street Vendors, Taxicabs, and Exclusion Zones: The Impact of Collateral Consequences of Criminal Convictions at the Local Level." *Ohio State Law Journal* 75, no. 1 (2014): 1–56.

Michalopoulos, Charles, Helen Lee, Anne Duggan, Erika Lundquist, Ada Tso, Sarah Shea Crowne, et al. *The Mother and Infant Home Visiting Program Evaluation: Early Findings on the Maternal, Infant, and Early Childhood Home Visiting Program.* OPRE Report 2015-11. Washington, DC: US Department of Health and Human Services, 2015.

Mielke, Howard W., and Sammy Zahran. "The Urban Rise and Fall of Air Lead (Pb) and the Latent Surge and Retreat of Societal Violence." *Environment International* 43 (2012): 48–55. https://doi.org/10.1016/j.envint.2012.03.005.

Miller, Cynthia, Megan Millenky, Lisa Schwartz, Lisbeth Goble, and Jillian Stein. *Building a Future: Interim Impact Findings from the YouthBuild Evaluation.* MDRC/ERIC, Nov. 2016. https://eric.ed.gov/?id=ED571142.

Miller, Reuben Jonathan. *Halfway Home: Race, Punishment, and the Afterlife of Mass Incarceration.* New York: Little, Brown, 2021.

Mills, John R., Anna Dorn, and Amelia Hritz. *Juvenile Life without Parole in Law and Practice: The End of Superpredator Era Sentencing.* Rochester, NY: Social Science Research Network, 2015. https://papers.ssrn.com/abstract=2663834.

Mizel, Matthew L., Jeremy N. V. Miles, Eric R. Pedersen, Joan S. Tucker, Brett A. Ewing, and Elizabeth J. D'Amico. "To Educate or to Incarcerate: Factors in Disproportionality in School Discipline." *Children and Youth Services Review* 70 (2016): 102–11. https://doi.org/10.1016/j.childyouth.2016.09.009.

Moody, Myles. "From Under-Diagnoses to Over-Representation: Black Children, ADHD, and the School-to-Prison Pipeline." *Journal of African American Studies* 20, no. 2 (2016): 152–63.

Morenoff, Jeffrey D., and Sam Norris. "Measuring Costs and Benefits of Incarceration." Unpublished congressional briefing presented at the Cost and Effect: Measuring the Impact of Incarceration on Individuals, Neighborhoods, and Society event. Washington, DC, Oct. 19, 2019.

Morrison, Toni. *Beloved.* New York: Alfred A. Knopf, 1987. Reprint, New York: Vintage, 2007.

Movement for Black Lives. "Vision for Black Lives." M4BL, 2020. https://m4bl
.org/policy-platforms.

Mowen, Thomas J., and Christy A. Visher. "Changing the Ties That Bind."
Criminology & Public Policy 15, no. 2 (2016): 503–28.

Muniz, Ana. "Maintaining Racial Boundaries: Criminalization, Neighborhood
Context, and the Origins of Gang Injunctions." *Social Problems* 61, no. 2
(2014): 216–36. https://doi.org/10.1525/sp.2014.12095.

Murphey, David, and P. Mae Cooper. *Parents behind Bars: What Happens to
Their Children?* Washington, DC: Child Trends, 2015. www.childtrends.org
/publications/parents-behind-bars-what-happens-to-their-children.

Murphy, J. Michael, Madelaine R. Abel, Sharon Hoover, Michael Jellinek, and
Mina Fazel. "Scope, Scale, and Dose of the World's Largest School-Based
Mental Health Programs." *Harvard Review of Psychiatry* 25, no. 5 (2017):
218–28. https://doi.org/10.1097/HRP.0000000000000149.

Musu-Gillette, Lauren, Anlan Zhang, Ke Wang, Jizhi Zhang, J. Kemp, M.
Diliberti, and Barbara Oudekerk. *Indicators of School Crime and Safety:
2017* (NCES 2018–036/NCJ 251413). Washington, DC: National Center for
Education Statistics, 2018. https://nces.ed.gov/pubs2018/2018036.pdf.

Musu-Gillette, Lauren, Anlan Zhang, Ke Wang, Jizhi Zhang, and Barbara A.
Oudekerk. *Indicators of School Crime and Safety: 2016.* Washington, DC:
National Center for Educational Statistics, 2017. https://nces.ed.gov/pubs2017
/2017064.pdf.

NASRO. "School Resource Officers: Frequently Asked Questions." National
Association of School Resource Officers. Hoover, AL: NASRO, 2018. https://
nasro.org/faq.

National Academies of Sciences, Engineering and Medicine. *The Effects of
Incarceration and Reentry on Community Health and Well-Being: Proceedings of a Workshop.* Washington, DC: National Academies Press, 2020.
https://doi.org/10.17226/25471.

National Institute of Justice. "State Responses to Mass Incarceration." In *Office
of Justice Programs.* Washington, DC: US Department of Justice, 2011.
www.ojp.gov/library/publications/state-responses-mass-incarceration-panel-
discussion-2011-nij-conference.

National Research Council. *Reforming Juvenile Justice: A Developmental
Approach.* Washington, DC: National Academies Press, 2013. https://doi
.org/10.17226/14685.

National Research Council and Institute of Medicine. *Juvenile Crime, Juvenile
Justice.* Washington, DC: National Academies Press, 2001. https://www
.nap.edu/catalog/9747/juvenile-crime-juvenile-justice.

Nelson, Jessica C., Glenn Adams, and Phia S. Salter. "The Marley Hypothesis:
Denial of Racism Reflects Ignorance of History." *Psychological Science* 24,
no. 2 (2013): 213–18. https://doi.org/10.1177/0956797612451466.

NeMoyer, Amanda, Sharon Kelley, Heather Zelle, and Naomi E. S. Goldstein. "Attorney Perspectives on Juvenile and Adult Clients' Competence to Plead Guilty." *Psychology, Public Policy, and Law* 24, no. 2 (2018): 171–79.

Nevin, Rick. "Understanding International Crime Trends: The Legacy of Preschool Lead Exposure." *Environmental Research* 104, no. 3 (2007): 315–36.

Nguyen, Quynh C., Dolores Acevedo-Garcia, Nicole M. Schmidt, and Theresa L. Osypuk. "The Effects of a Housing Mobility Experiment on Participants' Residential Environments." *Housing Policy Debate* 27, no. 3 (2017): 419–48.

Nichols, Emily B., Ann B. Loper, and J. Patrick Meyer. "Promoting Educational Resiliency in Youth with Incarcerated Parents: The Impact of Parental Incarceration, School Characteristics, and Connectedness on School Outcomes." *Journal of Youth and Adolescence* 45, no. 6 (2016): 1090–1109. https://doi.org/10.1007/s10964-015-0337-6.

Nicholson-Crotty, Sean, Zachary Birchmeier, and David Valentine. "Exploring the Impact of School Discipline on Racial Disproportion in the Juvenile Justice System." *Social Science Quarterly* 90, no. 4 (2009): 1003–18. https://doi.org/10.1111/j.1540-6237.2009.00674.x.

Nolan, Kathleen. *Police in the Hallways: Discipline in an Urban High School.* Minneapolis: University of Minnesota Press, 2011.

Novak, Abigail. "The Association between Experiences of Exclusionary Discipline and Justice System Contact: A Systematic Review." *Aggression and Violent Behavior* 40 (2018): 73–82.

Nowotny, Kathryn M., and Anastasiia Kuptsevych-Timmer. "Health and Justice: Framing Incarceration as a Social Determinant of Health for Black Men in the United States." *Sociology Compass* 12, no. 3 (2018): e12566. https://doi.org/10.1111/soc4.12566.

Nurse, Anne M. *Fatherhood Arrested: Parenting from within the Juvenile Justice System.* Nashville: Vanderbilt University Press, 2002.

Obama, Barack. "Remarks by the President on Sustainable Development Goals." Speech delivered at the United Nations, New York, Sept. 27, 2015. https://obamawhitehouse.archives.gov/the-press-office/2015/09/27/remarks-president-sustainable-development-goals.

O'Brien, Timothy L. "Arresting Confidence: Mass Incarceration and Black-White Differences in Perceptions of Legal Authorities." *Social Science Quarterly* 101, no. 5 (2020): 1905–19. https://doi.org/10.1111/ssqu.12842.

Ohio History Central. "Margaret Garner." www.ohiohistorycentral.org/w/Margaret_Garner.

Oldrup, Helene, and Signe Frederiksen. "Are the Children of Prisoners Socially Excluded?" In Condry and Scharff Smith, *Prisons, Punishment, and the Family,* 102–17.

Oleson, James. "The New Eugenics: Black Hyper-Incarceration and Human Abatement." *Social Sciences (Basel)* 5, no. 4 (2016): 66. https://doi.org/10.3390/socsci5040066.

Oliver, William, and Creasie Finney Hairston. "Intimate Partner Violence during the Transition from Prison to the Community: Perspectives of Incarcerated African American Men." *Journal of Aggression, Maltreatment & Trauma* 16, no. 3 (2008): 258–76. https://doi.org/10.1080/10926770801925577.

Orfield, Gary, and Erica Frankenberg. "Increasingly Segregated and Unequal Schools as Courts Reverse Policy." *Educational Administration Quarterly* 50, no. 5 (2014): 718–34. https://doi.org/10.1177/0013161x14548942.

Owens, Emily G. "Testing the School-to-Prison Pipeline." *Journal of Policy Analysis and Management* 36, no. 1 (2016): 11–37. https://doi.org/10.1002/pam.21954.

Pager, Devah. *Marked: Race, Crime, and Finding Work in an Era of Mass Incarceration*. Chicago: University of Chicago Press, 2007.

———. "The Mark of a Criminal Record." *American Journal of Sociology* 108, no. 5 (2003): 937–75.

Pager, Devah, and Lincoln Quillian. "Walking the Talk? What Employers Say versus What They Do." *American Sociological Review* 70, no. 3 (2005): 355–80.

Pager, Devah, Bruce Western, and Naomi Sugie. "Sequencing Disadvantage: Barriers to Employment Facing Young Black and White Men with Criminal Records." *ANNALS of the American Academy of Political and Social Science* 623, no. 1 (2009): 195–213.

Palmer, Catrina, and Johnna Christian. "Work Matters: Formerly Incarcerated Men's Resiliency in Reentry." *Equality, Diversity and Inclusion* 38, no. 5 (2019): 583–98. https://doi.org/10.1108/EDI-10-2018-0177.

Panter-Brick, Catherine. "Culture and Resilience: Next Steps for Theory and Practice." In *Youth Resilience and Culture*, edited by Linda C. Theron, Linda Liebenberg, and Michael Ungar, 233–44. Dordrecht: Springer, 2015. https://doi.org/10.1007/978-94-017-9415-2_17.

Parker, Gordon, Stacey McCraw, Dusan Hadzi-Pavlovic, and Kathryn Fletcher. "Costs of the Principal Mood Disorders: A Study of Comparative Direct and Indirect Costs Incurred by Those with Bipolar I, Bipolar II and Unipolar Disorders." *Journal of Affective Disorders* 149, no. 1 (2012): 46–55. https://doi.org/10.1016/j.jad.2012.10.002.

Parker, Lynette. "Schools and the No-Prison Phenomenon: Anti-Blackness and Secondary Policing in the Black Lives Matter Era." *Journal of Educational Controversy* 12, no. 1 (2017): 11.

Pascoe, John M., David L. Wood, James H. Duffee, Alice Kuo, Committee on Psychosocial Aspects of Child and Family Health, and Council on Community Pediatrics. "Mediators and Adverse Effects of Child Poverty in the

United States." *Pediatrics* 137, no. 4 (2016): e20160340. https://doi.org/10
.1542/peds.2016-0340.

Patterson, Evelyn J., and Christopher Wildeman. "Mass Imprisonment and the
Life Course Revisited: Cumulative Years Spent Imprisoned and Marked for
Working-Age Black and White Men." *Social Science Research* 53 (2015):
325–37. https://doi.org/10.1016/j.ssresearch.2015.06.011.

Pattillo, Mary, David Weiman, and Bruce Western. *Imprisoning America: The
Social Effects of Mass Incarceration.* New York: Russell Sage, 2004.

Payne, Allison Ann, and Kelly Welch. "How School and Education Impact the
Development of Criminal and Antisocial Behavior." In *The Development of
Criminal and Antisocial Behavior: Theory, Research, and Practical Applications,* edited by Julien Morizot and Lila Kazemian, 237–51. Cham: Springer,
2015. https://doi.org/10.1007/978-3-319-08720-7_15.

Peguero, Anthony A., Zahra Shekarkhar, Ann Marie Popp, and Dixie J. Koo.
"Punishing the Children of Immigrants: Race, Ethnicity, Generational
Status, Student Misbehavior, and School Discipline." *Journal of Immigrant
& Refugee Studies* 13, no. 2 (2015): 200–220. https://doi.org/10.1080/15562
948.2014.951136.

Pergamit, Michael, Mary Cunningham, and Devlin Hanson. "The Impact of
Family Unification Housing Vouchers on Child Welfare Outcomes." *American Journal of Community Psychology* 60, nos. 1–2 (2017): 103–13. https://
doi.org/10.1002/ajcp.12136.

Pettit, Becky. *Invisible Men: Mass Incarceration and the Myth of Black
Progress.* New York: Russell Sage, 2012.

Pettit, Becky, and Carmen Gutierrez. "Mass Incarceration and Racial Inequality." *American Journal of Economics and Sociology* 77, nos. 3–4 (2018):
1153–82. https://doi.org/10.1111/ajes.12241.

Pettit, Becky, and Bryan L. Sykes. "Civil Rights Legislation and Legalized Exclusion: Mass Incarceration and the Masking of Inequality." *Sociological Forum
(Randolph, NJ)* 30.S1 (2015): 589–611. https://doi.org/10.1111/socf.12179.

Pettit, Becky, and Bruce Western. "Mass Imprisonment and the Life Course:
Race and Class Inequality in U.S. Incarceration." *American Sociological
Review* 69 (2004): 151–69.

Pew Research Center. *On Views of Race and Inequality, Blacks and Whites Are
Worlds Apart.* Washington, DC: Pew Research Center, June 27, 2016. www
.pewsocialtrends.org/2016/06/27/on-views-of-race-and-inequality-blacks-
and-whites-are-worlds-apart.

Phelps, Michelle S. "Mass Probation from Micro to Macro: Tracing the Expansion and Consequences of Community Supervision." *Annual Review of
Criminology* 3, no. 1 (2020): 261–79.

Phillips, Deborah, William Gormley, and Sara Anderson. "The Effects of Tulsa's
CAP Head Start Program on Middle-School Academic Outcomes and

Progress." *Developmental Psychology* 52, no. 8 (2016): 1247–61. https://doi.org/10.1037/dev0000151.

Phillips, Scott W. "Myths, Militarism and the Police Patrol Rifle." *Policing & Society* 26, no. 2 (2016): 185–96. https://doi.org/10.1080/10439463.2014.922088.

Phillips, Susan D., and Trevor Gates. "A Conceptual Framework for Understanding the Stigmatization of Children of Incarcerated Parents." *Journal of Child and Family Studies* 20, no. 3 (2011): 286–94.

Pigott, Christina, Ami E. Stearns, and David N. Khey. "School Resource Officers and the School to Prison Pipeline: Discovering Trends of Expulsions in Public Schools." *American Journal of Criminal Justice* 43, no. 1 (2018): 120–38. https://doi.org/10.1007/s12103-017-9412-8.

Pinard, Michael. *Poor, Black and "Wanted": Criminal Justice in Ferguson and Baltimore.* Digital Commons@UM Carey Law, July 2015.

Pozen, Joanna, Richard Neugebauer, and Joseph Ntaganira. "Assessing the Rwanda Experiment: Popular Perceptions of Gacaca in Its Final Phase." *International Journal of Transitional Justice* 8, no. 1 (2014): 31–52. https://doi.org/10.1093/ijtj/ijt029.

Prins, Annabel, Paige Ouimette, Rachel Kimerling, Rebecca P. Camerond, Daniela S. Hugelshofer, Jennifer Shaw-Hegwer, et al. "The Primary Care PTSD Screen (PC-PTSD): Development and Operating Characteristics." *Primary Care Psychiatry* 9, no. 1 (2004): 9–14. https://doi.org/10.1185/135525703125002360.

Project WHAT. *We're Here and Talking.* Oakland, CA: Community Works West, 2016.

Provencher, Ashley, and James M. Conway. "Health Effects of Family Member Incarceration in the United States: A Meta-Analysis and Cost Study." *Children and Youth Services Review* 103 (2019): 87–99. https://doi.org/10.1016/j.childyouth.2019.05.029.

Prowse, Gwen, Vesla M. Weaver, and Tracey L. Meares. "The State from Below: Distorted Responsiveness in Policed Communities." *Urban Affairs Review* 56, no. 5 (2020): 1423–71. https://doi.org/10.1177/1078087419844831.

Pruitt Walker, Sheri. "The Effects of the Incarceration of Fathers on the Health and Wellbeing of Mothers and Children." PhD diss., University of Maryland, College Park, 2011. https://drum.lib.umd.edu/bitstream/handle/1903/12188/PruittWalker_umd_0117E_12530.pdf?sequence=1&isAllowed=y.

Quane, James M., William Julius Wilson, and Jackelyn Hwang. "Black Men and the Struggle for Work: Social and Economic Barriers Persist." *Education Next* 15, no. 2 (2015): 22–30.

Quinn, Joanna R. "Tractionless Transitional Justice in Uganda: The Potential for Thin Sympathetic Interventions as Ameliorating Factor." In *Transitional Justice in Comparative Perspective: Preconditions for Success,* edited by

Samar El-Masri, Tammy Lambert, and Joanna R. Quinn, 19–48. Cham: Springer, 2020.

Ramey, David M. "Recent Developments in School Social Control." *Sociology Compass* 14, no. 2 (2019): e12743. https://doi.org/10.1111/soc4.12743.

Randall, Robinson. *The Debt: What America Owes to Blacks.* New York: Dutton, 2000.

Raymond, Jaime. "Childhood Blood Lead Levels in Children Aged 5 Years—United States, 2009–2014." *Morbidity and Mortality Weekly Report: Surveillance Summaries* 66, no. 3 (2017): 1–7. https://doi.org/10.15585/mmwr.ss6603a1.

Redlich, Allison D. "The Susceptibility of Juveniles to False Confessions and False Guilty Pleas." *Rutgers Law Review* 62, no. 4 (2009): 943–58.

Reflective Democracy Campaign. *Reflective Democracy Research Findings,* 2017. https://wholeads.us/wp-content/uploads/2019/04/2017-report-corrected-4.2019.pdf.

Reyes, Jessica Wolpaw. "Environmental Policy as Social Policy? The Impact of Childhood Lead Exposure on Crime." *B.E. Journal of Economic Analysis & Policy* 7, no. 1 (2007): 51. https://doi.org/10.2202/1935-1682.1796.

Rice, Whitney S., Samantha S. Goldfarb, Anne E. Brisendine, Stevie Burrows, and Martha S. Wingate. "Disparities in Infant Mortality by Race among Hispanic and Non-Hispanic Infants." *Maternal and Child Health Journal* 21, no. 7 (2017): 1581–88. https://doi.org/10.1007/s10995-017-2290-3.

Richie, Beth E. "The Social Impact of Mass Incarceration on Women." In *Invisible Punishment: The Collateral Consequences of Mass Imprisonment,* edited by Marc Mauer and Meda Chesney-Lind, 136–49. New York: New Press, 2011.

Rios, Victor M. *Human Targets: Schools, Police, and the Criminalization of Latino Youth.* Chicago: University of Chicago Press, 2017.

———. "The Hyper-Criminalization of Black and Latino Male Youth in the Era of Mass Incarceration." *Souls: A Critical Journal of Black Politics, Culture, and Society* 8, no. 2 (2006): 40–54.

———. *Punished: Policing the Lives of Black and Latino Boys.* New York: New York University Press, 2011.

Roberts, Adrienne. *Gendered States of Punishment and Welfare: Feminist Political Economy, Primitive Accumulation and the Law.* London: Routledge, 2016. https://doi.org/10.4324/9781315542362.

Roberts, Dorothy. "The Social and Moral Cost of Mass Incarceration in African American Communities." *Stanford Law Review* 56, no. 5 (2004): 1271–1305.

Robst, John, Mary Armstrong, and Norin Dollard. "The Association between Type of Out-of-Home Mental Health Treatment and Juvenile Justice Recidivism for Youth with Trauma Exposure." *Criminal Behaviour and Mental Health* 27, no. 5 (2017): 501–13. https://doi.org/10.1002/cbm.2024.

Rocque, Michael, and Ray Paternoster. "Understanding the Antecedents of the 'School-to-Jail' Link: The Relationship between Race and School Discipline." *Journal of Criminal Law and Criminology* 101, no. 2 (2011): 633–65.

Rogers, Susan M., Maria R. Khan, Sylvia Tan, Charles F. Turner, William C. Miller, and Emily Erbelding. "Incarceration, High-Risk Sexual Partnerships and Sexually Transmitted Infections in an Urban Population." *Sexually Transmitted Infections* 88, no. 1 (2012): 63–68. https://doi.org/10.1136/sextrans-2011-050280.

Roman, John, Lisa Brooks, Erica Lagerson, Aaron Chalfin, and Bogdan Tereshchenko. *Impact and Cost Benefit Analysis of the Maryland Reentry Partnership Initiative*. Washington, DC: Urban Institute, 2007. http://webarchive.urban.org/UploadedPDF/311421_Maryland_Reentry.pdf.

Rose, Dina R., and Todd R. Clear. "Incarceration, Social Capital, and Crime: Examining the Unintended Consequences of Incarceration." *Criminology* 36, no. 3 (1998): 441–79.

Rosenblatt, Jennifer A., Abram Rosenblatt, and Edward E. Biggs. "Criminal Behavior and Emotional Disorder: Comparing Youth Served by the Mental Health and Juvenile Justice Systems." *Journal of Behavioral Health Services & Research* 27, no. 2 (2000): 227–37.

Ross, Martha, and Nicole Prchal Svajlenka. "Employment and Disconnection among Teens and Young Adults: The Role of Place, Race, and Education." *Brookings*, May 24, 2016. www.brookings.edu/research/employment-and-disconnection-among-teens-and-young-adults-the-role-of-place-race-and-education.

Rossi, Robert J. *Evaluation of Projects Funded by the School Dropout Demonstration Assistance Program: Final Evaluation Report*. Vol. 1, *Findings and Recommendations*. Washington, DC: US Department of Education, 1995.

Ryen, Linda, and Mikael Svensson. "The Willingness to Pay for a Quality Adjusted Life Year: A Review of the Empirical Literature." *Health Economics* 24, no. 10 (2015): 1289–1301. https://doi.org/10.1002/hec.3085.

Sama-Miller, Emily, Lauren Akers, Andrea Mraz-Esposito, Sarah Avellar, Diane Paulsell, and Patricia Del Grosso. *Home Visiting Programs: Reviewing Evidence of Effectiveness*. Washington, DC: US Department of Health and Human Services, 2017.

Sampson, Robert J. *Great American City*. Chicago: University of Chicago Press, 2012.

———. "The Incarceration Ledger: Toward a New Era in Assessing Societal Consequences." *Criminology and Public Policy* 10, no. 3 (2011): 819–28.

Sampson, Robert J., and Charles Loeffler. "Punishment's Place: The Local Concentration of Mass Incarceration." *Daedalus: The Journal of the American Academy of Arts & Sciences* 139, no. 3 (2010): 20–31.

Sampson, Robert J., and Alix S. Winter. "Poisoned Development: Assessing Childhood Lead Exposure as a Cause of Crime in a Birth Cohort Followed through Adolescence." *Criminology* 56, no. 2 (2018): 269–301. https://doi .org/10.1111/1745-9125.12171.

Samuel, Ignatius A. "Utilization of Mental Health Services among African-American Male Adolescents Released from Juvenile Detention: Examining Reasons for Within-Group Disparities in Help-Seeking Behaviors." *Child and Adolescent Social Work Journal* 32, no.1 (2015): 33–43. https://doi .org/10.1007/s10560-014-0357-1.

Sanchez, Amanda L., Danielle Cornacchio, Bridget Poznanski, Alejandra M. Golik, Tommy Chou, and Jonathan S. Comer. "The Effectiveness of School-Based Mental Health Services for Elementary-Aged Children: A Meta-Analysis." *Journal of the American Academy of Child & Adolescent Psychiatry* 57, no. 3 (2018): 153–65. https://doi.org/10.1016/j.jaac.2017.11.022.

Sawyer, Wendy. "Artist Collaboration: Visualizing 10.6 Million Jail Admissions Each Year." Northampton, MA: Prison Policy Initiative, 2018. www .prisonpolicy.org/blog/2018/03/22/chalabi.

———. *The Gender Divide: Tracking Women's State Prison Growth*. Northampton, MA: Prison Policy Initiative, 2018. www.prisonpolicy.org/reports /women_overtime.html.

———. *Youth Confinement: The Whole Pie 2019*. Northampton, MA: Prison Policy Initiative, 2019. www.prisonpolicy.org/reports/youth2019.html.

Sawyer, Wendy, and Peter Wagner. "Mass Incarceration: The Whole Pie 2020." Northampton, MA: Prison Policy Initiative, 2020. www.prisonpolicy.org /reports/pie2020.html.

Schiff, Mara. "Dignity, Disparity and Desistance: Effective Restorative Justice Strategies to Plug the 'School-to-Prison Pipeline.'" UCLA: The Civil Rights Project, Jan. 2013. https://escholarship.org/uc/item/6kw7w8s8.

Schiraldi, Vincent. "Will the Real John Dilulio Please Stand Up." *Washington Post*, Feb. 5, 2001.

Schmitt, John, Kris Warner, and Sarika Gupta. *The High Budgetary Cost of Incarceration*. Washington, DC: Center for Economic and Policy Research, 2010.

Schnepel, Kevin T. "Economics of Incarceration." *Australian Economic Review* 49, no. 4 (2016): 515–23.

Schnittker, Jason, Michael Massoglia, and Christopher Uggen. "Incarceration and the Health of the African American Community." *Dubois Review* 8, no. 1 (2011): 133–41.

———. "Out and Down: Incarceration and Psychiatric Disorders." *Journal of Health and Social Behavior* 53, no. 4 (2012): 448–64. https://doi.org/10.1177 /0022146512453928.

Schochet, Peter Z., John Burghardt, and Sheena McConnell. "Does Job Corps Work? Impact Findings from the National Job Corps Study." *American Economic Review* 98, no. 5 (2008): 1864–86. https://doi.org/10.1257/aer .98.5.1864.

Schoenfeld, Heather. *Building the Prison State: Race and the Politics of Mass Incarceration*. Chicago: University of Chicago Press, 2018.

Schwartz-Soicher, Ofira, Amanda Geller, and Irwin Garfinkel. "The Effect of Paternal Incarceration on Material Hardship." *Social Service Review* 85, no. 3 (2011): 447–73.

Scott, Eugene. "Black Lives Matter Protesters Confront Hillary Clinton at a Fundraiser." *CNNPolitics*, Feb. 25, 2016. www.cnn.com/2016/02/25/politics /hillary-clinton-black-lives-matter-whichhillary/index.html.

Scott-Hayward, Christine S. "Explaining Juvenile False Confessions: Adolescent Development and Policy Interrogation." *Law & Psychology Review* 31 (2007): 53–76.

Serwer, Adam. "The Fight over the 1619 Project Is Not about the Facts." *The Atlantic*, Dec. 23, 2019. www.theatlantic.com/ideas/archive/2019/12/historians-clash-1619-project/604093.

Sesame Street. "Little Children, Big Challenges: Incarceration." YouTube video, June 12, 2013. www.youtube.com/watch?v=QvMm7t29oeM.

Sewell, A. A., and Kevin A. Jefferson. "Collateral Damage: The Health Effects of Invasive Police Encounters in New York City." *Journal of Urban Health: Bulletin of the New York Academy of Medicine* 93, Suppl 1.S1 (2016): 42–67. https://doi.org/10.1007/s11524-015-0016-7.

Sewell, A. A., Kevin A. Jefferson, and Hedwig Lee. "Living under Surveillance: Gender, Psychological Distress, and Stop-Question-and-Frisk Policing in New York City." *Social Science & Medicine* 159 (2016): 1–13. https://doi.org /10.1016/j.socscimed.2016.04.024.

Shannon, Sarah K. S., Christopher Uggen, Jason Schnittker, Melissa Thompson, Sara Wakefield, and Michael Massoglia. "The Growth, Scope, and Spatial Distribution of People with Felony Records in the United States, 1948–2010." *Demography* 54, no. 5 (2017): 1795–1818. https://doi.org/10.1007/s13524-017-0611-1.

Sharkey, Patrick. "The Long Reach of Violence: A Broader Perspective on Data, Theory, and Evidence on the Prevalence and Consequences of Exposure to Violence." *Annual Review of Criminology* 1, no. 1 (2018): 85–102. https://doi .org/10.1146/annurev-criminol-032317-092316.

Shavell, Steven. "A Simple Model of Optimal Deterrence and Incapacitation." NBER Working Paper Series, Working Paper 20747, National Bureau of Economic Research, Cambridge, MA, Dec. 2014. https://doi.org/10.3386 /w20747.

Shavit, Shira, Jenerius A. Aminawung, Nathan Birnbaum, Scott Greenberg, Timothy Berthold, Amie Fishman, et al. "Transitions Clinic Network: Challenges and Lessons in Primary Care for People Released from Prison." *Health Affairs* 36, no. 6 (2017): 1006–15. https://doi.org/10.1377/hlthaff.2017.0089.

Sheats, Kameron J., Shalon M. Irving, Jim A. Mercy, Thomas R. Simon, Alex E. Crosby, Derek C. Ford, et al. "Violence-Related Disparities Experienced by Black Youth and Young Adults: Opportunities for Prevention." *American Journal of Preventive Medicine* 55, no. 4 (2018): 462–69. https://doi.org/10.1016/j.amepre.2018.05.017.

Shedd, Carla. *Unequal City: Race, Schools, and Perceptions of Injustice.* New York: Russell Sage, 2015.

Shollenberger, Tracey L. "Racial Disparities in School Suspension and Subsequent Outcomes." In *Closing the School Discipline Gap: Equitable Remedies for Excessive Exclusion,* edited by Daniel J. Losen, 31–44. New York: Teachers College Press, 2015.

Sickmund, Melissa, Anthony Sladky, and Wei Kang. "Easy Access to Juvenile Court Statistics: 1985–2011." Washington, DC: Office of Juvenile Justice and Delinquency Prevention, 2014.

Simmons, Lizbet. *The Prison School: Educational Inequality and School Discipline in the Age of Mass Incarceration.* Oakland: University of California Press, 2017.

Singh, Gopal K., Romuladus E. Azuine, Mohammad Siahpush, and Michael D. Kogan. "All-Cause and Cause-Specific Mortality among US Youth: Socioeconomic and Rural-Urban Disparities and International Patterns." *Journal of Urban Health* 90, no. 3 (2012): 388–405. https://doi.org/10.1007/s11524-012-9744-0.

Singh, Gopal K., and Michael D. Kogan. "Widening Socioeconomic Disparities in US Childhood Mortality, 1969 2000." *American Journal of Public Health* 97, no. 9 (2007): 1658–65. https://doi.org/10.2105/AJPH.2006.087320.

Sirois, Catherine. "The Strain of Sons' Incarceration on Mothers' Health." *Social Science & Medicine* 264 (2020): 113264.

Skiba, Russell J., Mariella I. Arredondo, and Natasha T. Williams. "More Than a Metaphor: The Contribution of Exclusionary Discipline to a School-to-Prison Pipeline." *Equity & Excellence in Education* 47, no. 4 (2014): 546–64. https://doi.org/10.1080/10665684.2014.958965.

Skiba, Russell J., Robert H. Horner, Choong-Geun Chung, M. Karega Rausch, Seth L. May, and Tary Tobin. "Race Is Not Neutral: A National Investigation of African American and Latino Disproportionality in School Discipline." *School Psychology Review* 40, no. 1 (2011): 85–107.

Skiba, Russell J., and Daniel J. Losen. "From Reaction to Prevention: Turning the Page on School Discipline." *American Educator* 39, no. 4 (2016): 4–11, 44.

Sloam, James. "New Voice, Less Equal: The Civic and Political Engagement of Young People in the United States and Europe." *Comparative Political Studies* 47, no. 5 (2014): 663–88. https://doi.org/10.1177/0010414012453441.

Smiley, CalvinJohn, and David Fakunle. "From 'Brute' to 'Thug': The Demonization and Criminalization of Unarmed Black Male Victims in America." *Journal of Human Behavior in the Social Environment* 26, nos. 3–4 (2016): 350–66. https://doi.org/10.1080/10911359.2015.1129256.

Smith, Clint. *How the Word Is Passed: A Reckoning with the History of Slavery across America.* New York: Little, Brown, 2021.

Soss, Joe, and Vesla Weaver. "Police Are Our Government: Politics, Political Science, and the Policing of Race-Class Subjugated Communities." *Annual Review of Political Science*, 20, no. 1 (2017): 565–91. https://doi.org/10.1146/annurev-polisci-060415-093825.

Sotero, Michelle. "A Conceptual Model of Historical Trauma: Implications for Public Health Practice and Research." *Journal of Health Disparities Research and Practice* 1, no. 1 (2006): 93–108.

Sousa, Cindy A. "Political Violence, Collective Functioning and Health: A Review of the Literature." *Medicine, Conflict, and Survival* 29, no. 3 (2013): 169–97.

Springboard to Opportunities. "The Magnolia Mother's Trust," 2020. http://springboardto.org/index.php/page/the-magnolia-mothers-trust.

Staggers-Hakim, Raja. "The Nation's Unprotected Children and the Ghost of Mike Brown, or the Impact of National Police Killings on the Health and Social Development of African American Boys." *Journal of Human Behavior in the Social Environment* 26, nos. 3–4 (2016): 390–99. https://doi.org/10.1080/10911359.2015.1132864.

Stargel, Lauren E., Rebecca C. Fauth, and M. Ann Easterbrooks. "Home Visiting Program Impacts on Reducing Homelessness among Young Mothers." *Journal of Social Distress and the Homeless* 27, no. 1 (2018): 89–92.

Stemple, Lara, and Ilan H. Meyer. "The Sexual Victimization of Men in America: New Data Challenge Old Assumptions." *American Journal of Public Health* 104, no. 6 (2014): e19–26. https://doi.org/10.2105/ajph.2014.301946.

Stevenson, Bryan. "Keynote Address by Mr. Bryan Stevenson." *DePaul Law Review* 53, no. 4 (2004): 1699. https://via.library.depaul.edu/cgi/viewcontent.cgi?article=1484&context=law-review.

Straus, Murray A., Sherry L. Hamby, Sue Boney-McCoy, and David B. Sugarman. "The Revised Conflict Tactics Scales (CTS2): Development and Preliminary Psychometric Data." *Journal of Family Issues* 17, no. 3 (1996): 283–316.

Stretesky, Paul B., and Michael J. Lynch. "The Relationship between Lead and Crime." *Journal of Health and Social Behavior* 45, no. 2 (2004): 214–29. https://doi.org/10.1177/002214650404500207.

————. "The Relationship between Lead Exposure and Homicide." *Archives of Pediatrics & Adolescent Medicine* 155, no. 5 (2001): 579–82.

Stuckler, David, Sanjay Basu, Martin McKee, and Lawrence King. "Mass Incarceration Can Explain Population Increases in TB and Multidrug-Resistant TB in European and Central Asian Countries." *Proceedings of the National Academy of Sciences—PNAS* 105, no. 36 (2008): 13280–85. https://doi.org/10.1073/pnas.0801200105.

Sugie, Naomi. "Punishment and Welfare: Paternal Incarceration and Families' Receipt of Public Assistance." *Social Forces* 90, no. 4 (2012): 1403–27.

Svetaz, Maria Veronica, Renne Sieving, Michele Allen, Rosemary Rodriguez Hager, Kara J. Beckman, Adriana Galvan, et al. "A Community Based Participatory Research (CBPR) Journey Bringing Culture and Family to the Center of an Intervention to Promote Positive Youth Development and Reproductive Health: The Encuentro Project." *Journal of Adolescent Health* 58, no. 2 (2016): S5. https://doi.org/10.1016/j.jadohealth.2015.10.026.

Swisher, Raymond R., and Unique R. Shaw-Smith. "Paternal Incarceration and Adolescent Well-Being: Life Course Contingencies and Other Moderators." *Journal of Criminal Law & Criminology* 104, no. 4 (2015): 929.

Sykes, Gresham. *The Society of Captives: A Study of a Maximum Security Prison.* Princeton, NJ: Princeton University Press, 1958.

Tamborini, Christopher R., ChangHwan Kim, and Arthur Sakamoto. "Education and Lifetime Earnings in the United States." *Demography* 52, no. 4 (2015): 1383–1407. https://doi.org/10.1007/s13524-015-0407-0.

Taylor, Philip. "Age and Work: International Perspectives." *Social Policy and Society* 3, no. 2 (2004): 163–70. https://doi.org/10.1017/S1474746403001623.

Teplin, Linda A., Karen M. Abram, Gary M. McClelland, Mina K. Dulcan, and Amy A. Mericle. "Psychiatric Disorders in Youth in Juvenile Detention." *Archives of General Psychiatry* 59, no. 12 (2002): 1133–43.

Teplin, Linda A., Gary M. McClelland, Karen M. Abram, Darinka Mileusnic-Polchan, Nichole D. Olson, and Anna J. Harrison. *Violent Death in Delinquent Youth after Detention.* Washington, DC: US Department of Justice, 2015.

Terrill, William, and Michael D. Reisig. "Neighborhood Context and Police Use of Force." *Journal of Research in Crime and Delinquency* 40, no. 3 (2016): 291–321. https://doi.org/10.1177/0022427803253800.

Theall, Katherine P., Elizabeth A. Shirtcliff, Andrew R. Dismukes, Maeve Wallace, and Stacy S. Drury. "Association between Neighborhood Violence and Biological Stress in Children." *JAMA Pediatrics* 171, no. 1 (2017): 53–60. https://doi.org/10.1001/jamapediatrics.2016.2321.

Theriot, Matthew T. "School Resource Officers and the Criminalization of Student Behavior." *Journal of Criminal Justice* 37, no. 3 (2009): 280–87.

Thompson, Heather Ann. "The Racial History of Criminal Justice in America." *Du Bois Review: Social Science Research on Race* 16, no. 1 (2020): 221–41. https://doi.org/10.1017/S1742058X19000183.

———. "Unmaking the Motor City in the Age of Mass Incarceration." *Journal of Law in Society* 15, no. 1 (2013): 41–61.

Thomson, Elizabeth, Thomas L. Hanson, and Sara S. McLanahan. "Family Structure and Child Well-Being: Economic Resources vs. Parental Behaviors." *Social Forces* 73, no. 1 (1994): 221–42.

Thomson, Susan. "The Darker Side of Transitional Justice: The Power Dynamics behind Rwanda's Gacaca Courts." *Africa* 81, no. 3 (2011): 373–90.

Tienda, Marta. "Thirteenth Annual Brown Lecture in Education Research: Public Education and the Social Contract: Restoring the Promise in an Age of Diversity and Division." *Educational Researcher* 46, no. 6 (2017): 271–83. https://doi.org/10.3102/0013189X17725499.

Tonry, Michael. "Remodeling American Sentencing: A Ten-Step Blueprint for Moving Past Mass Incarceration." *Criminology & Public Policy* 13, no. 4 (2014): 503–33. https://doi.org/10.1111/1745-9133.12097.

Travis, Jeremy, Bruce Western, and F. Stevens Redburn, eds. *The Growth of Incarceration in the United States: Exploring Causes and Consequences.* Washington, DC: National Academies Press, 2014.

Turner, Hana, Christine M. Rubie-Davies, and Melinda Webber. "Teacher Expectations, Ethnicity and the Achievement Gap." *New Zealand Journal of Educational Studies* 50, no. 1 (2015): 55–69.

Turney, Kristin. "Adverse Childhood Experiences among Children of Incarcerated Parents." *Children and Youth Services Review* 89 (2018): 218–25. https://doi.org/10.1016/j.childyouth.2018.04.033.

———. "The Consequences of Paternal Incarceration for Maternal Neglect and Harsh Parenting." *Social Forces* 92, no. 4 (2014): 1607–36.

———. "Depressive Symptoms among Adolescents Exposed to Personal and Vicarious Police Contact." *Society and Mental Health* 11, no. 2 (2021): 113–33.

———. "Hopelessly Devoted? Relationship Quality during and after Incarceration." *Journal of Marriage and Family* 77, no. 2 (2015): 480–95. https://doi.org/10.1111/jomf.12174.

———. "Stress Proliferation across Generations? Examining the Relationship between Parental Incarceration and Childhood Health." *Journal of Health and Social Behavior* 55, no. 3 (2014): 302–19. https://doi.org/10.1177/0022146514544173.

Turney, Kristin, and Anna Haskins. "Falling Behind? Children's Early Grade Retention after Paternal Incarceration." *Sociology of Education* 87, no. 4 (2014): 241–58. https://doi.org/10.1177/0038040714547086.

Turney, Kristin, Hedwig Lee, and Megan Comfort. "Discrimination and Psychological Distress among Recently Released Male Prisoners." *American Journal of Men's Health* 7, no. 6 (2013): 482–93.

Turney, Kristin, and Christopher Wildeman. "Adverse Childhood Experiences among Children Placed in and Adopted from Foster Care: Evidence from a Nationally Representative Survey." *Child Abuse & Neglect* 64 (2017): 117–29. https://doi.org/10.1016/j.chiabu.2016.12.009.

Tyler, Tom R., Jonathan Jackson, and Avital Mentovich. "The Consequences of Being an Object of Suspicion: Potential Pitfalls of Proactive Police Contact." *Journal of Empirical Legal Studies* 12, no. 4 (2015): 602–36. https://doi.org/10.1111/jels.12086.

Uggen, Christopher, Jeff Manza, and Melissa Thompson. "Citizenship, Democracy, and the Civic Reintegration of Criminal Offenders." *Annals of the American Academy of Political and Social Science* 605, no. 1 (2006): 281–310. https://doi.org/10.1177/0002716206286898.

Uggen, Christopher, Mike Vuolo, Sarah Lageson, Ebony Ruhland, and Hilary K. Whitham. "The Edge of Stigma: An Experimental Audit of the Effects of Low-Level Criminal Records on Employment." *Criminology* 52, no. 4 (2014): 627–54. https://doi.org/10.1111/1745-9125.12051.

Üngör, Uğur Ümit, and Nanci Adler. "Indonesia in the Global Context of Genocide and Transitional Justice." *Journal of Genocide Research* 19, no. 4 (2017): 609–17.

United Nations Secretary-General. *United Nations Approach to Transitional Justice: Guidance Note of the Secretary-General.* March 2010.

United States Department of Agriculture. "USDA Proposes to Close SNAP Automatic Eligibility Loophole." Press release, July 23, 2019. www.usda.gov/media/press-releases/2019/07/23/usda-proposes-close-snap-automatic-eligibility-loophole.

Upadhyayula, Satyasree, Megha Ramaswamy, Prabhakar Chalise, Jessie Daniels, and Nicholas Freudenberg. "The Association of Ethnic Pride with Health and Social Outcomes among Young Black and Latino Men after Release from Jail." *Youth & Society* 49, no. 8 (2017): 1057–76.

Valls, Andrew. "Racial Justice as Transitional Justice." *Polity* 36, no. 1 (2003): 53–71.

van der Merwe, Hugo, and Brinton Lykes. "Idealists, Opportunists and Activists: Who Drives Transitional Justice?" *International Journal of Transitional Justice* 12, no. 3 (2018): 381–85. https://doi.org/10.1093/ijtj/ijy022.

Visher, Christy A., Sara A. Debus-Sherrill, and Jennifer Yahner. "Employment after Prison: A Longitudinal Study of Former Prisoners." *Justice Quarterly* 28, no. 5 (2011): 698–718.

Visher, Christy, Pamela K. Lattimore, Kelle Barrick, and Stephen J. Tueller. "Evaluating the Long-Term Effects of Prisoner Reentry Services on Recidivism: What Types of Services Matter?" *Justice Quarterly* 34, no. 1 (2017): 136–65.

Visher, Christy A., and Jeremy Travis. "Life on the Outside: Returning Home after Incarceration." *Prison Journal* 91, no. 3_suppl (2011): 102S-19S.

Visher, Christy, Jennifer Yahner, and Nancy La Vigne. *Life after Prison: Tracking the Experiences of Male Prisoners Returning to Chicago, Cleveland, and Houston.* Washington, DC: Urban Institute, 2010.

Visser, M. Anne. "Beyond Labor Markets and Schools: Community-Based Youth Serving Organizations and the Integration of Puerto Rican and Dominican Disconnected Youth in New York City." *Centro Journal* 30, no. 1 (2018): 4–31.

Vukojevic, Vanja, Iris-T. Kolassa, Matthias Fastenrath, Leo Gschwind, Klara Spalek, Annette Milnik, et al. "Epigenetic Modification of the Glucocorticoid Receptor Gene Is Linked to Traumatic Memory and Post-Traumatic Stress Disorder Risk in Genocide Survivors." *Journal of Neuroscience* 34, no. 31 (2014): 10274–84. https://doi.org/10.1523/jneurosci.1526-14.2014.

Wacquant, Loïc. "The Curious Eclipse of Prison Ethnography in the Age of Mass Incarceration." *Ethnography* 3, no. 4 (2002): 371–97.

———. "Deadly Symbiosis: When Ghetto and Prison Meet and Mesh." *Punishment and Society* 3, no. 1 (2001): 95–134.

———. "Prisoner Reentry as Myth and Ceremony." *Dialectical Anthropology* 34, no. 4 (2010): 605–20. https://doi.org/10.1007/s10624-010-9215-5.

Wadhwa, Anita. *Restorative Justice in Urban Schools: Disrupting the School-to-Prison Pipeline.* New York: Routledge, 2015.

Wakefield, Sara. "Accentuating the Positive or Eliminating the Negative? Paternal Incarceration and Caregiver-Child Relationship Quality." *Journal of Criminal Law & Criminology* 104, no. 4 (2015): 905–27.

Wakefield, Sara, and Christopher Uggen. "Incarceration and Stratification." *Annual Review of Sociology* 36, no. 1 (2010): 387–406. https://doi.org/10.1146/annurev.soc.012809.102551.

Wakefield, Sara, and Christopher Wildeman. *Children of the Prison Boom: Mass Incarceration and the Future of American Inequality.* London: Oxford University Press, 2014.

———. "Mass Imprisonment and Racial Disparities in Childhood Behavioral Problems." *Criminology & Public Policy* 10, no. 3 (2011): 793–817.

Wald, Johanna, and Daniel J. Losen. "Defining and Redirecting a School-to-Prison Pipeline." *New Directions for Youth Development* 2003, no. 99 (2003): 9–15. https://doi.org/10.1002/yd.51.

Walkley, Meg, and Tory L. Cox. "Building Trauma-Informed Schools and Communities." *Children & Schools* 35, no. 2 (2013): 123–26. https://doi.org/10.1093/cs/cdt007.

Wallace, Danielle, Chantal Fahmy, Lindsy Cotton, Charis Jimmons, Rachel McKay, Sidney Stoffer, et al. "Examining the Role of Familial Support during

Prison and after Release on Post-Incarceration Mental Health." *International Journal of Offender Therapy and Comparative Criminology* 60, no. 1 (2016): 3–20. https://doi.org/10.1177/0306624X14548023.

Wang, Emily A., Clemens S. Hong, Liz Samuels, Shira Shavit, Ronald Sanders, and Margot Kushel. "Transitions Clinic: Creating a Community-Based Model of Health Care for Recently Released California Prisoners." *Public Health Reports* 125, no. 2 (2010): 171–77. https://doi.org/10.1177/003335491012500205.

Wang, Emily A., Mark Pletcher, Feng Lin, Eric Vittinghoff, Stefan G. Kertesz, Catarina I. Kiefe, et al. "Incarceration, Incident Hypertension, and Access to Health Care: Findings from the Coronary Artery Risk Development in Young Adults (CARDIA) Study." *Archives of Internal Medicine* 169, no. 7 (2009): 687–93.

Wang, Haidong, Chelsea A. Liddell, Matthew M. Coates, Meghan D. Mooney, Carly E. Levitz, Austin E. Schumacher, et al. "Global, Regional, and National Levels of Neonatal, Infant, and under-5 Mortality during 1990–2013: A Systematic Analysis for the Global Burden of Disease Study 2013." *The Lancet (British Edition)* 384, no. 9947 (2014): 957–79. https://doi.org/10.1016/S0140-6736(14)60497-9.

Ward, Geoff. "Living Histories of White Supremacist Policing: Towards Transformative Justice." *Du Bois Review: Social Science Research on Race* 15, no. 1 (2018): 167–84.

Wasserman, Gail A., Susan J. Ko, and Larkin S. McReynolds. "Assessing the Mental Health Status of Youth in Juvenile Justice Settings." *Juvenile Justice Bulletin*, August 2004.

Wasserman, Gail A., Larkin S. McReynolds, Christopher P. Lucas, Prudence Fisher, and Linda Santos. "The Voice DISC-IV with Incarcerated Male Youths: Prevalence of Disorder." *Journal of the American Academy of Child & Adolescent Psychiatry* 41, no. 3 (2002): 314–21.

Weaver, Vesla M. "Frontlash: Race and the Development of Punitive Crime Policy." *Studies in American Political Development* 21, no. 2 (2007): 230–65. https://doi.org/10.1017/S0898588X07000211.

———. "More Security May Actually Make Us Feel Less Secure." *Proceedings of the National Academy of Sciences—PNAS* 115, no. 39 (2018): 9649–51. https://doi.org/10.1073/pnas.1813014115.

Weaver, Vesla M., and Amanda Geller. "De-policing America's Youth: Disrupting Criminal Justice Policy Feedbacks That Distort Power and Derail Prospects." *ANNALS of the American Academy of Political and Social Science* 685, no. 1 (2019): 190–226. https://doi.org/10.1177/0002716219871899.

Weaver, Vesla M., and Amy E. Lerman. "Political Consequences of the Carceral State." *American Political Science Review* 104, no. 4 (2010): 817–33. https://doi.org/10.1017/S0003055410000456.

Weaver, Vesla M., Andrew Papachristos, and Michael Zanger-Tishler. "The Great Decoupling: The Disconnection between Criminal Offending and Experience of Arrest across Two Cohorts." *RSF: The Russell Sage Foundation Journal of the Social Sciences* 5, no. 1 (2019): 89–123. https://doi.org/10.7758/RSF.2019.5.1.05.

Weingarten, Kaethe. "Witnessing the Effects of Political Violence in Families: Mechanisms of Intergenerational Transmission and Clinical Interventions." *Journal of Marital and Family Therapy* 30, no. 1 (2004): 45–59.

Weinstein, James N., Amy Geller, Yamrot Negussie, and Alina Baciu, eds. *Communities in Action: Pathways to Health Equity.* Washington, DC: National Academies Press, 2017. https://doi.org/10.17226/24624.

Weisburd, David, Malay K. Majmundar, Hassan Aden, Anthony Braga, Jim Bueermann, Philip J. Cook, et al. "Proactive Policing: A Summary of the Report of the National Academies of Sciences, Engineering, and Medicine." *Asian Journal of Criminology* 14, no. 2 (2019): 145–77. https://doi.org/10.1007/s11417-019-09284-1.

Weisburst, Emily K. "Patrolling Public Schools: The Impact of Funding for School Police on Student Discipline and Long-Term Education Outcomes." *Journal of Policy Analysis and Management* 38, no. 2 (2019): 338–65. https://doi.org/10.1002/pam.22116.

Welch, Kelly, and Allison Ann Payne. "Racial Threat and Punitive School Discipline." *Social Problems* 57, no. 1 (2010): 25–48.

Western, Bruce. *Homeward: Life in the Year after Prison.* New York: Russell Sage, 2018.

———. "The Impact of Incarceration on Wage Mobility and Inequality." *American Sociological Review* 67, no. 4 (2002): 526–46. https://doi.org/10.2307/3088944.

———. *Punishment and Inequality in America.* New York: Russell Sage, 2006.

Western, Bruce, and Katherine Beckett. "How Unregulated Is the U.S. Labor Market? The Penal System as a Labor Market Institution." *American Journal of Sociology* 104, no. 4 (1999): 1030–60. https://doi.org/10.1086/210135.

Western, Bruce, Jeffrey R. Kling, and David F. Weiman. "The Labor Market Consequences of Incarceration." *NCCD News* 47, no. 3 (2001): 410–27.

Western, Bruce, and Becky Pettit. "Incarceration and Social Inequality." *Daedalus: The Journal of the American Academy of Arts & Sciences* 139, no. 3 (2010): 8–19.

Western, Bruce, Becky Pettit, and Josh Guetzkow. "Black Economic Progress in the Era of Mass Imprisonment." In *Invisible Punishment: The Collateral Consequences of Mass Imprisonment,* edited by Marc Mauer and Meda Chesney-Lind, 165–80. New York: New Press, 2002.

Western, Bruce, and Christopher Wildeman. "The Black Family and Mass Incarceration." *Annals of the American Academy of Political and Social Science* 621, no. 1 (2009): 221–42.

———. "Punishment, Inequality, and the Future of Mass Incarceration." *University of Kansas Law Review* 57, no. 4 (2008): 851–78.

Wexler, Lisa, Kalpana Poudel-Tandukar, Suzanne Rataj, Lucas Trout, Krishna C. Poudel, Michelle Woods, et al. "Preliminary Evaluation of a School-Based Youth Leadership and Prevention Program in Rural Alaska Native Communities." *School Mental Health* 9, no. 2 (2017): 172–83. https://doi.org/10.1007/s12310-016-9203-2.

Whitaker, Robert C., Shannon M. Phillips, and Sean M. Orzol. "Food Insecurity and the Risks of Depression and Anxiety in Mothers and Behavior Problems in Their Preschool-Aged Children." *Pediatrics* 118, no. 3 (2006): e859–68.

White House Council of Economic Advisors. *Economic Perspectives on Incarceration and the Criminal Justice System.* Washington, DC: Office of the Press Secretary, April 23, 2016. https://obamawhitehouse.archives.gov/the-press-office/2016/04/23/cea-report-economic-perspectives-incarceration-and-criminal-justice.

Wiegand, Andrew, Michelle Manno, Sengsouvanh Leshnick, Louisa Treskon, Christian Geckeler, Heather Lewis-Charp, et al. *Adapting to Local Context: Findings from the Youthbuild Evaluation Implementation Study.* MDRC/ERIC, Feb. 2015. https://eric.ed.gov/?id=ED558510.

Wildeman, Christopher. "Imprisonment and (Inequality in) Population Health." *Social Science Research* 41, no. 1 (2012): 74–91.

———. "Imprisonment and Infant Mortality." *Social Problems* 59, no. 2 (2012): 228–57.

———. "Incarceration and Population Health in Wealthy Democracies." *Criminology* 54, no. 2 (2016): 360–82. https://doi.org/10.1111/1745-9125.12107.

———. "Is It Better to Sit on Our Hands or Just Dive In? Cultivating Family-Friendly Criminal Justice Policy in the Contemporary Era." *Criminology and Public Policy* 15, no. 2 (2016): 497–502.

———. "Parental Incarceration, Child Homelessness, and the Invisible Consequences of Mass Imprisonment." *ANNALS of the American Academy of Political and Social Science* 651, no. 1 (2014): 74–96.

———. "Paternal Imprisonment, the Prison Boom, and the Concentration of Childhood Disadvantage." *Demography* 46, no. 2 (2009): 265–80.

———. "Paternal Incarceration and Children's Physically Aggressive Behaviors: Evidence from the Fragile Families and Child Wellbeing Study." *Social Forces* 89, no. 1 (2010): 285–309. https://doi.org/10.1353/sof.2010.0055.

Wildeman, Christopher, Maria D. Fitzpatrick, and Alyssa W. Goldman. "Conditions of Confinement in American Prisons and Jails." *Annual Review of Law and Social Science* 14, no. 1 (2018): 29–47. https://doi.org/10.1146/annurev-lawsocsci-101317-031025.

Wildeman, Christopher, Alyssa W. Goldman, and Hedwig Lee. "Health Consequences of Family Member Incarceration for Adults in the Household." *Public*

Health Reports 134, no. 1_suppl (2019): 15S-21S. https://doi.org/10.1177
/0033354918807974.

Wildeman, Christopher, Alyssa W. Goldman, and Kristin Turney. "Parental
Incarceration and Child Health in the United States." *Epidemiologic
Reviews* 40, no. 1 (2018): 146-56.

Wildeman, Christopher, and Hedwig Lee. "Women's Health in the Era of Mass
Incarceration." *Annual Review of Sociology* 47, no. 1 (2021): 543-65. https://
doi.org/10.1146/annurev-soc-081320-113303.

Wildeman, Christopher, Hedwig Lee, and Megan Comfort. "A New Vulnerable
Population? The Health of the Female Romantic Partners of Recently
Released Male Prisoners." *Women's Health Issues* 26, no. 3 (2013): 335-40.

Wildeman, Christopher, and Christopher Muller. "Mass Imprisonment and
Inequality in Health and Family Life." *Annual Review of Law and Social
Science* 8, no. 1 (2012): 11-30.

Wildeman, Christopher, Jason Schnittker, and Kristin Turney. "Despair by
Association? The Mental Health of Mothers with Children by Recently
Incarcerated Fathers." *American Sociological Review* 77, no. 2 (2012): 216-43.

Wildeman, Christopher, Kristin Turney, and Jason Schnittker. "The Hedonic
Consequences of Punishment Revisited." *Journal of Criminal Law &
Criminology* 104, no. 1 (2014): 133-63.

Wildeman, Christopher, and Emily A. Wang. "Mass Incarceration, Public
Health, and Widening Inequality in the USA." *The Lancet* 389, no. 10077
(2017): 1464-74. https://doi.org/10.1016/S0140-6736(17)30259-3.

Williams, Joanna L., and Nancy L. Deutsch. "Beyond Between-Group Differences: Considering Race, Ethnicity, and Culture in Research on Positive
Youth Development Programs." *Applied Developmental Science* 20, no. 3
(2016): 203-13. https://doi.org/10.1080/10888691.2015.1113880.

Wojciechowski, Thomas W. "Racial Disparities in Community Mental Health
Service Use among Juvenile Offenders." *Journal of Racial and Ethnic Health
Disparities* 6, no. 2 (2019): 393-400. https://doi.org/10.1007/s40615-018-
00536-x.

Yamato, Sharon. "Civil Liberties Act of 1988." In *Densho Encyclopedia*. Seattle,
WA: Densho, 2020. http://encyclopedia.densho.org/Civil_Liberties_Act_
of_1988.

Yaros, Anna, Derek Ramirez, Stephen Tueller, Tasseli McKay, Christine H.
Lindquist, Amy Helburn, Rose Feinberg, and Anupa Bir. "Child Well-Being
When Fathers Return from Prison." *Journal of Offender Rehabilitation* 57,
no. 2 (2018): 144-61. https://doi.org/10.1080/10509674.2018.1441204.

Yehuda, Rachel, and Linda M. Bierer. "Transgenerational Transmission of
Cortisol and PTSD Risk." *Progress in Brain Research* 167 (2007): 121-35.

Yehuda, Rachel, Nikolaos P. Daskalakis, Linda M. Bierer, Heather N. Bader,
Torsten Klengel, Florian Holsboer, et al. "Holocaust Exposure Induced

Intergenerational Effects on FKBP5 Methylation." *Biological Psychiatry* 80, no. 5 (2016): 372–80.

Yoshikawa, Hirokazu, J. Lawrence Aber, and William R. Beardslee. "The Effects of Poverty on the Mental, Emotional, and Behavioral Health of Children and Youth: Implications for Prevention." *American Psychologist* 67, no. 4 (2012): 272–84. https://doi.org/10.1037/a0028015.

YouthBuild. "YouthBuild." https://www.youthbuild.org.

Zatz, Noah D. "Get to Work or Go to Jail: State Violence and the Racialized Production of Precarious Work." *Law & Social Inquiry* 45, no. 2 (2020): 304–38. https://doi.org/10.1017/lsi.2019.56.

Zaw, Khaing, Darrick Hamilton, and William Darity. "Race, Wealth and Incarceration: Results from the National Longitudinal Survey of Youth." *Race and Social Problems* 8, no. 1 (2016): 103–15.

Zeldin, Shepherd, Josset Gauley, Steven Eric Krauss, Mariah Kornbluh, and Jessica Collura. "Youth-Adult Partnership and Youth Civic Development: Cross-National Analyses for Scholars and Field Professionals." *Youth & Society* 49, no. 7 (2017): 851–78. https://doi.org/10.1177/0044118X15595153.

Zeman, Janice, Danielle Dallaire, Johanna Folk, and Todd Thrash. "Maternal Incarceration, Children's Psychological Adjustment, and the Mediating Role of Emotion Regulation." *Journal of Abnormal Child Psychology* 46, no. 2 (2018): 223–36.

Zewde, Naomi. "Universal Baby Bonds Reduce Black-White Wealth Inequality, Progressively Raise Net Worth of All Young Adults." *Review of Black Political Economy* 47, no. 1 (2020): 3–19. https://doi.org/10.1177/0034644619885321.

Zottoli, Tina M., Tarika Daftary-Kapur, Georgia M. Winters, and Conor Hogan. "Plea Discounts, Time Pressures, and False-Guilty Pleas in Youth and Adults Who Pleaded Guilty to Felonies in New York City." *Psychology, Public Policy, and Law* 22, no. 3 (2016): 250–59.

Index

292

biomarkers: of collective trauma, 5; of stress, 136
birth cohorts, mass incarceration-era, 37–39
Black Lives Matter. *See* Movement for Black Lives
Black Reconstruction (Du Bois), 166–67
Black youth: barriers to educational attainment of, 150; disproportionate disconnection from social institutions among, 31–33; engaging the power of youthful challenge among, 45–46; high gun-related injury and mortality among, 143; incarceration rate among, 40; losses associated with racial criminalization of, 41, 169; placed on probation, 32–33; prosecuted for drug-related activity, 35–36; reparations for childhood criminalization of, 41–45; social exclusion of, 31–33; systematic removal of, 138
boarding schools, trauma to Native children in, 136
Booker, Cory, 158
Brave Heart, Maria Yellow Horse, 135–36

cardiovascular disease, 145
caregivers of children of incarcerated parents, 123–24, 126, 127
cash-value reparations. *See* reparations
Center for Urban Families, 157
Centers for Disease Control and Prevention (CDC), 38
Cheliotis, Leonidas, 133
Child and Dependent Care Credit, 126
childcare assistance, direct-subsidy for, 126
childhood cognitive difficulties, 115, 142
Circle of Parents, 126
civic engagement, 43, 46, 48
Civil Rights Act, 135
Clear, Todd, 3
Clinton, Hillary, 24, 34, 37–38, 47–48
Clinton-era political agenda, 23–24
closure, 13. *See also* reparations
Cluster Plan for Dropout Prevention, 154
Coates, Ta-Nehisi, 23
coerced labor, Black women's, 78–85
Cognitive Behavioral Intervention for Trauma in Schools, 44–45
collective consciousness, 5
collective effects of mass incarceration, 131–62; collective health of Black communities, 142–46; community and collective harms, adding up, 146–51; economic damage to Black communities, 137–41;

legacy of collective violence, 135–37; systematic reconstruction, 151–59
collective memory, 6, 11
collective trust, 13
collective violence, mass incarceration as, 132–35; effects of, 136–37
community-based primary health care, 155
community-based youth organizations, 42
computer-assisted personal interviewing, 187
conviction-related discrimination, 56
coparent incarceration, 86
coping, 55; developing healthy coping options in youth, 44–45; with incarceration and reentry, 124; interpersonal, 66; relationship conflict and couples' coping skills, 87; skills of children, 112, 124, 126–27, 128, 176; skills of families, 124
correctional officers, 49, 124, 133
cortisol patterns and collective violence, 136
counseling, 43, 124, 154, 176
criminalization of Black children, 20–24, 37–41
Crow, Jim, 178, 179–80
cultural identity development, 44
culturally competent health care, 155
cultural supremacy, 44

Darity, Sandy, 15, 41, 179, 180
Davis, Emani, 129
deaths, mass incarceration-related, 148–49
depression, 28, 36, 108–10, 121, 142
developmental inappropriateness of contemporary juvenile justice, 34–35. *See also* adolescents
developmental timing and juvenile sentences, 25. *See also* adolescents
diabetes, 145
Dilulio, John, 23–24, 33–34
disability and hyper incarceration, 144
disciplinary practices, 30–31. *See also* schools
disengagement, 30, 111–12
dispersal-oriented programs, 156. *See also* housing
divorce and returning prisoners, 54
Du Bois, W. E. B., 166–67

earnings: lifetime, 118–20; losses due to mass incarceration, 63, 93. *See also* wages
East Coast cities, policing in, 24, 27
economic damage to Black communities and mass incarceration, 137–41

Founded in 1893,
UNIVERSITY OF CALIFORNIA PRESS
publishes bold, progressive books and journals
on topics in the arts, humanities, social sciences,
and natural sciences—with a focus on social
justice issues—that inspire thought and action
among readers worldwide.

The UC PRESS FOUNDATION
raises funds to uphold the press's vital role
as an independent, nonprofit publisher, and
receives philanthropic support from a wide
range of individuals and institutions—and from
committed readers like you. To learn more, visit
ucpress.edu/supportus.